Marijuana

Recent Titles in Contemporary Debates

The Affordable Care Act: Examining the Facts
Purva H. Rawal

Climate Change: Examining the Facts
Daniel Bedford and John Cook

Immigration: Examining the Facts
Cari Lee Skogberg Eastman

MARIJUANA

❖❖❖

Examining the Facts

Karen T. Van Gundy and Michael S. Staunton

Contemporary Debates

An Imprint of ABC-CLIO, LLC
Santa Barbara, California • Denver, Colorado

Library of Congress Cataloging-in-Publication Data

Names: Van Gundy, Karen T., author. | Staunton, Michael S., author.
Title: Marijuana : examining the facts / Karen T. Van Gundy and
    Michael S. Staunton.
Description: Santa Barbara, California : ABC-CLIO, [2017] |
    Series: Contemporary debates | Includes bibliographical references
    and index.
Identifiers: LCCN 2017016411 (print) | LCCN 2017026593 (ebook) |
    ISBN 9781440836732 (ebook) | ISBN 9781440836725 (alk. paper)
Subjects: LCSH: Marijuana—Social aspects. | Marijuana—Therapeutic use. |
    Marijuana—Government policy.
Classification: LCC HV5822.M3 (ebook) | LCC HV5822.M3 V36 2017 (print) |
    DDC 362.29/5—dc23
LC record available at https://lccn.loc.gov/2017016411

ISBN: 978-1-4408-3672-5
EISBN: 978-1-4408-3673-2

21   20   19   18   2   3   4   5

This book is also available as an eBook.

ABC-CLIO
An Imprint of ABC-CLIO, LLC

ABC-CLIO, LLC
130 Cremona Drive, P.O. Box 1911
Santa Barbara, California 93116-1911
www.abc-clio.com

This book is printed on acid-free paper ∞

Manufactured in the United States of America

Contents

How to Use This Book   vii

Introduction   ix

1 Patterns and Trends   1

Q1. Is Marijuana Use or Misuse More Widespread
    Than Ever Before?   1

Q2. Does Marijuana Use or Misuse Vary
    by Race or Ethnicity?   13

Q3. Does Marijuana Use or Misuse Vary
    by Population Density?   24

Q4. Does Marijuana Use or Misuse Vary
    by Family Income Level?   34

Q5. Does Marijuana Use or Misuse Vary
    by Employment Status?   45

Q6. Does Marijuana Use or Misuse Vary
    by Education Level?   55

Q7. Does Marijuana Use or Misuse Vary
    by Marital Status?   64

2 Risks and Benefits   75

Q8. Is Accurate Information about the Risks and
    Benefits of Marijuana Widely Available?   75

Q9. Does Marijuana Use or Misuse Increase Risk for
     Physical Health Problems?   80
Q10. Does Marijuana Pose More of a Health Risk than
     Tobacco or Alcohol?   92
Q11. Does Marijuana Pose Less of a Health Risk than
     Other Illicit Drugs?   102
Q12. Is Marijuana Safe and Effective for Treating
     Medical Disorders?   113
Q13. Are All Medical Uses for Marijuana Substantiated
     by Research?   126
Q14. Does Marijuana Cause Cancer?   137
Q15. Is Marijuana Addictive?   144

3 **Policy Considerations**   **157**
Q16. Was Marijuana Criminalized to Protect Public Health
     and Safety?   157
Q17. Do Most Americans Support the Criminalization
     of Marijuana?   174
Q18. Is Marijuana Use a "Gateway" to Other Illicit
     Drug Use or Misuse?   183
Q19. Does Marijuana Use or Misuse Increase
     Criminal Behavior?   196
Q20. Is Driving under the Influence of Marijuana Safe?   205
Q21. Are Marijuana Infractions Fairly Punished?   217
Q22. Is Treatment for Marijuana Misuse Needed?   232
Q23. Is Treatment for Marijuana Misuse Effective?   241
Q24. Is Marijuana Prohibition Effective?   250

Index   265

About the Authors   283

How to Use This Book

Marijuana: Examining the Facts is one of the first volumes in ABC-CLIO's new Contemporary Debates reference series. Each title in this new series, which is intended for use by high school and undergraduate students as well as members of the general public, examines the veracity of controversial claims or beliefs surrounding a major political/cultural issue in the United States. The purpose of the series is to give readers a clear and unbiased understanding of current issues by informing them about falsehoods, half-truths, and misconceptions—and confirming the factual validity of other assertions—that have gained traction in America's political and cultural discourse. Ultimately, this series has been crafted to give readers the tools for a fuller understanding of controversial issues, policies, and laws that occupy center stage in American life and politics.

Each volume in this series identifies questions swirling about the larger topic under discussion. These questions are examined in individualized entries, which are in turn arranged in broad subject chapters that cover certain aspects of the issue being examined, that is, history of concern about the issue, potential economic or social impact, findings of latest scholarly research, and others.

Each chapter features 4–10 individual entries. Each entry begins by stating an important and/or well-known **Question** about the issue being studied. The entry then provides a concise and objective one- or two-paragraph **Answer** to the featured question, followed by a more comprehensive, detailed explanation of **The Facts**. This latter portion of each entry uses quantifiable, evidence-based information from respected sources to fully address each question and provide readers with the information they need to be informed citizens. Importantly, entries will also acknowledge instances in which conflicting data exist or data are incomplete. Finally, each entry concludes with a **Further Reading** section providing users with information on other important and/or influential resources.

The ultimate purpose of every book in the Contemporary Debates series is to reject "false equivalence," in which demonstrably false beliefs or statements are given the same exposure and credence as the facts; to puncture myths that diminish our understanding of important policies and positions; to provide needed context for misleading statements and claims; and to confirm the factual accuracy of other assertions. In other words, volumes in this series are being crafted to clear the air surrounding some of the most contentious and misunderstood issues of our time—not just add another layer of obfuscation and uncertainty to the debate.

Introduction

According to current U.S. federal law, marijuana is a Schedule I controlled substance, suggesting that it has a high potential for misuse (abuse or dependence), no currently accepted medical use, and a lack of accepted safety for use under medical supervision. Many state-level laws, however, do allow for medical marijuana use, and some states have legalized marijuana for recreational use. As of the 2016 U.S. election, comprehensive medical marijuana laws existed in 29 states, the District of Columbia, Guam, and Puerto Rico, and in 8 states—Alaska, California, Colorado, Maine, Massachusetts, Nevada, Oregon, and Washington—recreational use of marijuana had been legalized. Although such laws are at odds with the federal laws about marijuana, the federal government has not actively prosecuted medical marijuana distributors in states with medical marijuana provisions, and it has deferred its "right to challenge . . . legalization laws" in states like Colorado or Washington (National Conference of State Legislators 2016). With recent changes in the composition of the federal government, however, the conflict between state and federal government approaches to marijuana policy could become more contentious. When making decisions about marijuana-related practice and policy, it is thus crucial to consider carefully "the facts" about the possible benefits or harms associated with marijuana use or misuse.

CONTROLLED SUBSTANCE SCHEDULES

Schedule I Controlled Substances	Substances in this schedule have no currently accepted medical use in the United States, a lack of accepted safety for use under medical supervision, and a high potential for abuse. Examples: heroin, lysergic acid diethylamide (LSD), marijuana (cannabis), peyote, methaqualone, and 3,4-methylenedioxymethamphetamine ("Ecstasy").
Schedule II/IIN Controlled Substances (2/2N)	Substances in this schedule have a high potential for abuse, which may lead to severe psychological or physical dependence. Examples: hydromorphone (Dilaudid), methadone (Dolophine), oxycodone (OxyContin, Percocet), fentanyl (Sublimaze, Duragesic), morphine, opium, amphetamine (Dexedrine, Adderall), methamphetamine (Desoxyn), and methylphenidate (Ritalin).
Schedule III/IIIN Controlled Substances (3/3N)	Substances in this schedule have a potential for abuse less than substances in Schedules I or II and abuse may lead to moderate or low physical dependence or high psychological dependence. Examples: products containing not more than 90 milligrams of codeine per dosage unit (Tylenol with Codeine), buprenorphine (Suboxone), ketamine, and anabolic steroids such as Depo-Testosterone.
Schedule IV Controlled Substances	Substances in this schedule have a low potential for abuse relative to substances in Schedule III. Examples: alprazolam (Xanax), clonazepam (Klonopin), diazepam (Valium), lorazepam (Ativan), midazolam (Versed), temazepam (Restoril), and triazolam (Halcion).

(*Continued*)

Schedule V Controlled Substances	Substances in this schedule have a low potential for abuse relative to substances listed in Schedule IV and consist primarily of preparations containing limited quantities of certain narcotics.
	Examples: cough preparations containing not more than 200 milligrams of codeine per 100 milliliters or per 100 grams (Robitussin AC, Phenergan with Codeine), and ezogabine.

Source: http://www.deadiversion.usdoj.gov/schedules/.

Unfortunately, the national discourse on marijuana is often oversimplified and sensationalized. In many cases, the debate is reduced to overgeneralized arguments between marijuana prohibitionists (those who support the criminalization of marijuana production, sale, and use) and marijuana protagonists (those who support lifting criminal sanctions for marijuana-related offenses), with each side being identified according to particular talking points and supported by selected pieces of scientific evidence. Some people might wonder how both prohibitionists and protagonists are able to present scientific evidence to support their positions. The reason has to do with the fact that no single piece of scientific evidence is enough to prove or disprove a claim about marijuana. In fact, many myths and mistruths about marijuana exist because there *is* scientific evidence that can be used to support the myth. In the national debate over marijuana, it is often the case that scientific evidence is presented only partially, or presented out of context, in such a way that reifies myths and propagates mistruths about marijuana.

The reader of this book must therefore be cautioned that the "truth" about marijuana will almost never be neat and clean. The real world is rarely neat and clean. Newsmakers and politicians often try to make absolute claims about marijuana, as if, at one point in time, there may finally be answer to whether marijuana is "good" or "bad." The reader of this book, and the student of any science, will need to become comfortable with the fact that empirical evidence is useful in supporting or refuting hypotheses about marijuana, but it is surprisingly limited in its ability to prove some things to be true or false. Evidence provided in this book will document patterns of marijuana use and misuse; show that marijuana is associated with both risks and benefits; and suggest that some commonly held beliefs about marijuana may have an ounce of truth, while others have almost no scientific basis.

Because this book uses scientific evidence to support or refute commonly held beliefs about marijuana, portions of the book are dedicated to various aspects of the scientific process. Differing scientific methodologies have different strengths and weaknesses, and it is often true that misinformation about marijuana exists because conclusions are extended beyond the limits of the methodology. Moreover, it is often the case that statistics about marijuana are presented without any reference to the methods used to generate those statistics. The conscientious citizen-scientist needs to recognize that it *is* possible to find a single statistic to support almost any claim about marijuana. Accordingly, great care has been taken in this book to explain how analyses were performed and when conflicting evidence exists. In contrast to how some statistics are presented in the popular media, statistics here will be presented with a healthy degree of skepticism to ensure that unwarranted conclusions do not extend beyond the limits of the data.

This book is divided into three parts. Part 1 considers "patterns and trends" with regard to marijuana use and misuse (i.e., marijuana abuse or dependence) in the general population. Specifically, it uses data from the National Survey of Drug Use and Health (NSDUH 2016) to examine if marijuana use or marijuana misuse is more widespread today than ever before, and whether use or misuse varies by age, sex, race or ethnicity, population density, family income level, employment status, education level, and marital status. The NSDUH is considered by experts to be one of the best sources for estimating the prevalence of substance use and misuse in the general population, as well as for examining trends in use and misuse over time. Unlike national studies on youth populations, like Monitoring the Future (MTF 2016), it considers use and misuse for a wider age range (ages 12 and older), thereby allowing for the analysis of a sizable portion of American marijuana users—adults. Although youth estimates from the NSDUH tend to be somewhat lower than estimates from MTF, overall trends from both studies are quite consistent. NSDUH estimates include data from noninstitutionalized civilians with household addresses; as such, estimates do not include active-duty military personnel, homeless people who are not living in shelters, or residents of correctional, psychiatric, or long-term nursing or health care facilities or institutions. Yet, Parts 2 and 3 of this book consider relevant findings about marijuana use and misuse among such populations in emergency rooms, substance treatment centers, and the criminal justice system (i.e., prisons).

Parts 2 and 3 rely primarily on findings and information published in scholarly and peer-reviewed sources, as well as some publicly available data (like opinion polls). Part 2 considers the "risks and benefits" associated with marijuana use or misuse. It considers whether accurate information about marijuana's risks and benefits is available, and if so, whether marijuana increases risk for health problems, if marijuana is more dangerous than other types of psychoactive substances, whether it has medicinal value, or if it is addictive. Part 3 covers a range of "policy considerations" with regard to marijuana. These include whether marijuana was criminalized to protect public health and safety, whether most Americans now support marijuana criminalization, whether marijuana use is a "gateway" to the use of other illicit drugs, whether marijuana use increases criminal behavior, whether marijuana infractions are fairly punished, whether treatment for marijuana misuse is needed, whether marijuana treatment is effective, and whether marijuana prohibition is an effective drug control policy.

FURTHER READING

National Conference of State Legislators (NCSL). 2016. State Medical Marijuana Laws. 2017. http://www.ncsl.org/research/health/state-medical-marijuana-laws.aspx

National Institute on Drug Abuse. "Monitoring the Future Results (MTF)." 2016. https://www.drugabuse.gov/related-topics/trends-statistics/monitoring-future

National Survey on Drug Use and Health (NSDUH). 2016. United States Department of Health and Human Services. Substance Abuse and Mental Health Services Administration. Center for Behavioral Health Statistics and Quality. National Survey on Drug Use and Health, 2014. ICPSR36361-v1. Ann Arbor, MI: Inter-university Consortium for Political and Social Research [distributor], 2016–03–22. http://doi.org/10.3886/ICPSR36361.v1

U.S. Department of Justice. Drug Enforcement Administration. "Diversion Control Division. Definition of Controlled Substance Schedules." http://www.deadiversion.usdoj.gov/schedules/

1

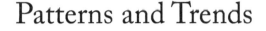

Patterns and Trends

Q1. IS MARIJUANA USE OR MISUSE MORE WIDESPREAD THAN EVER BEFORE?

Answer: No. Although there has been an increase in marijuana use in recent years, marijuana use percentages are still not as high as their peak in 1979. In addition, marijuana misuse (i.e., abuse of or dependence on marijuana) has remained stable for over a decade. Considering such patterns within key age categories, however, reveals some notable changes in marijuana use and misuse over the 2004–2014 decade. For youth (ages 12 to 17), marijuana use and misuse were significantly lower in 2014 than in 2004. For young adults (ages 18 to 25) use was higher in 2014 than in 2004, but misuse was lower in 2014 than in 2004. For adults ages 26 to 49, rates of marijuana use increased during this time, but there were no significant changes in marijuana misuse for this age group. In youth, there were very few differences in marijuana use or misuse by sex (i.e., being female or male), but across all the adult ages considered here (ages 18 to 49), women used and misused marijuana at significantly lower rates than men did (National Survey on Drug Use and Health, 2016).

The Facts: Marijuana is the most commonly used illicit drug in the United States. In 2014, an estimated 13.3 percent of the population of U.S. household residents ages 12 and older (about 35 million people) had used marijuana at least once during the prior 12 months, and

1.5 percent of that population (about 4 million people) met the American Psychiatric Association's (APA's) diagnostic criteria for marijuana abuse or dependence (those criteria are published in the APA's *Diagnostic and Statistical Manual of Mental Disorders*, also called the DSM). In order to determine if currently observed rates of marijuana use or misuse are higher than prior rates, this chapter used data from the National Survey on Drug Use and Health (NSDUH; formerly the National Household Survey on Drug Abuse or NHSDA), which is a large, representative, ongoing survey of U.S. household residents ages 12 years and older. In 1979, the survey began asking participants about their alcohol, tobacco, and other drug use, and beginning in 2000, it began also collecting data about self-reported symptoms (criteria) like those used by the APA to diagnose marijuana abuse or marijuana dependence. Since the 1990s, these national, cross-sectional surveys have been administered on a yearly basis. The most recent NSDUH data set available at the time this chapter was written was from 2014.

DSM DIAGNOSTIC CRITERIA FOR MARIJUANA ABUSE AND DEPENDENCE

MEASURING MARIJUANA MISUSE

In the fourth edition of the *Diagnostic and Statistical Manual of Mental Disorders* (DSM-IV), marijuana "abuse" and marijuana "dependence" are independent diagnoses. Accordingly, the National Survey of Drug Use and Health (NSDUH) measures each of these concepts individually.

A respondent was defined as having marijuana (cannabis) dependence if he or she met three or more of the following criteria: (1) Spent great deal of time obtaining, using, or recovering from marijuana; (2) Used marijuana more often than intended; (3) Needed to use marijuana more than before to get desired effects; (4) Unable to cut down or stop using marijuana; (5) Continued to use marijuana even though it was causing problems with nerves, mental health, or physical health; (6) Marijuana use reduced or eliminated involvement or participation in important activities.

A respondent was defined as having abused marijuana if he or she met one or more of the following criteria: (1) Serious problems at home, work, or school caused by marijuana; (2) Used marijuana regularly in hazardous situations; (3) Use of marijuana repeatedly caused problems with the law; (4) Had problems with family or friends that were probably caused by using marijuana and continued to use marijuana in spite of these problems.

Unless otherwise noted, this book uses the term marijuana misuse to refer to the constellation of behaviors and symptoms that meet the DSM-IV criteria for *either* "abuse" *or* "dependence" in the prior 12 months.

Confusion about current and previous patterns of marijuana use and marijuana misuse appears to stem from several sources. One source involves how people define or measure marijuana *use* as opposed to marijuana *misuse*. Due in part to the federal placement of marijuana on its list of illicit or illegal substances, many people mistakenly define marijuana "abuse" (or misuse) as any "use" of marijuana—that is, they do not distinguish infrequent, medicinal, or otherwise low-risk use of marijuana from marijuana misuse, which is more serious, dangerous, unhealthy, or otherwise problematic. The risks and benefits associated with simply using marijuana are often quite different from those of marijuana misuse. This chapter draws from the NSDUH data to define marijuana *use* as the self-reported nonmedical use of that substance over a defined period of time, such as during the 12 months or 30 days prior to the survey. *Misuse* is defined as meeting the APA's diagnostic criteria for DSM-IV marijuana abuse or dependence in the 12 months prior to the survey.

Part of the confusion about U.S. marijuana use and/or misuse patterns and trends can also come from how statistics about marijuana use behaviors are estimated and reported to the public. Relying on individuals' "lifetime" use estimates, rather than recent use estimates (e.g., during the 30 days or 12 months prior to their surveys), can artificially inflate rates of marijuana use, thus leading to the false conclusion that marijuana use is more widespread today than ever before. This distortion results, in part, from historical changes in marijuana use patterns. Today's adults are more likely than adults from earlier generations to have tried marijuana when they were younger, but that does not necessarily mean that current marijuana use or marijuana misuse is higher now than previously.

Another potential source of confusion about marijuana use patterns and trends has to do with the tendency for many researchers (and the public) to focus mostly on the study of youth or young adult populations. In part, this tendency makes sense because marijuana use and misuse typically begin in adolescence and peak in young adulthood. However, the failure to consider marijuana use patterns beyond young adulthood can limit our understanding about a significant portion of the U.S. population's marijuana users. In addition, the failure to consider the role and significance of sex (i.e., being male or female) can detract from our understanding of the landscape of marijuana use and misuse in America.

THE DATA

As described earlier, some of the confusion surrounding marijuana use trends likely stems from the different ways in which marijuana use and misuse are estimated and reported. As Figure 1.1 shows, since 1979 there has been a steady and statistically significant rise in the percentage of U.S. household residents who have reported *ever* using marijuana. In 1979, nearly 30 percent of residents ages 12 and older reported that they had used marijuana at least once during their lifetimes, and by 2000 that percentage had increased to just over 34. Although not directly comparable

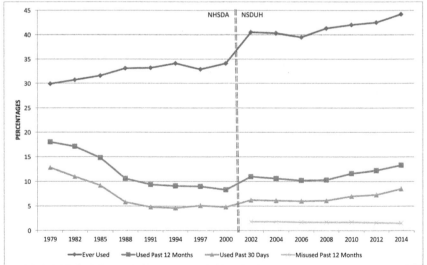

Note: Data are from the National Survey on Drug Use and Health (NSDUH; formerly the National Household Survey on Drug Abuse or NHSDA). In 2002, the study methodology (and the name of the study) was changed to better estimate substance use patterns in the population (and to highlight the new broader focus of the study). As such, percentage estimates from before 2002 (the NHSDA) cannot be directly compared to estimates from 2002 and later (the NSDUH).

Figure 1.1 Marijuana Use Patterns among U.S. Residents Age 12 and Older from 1979 to 2014

to rates before 2002 (see the NSDUH codebook), during the most recent year for which data were available (in 2014), the percentage of residents who reported ever using marijuana was just over 44 percent—that is, nearly a one-third increase since 1979. Based on this type of estimate, one might falsely conclude that marijuana use is higher than it has ever been, or at least within the past 35 years. Notably, even at its highest percentage (in 2014), less than half of all NSDUH respondents ages 12 and older reported having ever used marijuana in their lifetimes. If these percentage estimates are correct, then as of 2014, the *majority* of U.S. household residents had *never* used marijuana. Yet interestingly, as Q17 explains, a majority (over half) of U.S. citizens support the legalization of marijuana for recreational use.

When marijuana use is estimated based on *recent* use (i.e., use in the previous 30 days or the previous 12 months), however, a different and more accurate picture emerges. In 1979, 18.0 percent of respondents ages 12 and older reported that they had used marijuana in the previous 12 months, and 12.8 percent had used it in the prior 30 days. By 2000, those respective percentages had fallen to 8.3 and 4.8—that is, to less than *half* the rates observed two decades before. This decline mirrors a general reduction in the use of various illicit substances during this same time period. Between 2002 and 2014, statistically significant increases in percentages were observed for both past 12-month use (from 11.0 percent to 14.3 percent) and past 30-day use (from 6.2 percent to 8.5 percent). Yet these rates were still *lower* than the rates observed in 1979—thus, the *use* of marijuana does not appear to be more widespread today than it was just three-and-one-half decades ago.

Unfortunately, the NSDUH (formerly the NHSDA) did not contain measures of marijuana abuse or dependence prior to the 2000s, so estimating marijuana misuse during those earlier years is not possible. In addition, due to changes in the NSDUH study methodology, marijuana abuse and dependence estimates from before 2002 cannot be reliably compared to estimates in 2002 and later (see the NSDUH codebook). Therefore, for purposes of this chapter, measures of DSM marijuana abuse and dependence, beginning in 2002 and ending in 2014, were used to estimate marijuana misuse. That is, based on their survey responses, respondents who met DSM criteria for past 12-month marijuana abuse or dependence in 2002, 2004, 2006, 2008, 2010, 2012, and 2014 were categorized as misusers of marijuana. Then the marijuana misuse percentages across those years were compared to reveal any changes (see Figure 1.1).

As Figure 1.1 shows, marijuana misuse percentages among U.S. household residents ages 12 and older have remained below 2 percent for over a decade. This percentage is much lower than for the self-reported *use* of marijuana in the prior year, which has ranged from 10.2 percent to 13.3 percent over this 12-year period. Although there had been statistically significant increases in the rates of past 12-month marijuana *use* between 2002 and 2014, there had not been similarly significant changes in marijuana *misuse* during that same period. Thus, there is *no* evidence to suggest that marijuana misuse is more widespread today. In fact, marijuana misuse seems to have remained remarkably and consistently low for more than a decade, at least when rates among U.S. residents ages 12 and older were considered together.

Patterns by Age

One of the most reliable predictors of substance use and misuse is *age*. The use or misuse of illicit substances like marijuana begins in early adolescence, increases into late adolescence, peaks in young adulthood, and subsides thereafter. Because of this, it is important that estimates of marijuana use and marijuana misuse consider patterns within key age categories. Although the estimates reported earlier (among U.S. residents ages 12 and older) provide useful information about general trends, average percentage estimates at key risk periods, like during youth and young adulthood, can provide nuanced insight into the nature of marijuana use and marijuana misuse patterns and trends.

Using data from the NSDUH study in 2004 and 2014, Table 1.1 provides average percentages of marijuana use and marijuana misuse within four age categories: ages 12 to 17 years (youth), ages 18 to 25 years (young adults), ages 26 to 34 years (pre-middle-aged adults), and ages 35 to 49 years (middle-aged adults). As the table shows, age was statistically significantly related to both marijuana use and marijuana misuse in both 2004 and 2014. As expected, young adults showed the highest percentages of past 12-month marijuana use and marijuana misuse in both 2004 (when young adult use was 27.8 percent and misuse was 6.0 percent) and 2014 (when young adult use was 32.2 percent and misuse was 4.9 percent). Over the course of the decade, marijuana *use* rates changed significantly for all of the age categories considered, while marijuana *misuse* rates changed significantly only for youth and young adults.

Table 1.1 Past 12-Month Marijuana Use and Misuse Percentages by Age in 2004 and 2014

	Marijuana Use		Marijuana Misuse	
	2004	2014	2004	2014
Age 12 to 17	14.5%	13.2*	3.9	2.7***
Age 18 to 25	27.8	32.2***	6.0	4.9***
Age 26 to 34	13.8	20.2***	2.0	2.2
Age 35 to 49	9.2	11.1**	0.9	1.0
	(p < .001)	(p < .001)	(p < .001)	(p < .001)

Note: Data are from the 2004 and 2014 NSDUH.
* p < .05; ** p < .01; *** p < .001.

Youth patterns showed a slight but statistically significant *decline* in past 12-month marijuana use between 2004 and 2014, while the data for all of the adult age groups indicated *increases* in marijuana use during that same period. From these results, it can be inferred that the increases in marijuana consumption observed over this decade are largely attributable to changes in U.S. adult marijuana use behaviors and not the marijuana use behaviors of U.S. youth. With regard to marijuana misuse, average percentages have either decreased or stayed the same, depending on the age category considered. That is, for youth and young adults, marijuana misuse rates were significantly *lower* in 2014 than they were in 2004, while for pre-middle and middle-aged adults, there were no significant changes in marijuana misuse percentages over that same 10-year period. Notably, increases in marijuana use were *not* accompanied by concomitant rises in marijuana misuse.

Patterns by Sex

Sex (i.e., being male or female) is a persistent and strong correlate of substance use and misuse both nationally and cross-nationally, at least in adulthood. In particular, men tend to use and misuse substances at higher rates than women. Similarly, as Figure 1.2 and Table 1.2 show, over the 2004–2014 decade there had been consistent, statistically significant sex differences in both marijuana use and marijuana misuse for U.S. young adults, pre-middle-aged adults, and middle-aged adults, with males reporting greater use and misuse of marijuana than their female counterparts.

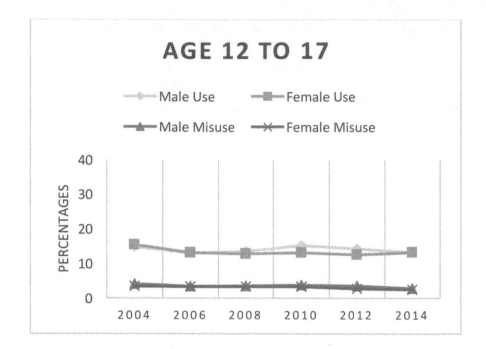

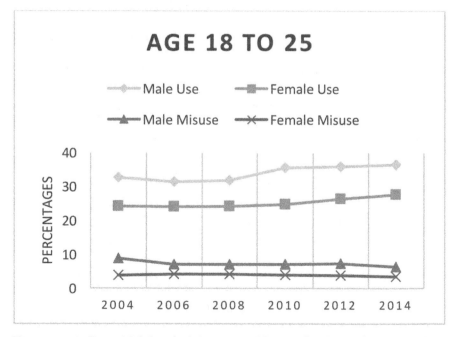

Figure 1.2 Past 12-Month Marijuana Use and Misuse by Age, Year, and Sex

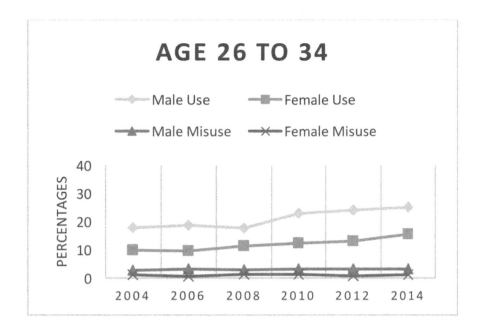

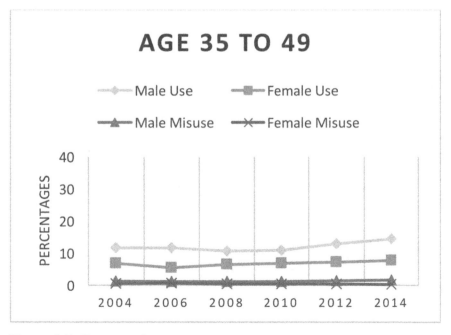

Figure 1.2 Continued

Table 1.2 Past 12-Month Marijuana Use and Misuse: Within Year Percentage Differences by Age and Sex

		Age 12 to 17		Age 18 to 25		Age 26 to 34		Age 35 to 49	
		Use	Misuse	Use	Misuse	Use	Misuse	Use	Misuse
2004	Male	14.8%	4.2	32.7	8.8	17.8	2.8	11.7	1.3
	Female	15.4	3.5	24.2	3.8	9.9	1.2	6.8	0.5
		(ns)	(ns)	(p < .001)	(p < .001)	(p < .001)	(p < .01)	(p < .001)	(p < .01)
2006	Male	13.0	3.5	31.4	7.1	18.7	3.3	11.7	1.2
	Female	13.1	3.4	24.0	4.2	9.6	0.6	5.4	0.6
		(ns)	(ns)	(p < .001)	(p < .001)	(p < .001)	(p < .001)	(p < .001)	(p < .05)
2008	Male	13.5	3.6	31.8	7.1	17.7	3.0	10.6	1.2
	Female	12.8	3.3	24.2	4.2	11.3	1.4	6.5	0.4
		(ns)	(ns)	(p < .001)	(p < .001)	(p < .001)	(p < .01)	(p < .001)	(p < .01)
2010	Male	15.2	3.8	35.5	7.1	22.9	3.2	10.9	1.1
	Female	13.1	3.3	24.7	4.0	12.3	1.4	6.8	0.4
		(p < .01)	(ns)	(p < .001)	(p < .001)	(p < .001)	(p < .01)	(p < .001)	(p < .01)
2012	Male	14.3	3.6	35.9	7.3	24.1	3.3	12.9	1.4
	Female	12.6	2.8	26.4	3.8	13.1	0.8	7.2	0.4
		(p < .05)	(p < .05)	(p < .001)	(p < .001)	(p < .001)	(p < .001)	(p < .001)	(p < .01)
2014	Male	13.3	2.9	36.5	6.4	25.1	3.3	14.5	1.7
	Female	13.2	2.5	27.7	3.5	15.5	1.2	7.7	0.3
		(ns)	(ns)	(p < .001)	(p < .001)	(p < .001)	(p < .001)	(p < .001)	(p < .001)

Note: Data are from the National Survey on Drug Use and Health (NSDUH 2004–2014).
ns = not statistically significant at p < .05.

Specifically, among young adults (ages 18 to 25) during the 2004–2014 decade, rates of past 12-month marijuana use ranged from 31.4 percent to 36.5 percent for males and from 24.0 percent to 27.7 percent for females. Among pre-middle-aged adults (ages 26 to 34), such rates ranged from 17.7 percent to 25.1 percent for males and from 9.6 percent to 15.5 percent for females. Among middle-aged adults (ages 35 to 49), percentages of past 12-month marijuana use during that same decade ranged from 10.6 percent to 14.5 percent for males and from 6.5 percent to 7.7 percent for females.

In addition, marijuana misuse was significantly higher for males than for females in all three of the adult age categories and for all of the years (2004 to 2014) considered. Among young adults, the average percentages of past 12-month marijuana misuse ranged from 6.4 percent to 8.8 percent for males and from 3.5 percent to 4.2 percent for females. Among pre-middle-aged adults, rates ranged from 2.8 percent to 3.3 percent for males and from 0.6 percent to 1.4 percent for females. Among middle-aged adults, percentages ranged from 1.1 percent to 1.7 percent for males and from 0.3 percent and 0.6 percent for females.

Among youth (ages 12 to 17), however, it was during only two of the years considered, 2010 and 2012, when the data showed significant sex differences in marijuana use, and it was in only one year (2012) that sex differences in marijuana *misuse* were observed for this age group. In those years where significant differences emerged, the pattern was similar to adult patterns; that is, boys used and misused marijuana at significantly higher rates than girls did. Yet, the bulk of the evidence here suggests that sex differences in marijuana use and marijuana misuse do not typically emerge until adulthood.

Finally, over the 2004–2014 decade, girls' (ages 12 to 17) rates of marijuana use did not change, but girls were significantly *less* likely to misuse marijuana later that decade than earlier in the decade. For boys, both marijuana use and marijuana misuse *decreased* significantly during that same time period. Young-adult (ages 18 to 25) marijuana use *increased* significantly for both men and women, and although young women's marijuana misuse did not change during this period, young men's rates of marijuana misuse *decreased* significantly between 2004 and 2014. For pre-middle-aged adults (ages 26 to 34), marijuana use *increased* significantly for both men and women, while marijuana misuse rates remained largely the same for men and women (except that for women, misuse was significantly higher in 2014 than in 2006). For middle-aged adults (ages 35 to 49), marijuana use *increased* significantly among males, and for females, marijuana use in 2014 was significantly greater than use in 2006; with regard to marijuana misuse, rates for this age group remained quite low and did not change.

ACKNOWLEDGMENT

The National Survey on Drug Use and Health (NSDUH), which is made available by the Inter-University Consortium for Political and Social Science, is supported by the Substance Abuse and Mental Health Services Administration and the U.S. Department of Health and Human Services. Any opinions, findings, conclusions, or recommendations expressed in this chapter are those of the authors and do not necessarily reflect the views of the funders.

FURTHER READING

American Psychiatric Association (APA). *Diagnostic and statistical manual of mental disorders*. 4th ed. Washington, DC: American Psychiatric Association, 1994.

Centers for Disease Control and Prevention (CDC). "National estimates of marijuana use and related indicators—National Survey on Drug Use and Health, United States, 2002–2014." *Surveillance Summaries* 65, no. 11 (2016): 1–25. https://www.cdc.gov/mmwr/volumes/65/ss/ss6511a1.htm

Compton, Wilson M., Beth Han, Christopher M. Jones, Carlos Blanco, and Arthur Hughes. "Marijuana use and use disorders in adults in the USA, 2002–14: analysis of annual cross-sectional surveys." *The Lancet Psychiatry* 3, no. 10 (2016): 954–964.

Evans-Polce, Rebecca J., Sara A. Vasilenko, and Stephanie T. Lanza. "Changes in gender and racial/ethnic disparities in rates of cigarette use, regular heavy episodic drinking, and marijuana use: ages 14 to 32." *Addictive Behaviors* 41 (2015): 218–222.

Haberstick, Brett C., Susan E. Young, Joanna S. Zeiger, Jeffrey M. Lessem, John K. Hewitt, and Christian J. Hopfer. "Prevalence and correlates of alcohol and cannabis use disorders in the United States: results from the longitudinal study of adolescent health." *Drug and Alcohol Dependence* 136 (2014): 158–161.

Hasin, Deborah S., Bradley T. Kerridge, Tulshi D. Saha, Boji Huang, Roger Pickering, Sharon M. Smith, Jeesun Jung, Haitao Zhang, and Bridget F. Grant. "Prevalence and correlates of DSM-5 cannabis use disorder, 2012–2013: findings from the National Epidemiologic Survey on Alcohol and Related Conditions–III." *The American Journal of Psychiatry* 173, no. 6 (2016): 588–599.

Hasin, Deborah S., Tulshi D. Saha, Bradley T. Kerridge, Risë B. Goldstein, S. Patricia Chou, Haitao Zhang, Jeesun Jung, Roger P. Pickering, W. June Ruan, Sharon M. Smith, Boji Huang, and Bridget F. Grant. "Prevalence of marijuana use disorders in the United States between 2001–2002 and 2012–2013." *JAMA Psychiatry* 72, no. 12, (2015): 1235–1242.

National Survey on Drug Use and Health (NSDUH). United States Department of Health and Human Services. Substance Abuse and Mental Health Services Administration. Center for Behavioral Health Statistics and Quality. National Survey on Drug Use and Health, 2014. ICPSR36361-v1. Ann Arbor, MI: Inter-university Consortium for Political and Social Research [distributor], March 22, 2016. http://doi .org/10.3886/ICPSR36361.v1

Substance Abuse and Mental Health Services Administration. Center for Behavioral Statistics and Quality. 2014 National Survey on Drug Use and Health. "Methodological Summary and Definitions." September 2015. https://www.samhsa.gov/data/sites/default/files/NSDUH-Method SummDefs2014/NSDUH-MethodSummDefs2014.htm#b4–2

Q2. DOES MARIJUANA USE OR MISUSE VARY BY RACE OR ETHNICITY?

Answer: Yes. When comparing the three largest U.S. racial or ethnic groups (Whites, Hispanics, and African Americans), there are statistically significant differences in marijuana use and misuse (i.e., abuse of or dependence on marijuana), but the nature of those patterns varies by age and sex and over time. In general, racial or ethnic differences do not emerge until young adulthood. Until recently, White Americans, especially men, tended to use marijuana at rates higher than both African Americans and Hispanic Americans, but in 2014, both White and African American men tended to show the highest use rates, and Hispanic women showed the lowest use rates. With regard to marijuana misuse, racial and ethnic differences were less consistent. When differences emerged, African American men showed the highest rates of marijuana misuse, and misuse tended to be lowest for women regardless of race or ethnicity.

The Facts: Many people assume that U.S. racial or ethnic minorities use or misuse illicit substances, like marijuana, at higher rates than do nonminority populations. In order to examine this assumption, this chapter used data from the ongoing National Survey on Drug Use and Health (NSDUH 2016), a large and nationally representative survey of U.S. household residents ages 12 and older, between the years 2004 and 2014. These yearly, cross-sectional, self-administered surveys asked participants to answer confidential questions about their use or misuse of marijuana in the 12 months prior to the survey. *Marijuana users* included those who reported that they had used marijuana at all in that 12-month period, and *marijuana misusers* included those who reported that during that time they experienced symptoms (criteria) like those used by the American Psychiatric Association to diagnose marijuana abuse or dependence (those criteria are presented in Q1). Racial and ethnic statuses were defined based on the NSDUH respondents' self-reported identification with one of three racial or ethnic groups: White, Hispanic, or African American.

Among household residents ages 12 and older in 2014, the most recent year for which data were available when this book was written, estimates of marijuana use were highest for African Americans (16.1 percent), followed by Whites (13.9 percent), followed by Hispanics (11.0 percent). Marijuana misuse was highest among African Americans (2.5 percent), but roughly the same for Whites (1.4 percent) and Hispanics (1.7 percent). Although these estimates suggest elevated percentages of marijuana use and marijuana misuse among African Americans relative to Whites and Hispanics, such patterns vary importantly by age and sex, and they have changed significantly over the past decade.

PATTERNS BY AGE

Age is one of the most reliable predictors of the use and misuse of marijuana. That is, marijuana use and misuse tend to begin in early adolescence, increase into late adolescence, peak in young adulthood, and subside thereafter. Therefore, this chapter examines racial or ethnic differences in marijuana use and marijuana misuse within four key age categories: ages 12 to 17 years (youth), ages 18 to 25 years (young adults), ages 26 to 34 years (pre-middle-aged adults), and ages 35 to 49 years (middle-aged adults). As Figure 1.3 and Table 1.3 reveal, patterns of racial or ethnic differences in marijuana use and marijuana misuse vary depending on the age categories and years (between 2004 and 2014) considered.

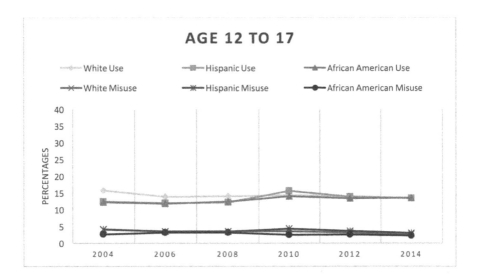

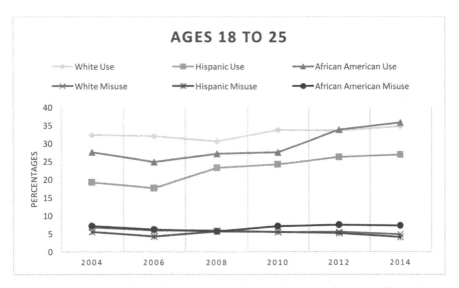

Figure 1.3 Past 12-Month Marijuana Use and Misuse by Age, Year, Race, and Ethnicity

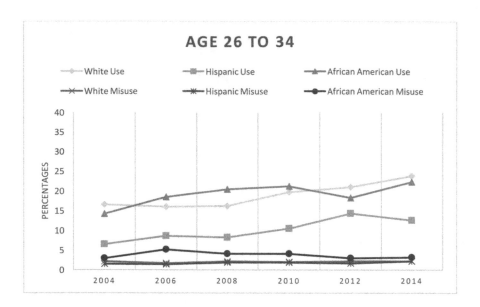

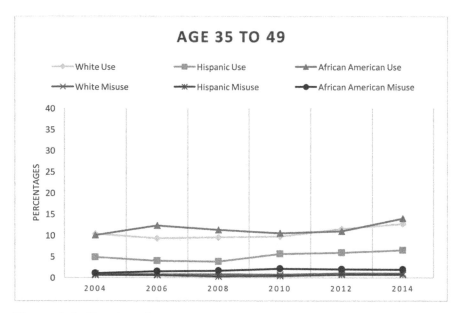

Figure 1.3 Continued

Table 1.3 Past 12-Month Marijuana Use and Misuse: Within-Year Percentage Estimates by Race and Ethnicity

	Age 12 to 17		Age 18 to 25		Age 26 to 34		Age 35 to 49	
	Use	Misuse	Use	Misuse	Use	Misuse	Use	Misuse
2004								
White	15.8%	4.1	32.3	6.7	16.5	2.1	10.3	0.9
Hispanic	12.4	4.2	19.2	5.5	6.5	1.5	4.8	0.6
African American	12.3	2.7	27.5	7.1	14.2	2.9	10.0	1.0
	(p < .05)	(p < .05)	(p < .05)	(ns)	(p < .05)	(ns)	(p < .05)	(ns)
2006								
White	13.9	3.6	32.0	5.9	16.0	1.7	9.3	0.8
Hispanic	12.0	3.5	17.6	4.2	8.6	1.4	4.0	0.6
African American	11.8	3.2	24.8	6.1	18.5	5.2	12.3	1.5
	(p < .05)	(ns)	(p < .05)	(p < .05)	(p < .05)	(p < .05)	(p < .05)	(ns)
2008								
White	14.0	3.6	30.5	5.9	16.2	2.1	9.5	0.8
Hispanic	12.2	3.5	23.2	5.6	8.2	1.9	3.8	0.3
African American	12.4	3.2	27.1	5.6	20.4	4.1	11.3	1.6
	(ns)	(ns)	(p < .05)	(ns)	(p < .05)	(p < .05)	(p < .05)	(p < .05)

(Continued)

Table 1.3 Continued

		Age 12 to 17		Age 18 to 25		Age 26 to 34		Age 35 to 49	
		Use	Misuse	Use	Misuse	Use	Misuse	Use	Misuse
2010	White	14.3	3.6	33.7	5.4	19.7	2.0	9.7	0.7
	Hispanic	15.6	4.4	24.2	5.5	10.5	1.9	5.6	0.4
	African American	14.0	2.5	27.5	7.1	21.2	4.1	10.5	2.1
		(ns)	(p < .05)	(p < .05)	(p < .05)	(p < .05)	(p < .05)	(p < .05)	(p < .05)
2012	White	14.0	3.2	33.5	5.5	21.0	2.2	11.5	1.0
	Hispanic	13.9	3.7	26.2	5.1	14.3	1.7	5.9	0.7
	African American	13.4	2.6	33.8	7.4	18.3	3.0	11.0	1.9
		(ns)	(ns)	(p < .05)	(p < .05)	(p < .05)	(ns)	(p < .05)	(p < .05)
2014	White	13.5	2.8	34.7	4.8	23.8	2.2	12.7	1.0
	Hispanic	13.4	3.1	26.8	4.0	12.6	2.2	6.5	0.7
	African American	13.6	2.3	35.7	7.2	22.3	3.2	14.0	1.9
		(ns)	(ns)	(p < .05)	(p < .05)	(p < .05)	(ns)	(p < .05)	(p < .05)

Note: Data are from the National Survey on Drug Use and Health (NSDUH 2004–2014).
ns = not statistically significant at p < .05.

Marijuana Use

Among youth (ages 12 to 17) during the 2004–2014 decade, rates of past 12-month use of marijuana ranged from 13.5 percent to 15.8 percent for Whites, 12.0 percent to 15.6 percent for Hispanics, and 11.8 percent to 14.0 percent for African Americans. In only two years (2004 and 2006) were statistically significant differences by race or ethnicity observed for youth, and in both of those years, it was White youth who reported the *highest* percentages of marijuana use in the prior year. These findings suggest that there were few differences by race or ethnicity in marijuana use among youth during the 2004–2014 decade, at least when considering rates among the three largest U.S. racial or ethnic groups. When differences did emerge, they did *not* support the notion that racial or ethnic minorities use marijuana at levels higher than their nonminority counterparts. If anything, White youth tended to use marijuana at higher rates. The overall evidence, however, suggests that youth marijuana use does not vary meaningfully by race or ethnicity.

Although clear racial or ethnic differences in marijuana use were not found among youth, past 12-month use did vary significantly by race or ethnicity among adults in every year considered (2004, 2006, 2008, 2010, 2012, and 2014). For young adults (ages 18 to 25), marijuana use rates ranged from 30.5 percent to 34.7 percent for Whites, 17.6 percent to 26.8 percent for Hispanics, and 24.8 percent to 35.7 percent for African Americans. In every year considered, Hispanic use rates were statistically significantly lower than the marijuana use rates of both Whites and African Americans in young adulthood. Marijuana use rates among African American young adults were statistically significantly lower than use rates among White young adults until 2012; however, in both 2012 and 2014, White and African American young adults reported using marijuana at essentially equivalent rates.

For pre-middle-aged adults (ages 26 to 34), marijuana use rates ranged from 16.0 percent to 23.8 percent for Whites, 6.5 percent to 14.3 percent for Hispanics, and 14.2 percent to 22.3 percent for African Americans over the 2004–2014 decade. Hispanic marijuana use rates were statistically significantly lower than rates for both African Americans and Whites in every year considered with one exception; in 2012, Hispanic use was significantly lower than White use but not African American use. In all but one year (2008), African American and White pre-middle-aged adults showed nearly equal rates of use. For middle-aged adults (ages 35 to 49), marijuana use rates ranged from 9.3 percent to 12.7 percent for Whites, 3.8 percent to 6.5 percent for Hispanics, and

10.0 percent to 14.0 percent for African Americans. Again, the patterns showed consistent and statistically significantly lower marijuana use rates for Hispanics relative to Whites and African Americans, and White and African American middle-aged adults showed essentially equal rates in every year considered but one; in 2006, African Americans reported significantly higher marijuana use rates than Whites.

In sum, with regard to marijuana use, there were few meaningful racial or ethnic differences in youth; however, differences did surface among adults. In nearly all of the years considered between 2004 and 2014, Hispanic adults showed significantly lower rates of marijuana use relative to their White and African American counterparts. In young adulthood, Whites reported significantly higher percentages of use than African Americans until 2012, when White and African American rates of use converged. In addition, Whites and African Americans reported comparable rates of use within the pre-middle and middle-age adult categories. Although there were racial or ethnic differences in adult marijuana use, the notion that racial or ethnic minorities used marijuana more than non-minorities was *not* supported by these data.

Marijuana Misuse

Among youth in the 2004–2014 decade, rates of marijuana misuse ranged from 2.8 percent to 4.1 percent for Whites, 3.1 percent to 4.4 percent for Hispanics, and 2.6 percent to 3.2 percent for African Americans. It was during only two years considered (2004 and 2010) that the misuse of marijuana varied by race or ethnicity to a statistically significant degree; in both cases, African American youth showed the *lowest* rates of marijuana misuse. Similar to marijuana *use*, however, the bulk of the evidence shows that marijuana *misuse* does not vary importantly by race or ethnicity among U.S. youth.

In adulthood, however, a trend toward higher misuse among African Americans emerged. Among young adults (ages 18 to 25), rates of marijuana misuse ranged from 4.8 percent to 6.7 percent for Whites, 4.0 percent to 5.6 percent for Hispanics, and 5.6 percent to 7.4 percent for African Americans. In four of the years considered (2006, 2010, 2012, and 2014), African American young adults misused marijuana at statistically significantly higher rates than White young adults, and in three of those same years (2006, 2012, and 2014), African American young adults misused marijuana at significantly higher rates than Hispanic young adults.

Among pre-middle-aged adults (ages 26 to 34), rates of marijuana misuse ranged from 1.7 percent to 2.2 percent for Whites, 1.4 percent to 2.2 percent for Hispanics, and 2.9 percent to 5.2 percent for African Americans. Rates of misuse for African Americans in this age category were significantly higher than rates for their White and Hispanic counterparts in 2006, 2008, and 2010. Among middle-aged adults (ages 35 to 49), misuse rates ranged from 0.7 percent to 1.0 percent for Whites, 0.3 percent to 0.7 percent for Hispanics, and 1.0 percent to 2.1 percent for African Americans. From 2008 to 2014, African Americans in this age group showed statistically significantly higher rates of marijuana misuse than Hispanics, and from 2010 to 2014, African Americans showed significantly higher rates of marijuana misuse than Whites.

In sum, the findings suggest that with regard to marijuana misuse, there are some racial or ethnic differences, at least in adulthood. When differences surfaced, African American adults tended to show the highest rates of marijuana misuse. That is, even though a sizeable U.S. racial minority population (African American adults) did not *use* marijuana at higher rates than their nonminority counterparts, they did *misuse* marijuana at rates higher than their nonminority counterparts in roughly half of the years considered over the 2004–2014 decade.

Recent Changes

Increases in marijuana use over the 2004–2014 decade did not seem to correspond with concomitant increases in marijuana misuse during that same time; yet, patterns did vary somewhat by age and sex. Similarly, changes in marijuana use and marijuana misuse varied by age and race or ethnicity. In youth (ages 12 to 17), marijuana use changed significantly only for Whites; in 2014, White youth were significantly less likely to report using marijuana in the previous 12 months than they were in 2004, while use rates among Hispanic and African American youth did not change during the decade. With regard to marijuana misuse, White youth showed significantly lower rates in 2014 than in 2004, 2006, 2008, and 2010, Hispanic youth showed a lower rate in 2014 than in 2010, and no significant changes in marijuana misuse were observed for African American youth during this time period.

In contrast, adult marijuana use tended to increase for all racial or ethnic groups over the 2004–2014 decade, and in most adult age groups, marijuana misuse remained relatively stable during that time. For young adults (ages 18 to 25), regardless of race or ethnicity, rates of marijuana use were significantly higher in 2014 than they were in 2004, 2006, and 2008; in addition, African American use was significantly higher in 2014 than it was in 2010. In young adulthood, marijuana misuse decreased for Whites (2014 rates were significantly lower than rates in 2004, 2006, and 2008) and Hispanics (2014 rates were significantly lower than 2008 rates); no changes in African American misuse were observed for young adults during this time period.

For pre-middle-aged adults (ages 26 to 34), marijuana use rates for Whites in 2014 were statistically significantly higher than rates in all the other years considered (2004 to 2012); for Hispanics, 2014 use rates were significantly higher than rates in 2004 to 2008; and for African Americans, 2014 rates were significantly higher than 2004 rates. For middle-aged adults (ages 25 to 49), marijuana use rates for Whites in 2014 were statistically significantly higher than their rates in 2004–2010; for Hispanics, 2014 marijuana use rates were higher than rates in 2006; and for African Americans, 2014 marijuana use rates were higher than rates in 2004. No changes in marijuana misuse were observed for pre-middle or middle-aged adults regardless of race or ethnicity during the 2004–2014 decade.

PATTERNS BY SEX

Finally, self-reported sex (as female or male) is related to marijuana use and marijuana misuse strongly and consistently, at least in adulthood. In Table 1.4, estimates of past 12-month marijuana use and marijuana

Table 1.4 Past 12-Month Marijuana Use and Misuse Percentages by Age, Sex, Race, and Ethnicity in 2014

| | | Marijuana Use | | Marijuana Misuse | |
		Males	Females	Males	Females
Age 12 to 17	White	13.8%	13.2	2.7	2.8
	Hispanic	12.3	14.6	3.4	2.7
	African American	14.3	12.9	3.3	1.2*
Age 18 to 25	White	38.8	30.5*	6.6	2.9*
	Hispanic	32.1	21.1*	4.2	3.8
	African American	40.9	31.1*	9.7	5.0*
Age 26 to 34	White	29.7	18.0*	2.9	1.5*
	Hispanic	14.9	10.2*	3.9	0.5*
	African American	28.2	17.1*	4.9	1.7*
Age 35 to 49	White	16.1	9.2*	1.5	0.4*
	Hispanic	9.5	3.5*	1.4	N/A
	African American	20.1	8.7*	4.0	0.2*

Note: Data are from the National Survey on Drug Use and Health (NSDUH 2014).
* p < .05 (sex differences).

misuse by age, sex, and race or ethnicity are presented using data from 2014, the most recent year data available when this book was written. For youth (ages 12 to 17) there were no sex differences in marijuana use or marijuana misuse with one exception; African American girls tended to misuse marijuana at significantly lower rates than their male counterparts. Regardless of race or ethnicity, young adult men (ages 18 to 25) tended to use and misuse marijuana at statistically significantly higher rates than women with one exception; rates of marijuana misuse among Hispanic young adults did not vary significantly by sex. Finally, for pre-middle and middle-aged adults (ages 26 to 34 and 35 to 49), White, Hispanic, and African American men used and misused marijuana at significantly higher rates than did White, Hispanic, and African American women, respectively.

ACKNOWLEDGMENT

The National Survey on Drug Use and Health (NSDUH), which is made available by the Inter-University Consortium for Political and Social Science, is supported by the Substance Abuse and Mental Health Services Administration and the U.S. Department of Health and Human Services. Any opinions, findings, conclusions, or recommendations expressed in this chapter are those of the authors and do not necessarily reflect the views of the funders.

FURTHER READING

Centers for Disease Control and Prevention (CDC). "National estimates of marijuana use and related indicators—National Survey on Drug Use and Health, United States, 2002–2014." *Surveillance Summaries* 65, no. 11 (2016): 1–25. https://www.cdc.gov/mmwr/volumes/65/ss/ss6511a1 .htm

Compton, Wilson M., Beth Han, Christopher M. Jones, Carlos Blanco, and Arthur Hughes. "Marijuana use and use disorders in adults in the USA, 2002–14: analysis of annual cross-sectional surveys." *The Lancet Psychiatry* 3, no. 10 (2016): 954–964.

Evans-Polce, Rebecca J., Sara A. Vasilenko, and Stephanie T. Lanza. "Changes in gender and racial/ethnic disparities in rates of cigarette use, regular heavy episodic drinking, and marijuana use: ages 14 to 32." *Addictive Behaviors* 41 (2015): 218–222.

Haberstick, Brett C., Susan E. Young, Joanna S. Zeiger, Jeffrey M. Lessem, John K. Hewitt, and Christian J. Hopfer. "Prevalence and correlates of alcohol and cannabis use disorders in the United States: results from the longitudinal study of adolescent health." *Drug and Alcohol Dependence* 136 (2014): 158–161.

Hasin, Deborah S., Bradley T. Kerridge, Tulshi D. Saha, Boji Huang, Roger Pickering, Sharon M. Smith, Jeesun Jung, Haitao Zhang, and Bridget F. Grant. "Prevalence and correlates of DSM-5 cannabis use disorder, 2012–2013: findings from the National Epidemiologic Survey on Alcohol and Related Conditions–III." *The American Journal of Psychiatry* 173, no. 6 (2016): 588–599.

Hasin, Deborah S., Tulshi D. Saha, Bradley T. Kerridge, Risë B. Goldstein, S. Patricia Chou, Haitao Zhang, Jeesun Jung, Roger P. Pickering, W. June Ruan, Sharon M. Smith, Boji Huang, and Bridget F. Grant. "Prevalence of marijuana use disorders in the United States between 2001–2002 and 2012–2013." *JAMA Psychiatry* 72, no. 12 (2015): 1235–1242.

National Survey on Drug Use and Health (NSDUH). United States Department of Health and Human Services. Substance Abuse and Mental Health Services Administration. Center for Behavioral Health Statistics and Quality. National Survey on Drug Use and Health, 2014. ICPSR36361-v1. Ann Arbor, MI: Inter-university Consortium for Political and Social Research [distributor], March 22, 2016. http://doi.org/10.3886/ICPSR36361.v1

Q3. DOES MARIJUANA USE OR MISUSE VARY BY POPULATION DENSITY?

Answer: Yes and no. U.S. rates of marijuana *use* tend to be lower in rural areas relative to suburban and urban areas, and such differences are most pronounced in young adulthood; yet, marijuana *misuse* (abuse or dependence) is generally low and varies little by population density. Women tend to use and misuse marijuana at rates lower than men; however, sex differences are somewhat less evident in rural areas relative to urban and suburban areas. Across the adult ages considered (18 to 49 years), marijuana use increased during the 2004 to 2014 decade, though such differences were most apparent for urban and suburban adults. Few changes in marijuana misuse emerged, but when changes did surface, patterns tended to show that, regardless of population density, misuse in 2014 was lower than in the prior years considered.

The Facts: According to the United Nations Office on Drug Use and Crime (2016), the United States has among the highest rates of marijuana consumption worldwide; yet within the nation, variation by population density is important to consider. To examine differences in marijuana use or marijuana misuse by population density, this chapter used data from the ongoing National Survey on Drug Use and Health (NSDUH 2016), a large and nationally representative survey of U.S. household residents ages 12 and older, between the years 2004 and 2014. These yearly, cross-sectional, self-administered surveys asked participants to answer confidential questions about their use or misuse of marijuana in the 12 months prior to the survey. In the NSDUH survey, *marijuana users* included those who reported that they had used marijuana during that 12-month period, and *marijuana misusers* included those who reported that during that time they experienced symptoms (criteria) like those used by the American Psychiatric Association to diagnose marijuana abuse or marijuana dependence (see Q1 to view those criteria).

Population density is defined in terms of core based statistical areas (CBSAs) classified by the U.S. Census Bureau (2016) in 2000. Urban participants include people who lived in a CBSA with more than one million residents, suburban participants include people who lived in a CBSA with fewer than one million residents, and rural participants include people who did not live in a CBSA. When considering the U.S. population of household residents ages 12 and older in 2014 (NSDUH 2016), rural rates of marijuana use and marijuana misuse were the lowest (9.9 percent and 1.1 percent, respectively), followed by suburban (13.2 percent and 1.5 percent, respectively) and urban (13.9 percent and 1.6 percent, respectively) rates, which were essentially the same. Experts caution, however, that within such patterns, considerable variability can be found by age, sex, and year.

PATTERNS BY AGE

Age is one of the most reliable predictors of the use and misuse of marijuana. That is, marijuana use and misuse tend to begin in early adolescence, increase into late adolescence, peak in young adulthood, and subside thereafter. Therefore, this chapter examines population density differences in marijuana use and marijuana misuse within four key age categories: ages 12 to 17 years (youth), ages 18 to 25 years (young adults), ages 26 to 34 years (pre-middle-aged adults), and ages 35 to 49 years (middle-aged adults). As Figure 1.4 and Table 1.5 reveal, patterns by population density in marijuana use and marijuana misuse vary depending on the age categories and years (between 2004 and 2014) considered.

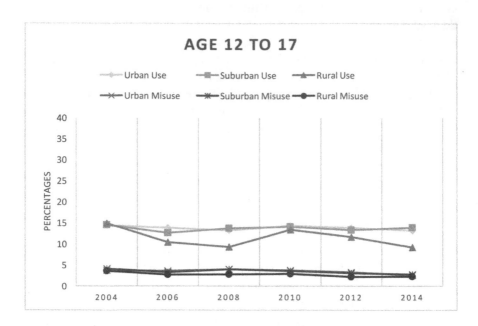

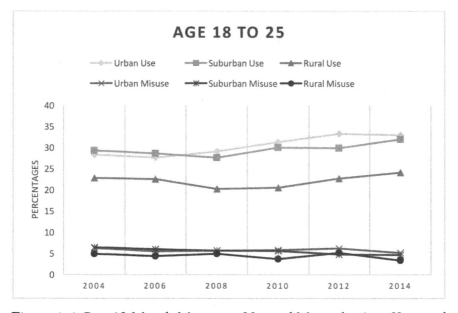

Figure 1.4 Past 12-Month Marijuana Use and Misuse by Age, Year, and Population Density

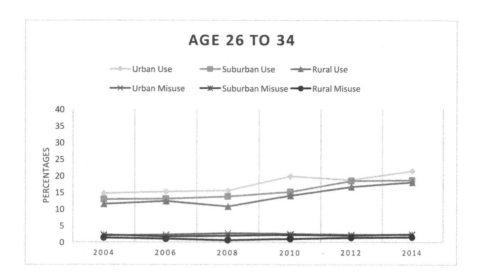

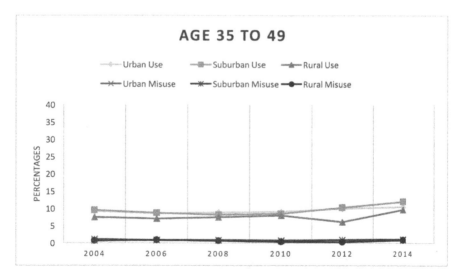

Figure 1.4 Continued

Table 1.5 Past 12-Month Marijuana Use and Misuse: Within-Year Percentage Differences by Population Density

		Age 12 to 17		Age 18 to 25		Age 26 to 34		Age 35 to 49	
		Use	Misuse	Use	Misuse	Use	Misuse	Use	Misuse
2004	Urban	14.4%	3.7	28.3	6.3	14.7	2.0	9.2	0.7
	Suburban	14.5	4.1	29.3	6.5	12.9	2.2	9.5	1.1
	Rural	14.9	3.6	22.8	4.9	11.5	1.3	7.5	0.7
		(ns)	(ns)	(p < .05)	(ns)	(ns)	(ns)	(ns)	(ns)
2006	Urban	13.8	3.6	27.6	5.5	15.2	2.2	8.6	0.9
	Suburban	12.6	3.3	28.6	6.0	13.0	1.7	8.7	0.8
	Rural	10.4	2.7	22.5	4.4	12.4	1.0	7.1	0.9
		(p < .05)	(ns)	(p < .05)	(ns)	(ns)	(ns)	(ns)	(ns)
2008	Urban	13.2	4.0	29.1	5.7	15.5	2.7	8.9	0.9
	Suburban	13.7	4.0	27.6	5.7	13.7	1.9	8.2	0.8
	Rural	9.3	2.8	20.2	4.9	10.7	0.6	7.5	0.7
		(p < .05)	(p < .05)	(p < .05)	(ns)	(ns)	(p < .05)	(ns)	(ns)
2010	Urban	14.3	3.7	31.3	5.8	19.8	2.5	9.1	0.8
	Suburban	14.1	3.6	30.0	5.6	15.1	2.2	8.5	0.7
	Rural	13.4	2.9	20.5	3.7	14.0	1.0	8.0	0.4
		(ns)	(ns)	(p < .05)	(p < .05)	(p < .05)	(ns)	(ns)	(ns)

2012	Urban	13.8	3.3	33.3	5.2	18.7	2.2	10.0	0.9
	Suburban	13.3	3.1	29.9	4.8	18.4	2.0	10.3	1.0
	Rural	11.7	2.2	22.7	5.2	16.6	1.3	6.1	0.3
		(ns)	(ns)	($p < .05$)	($p < .05$)	(ns)	(ns)	($p < .05$)	(ns)
2014	Urban	13.2	2.6	33.0	5.2	21.4	2.2	10.5	0.9
	Suburban	13.9	2.8	32.0	4.7	18.6	2.4	12.0	1.1
	Rural	9.2	2.3	24.1	3.4	18.0	1.5	9.7	0.9
		($p < .05$)	(ns)	($p < .05$)	(ns)	($p < .05$)	(ns)	(ns)	(ns)

Note: Data are from the National Survey on Drug Use and Health (NSDUH 2004–2014).
ns = not statistically significant at $p < .05$.

Marijuana Use

Among youth (ages 12 to 17) during the 2004–2014 decade, rates of past 12-month marijuana use ranged from 13.2 percent to 14.4 percent for urban youth, 12.6 percent to 14.5 percent for suburban youth, and 9.2 percent to 14.9 percent for rural youth. Consistent use differences by population density were not apparent in youth, but when differences emerged, rural youth percentages of marijuana use tended to be the lowest. In half of the years considered (2006, 2008, and 2014), rates of use were statistically significantly lower for rural youth than for urban youth, and in two of those years (2008 and 2014), rural marijuana use rates were also significantly lower than rates for suburban youth.

In young adulthood (ages 18 to 25), differences in marijuana use by population density were more apparent and consistent than they were in youth. Rates of marijuana use ranged from 27.6 percent to 33.3 percent for urban young adults, 27.6 percent to 32.0 percent for suburban young adults, and 20.2 percent to 24.1 percent for rural young adults. In every year considered between 2004 and 2014, young adult marijuana use varied significantly by population density. Rural use was significantly lower than use among both urban and suburban young adults in every year considered, and in 2012, suburban marijuana use was significantly lower than it was among urban young adults.

For pre-middle-aged adults (ages 26 to 34), marijuana use rates ranged over the 2004–2014 decade from 14.7 percent to 21.4 percent for urban adults, 12.9 percent to 18.6 percent for suburban adults, and 10.7 percent to 18.0 percent for rural adults. Significant differences by population density for this age group were observed in only two of the years considered: in 2010, urban rates were significantly higher than both rural and suburban rates; and in 2014, urban rates were higher than suburban rates. For middle-aged adults (ages 35 to 49), use rates ranged from 8.6 percent to 10.5 percent for urban adults, 8.2 percent to 12.0 percent for suburban adults, and 6.1 percent to 9.7 percent for rural adults. Significant differences by population density surfaced in only one year (2012), such that rural rates of marijuana use were lower than the marijuana use rates observed for both urban and suburban middle-aged adults.

Marijuana Misuse

During the 2004–2014 decade, youth (ages 12 to 17) rates of marijuana misuse ranged from 2.6 percent to 4.0 percent for urban youth, 2.8 percent to 4.1 percent for suburban youth, and 2.2 percent to 3.6 percent for rural youth. Rates varied by population density among youth in only one year considered (2008), such that rural youth showed significantly lower rates of misuse than urban or suburban youth. Young adult (ages 18 to 25) rates of marijuana misuse ranged from 5.2 percent to 6.3 percent for urban young adults, 4.7 percent to 6.5 percent for suburban young adults, and 3.4 percent to 5.2 percent for rural young adults. Rates varied significantly by population density in two of the years considered: in 2010, misuse among urban young adults was higher than misuse among rural young adults; and in 2012, misuse among urban young adults was greater than misuse among suburban young adults.

For early middle-aged adults (ages 26 to 34), between 2004 and 2014, marijuana misuse rates ranged from 2.0 percent to 2.7 percent among urban adults, 1.7 percent to 2.4 percent among suburban adults, and 0.6 percent to 1.5 percent among rural adults. Statistically significant differences in misuse by population density for early middle-aged adults were observed in only one year (2008), when rural rates were lower than urban and suburban rates. During that same decade, marijuana misuse among middle-aged adults (ages 35 to 49) ranged from 0.9 percent to 0.7 percent for urban adults, 0.7 percent to 1.1 percent for suburban adults, and 0.3 percent to 0.9 percent for rural adults. No statistically significant differences by population density in marijuana misuse were observed for middle-aged adults.

Recent Changes

Increases in marijuana use over the 2004–2014 decade do not necessarily correspond with increases in marijuana misuse; yet, changes in marijuana use and misuse did vary by population density and age. For the most part, youth (ages 12 to 17) use did not change over the decade, but among rural youth, marijuana use was significantly lower in 2014 than in 2004 and 2010. For urban youth, marijuana misuse in 2014 was lower than it was in 2004, 2006, and 2010. For suburban youth, misuse was lower in 2014 than it was in 2004 or 2008. No changes in marijuana misuse were observed for rural youth during this decade.

In young adulthood (ages 18 to 25), significant changes in marijuana use and marijuana misuse were evident for urban and suburban respondents only. For urban young adults, marijuana use rates were higher in 2014 than they were in 2004, 2006, and 2008, and marijuana misuse rates were lower in 2014 than they were in 2004. For suburban young adults, rates of marijuana use were higher in 2014 than they were in every other year considered, and marijuana misuse rates were lower in 2014 than they were in 2004, 2006, and 2008. No significant changes in the use or misuse of marijuana were observed for rural young adults between 2004 and 2014.

Among pre-middle-aged adults (ages 26 to 34), rural marijuana use was significantly higher in 2014 than it was in 2008. For urban and suburban respondents, however, 2014 marijuana use rates among pre-middle-aged adults were significantly higher than the rates observed in all of the prior years considered with two exceptions: in 2014, marijuana use rates were statistically similar to 2012 rates among urban respondents, and 2014 rates were statistically similar to 2010 rates among suburban respondents. Among middle-aged adults (ages 35 to 49): urban marijuana use was higher in 2014 than it was in 2006 and 2008; suburban use was significantly higher in 2014 than it was between 2004 and 2010; and rural marijuana use was significantly higher in 2014 than it was in 2012. In all years considered, within early middle and middle-aged categories, marijuana misuse rates were statistically similar irrespective of population density.

PATTERNS BY SEX

Finally, self-reported sex (as female or male) is related to marijuana use and marijuana misuse strongly and consistently, at least in adulthood. In Table 1.6, estimates of past 12-month marijuana use and misuse by

Table 1.6 Past 12-Month Marijuana Use and Misuse Percentages by Age, Sex, and Population Density in 2014

		Marijuana Use		Marijuana Misuse	
		Males	Females	Males	Females
Age 12 to 17	Urban	13.5%	12.8	2.8	2.4
	Suburban	13.7	14.1	3.1	2.5
	Rural	8.1	10.3	2.3	2.3
Age 18 to 25	Urban	37.8	28.0*	6.8	3.6*
	Suburban	35.6	28.3*	6.1	3.3*
	Rural	29.3	18.4*	3.9	3.0
Age 26 to 34	Urban	26.0	16.9*	3.4	1.1*
	Suburban	23.9	13.5*	3.5	1.3*
	Rural	22.1	13.8	1.2	1.8
Age 35 to 49	Urban	13.1	8.0*	1.5	0.3*
	Suburban	16.7	7.6*	2.0	0.2*
	Rural	15.2	4.6*	1.6	0.3

Note: Data are from the National Survey on Drug Use and Health (NSDUH 2014).
* $p < .05$ (sex differences).

age, sex, and population density are presented using data from 2014, the most recent year data available when this book was written. As shown, regardless of population density, no sex differences in marijuana use or marijuana misuse are apparent among youth (ages 12 to 17). Yet, sex differences in both use and misuse are evident among urban and suburban adults ages 18 to 49—that is, women used and misused marijuana at lower rates than did men. With regard to rural marijuana use, there were no sex differences observed for pre-middle-aged adults (ages 26 to 34), and there were no sex differences in rural marijuana misuse within any of the age categories considered in 2014.

ACKNOWLEDGMENT

The National Survey on Drug Use and Health (NSDUH), which is made available by the Inter-University Consortium for Political and Social Science, is supported by the Substance Abuse and Mental Health Services Administration and the U.S. Department of Health and Human Services. Any opinions, findings, conclusions, or recommendations expressed in this chapter are those of the authors and do not necessarily reflect the views of the funders.

FURTHER READING

Centers for Disease Control and Prevention (CDC). "National estimates of marijuana use and related indicators—National Survey on Drug Use and Health, United States, 2002–2014." *Surveillance Summaries* 65, no. 11 (2016): 1–25. https://www.cdc.gov/mmwr/volumes/65/ss/ss6511a1 .htm

Compton, Wilson M., Beth Han, Christopher M. Jones, Carlos Blanco, and Arthur Hughes. "Marijuana use and use disorders in adults in the USA, 2002–14: analysis of annual cross-sectional surveys." *The Lancet Psychiatry* 3, no. 10 (2016): 954–964.

Evans-Polce, Rebecca J., Sara A. Vasilenko, and Stephanie T. Lanza. "Changes in gender and racial/ethnic disparities in rates of cigarette use, regular heavy episodic drinking, and marijuana use: ages 14 to 32." *Addictive Behaviors* 41 (2015): 218–222.

Haberstick, Brett C., Susan E. Young, Joanna S. Zeiger, Jeffrey M. Lessem, John K. Hewitt, and Christian J. Hopfer. "Prevalence and correlates of alcohol and cannabis use disorders in the United States: results from the longitudinal study of adolescent health." *Drug and Alcohol Dependence* 136 (2014): 158–161.

Hasin, Deborah S., Bradley T. Kerridge, Tulshi D. Saha, Boji Huang, Roger Pickering, Sharon M. Smith, Jeesun Jung, Haitao Zhang, and Bridget F. Grant. "Prevalence and correlates of DSM-5 cannabis use disorder, 2012–2013: findings from the National Epidemiologic Survey on Alcohol and Related Conditions–III." *The American Journal of Psychiatry* 173, no. 6 (2016): 588–599.

Hasin, Deborah S., Tulshi D. Saha, Bradley T. Kerridge, Risë B. Goldstein, S. Patricia Chou, Haitao Zhang, Jeesun Jung, Roger P. Pickering, W. June Ruan, Sharon M. Smith, Boji Huang, and Bridget F. Grant. "Prevalence of marijuana use disorders in the United States between 2001–2002 and 2012–2013." *JAMA Psychiatry* 72, no. 12, (2015): 1235–1242.

National Survey on Drug Use and Health (NSDUH). United States Department of Health and Human Services. Substance Abuse and Mental Health Services Administration. Center for Behavioral Health Statistics and Quality. National Survey on Drug Use and Health, 2014. ICPSR36361-v1. Ann Arbor, MI: Inter-university Consortium for Political and Social Research [distributor], March 22, 2016. http://doi.org/10.3886/ICPSR36361.v1

United Nations Office on Drug Use and Crime. 2016. *World Drug Report 2016*. http://www.unodc.org/doc/wdr2016/WDR_2016_Chapter_1_Cannabis.pdf

United States Census Bureau. "Geographic Terms and Concepts—Core Based Statistical Areas and Related Statistical Areas." 2016. https://www.census.gov/geo/reference/gtc/gtc_cbsa.html

Q4. DOES MARIJUANA USE OR MISUSE VARY BY FAMILY INCOME LEVEL?

Answer: Yes. When comparing family income levels among U.S. residents that are low (less than $20,000 per year), middle range ($20,000 to $74,999 per year), or high ($75,000 or more per year), there are statistically significant differences in marijuana use and misuse (i.e., abuse of or dependence on marijuana), but the nature of those patterns varies by age and over time. Early in the decade considered here (2004 to 2014), there were few income-level-related differences in marijuana use or misuse for youth; yet later in that decade, high-income youth tended to show relatively lower rates of use and misuse than middle- and low-income youth. Among young adults, in contrast, marijuana use was lowest for middle-income respondents throughout that decade, but marijuana misuse varied little by family income level during that time. Among adults ages

26 to 49 years old, marijuana use tended to be highest among low-income respondents and lowest among high-income respondents. Throughout the decade, especially among middle-aged adults (ages 35 to 49), marijuana misuse was elevated among low-income respondents. Regardless of income level, adult women showed significantly lower marijuana use and misuse than their male counterparts in all but one case considered.

The Facts: To examine whether there are differences in marijuana use or marijuana misuse by income level, this chapter used data from the ongoing National Survey on Drug Use and Health (NSDUH 2016), a large and nationally representative survey of U.S. household residents ages 12 and older, between the years 2004 and 2014. These yearly, cross-sectional, self-administered surveys asked participants to answer confidential questions about their use or misuse of marijuana in the 12 months prior to the survey. *Marijuana users* included those who reported that they had used marijuana at all in that 12-month period, and *marijuana misusers* included those who reported that during that time they experienced symptoms (criteria) like those used by the American Psychiatric Association to diagnose marijuana abuse or dependence (see Q1). Family income level was divided into three yearly categories: low-income (less than $20,000), middle-income ($20,000 to $74,999), and high-income ($75,000 or more).

Among household residents ages 12 and older in 2014, rates of marijuana use and marijuana misuse were highest among low-income residents (18.7 percent and 2.4 percent, respectively), followed by middle-income residents (12.9 percent and 1.6 percent, respectively), followed by high-income residents (11.1 percent and 1.1 percent, respectively). Those percentages vary importantly by age category, however, and, in some cases, changed during the 2004 to 2014 decade.

PATTERNS BY AGE

As discussed in Q1, *age* is one of the most reliable predictors of the use and misuse of marijuana. That is, marijuana use and misuse tend to begin in early adolescence, increase into late adolescence, peak in young adulthood, and subside thereafter. Therefore, this chapter examines differences by family income level in marijuana use and marijuana misuse within four key age categories: ages 12 to 17 years (youth), ages 18 to 25 years (young adults), ages 26 to 34 years (pre-middle-aged adults), and ages 35 to 49 years (middle-aged adults). As Figure 1.5 and Table 1.7 reveal, family income differences in marijuana use and marijuana misuse vary depending on the age categories and years (between 2004 and 2014) considered.

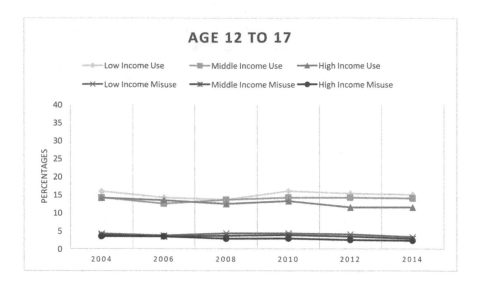

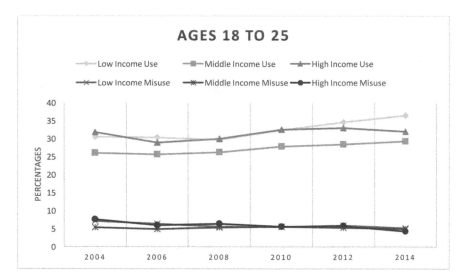

Figure 1.5 Past 12-Month Marijuana Use and Misuse by Age, Year, and Family Income

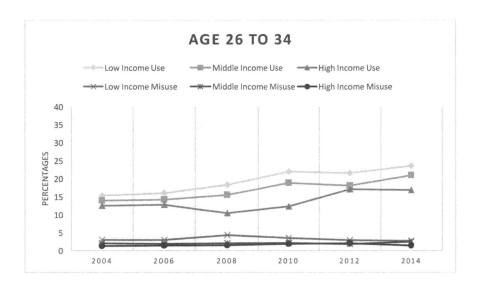

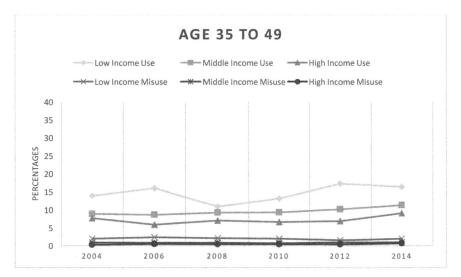

Figure 1.5 Continued

Table 1.7 Past 12-Month Marijuana Use and Misuse: Within-Year Percentage Differences by Family Income

		Age 12 to 17		Age 18 to 25		Age 26 to 34		Age 35 to 49	
		Use	Misuse	Use	Misuse	Use	Misuse	Use	Misuse
2004	Low Income	15.9%	4.2	30.5	7.1	15.3	3.0	13.9	2.0
	Middle Income	14.2	3.9	26.0	5.4	13.9	2.0	8.9	0.9
	High Income	14.1	3.5	31.8	7.6	12.5	1.3	7.7	0.3
		(ns)	(ns)	(p < .05)	(p < .05)	(ns)	(ns)	(p < .05)	(p < .05)
2006	Low Income	14.2	3.7	30.3	6.4	16.0	3.0	16.0	2.4
	Middle Income	12.5	3.4	25.6	4.9	14.2	1.9	8.6	0.8
	High Income	13.4	3.4	28.9	6.0	12.8	1.4	5.9	0.5
		(ns)	(ns)	(p < .05)	(p < .05)	(ns)	(ns)	(p < .05)	(p < .05)
2008	Low Income	13.6	4.3	29.7	5.6	18.3	4.3	10.9	2.1
	Middle Income	13.6	3.6	26.2	5.4	15.5	2.0	9.2	0.8
	High Income	12.4	2.8	30.0	6.4	10.4	1.5	7.0	0.5
		(ns)	(p < .05)	(p < .05)	(ns)	(p < .05)	(p < .05)	(p < .05)	(p < .05)
2010	Low Income	16.0	4.3	32.4	5.5	22.0	3.5	13.1	2.0
	Middle Income	14.2	3.8	27.8	5.6	18.8	2.1	9.3	0.7
	High Income	13.2	2.9	32.5	5.6	12.3	1.9	6.6	0.4
		(p < .05)	(p < .05)	(p < .05)	(ns)	(p < .05)	(ns)	(p < .05)	(p < .05)

2012	Low Income	15.3	4.0	34.6	5.9	21.6	2.9	17.3	1.6
	Middle Income	14.2	3.4	28.4	5.3	18.1	1.8	10.2	1.0
	High Income	11.5	2.5	33.0	5.8	17.1	2.0	6.9	0.4
		(p < .05)	(p < .05)	(p < .05)	(ns)	(p < .05)	(ns)	(p < .05)	(p < .05)
2014	Low Income	15.0	3.3	36.5	5.2	23.6	2.7	16.4	2.0
	Middle Income	14.0	2.8	29.3	5.0	21.0	2.5	11.3	1.0
	High Income	11.5	2.3	32.0	4.3	16.9	1.4	9.1	0.7
		(p < .05)	(p < .05)	(p < .05)	(ns)	(p < .05)	(p < .05)	(p < .05)	(p < .05)

Note: Data are from the National Survey on Drug Use and Health (NSDUH 2004–2014).
ns = not statistically significant at p < .05.

Marijuana Use

Between 2004 and 2014, marijuana use among youth (ages 12 to 17) ranged from 13.6 percent to 16.0 percent for low-income youth, 12.5 percent to 14.2 percent for middle-income youth, and 11.5 percent to 14.1 percent for high-income youth. No significant differences in youth use were observed until 2010, when high-income use was significantly lower than low-income use. In 2012 and 2014, high-income youth showed significantly lower marijuana use than both low- and middle-income youth.

By contrast, in young adulthood (ages 18 to 25), marijuana use rates tended to be lowest among *middle*-income respondents. Rates ranged from 29.7 percent to 36.5 percent for low-income young adults, 25.6 percent to 29.3 percent for middle-income young adults, and 28.9 percent to 33.0 percent for high-income young adults. In every year considered, middle-income young adults showed significantly lower marijuana use rates than low-income young adults, and in all but one year (2014), those rates also were lower than were high-income young adult rates. In that same year, low-income young adults showed significantly higher use rates than both middle- and high-income young adults.

For pre-middle-aged adults (ages 26 to 34), percentages from 2004 to 2014 ranged from 15.3 percent to 23.6 percent for low-income respondents, 13.9 percent to 21.0 percent for middle-income respondents, and 10.4 percent to 17.1 percent for high-income respondents. In pre-middle age, low-income adults showed significantly higher rates of marijuana use than high-income adults in four of the six years considered (2008, 2010, 2012, and 2014), and middle-income adults showed significantly higher rates than high-income adults in three of those same years (2008, 2010, and 2014).

For middle-aged adults (ages 35 to 49), marijuana use rates ranged from 10.9 percent to 17.3 percent for low-income respondents, 8.6 percent to 11.3 percent for middle-income respondents, and 5.9 percent to 9.1 percent for high-income respondents. Quite consistently, low-income middle-aged adults showed the highest rates of use and high-income middle-aged adults showed the lowest rates of use. Here, low-income use was significantly higher than high-income use in every year considered, and it was significantly higher than middle-income use in every year but one (2008). Middle-income marijuana use was significantly higher than high-income use in every year but one (2004).

Marijuana Misuse

During the 2004 to 2014 decade, youth (ages 12 to 17) misuse of marijuana ranged from 3.3 percent to 4.3 percent for low-income youth, 2.8 percent to 3.9 percent for middle-income youth, and 2.3 percent to 3.5 percent for high-income youth. Early in the decade (2004 to 2006), there were no observed statistically significant differences in marijuana misuse by family income level, but differences did emerge in 2008. From 2008 to 2012, high-income youth showed significantly lower marijuana misuse rates than did middle-income youth, and from 2008 to 2014, high-income percentages were significantly lower than low-income percentages among youth.

In young adulthood (ages 18 to 25), few differences by family income level in marijuana misuse surfaced. Percentages ranged from 5.2 percent to 7.1 percent for low-income young adults, 4.9 percent to 5.6 percent for middle-income young adults, and 4.3 percent to 7.6 percent for high-income young adults. In 2004, middle-income young adults showed significantly lower misuse than high-income young adults did, and in 2004 and 2006, they showed significantly lower misuse than low-income young adults did.

Few differences by family income level were observed also in pre-middle-aged adulthood (ages 26 to 34). During the 2004 to 2014 decade, rates of pre-middle-aged adult misuse ranged from 2.7 percent to 4.3 percent for low-income respondents, 1.8 percent to 2.5 percent for middle-income respondents, and 1.3 percent to 2.0 percent for high-income respondents. Differences emerged for pre-middle-aged adults in only two years considered (2008 and 2014); in both cases, low-income respondents showed significantly higher marijuana misuse than both middle- and high-income respondents.

In middle age (ages 35 to 49), however, marijuana misuse varied significantly by family income level in every year considered. Middle-age misuse percentages ranged from 1.6 percent to 2.4 percent for low-income respondents, 0.7 percent to 1.0 percent for middle-income respondents, and 0.3 percent to 0.7 percent for high-income respondents. In every year considered, middle-aged respondents in the low-income range showed significantly higher rates of marijuana misuse than both middle- and high-income middle-aged respondents; in 2004 only, middle-income respondents showed significantly higher rates of marijuana misuse than high-income respondents in middle age.

Recent Changes

Increases in marijuana use over the 2004–2014 decade do not necessarily correspond with concomitant increases in marijuana misuse. Patterns of change in marijuana use and misuse, however, do appear to vary by the age category and family income level of respondents. Among youth (ages 12 to 17), significant differences in both use and misuse did not seem to surface until the latter half of the decade. Such differences seemed to be due primarily to a *lack of change* in use or misuse among low-income youth. Unlike low-income youth, middle-income youth reported lower marijuana use in 2014 than they did in 2006, and high-income youth reported lower marijuana use in 2014 than they did in 2004, 2006, and 2010. Similarly, while low-income youth misuse rates remained unchanged, middle-income youth showed lower marijuana misuse in 2014 than in 2004, 2008, and 2010, and high-income youth showed lower rates of misuse in 2014 than they did in 2004 and 2006.

In young adulthood (ages 18 to 25), rates of marijuana use remained stable among high-income respondents, but increases in use emerged for both low- and middle-income young adults. For low-income young adults, 2014 rates of marijuana use were significantly higher than rates in 2004, 2006, 2008, and 2010. For middle-income young adults, 2014 rates of use were greater than use rates in 2004, 2006, and 2008. With regard to marijuana misuse, however, marijuana misuse was significantly lower in 2014 than it was in 2004 for low-income young adults, and it was lower in 2014 than it was in 2004, 2006, and 2008 for high-income young adults. For middle-income young adults, rates of marijuana misuse remained unchanged.

In pre-middle-aged adulthood (ages 26 to 34) and middle-aged adulthood (ages 35 to 49), the use of marijuana increased over the 2004 to 2014 decade for every family income level group. For early middle-aged adult respondents, low-income rates of use in 2014 were significantly higher than rates in 2004, 2006, and 2008; middle-income rates of use in 2014 were significantly higher than rates in 2004, 2006, 2008, and 2012, and; high-income rates of use in 2014 were significantly higher than rates in 2004, 2006, 2008, and 2010. Among middle-aged adults, low-income rates of use were significantly higher in 2014 than rates in 2008 and 2010; middle-income rates of use were significantly higher in 2014 than rates in 2004, 2006, 2008, and 2010, and; high-income rates of use in 2014 were significantly higher than rates in 2006, 2008, 2010, and 2012. Yet with regard to marijuana misuse, there were no changes in pre-middle age or middle age; that is, regardless of family income level, rates of marijuana misuse for adults ages 26 to 49 were essentially the same in every year considered.

PATTERNS BY SEX

Finally, as observed in Q1, self-reported sex (as female or male) is related to marijuana use and marijuana misuse strongly and consistently, at least in adulthood. In Table 1.8, estimates of past 12-month marijuana use and marijuana misuse by age, sex, and family income level are presented using data from 2014, the most recent year data available when this book was written. For youth (ages 12 to 17), there were no significant sex differences in marijuana use or misuse across family income level with one only exception: high-income boys reported significantly higher rates of marijuana use than high-income girls. In contrast, women in every adult age category across family income level used and misused marijuana at significantly lower rates than men with only one exception: low-income men and women in pre-middle age reported statistically equivalent rates of marijuana misuse.

Table 1.8 Past 12-Month Marijuana Use and Misuse by Age, Sex, and Family Income in 2014

		Marijuana Use		Marijuana Misuse	
		Males	**Females**	**Males**	**Females**
Age 12 to 17	Low Income	14.6%	15.4	3.6	3.1
	Middle Income	13.2	14.8	2.9	2.6
	High Income	12.8	10.3*	2.5	2.1
Age 18 to 25	Low Income	43.2	31.1*	7.1	3.8*
	Middle Income	34.0	24.5*	6.7	3.3*
	High Income	34.0	29.3*	5.1	3.3*
Age 26 to 34	Low Income	30.7	18.4*	3.1	2.4
	Middle Income	26.2	15.5*	3.9	1.1*
	High Income	20.3	13.5*	2.4	0.5*
Age 35 to 49	Low Income	21.8	12.0*	3.4	0.8*
	Middle Income	15.6	7.4*	1.8	0.3*
	High Income	11.6	6.4*	1.2	0.1*

Note: Data are from the National Survey on Drug Use and Health (NSDUH 2014).
* $p < .05$ (sex differences).

ACKNOWLEDGMENT

The National Survey on Drug Use and Health (NSDUH), which is made available by the Inter-University Consortium for Political and Social Science, is supported by the Substance Abuse and Mental Health Services Administration and the U.S. Department of Health and Human Services. Any opinions, findings, conclusions, or recommendations expressed in this chapter are those of the authors and do not necessarily reflect the views of the funders.

FURTHER READING

Centers for Disease Control and Prevention (CDC). "National estimates of marijuana use and related indicators—National Survey on Drug Use and Health, United States, 2002–2014." *Surveillance Summaries* 65, no. 11 (2016): 1–25. https://www.cdc.gov/mmwr/volumes/65/ss/ss6511a1 .htm

Compton, Wilson M., Beth Han, Christopher M. Jones, Carlos Blanco, and Arthur Hughes. "Marijuana use and use disorders in adults in the USA, 2002–14: analysis of annual cross-sectional surveys." *The Lancet Psychiatry* 3, no. 10 (2016): 954–964.

Evans-Polce, Rebecca J., Sara A. Vasilenko, and Stephanie T. Lanza. "Changes in gender and racial/ethnic disparities in rates of cigarette use, regular heavy episodic drinking, and marijuana use: ages 14 to 32." *Addictive Behaviors* 41 (2015): 218–222.

Haberstick, Brett C., Susan E. Young, Joanna S. Zeiger, Jeffrey M. Lessem, John K. Hewitt, and Christian J. Hopfer. "Prevalence and correlates of alcohol and cannabis use disorders in the United States: results from the longitudinal study of adolescent health." *Drug and Alcohol Dependence* 136 (2014): 158–161.

Hasin, Deborah S., Bradley T. Kerridge, Tulshi D. Saha, Boji Huang, Roger Pickering, Sharon M. Smith, Jeesun Jung, Haitao Zhang, and Bridget F. Grant. "Prevalence and correlates of DSM-5 cannabis use disorder, 2012–2013: findings from the National Epidemiologic Survey on Alcohol and Related Conditions–III." *The American Journal of Psychiatry* 173, no. 6 (2016): 588–599.

Hasin, Deborah S., Tulshi D. Saha, Bradley T. Kerridge, Risë B. Goldstein, S. Patricia Chou, Haitao Zhang, Jeesun Jung, Roger P. Pickering, W. June Ruan, Sharon M. Smith, Boji Huang, and Bridget F. Grant. "Prevalence of marijuana use disorders in the United States between 2001–2002 and 2012–2013." *JAMA Psychiatry* 72, no. 12, (2015): 1235–1242.

National Survey on Drug Use and Health (NSDUH). United States Department of Health and Human Services. Substance Abuse and Mental Health Services Administration. Center for Behavioral Health Statistics and Quality. National Survey on Drug Use and Health, 2014. ICPSR36361-v1. Ann Arbor, MI: Inter-university Consortium for Political and Social Research [distributor], March 22, 2016. http://doi.org/10.3886/ICPSR36361.v1

Q5. DOES MARIJUANA USE OR MISUSE VARY BY EMPLOYMENT STATUS?

Answer: Yes. There are statistically significant differences in both marijuana use and marijuana misuse (i.e., abuse of or dependence on marijuana) among U.S. residents depending on whether they are employed, unemployed, or non-workforce (e.g., retirees, homemakers, students, disabled). In general, the unemployed show the highest rates of marijuana use and misuse, followed by the employed, followed by those not in the workforce. The nature of those differences is mostly consistent across age category, as is the tendency for women to use or misuse marijuana at lower rates than men. Over the 2004 to 2014 decade, marijuana use among the employed increased significantly for all age groups considered, and use among the unemployed remained generally stable; however, although non-workforce marijuana use was relatively stable in youth and young adulthood, among adults ages 26 to 49, non-workforce use increased. In youth, marijuana misuse decreased significantly for the unemployed and for non-workforce respondents, and among young adults, misuse decreased for respondents regardless of employment status. Yet among adults ages 26 to 49, and irrespective of employment status, marijuana misuse rates remained unchanged across all of the years considered.

The Facts: To examine if there are differences in marijuana use or misuse by employment status, this chapter used data from the ongoing National Survey on Drug Use and Health (NSDUH 2016), a large and representative survey of U.S. household residents ages 12 and older, between the years 2004 and 2014. These yearly, cross-sectional, self-administered surveys asked participants to answer questions about their use or misuse of marijuana in the 12 months prior to the survey. *Marijuana users* included those who reported that they had used marijuana during that 12-month period, and *marijuana misusers* included those who reported that during that time they experienced symptoms (criteria) like those used by the

American Psychiatric Association to diagnose marijuana abuse or dependence (see Q1 for those criteria). The NSDUH includes employment
data for respondents ages 15 and older.

Employment status was divided by the NSDUH into three categories: employed (those who were working full- or part-time in the previous week); unemployed (those who were not working, but were making
specific efforts to obtain employment); and non-workforce (those who
were not employed but were not looking for work, such as retirees, homemakers, full-time students, the disabled). When considering the U.S.
population of household residents ages 15 and older in 2014, rates of
marijuana use and marijuana misuse were highest among the unemployed
(24.7 percent and 4.4 percent, respectively), followed by the employed
(15.1 percent and 1.6 percent, respectively), followed by those not in the
workforce (9.5 percent and 1.1 percent, respectively). Yet, it is important
to consider those patterns by age, sex, and year.

PATTERNS BY AGE

As discussed in Q1, *age* is one of the most reliable predictors of the use
and misuse of marijuana. That is, marijuana use and misuse tend to begin
in early adolescence, increase into late adolescence, peak in young adulthood, and subside thereafter. Thus, this chapter examines differences by
employment status in marijuana use and misuse within four age categories: ages 15 to 17 years (youth), ages 18 to 25 years (young adults), ages
26 to 34 years (pre-middle-aged adults), and ages 35 to 49 years (middle-
aged adults). Figure 1.6 and Table 1.9 show patterns of marijuana use
and marijuana misuse by employment status and age between 2004
and 2014.

Marijuana Use

Over the 2004 to 2014 decade, there were statistically significant differences in marijuana use by employment status in every year and for every
age group considered. In youth (ages 15 to 17), past 12-month marijuana use rates ranged from 26.0 percent to 30.0 percent for employed
youth, 29.3 percent to 36.3 percent for unemployed youth, and 17.2 percent to 19.3 percent for non-workforce youth. In every year considered,
non-workforce youth used marijuana at significantly lower rates than
both employed and unemployed youth. In three of the six years (2004,
2010, and 2012), unemployed youth also showed significantly higher rates
of marijuana use than employed youth.

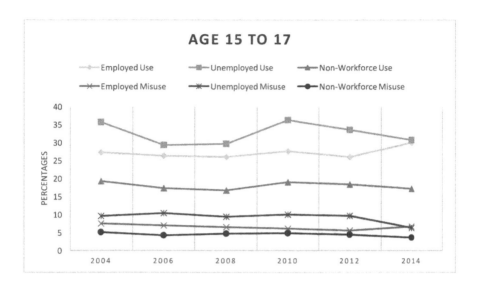

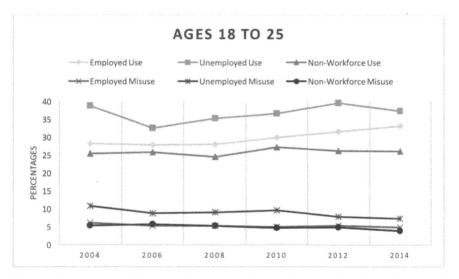

Figure 1.6 Past 12-Month Marijuana Use and Misuse by Age, Year, and Employment Status

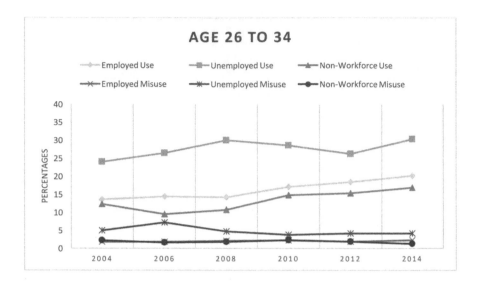

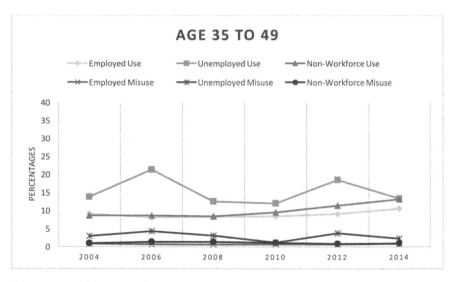

Figure 1.6 Continued

Table 1.9 Past 12-Month Marijuana Use and Misuse: Within-Year Percentage Differences by Employment Status

		Age 15 to 17		Age 18 to 25		Age 26 to 34		Age 35 to 49	
		Use	Misuse	Use	Misuse	Use	Misuse	Use	Misuse
2004	Employed	27.3%	7.5	28.2	6.1	13.6	1.8	9.1	0.8
	Unemployed	35.7	9.6	38.8	10.8	24.0	5.0	13.8	3.0
	Non-Workforce	19.3	5.1	25.4	5.4	12.3	2.2	8.6	1.0
		($p < .05$)	($p < .05$)	($p < .05$)	($p < .05$)	($p < .05$)	($p < .05$)	($p < .05$)	($p < .05$)
2006	Employed	26.3	7.0	27.8	5.3	14.4	1.8	8.1	0.7
	Unemployed	29.3	10.4	32.5	8.8	26.4	7.2	21.3	4.3
	Non-Workforce	17.3	4.2	25.8	5.7	9.5	1.6	8.6	1.4
		($p < .05$)	($p < .05$)	($p < .05$)	($p < .05$)	($p < .05$)	($p < .05$)	($p < .05$)	($p < .05$)
2008	Employed	26.0	6.5	28.0	5.3	14.2	2.1	8.3	0.6
	Unemployed	29.6	9.4	35.3	9.1	30.0	4.7	12.5	3.1
	Non-Workforce	16.7	4.7	24.5	5.3	10.7	1.8	8.4	1.4
		($p < .05$)	($p < .05$)	($p < .05$)	($p < .05$)	($p < .05$)	($p < .05$)	($p < .05$)	($p < .05$)
2010	Employed	27.6	6.1	29.9	5.0	17.1	2.2	8.4	0.7
	Unemployed	36.3	10.0	36.6	9.6	28.6	3.8	12.0	1.2
	Non-Workforce	19.0	4.8	27.2	4.7	14.8	2.3	9.5	1.1
		($p < .05$)	($p < .05$)	($p < .05$)	($p < .05$)	(ns)	(ns)	($p < .05$)	(ns)

(Continued)

Table 1.9 Continued

		Age 15 to 17		Age 18 to 25		Age 26 to 34		Age 35 to 49	
		Use	Misuse	Use	Misuse	Use	Misuse	Use	Misuse
2012	Employed	26.0	5.6	31.6	5.4	18.4	1.9	9.1	0.7
	Unemployed	33.5	9.7	39.6	7.9	26.2	4.2	18.5	3.8
	Non-Workforce	18.4	4.4	26.2	4.9	15.3	1.9	11.4	0.8
		(p < .05)	(p < .05)	(p < .05)	(p < .05)	(p < .05)	(p < .05)	(p < .05)	(p < .05)
2014	Employed	30.0	6.7	33.1	4.9	20.2	2.3	10.6	0.9
	Unemployed	30.7	6.3	37.3	7.3	30.3	4.2	13.3	2.3
	Non-Workforce	17.2	3.6	26.1	3.9	16.9	1.3	13.2	1.0
		(p < .05)	(p < .05)	(p < .05)	(p < .05)	(p < .05)	(p < .05)	(p < .05)	(p < .05)

Note: Data are from the National Survey on Drug Use and Health (NSDUH 2004–2014).

ns = not statistically significant at p < .05.

In young adulthood (ages 18 to 25), marijuana use rates ranged from 27.8 percent to 33.1 percent for employed young adults, 32.5 percent to 39.6 percent for unemployed young adults, and 24.4 percent to 27.2 percent for non-workforce young adults. In every year considered, unemployed young adults showed statistically significantly higher rates of marijuana use than young adults who were employed or not in the workforce. In addition, employed young adults showed significantly higher use rates than non-workforce young adults in all but one year (2006) considered here.

For pre-middle-age adults (ages 26 to 34) between 2004 and 2014, past 12-month marijuana use percentages ranged from 13.6 percent to 20.2 percent for the employed, from 24.0 percent to 30.3 percent for the unemployed, and from 9.5 percent to 16.9 percent for those not in the workforce. Unemployed pre-middle-aged adults showed statistically significantly higher marijuana use rates than their employed and non-workforce counterparts in every year considered, and the employed showed significantly higher rates than those not in the workforce in three years (2006, 2008, and 2014).

Among middle-aged adults (ages 35 to 49), marijuana use percentages ranged from 8.1 percent to 10.6 percent for employed adults, 12.0 percent to 21.3 percent for unemployed adults, and 8.4 percent to 13.2 percent for non-workforce adults. In every year but one (2014), marijuana use among the unemployed was significantly higher than marijuana use among the employed. Middle-aged marijuana use among the unemployed was also significantly higher than marijuana use among non-workforce middle-aged adults in 2004, 2006, and 2012. In 2012 and 2014, employed middle-aged adults used marijuana at statistically significantly *lower* rates than non-workforce middle-aged adults.

Marijuana Misuse

During the 2004 to 2014 decade, regardless of age, marijuana misuse varied by employment status to a statistically significant degree in every year considered except one (2010). Among youth (ages 15 to 17), marijuana misuse ranged from 5.6 percent to 7.5 percent for the employed, 6.3 percent to 10.4 percent for the unemployed, and 3.6 percent to 5.1 percent for youth not in the workforce. Unemployed youth showed significantly higher rates of marijuana misuse than non-workforce youth in every year considered, and unemployed rates were also higher than rates among employed youth in every year but two (2004 and 2014). Marijuana misuse rates among non-workforce youth were significantly lower than rates among employed youth in every year but two (2010 and 2012).

Marijuana misuse rates among young adults (ages 18 to 25) ranged from 4.9 percent to 6.1 percent for the employed, 7.3 percent to 10.8 percent for the unemployed, and 3.9 percent to 5.7 percent for young adults not in the workforce. In every year considered, unemployed young adults showed statistically significantly higher rates of marijuana misuse than those who were employed or not in the workforce.

In pre-middle-aged adulthood (ages 26 to 34), marijuana misuse rates ranged from 1.8 percent to 2.3 percent for the employed, 3.8 percent to 7.2 percent for the unemployed, and 1.3 percent to 2.3 percent for those not in the workforce. In every year considered except one (2010), unemployed pre-middle-aged adults misused marijuana at rates significantly higher than the unemployed; unemployed rates were also significantly higher than non-workforce marijuana misuse rates in 2006 and 2014.

For middle-aged adults (ages 35 to 49), marijuana misuse rates ranged from 0.6 percent to 0.9 percent for the employed, 1.2 percent to 4.3 percent for the unemployed, and 0.8 percent to 1.4 percent for those not in the workforce. In all but one year considered (2010), marijuana misuse rates for unemployed middle-aged adults were statistically significantly higher than misuse rates for those who were employed, and in all but two years (2010 and 2014) considered, unemployed misuse rates were significantly higher than rates for those not in the workforce. In 2006 and 2008, employed middle-aged adults showed significantly *lower* misuse than non-workforce middle-aged adults.

Recent Changes

Increases in marijuana use over the 2004–2014 decade did not necessarily correspond with increases in marijuana misuse. Patterns of change in marijuana use and misuse, however, do appear to vary by the age and employment status of respondents. For youth (ages 15 to 17), marijuana use among the employed in 2014 was statistically significantly higher than it was for employed youth in 2006, 2008, and 2012; however, marijuana misuse did not change significantly among employed youth during the decade. Among unemployed youth, marijuana use was statistically significantly lower in 2014 than it was in 2010, and marijuana misuse was significantly lower in 2014 than it was for youth in all other years considered. For non-workforce youth, marijuana use was statistically significantly lower in 2014 than it was in 2004, and marijuana misuse was significantly lower in 2014 than in 2004, 2008, and 2010.

In young adulthood (ages 18 to 25), marijuana use rates among the employed increased over the course of the decade such that rates were statistically significantly higher among employed young adults in 2014 than they were in every prior year considered except 2012; yet, marijuana misuse was significantly *lower* among employed young adults in 2014 relative to 2004. Rates of marijuana use among unemployed young adults were significantly higher in 2014 than in 2006, but rates of marijuana misuse were significantly lower among unemployed young adults in 2014 than in 2004. For young adults not in the workforce, there were no significant changes in marijuana use, but marijuana misuse rates were significantly lower for non-workforce young adults in 2014 than they were in 2004, 2006, and 2008.

Among pre-middle-aged (ages 26 to 34) and middle-aged (ages 35 to 49) adults, there were no statistically significant changes in marijuana *misuse* regardless of employment status, but marijuana *use* rates did tend to increase, especially among employed and non-workforce adults. Rates of marijuana use among the employed were statistically significantly higher in 2014 than for every other year considered among middle-aged adults, and for every year but one (2012) among pre-middle-aged adults. For non-workforce middle-aged adults, rates of marijuana use were higher in 2014 than in four of the six years considered (2004, 2006, 2008, and 2010), and for non-workforce pre-middle-aged adults, use rates were higher in 2014 than rates in three of those same years (2004, 2006, and 2008). No changes in pre-middle-aged marijuana use were observed for the unemployed, and for unemployed middle-aged adults, use rates in 2014 were significantly different from use rates in only one other year (2006).

PATTERNS BY SEX

Finally, as observed in Q1, self-reported sex (as female or male) is related to marijuana use and marijuana misuse strongly and consistently, at least in adulthood. In Table 1.10, estimates of past 12-month marijuana use and marijuana misuse by age, sex, and employment status are presented using data from 2014, the most recent year data were available when this chapter was written. Among youth (ages 15 to 17), there were no significant sex differences by employment status in marijuana use or misuse with one exception: unemployed girls showed significantly lower rates of marijuana misuse than did unemployed boys. In young adulthood (ages 18 to 25), women tended to use and misuse marijuana at lower rates than men regardless of employment status. For pre-middle-aged adults (ages 26 to 34), women tended to use and misuse marijuana at rates lower than men with two exceptions: unemployed men and women used marijuana at statistically similar rates, and non-workforce men and women misused marijuana at statistically similar rates. Among

Table 1.10 Past 12-Month Marijuana Use and Misuse by Age, Sex, and Employment Status in 2014

		Marijuana Use		Marijuana Misuse	
		Males	Females	Males	Females
Age 15 to 17	Employed	28.6%	31.8	7.0	6.4
	Unemployed	33.9	27.4	8.5	4.1*
	Non-Workforce	17.9	16.4	3.7	3.5
Age 18 to 25	Employed	36.5	29.6*	5.9	3.8*
	Unemployed	42.0	31.4*	9.8	4.0*
	Non-Workforce	32.8	21.0*	5.8	2.4*
Age 26 to 34	Employed	21.4	15.6*	3.3	1.0*
	Unemployed	34.2	25.9	4.9	3.4*
	Non-Workforce	31.6	12.9*	2.2	1.1
Age 35 to 49	Employed	13.3	7.5*	1.5	0.2*
	Unemployed	18.9	7.2*	3.4	1.1
	Non-Workforce	27.5	8.4*	3.0	0.3*

Note: Data are from the National Survey on Drug Use and Health (NSDUH 2014). * $p < .05$ (sex differences).

middle-aged adults (ages 35 to 49), women used and misused marijuana at lower rates than men with one exception: unemployed women and men showed nearly equivalent rates of marijuana misuse.

ACKNOWLEDGMENT

The National Survey on Drug Use and Health (NSDUH), which is made available by the Inter-University Consortium for Political and Social Science, is supported by the Substance Abuse and Mental Health Services Administration and the U.S. Department of Health and Human Services. Any opinions, findings, conclusions, or recommendations expressed in this chapter are those of the authors and do not necessarily reflect the views of the funders.

FURTHER READING

Centers for Disease Control and Prevention (CDC). "National estimates of marijuana use and related indicators—National Survey on Drug Use and Health, United States, 2002–2014." *Surveillance Summaries* 65, no. 11 (2016): 1–25. https://www.cdc.gov/mmwr/volumes/65/ss/ss6511a1.htm

Compton, Wilson M., Beth Han, Christopher M. Jones, Carlos Blanco, and Arthur Hughes. "Marijuana use and use disorders in adults in the USA, 2002–14: analysis of annual cross-sectional surveys." *The Lancet Psychiatry* 3, no. 10 (2016): 954–964.

Evans-Polce, Rebecca J., Sara A. Vasilenko, and Stephanie T. Lanza. "Changes in gender and racial/ethnic disparities in rates of cigarette use, regular heavy episodic drinking, and marijuana use: ages 14 to 32." *Addictive Behaviors* 41 (2015): 218–222.

Haberstick, Brett C., Susan E. Young, Joanna S. Zeiger, Jeffrey M. Lessem, John K. Hewitt, and Christian J. Hopfer. "Prevalence and correlates of alcohol and cannabis use disorders in the United States: results from the longitudinal study of adolescent health." *Drug and Alcohol Dependence* 136 (2014): 158–161.

Hasin, Deborah S., Bradley T. Kerridge, Tulshi D. Saha, Boji Huang, Roger Pickering, Sharon M. Smith, Jeesun Jung, Haitao Zhang, and Bridget F. Grant. "Prevalence and correlates of DSM-5 cannabis use disorder, 2012–2013: findings from the National Epidemiologic Survey on Alcohol and Related Conditions–III." *The American Journal of Psychiatry* 173, no. 6 (2016): 588–599.

Hasin, Deborah S., Tulshi D. Saha, Bradley T. Kerridge, Risë B. Goldstein, S. Patricia Chou, Haitao Zhang, Jeesun Jung, Roger P. Pickering, W. June Ruan, Sharon M. Smith, Boji Huang, and Bridget F. Grant. "Prevalence of marijuana use disorders in the United States between 2001–2002 and 2012–2013." *JAMA Psychiatry* 72, no. 12, (2015): 1235–1242.

National Survey on Drug Use and Health (NSDUH). United States Department of Health and Human Services. Substance Abuse and Mental Health Services Administration. Center for Behavioral Health Statistics and Quality. National Survey on Drug Use and Health, 2014. ICPSR36361-v1. Ann Arbor, MI: Inter-university Consortium for Political and Social Research [distributor], March 22, 2016. http://doi.org/10.3886/ICPSR36361.v1

Q6. DOES MARIJUANA USE OR MISUSE VARY BY EDUCATION LEVEL?

Answer: Yes. In a majority of the years considered here, U.S. adults (ages 18 to 49) who were postgraduates of high school (i.e., they continued their education after graduating from high school) showed significantly lower rates of marijuana misuse (abuse or dependence) than high school graduates (who did not pursue education after high school) and non-graduates (who did not graduate from high school). Fewer differences by education level were observed for marijuana use, but when they emerged, the highest use rates were among nongraduates, and the lowest use rates were among postgraduates. With few exceptions, rates of marijuana use in 2014 tended to be higher than earlier in the decade regardless of age or education level, and marijuana misuse did not change among pre-middle or middle-aged adults (ages 26 to 49). Among young adults (ages 18 to 25), marijuana misuse was lower among high school graduates in 2014 than in half of the prior years considered. In all but one case, women used or misused marijuana less than men did within every age category and education level considered in 2014.

The Facts: To examine if there are differences in marijuana use or misuse by education level, this chapter used data from the National Survey on Drug Use and Health (NSDUH 2016), a large and representative survey of U.S. household residents ages 12 and older, between the years 2004 and 2014. These yearly, cross-sectional, self-administered surveys asked participants to answer questions about their use or misuse of marijuana in the 12 months prior to the survey. *Marijuana users* included those who reported that they used marijuana during that 12-month period, and *marijuana misusers* included those who reported that during that time they experienced symptoms (criteria) like those used by the American Psychiatric Association to diagnose marijuana abuse or dependence (see Q1 for those criteria).

Education level was divided into three categories by the NSDUH: nongraduates (i.e., respondents who did not earn a high school degree), graduates (i.e., respondents who graduated from high school but did not continue their education), and postgraduates (i.e., respondents who continued their education beyond high school, regardless of whether they earned additional degrees). Analyses here focused on adults. When considering the U.S. population of household residents ages 18 and older in 2014, rates of marijuana use were remarkably similar (ranging from 13.1 percent to 13.7 percent) across the three education levels considered. Marijuana misuse rates were lowest among post high school-grads (1.2 percent), but nearly equivalent for high school graduates (1.6 percent) or those who did not graduate from high school (1.9 percent). There were, however, some variations across age, sex, and year.

PATTERNS BY AGE

Age is one of the most reliable predictors of the use and misuse of marijuana. Therefore, this chapter examines differences by education level in marijuana use and misuse within three adult age categories: ages 18 to 25 years (young adults), ages 26 to 34 years (pre-middle-aged adults), and ages 35 to 49 years (middle-aged adults). Figure 1.7 and Table 1.11 show patterns of marijuana use and marijuana misuse by education level and age between 2004 and 2014.

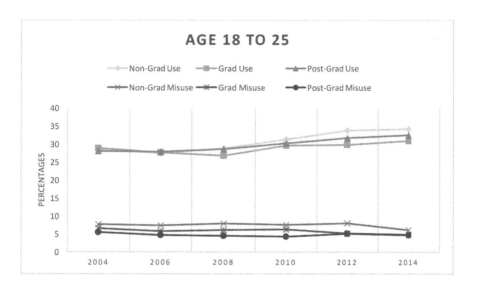

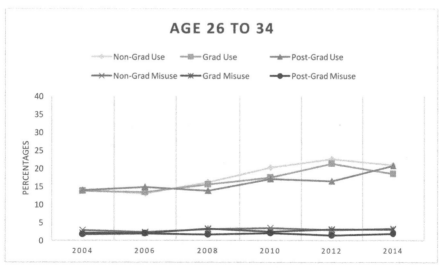

Figure 1.7 Past 12-Month Marijuana Use and Misuse by Age, Year, and Education Level

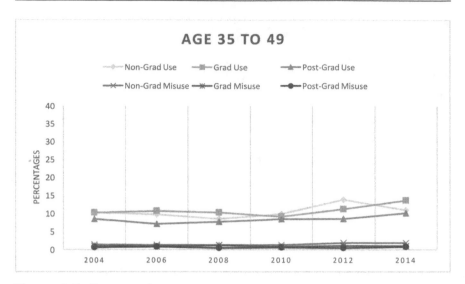

Figure 1.7 Continued

Marijuana Use

Between 2004 and 2014, rates of marijuana use among young adults (ages 18 to 25) ranged from 27.5 percent to 34.2 percent for nongraduates, 26.8 percent to 30.9 percent for graduates, and 27.9 percent to 32.5 percent for postgraduates. Marijuana use differences were observed in only two years (2012 and 2014), wherein young adult nongraduates showed significantly higher rates of marijuana use than postgraduates. For pre-middle-aged adults (ages 26 to 34), rates of marijuana use ranged from 13.0 percent to 22.6 percent for nongraduates, 13.4 percent to 21.3 percent for graduates, and 13.8 percent to 20.8 percent for postgraduates. Statistically significant marijuana use differences by education level were observed only in one year (2012), such that postgraduates showed lower marijuana use rates than nongraduates or graduates.

For middle-aged adults (ages 35 to 49) over the 2004 to 2014 decade, rates of marijuana use ranged from 8.5 percent to 13.8 percent for non-graduates, 9.1 percent to 13.6 percent for graduates, and 7.1 percent to 10.1 percent for postgraduates. Rates of use for this age group varied by education level in four of the six years considered: nongraduates showed higher rates than postgraduates in 2006 and 2012; gradates showed higher rates than post-graduates in 2006, 2008, 2012, and 2014; nongraduates showed higher rates than graduates in 2012, and; graduates showed higher rates than both nongraduates and postgraduates in 2014.

Table 1.11 Past 12-Month Marijuana Use and Misuse: Within-Year Percentage Differences by Education Level

		Age 18 to 25		Age 26 to 34		Age 35 to 49	
		Use	Misuse	Use	Misuse	Use	Misuse
2004	Nongraduate	28.6%	7.7	14.0	2.8	10.2	1.4
	Graduate	28.9	6.6	13.7	2.1	10.2	1.0
	Postgraduate	28.1	5.5	13.9	1.7	8.5	0.7
		ns	(p < .05)	ns	ns	ns	ns
2006	Nongraduate	27.5	7.4	13.0	2.3	9.7	1.3
	Graduate	27.7	5.8	13.4	2.0	10.6	0.9
	Postgraduate	27.9	4.7	14.8	1.9	7.1	0.8
		ns	(p < .05)	ns	ns	(p < .05)	ns
2008	Nongraduate	28.8	7.9	16.1	3.1	8.5	1.3
	Graduate	26.8	6.1	15.5	3.2	10.2	1.2
	Postgraduate	28.6	4.5	13.8	1.6	7.7	0.5
		ns	(p < .05)	ns	(p < .05)	P < .05)	(p < .05)
2010	Nongraduate	31.3	7.6	20.2	3.4	9.8	1.3
	Graduate	29.6	6.3	17.5	2.4	9.1	0.8
	Postgraduate	30.2	4.3	17.1	2.0	8.4	0.6
		ns	(p < .05)	ns	ns	ns	ns

(Continued)

Table 1.11 Continued

		Age 18 to 25		Age 26 to 34		Age 35 to 49	
		Use	Misuse	Use	Misuse	Use	Misuse
2012	Nongraduate	33.8	8.0	22.6	2.9	13.8	1.9
	Graduate	29.8	5.2	21.3	3.1	11.2	1.1
	Postgraduate	31.7	5.1	16.5	1.4	8.5	0.5
		(p < .05)	(p < .05)	(p < .05)	(p < .05)	(p < .05)	(p < .05)
2014	Nongraduate	34.2	6.1	20.9	3.2	10.9	1.9
	Graduate	30.9	4.8	18.5	3.0	13.6	1.0
	Postgraduate	32.5	4.7	20.8	1.8	10.1	0.8
		(p < .05)	ns	ns	(p < .05)	(p < .05)	(p < .05)

Note: Data are from the National Survey on Drug Use and Health (NSDUH 2004–2014).

ns = not statistically significant at p < .05.

Marijuana Misuse

In young adulthood (ages 18 to 25), differences in marijuana misuse by education level were observed in all years considered but one (2014) between 2004 and 2014. Misuse rates ranged from 6.1 percent to 8.0 percent for nongraduates, 4.8 percent to 6.6 percent for graduates, and 4.3 percent to 5.5 percent for postgraduates. Nongraduates showed significantly higher rates of marijuana misuse than postgraduates from 2004 to 2012, and significantly higher rates than graduates in 2006 and 2008. Graduates showed significantly higher misuse rates than postgraduates in 2008 and 2010.

For pre-middle-aged adults (ages 26 to 34), marijuana misuse rates ranged from 2.3 percent to 3.4 percent for nongraduates, 2.0 percent to 3.2 percent for graduates, and 1.4 percent to 2.0 percent for postgraduates. Rates for this age group varied by education level in three of the six years considered (2008, 2012, and 2014) such that postgraduates showed significantly lower marijuana misuse than either nongraduates or graduates. For middle-aged adults (ages 35 to 49), marijuana misuse rates ranged from 1.3 percent to 1.9 percent for nongraduates, 0.8 percent to 1.2 percent for graduates, and 0.5 percent to 0.8 percent for postgraduates. Misuse rates varied by education level for middle-aged adults in three of the six years considered (2008, 2012, and 2014). In all three years, middle-aged postgraduates showed significantly lower misuse than nongraduates, and in two of those years (2008 and 2012), postgraduate rates were also significantly lower than graduate misuse rates.

Recent Changes

Increases in marijuana use over the 2004–2014 decade did not necessarily correspond with increases in marijuana misuse. Patterns of change in marijuana use and misuse, however, do vary somewhat by the age and education level of respondents. In 2014, young adults (ages 18 to 25) who were nongraduates showed higher rates of marijuana use than they did in 2004, 2006, and 2008; however, their rates of marijuana misuse did not change significantly over the decade. Among young adults who graduated from high school, 2014 rates of marijuana use were higher than they were in 2006 and 2008, and marijuana misuse rates were significantly lower in 2014 than they were in 2004, 2008, and 2010. For postgraduate young adults, marijuana use was significantly higher in 2014 than it was in 2004, 2006, 2008 and 2010; however, their rates of marijuana misuse did not change over the decade.

Among pre-middle-aged adults (ages 26 to 34), 2014 rates of marijuana use were statistically significantly higher for nongraduates than they were in 2004, 2006, and 2008. For pre-middle-aged graduates, 2014 use rates were significantly higher than their rates in 2004 and 2006. For pre-middle-aged postgraduates, marijuana use in 2014 was significantly higher than every other year considered over the 2004–2014 decade. Among middle-aged adults (ages 35 to 49), 2014 rates of marijuana use did not change significantly for nongraduates; however, for both graduates and postgraduates, 2014 rates of marijuana use were significantly higher than use rates in every other year considered. No changes in marijuana misuse were observed for pre-middle- or middle-aged adults between 2004 and 2014.

PATTERNS BY SEX

Finally, self-reported sex (as female or male) is consistently related to marijuana use and misuse in adulthood. In Table 1.12, estimates of past 12-month marijuana use and marijuana misuse by age, sex, and education level are presented using data from 2014, the most recent year data available when this chapter was written. Regardless of age category or education level, rates of marijuana use and misuse were significantly lower

Table 1.12 Past 12-Month Marijuana Use and Misuse Percentages by Age, Sex, and Education Level in 2014

		Marijuana Use		Marijuana Misuse	
		Males	Females	Males	Females
Age 18 to 25	Nongraduate	40.4%	25.7*	7.6	4.0*
	Graduate	35.4	25.6*	5.9	3.5*
	Postgraduate	36.1	29.4*	6.3	3.4*
Age 26 to 34	Nongraduate	26.9	12.9*	4.5	1.4*
	Graduate	21.3	15.3*	4.0	1.9*
	Postgraduate	26.3	15.9*	2.8	0.9*
Age 35 to 49	Nongraduate	14.7	6.0*	2.9	0.7*
	Graduate	16.4	10.3*	1.5	0.4
	Postgraduate	13.6	7.0*	1.5	0.2*

Note: Data are from the National Survey on Drug Use and Health (NSDUH 2014).
* $p < .05$ (sex differences).

among women than among men with only one exception: middle-aged women and men who were high school graduates misused marijuana at statistically similar rates.

ACKNOWLEDGMENT

The National Survey on Drug Use and Health (NSDUH), which is made available by the Inter-University Consortium for Political and Social Science, is supported by the Substance Abuse and Mental Health Services Administration and the U.S. Department of Health and Human Services. Any opinions, findings, conclusions, or recommendations expressed in this chapter are those of the authors and do not necessarily reflect the views of the funders.

FURTHER READING

Centers for Disease Control and Prevention (CDC). "National estimates of marijuana use and related indicators—National Survey on Drug Use and Health, United States, 2002–2014." *Surveillance Summaries* 65, no. 11 (2016): 1–25. https://www.cdc.gov/mmwr/volumes/65/ss/ss6511a1 .htm

Compton, Wilson M., Beth Han, Christopher M. Jones, Carlos Blanco, and Arthur Hughes. "Marijuana use and use disorders in adults in the USA, 2002–14: analysis of annual cross-sectional surveys." *The Lancet Psychiatry* 3, no. 10 (2016): 954–964.

Evans-Polce, Rebecca J., Sara A. Vasilenko, and Stephanie T. Lanza. "Changes in gender and racial/ethnic disparities in rates of cigarette use, regular heavy episodic drinking, and marijuana use: ages 14 to 32." *Addictive Behaviors* 41 (2015): 218–222.

Haberstick, Brett C., Susan E. Young, Joanna S. Zeiger, Jeffrey M. Lessem, John K. Hewitt, and Christian J. Hopfer. "Prevalence and correlates of alcohol and cannabis use disorders in the United States: results from the longitudinal study of adolescent health." *Drug and Alcohol Dependence* 136 (2014): 158–161.

Hasin, Deborah S., Bradley T. Kerridge, Tulshi D. Saha, Boji Huang, Roger Pickering, Sharon M. Smith, Jeesun Jung, Haitao Zhang, and Bridget F. Grant. "Prevalence and correlates of DSM-5 cannabis use disorder, 2012–2013: findings from the National Epidemiologic Survey on Alcohol and Related Conditions–III." *The American Journal of Psychiatry* 173, no. 6 (2016): 588–599.

Hasin, Deborah S., Tulshi D. Saha, Bradley T. Kerridge, Risë B. Gold-
stein, S. Patricia Chou, Haitao Zhang, Jeesun Jung, Roger P. Pickering,
W. June Ruan, Sharon M. Smith, Boji Huang, and Bridget F. Grant.
"Prevalence of marijuana use disorders in the United States between
2001–2002 and 2012–2013." *JAMA Psychiatry* 72, no. 12, (2015):
1235–1242.
National Survey on Drug Use and Health (NSDUH). United States
Department of Health and Human Services. Substance Abuse and
Mental Health Services Administration. Center for Behavioral Health
Statistics and Quality. National Survey on Drug Use and Health, 2014.
ICPSR36361-v1. Ann Arbor, MI: Inter-university Consortium for
Political and Social Research [distributor], March 22, 2016. http://doi
.org/10.3886/ICPSR36361.v1

Q7. DOES MARIJUANA USE OR MISUSE VARY BY MARITAL STATUS?

Answer: Yes. Across adulthood (ages 18 to 49) and in every year considered over the 2004–2014 decade, both marijuana use and misuse (abuse
or dependence) varied by the marital status of U.S. household residents.
Quite consistently, married adults showed the lowest rates of use and misuse, followed by divorced adults, followed by never-married adults. Marijuana use rates tended to increase over the decade, particularly among the
never married, and misuse rates did not change for adults ages 26 to 49,
regardless of marital status. Among never-married young adults (ages 18
to 25), marijuana misuse decreased over the decade. Irrespective of marital status, women tended to use marijuana at rates lower than men did;
however, with regard to the misuse of marijuana, sex differences were less
apparent especially among married adults.

The Facts: To examine if there are differences in marijuana use
or misuse by marital status, this chapter used data from the ongoing
National Survey on Drug Use and Health (NSDUH 2016), a large and
representative survey of U.S. household residents ages 12 and older,
between the years 2004 and 2014. These yearly, cross-sectional, self-
administered surveys asked participants to answer questions about their
use or misuse of marijuana in the 12 months prior to the survey. *Marijuana
users* included those who reported that they used marijuana during that
12-month period, and *marijuana misusers* included those who reported
that during that time they experienced symptoms (criteria) like those

used by the American Psychiatric Association to diagnose marijuana abuse or dependence (see Q1 for those criteria).

Current marital status was divided into three categories: married, divorced or separated (henceforth referred to as "divorced"), and never married. Analyses focused on adults and did not include widowed respondents. Among the U.S. population of household residents ages 18 and older in 2014, rates of marijuana use and misuse were lowest for married respondents (6.9 percent and 0.4 percent, respectively), followed by respondents who were divorced (13.1 percent and 1.0 percent, respectively), followed by respondents who were never married (27.6 percent and 3.8 percent, respectively). There were, however, some variations across age, sex, and year.

PATTERNS BY AGE

This chapter examines differences by marital status in marijuana use and misuse within three adult age categories: ages 18 to 25 years (young adults), ages 26 to 34 years (pre-middle-aged adults), and ages 35 to 49 years (middle-aged adults). Figure 1.8 and Table 1.13 show patterns of marijuana use and marijuana misuse by marital status and age between 2004 and 2014.

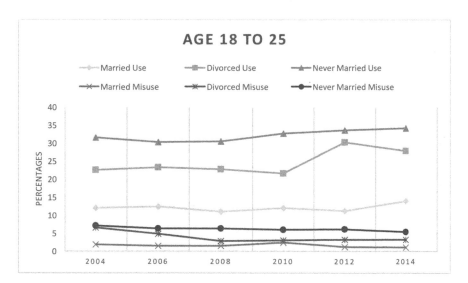

Figure 1.8 Past 12-Month Marijuana Use and Misuse by Age, Year, and Marital Status

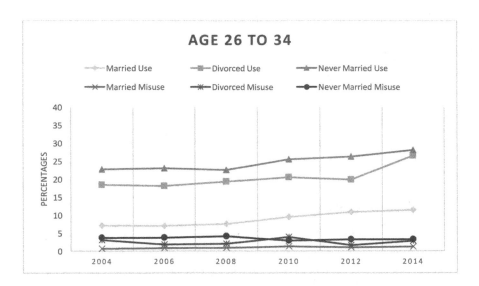

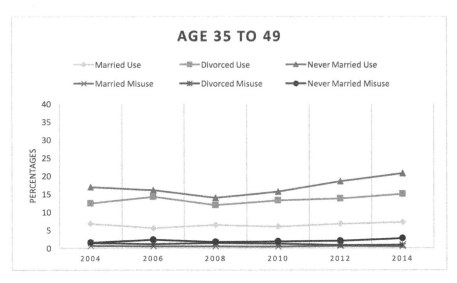

Figure 1.8 Continued

Table 1.13 Past 12-Month Marijuana Use and Misuse: Within-Year Percentage Differences by Marital Status

		Age 18 to 25		Age 26 to 34		Age 35 to 49	
		Use	Misuse	Use	Misuse	Use	Misuse
2004	Married	12.0%	1.9	7.1	0.7	6.7	0.6
	Divorced	22.6	6.6	18.4	3.1	12.4	1.4
	Never Married	31.6	7.1	22.7	3.7	16.9	1.5
		(p < .05)	(p < .05)	(p < .05)	(p < .05)	(p < .05)	(p < .05)
2006	Married	12.4	1.5	7.0	0.8	5.5	0.5
	Divorced	23.3	4.8	18.1	1.8	14.2	1.1
	Never Married	30.3	6.3	23.0	3.7	16.0	2.3
		(p < .05)	(p < .05)	(p < .05)	(p < .05)	(p < .05)	(p < .05)
2008	Married	11.0	1.5	7.5	0.9	6.4	0.5
	Divorced	22.8	2.8	19.3	2.0	11.9	1.4
	Never Married	30.5	6.3	22.5	4.1	13.9	1.7
		(p < .05)	(p < .05)	(p < .05)	(p < .05)	(p < .05)	(p < .05)

(Continued)

Table 1.13 Continued

		Age 18 to 25		Age 26 to 34		Age 35 to 49	
		Use	Misuse	Use	Misuse	Use	Misuse
2010	Married	12.0	2.4	9.5	1.3	5.9	0.4
	Divorced	21.6	3.0	20.5	3.9	13.2	1.2
	Never Married	32.7	6.0	25.5	2.9	15.6	1.8
		(p < .05)	(p < .05)	(p < .05)	(p < .05)	(p < .05)	(p < .05)
2012	Married	11.2	1.2	10.8	1.0	6.7	0.6
	Divorced	30.2	3.2	19.8	1.6	13.7	0.8
	Never Married	33.6	6.1	26.2	3.2	18.5	2.0
		(p < .05)	(p < .05)	(p < .05)	(p < .05)	(p < .05)	(p < .05)
2014	Married	14.0	1.1	11.4	1.2	7.2	0.5
	Divorced	27.9	3.2	26.5	2.8	15.0	0.9
	Never Married	34.2	5.4	28.0	3.2	20.7	2.7
		(p < .05)	(p < .05)	(p < .05)	(p < .05)	(p < .05)	(p < .05)

Note: Data are from the National Survey on Drug Use and Health (NSDUH 2004–2014).

ns = not statistically significant at p < .05.

Marijuana Use

In young adulthood (ages 18 to 25), rates of marijuana use ranged from 11.0 percent to 14.0 percent for married respondents, 21.6 percent to 30.2 percent for divorced respondents, and 30.2 percent to 34.2 percent for never-married respondents during the 2004–2014 decade. In every year considered, married young adults showed significantly lower rates of marijuana use than their divorced or never-married counterparts. In addition, divorced young adults showed significantly lower rates of marijuana use than their never married counterparts in four of the six years considered (2004 to 2010).

Between 2004 and 2014, rates of marijuana use among pre-middle-aged adults (ages 26 to 34) ranged from 7.0 percent to 11.4 percent for married respondents, 18.1 percent to 26.5 percent for divorced respondents, and 22.5 percent to 28.0 percent for never-married respondents. Similar to married young adults, married pre-middle-aged adults showed significantly lower rates of marijuana use than their divorced or never-married counterparts in every year considered. In one of those years (2012), divorced pre-middle-aged adults showed significantly lower rates of use than never-married adults.

Among middle-aged adults (ages 35 to 49), rates of marijuana use ranged from 5.5 percent to 7.2 percent for married respondents, 11.9 percent to 15.0 percent for divorced respondents, and 13.7 percent to 20.7 percent for never-married respondents. Again, married respondents showed significantly lower rates of use than divorced or never-married respondents in all years considered. In 2004, 2012, and 2014, middle-aged adults who were divorced showed lower rates of use than those who were never married.

Marijuana Misuse

Over the 2004–2014 decade, young adult (ages 18 to 25) rates of marijuana misuse ranged from 1.1 percent to 2.4 percent for married young adults, 2.8 percent to 6.6 percent for divorced young adults, and 5.4 percent to 7.1 percent for never-married young adults. Married misuse rates were significantly lower than never-married rates among young adults in every year considered. In 2004 and 2006, married rates of marijuana misuse were also lower than marijuana misuse rates among divorced young adults.

For pre-middle-aged adults (ages 26 to 34) during this decade, marijuana misuse rates ranged from 0.7 percent to 1.3 percent for married respondents, 1.6 percent to 3.9 percent for divorced respondents, and 2.9 percent to 4.1 percent for never-married respondents. Similar to married young adults, married pre-middle-aged adults showed significantly lower misuse rates than their never-married counterparts in every year considered, and they showed significantly lower misuse rates than their divorced counterparts in three of those years (2004, 2010, and 2014). In 2006, divorced pre-middle-aged adults showed lower marijuana misuse rates than never-married pre-middle-aged adults.

Among middle-aged adults (ages 35 to 49), rates of marijuana misuse ranged from 0.4 percent to 0.6 percent for married respondents, 0.8 percent to 1.4 percent for divorced respondents, and 1.5 percent to 2.7 percent for never-married respondents. Again, married marijuana misuse rates were lower than rates for never-married respondents in every year considered. Middle-aged adults who were married showed significantly lower rates of marijuana misuse than divorced middle-aged adults from 2004 to 2010. Middle-aged adults who were divorced in 2012 and 2014 showed significantly lower misuse rates than their never-married counterparts.

Recent Changes

Increases in marijuana use over the 2004–2014 decade did not necessarily correspond with increases in marijuana misuse. Patterns of change in marijuana use and misuse, however, do appear to vary by the age and marital status of respondents. In 2014, married young adults (ages 18 to 25) showed significantly higher rates of marijuana use than they did in 2008, but they showed significantly *lower* rates of marijuana misuse than they did in 2010. For divorced young adults, rates of marijuana use and misuse remained unchanged over the years considered here. For never-married young adults, the 2014 marijuana use rate was significantly higher than rates in 2004, 2006, and 2008; however, the 2014 rate of misuse for never-married young adults was significantly *lower* than misuse rates in those same years.

For pre-middle-aged adults (ages 26 to 34), marijuana use in 2014 was significantly higher than use in 2004, 2006, and 2008 regardless of marital status. For middle-aged adults (ages 35 to 49), married marijuana use was higher in 2014 than use in 2006 and 2010, divorced use was higher in 2014 than use in 2008, and marijuana use among never-married middle-aged adults was higher in 2014 than marijuana use in 2004, 2006, 2008, and 2010. Marijuana misuse among pre-middle- and middle-aged adults remained unchanged throughout the 2004 to 2014 decade.

PATTERNS BY SEX

Finally, self-reported sex (as female or male) is consistently related to marijuana use and misuse in adulthood. In Table 1.14, estimates of past 12-month marijuana use and marijuana misuse by age, sex, and marital status are presented using data from 2014, the most recent year data available when this chapter was written. Women used marijuana at significantly lower rates than did men, across marital status, and within every adult age category considered, except for one: for divorced young adults, sex differences were not statistically significant. Sex differences in marijuana misuse were somewhat less consistent. For married young adults and middle-aged adults, no sex differences in marijuana misuse were observed, and divorced misuse did not vary significantly by sex in pre-middle age. Across age, however, never-married men misused marijuana at rates higher than women did.

ACKNOWLEDGMENT

The National Survey on Drug Use and Health (NSDUH), which is made available by the Inter-University Consortium for Political and Social

Table 1.14 Past 12-Month Marijuana Use and Misuse Percentages by Age, Sex, and Marital Status in 2014

		Marijuana Use		Marijuana Misuse	
		Males	Females	Males	Females
Age 18 to 25	Married	18.8%	11.3*	1.4	1.0
	Divorced	37.1	22.6	8.5	0.1*
	Never Married	37.8	30.2*	6.7	3.9*
Age 26 to 34	Married	13.9	9.2*	1.9	0.5*
	Divorced	33.1	21.9*	4.5	1.6
	Never Married	33.5	21.5*	4.4	1.8*
Age 35 to 49	Married	9.4	5.0*	0.7	0.3
	Divorced	21.7	10.1*	2.3	4.4*
	Never Married	25.7	14.9*	4.4	0.8*

Note: Data are from the National Survey on Drug Use and Health (NSDUH 2014).
* $p < .05$ (sex differences).

Science, is supported by the Substance Abuse and Mental Health Services Administration and the U.S. Department of Health and Human Services. Any opinions, findings, conclusions, or recommendations expressed in this chapter are those of the authors and do not necessarily reflect the views of the funders.

FURTHER READING

Centers for Disease Control and Prevention (CDC). "National estimates of marijuana use and related indicators—National Survey on Drug Use and Health, United States, 2002–2014." *Surveillance Summaries* 65, no. 11 (2016): 1–25. https://www.cdc.gov/mmwr/volumes/65/ss/ss6511a1.htm

Compton, Wilson M., Beth Han, Christopher M. Jones, Carlos Blanco, and Arthur Hughes. "Marijuana use and use disorders in adults in the USA, 2002–14: analysis of annual cross-sectional surveys." *The Lancet Psychiatry* 3, no. 10 (2016): 954–964.

Evans-Polce, Rebecca J., Sara A. Vasilenko, and Stephanie T. Lanza. "Changes in gender and racial/ethnic disparities in rates of cigarette use, regular heavy episodic drinking, and marijuana use: ages 14 to 32." *Addictive Behaviors* 41 (2015): 218–222.

Haberstick, Brett C., Susan E. Young, Joanna S. Zeiger, Jeffrey M. Lessem, John K. Hewitt, and Christian J. Hopfer. "Prevalence and correlates of alcohol and cannabis use disorders in the United States: results from the longitudinal study of adolescent health." *Drug and Alcohol Dependence* 136 (2014): 158–161.

Hasin, Deborah S., Bradley T. Kerridge, Tulshi D. Saha, Boji Huang, Roger Pickering, Sharon M. Smith, Jeesun Jung, Haitao Zhang, and Bridget F. Grant. "Prevalence and correlates of DSM-5 cannabis use disorder, 2012–2013: findings from the National Epidemiologic Survey on Alcohol and Related Conditions–III." *The American Journal of Psychiatry* 173, no. 6 (2016): 588–599.

Hasin, Deborah S., Tulshi D. Saha, Bradley T. Kerridge, Risë B. Goldstein, S. Patricia Chou, Haitao Zhang, Jeesun Jung, Roger P. Pickering, W. June Ruan, Sharon M. Smith, Boji Huang, and Bridget F. Grant. "Prevalence of marijuana use disorders in the United States between 2001–2002 and 2012–2013." *JAMA Psychiatry* 72, no. 12, (2015): 1235–1242.

National Survey on Drug Use and Health (NSDUH). United States Department of Health and Human Services. Substance Abuse and Mental Health Services Administration. Center for Behavioral Health Statistics and Quality. National Survey on Drug Use and Health, 2014. ICPSR36361-v1. Ann Arbor, MI: Inter-university Consortium for Political and Social Research [distributor], March 22, 2016. http://doi .org/10.3886/ICPSR36361.v1

2

❖

Risks and Benefits

Q8. IS ACCURATE INFORMATION ABOUT THE RISKS AND BENEFITS OF MARIJUANA WIDELY AVAILABLE?

Answer: Yes, but the information often exists outside of mainstream information sources. The risks and benefits of marijuana use are debated in the news, in academic institutions, in Congress, and in families. Unfortunately, many of these discussions and debates take place in the absence of accurate, reliable, and valid scientific evidence. Marijuana has at times been held in high esteem due to its medicinal properties, while at other times it has been demonized along with other illicit substances because of its potential to be misused. As a result, many people are misinformed about marijuana. However, researchers and scientists from diverse fields investigate the risks and benefits of marijuana, and their research provides the accurate information on marijuana that can help people become better informed.

The Facts: In the current task of investigating commonly held beliefs about marijuana, particular types of information are given precedence. Whenever possible, this book presents empirical evidence, gathered systematically through scientific research, as the chief source of accurate information about marijuana. In the most general sense, empirical evidence is evidence based on observation or experience. In scientific research, observations are made according to rigorous scientific methods, and conclusions drawn from these observations are made carefully and cautiously.

Other forms of observational evidence exist, including the evidence gathered from personal experiences during the course of everyday life. These types of personal experiences are of course helpful in allowing people to make sense of the world. However, everyday experiences can sometimes be misleading. For example, many people in the world have only seen swans that are white. For these people, there is ample evidence—in the form of everyday observations—that all swans are white, but in reality, not all swans are white. *Cygnus atratus* is a large species of black-feathered swan that lives in Australia and elsewhere. Many people do not know that black swans exist. Similarly, many people have smoked marijuana without ever having negative experiences or consequences. These benign experiences may lead the occasional marijuana user to believe that the drug is harmless. Yet there is a small but significant proportion of the population for whom marijuana has caused serious problems. Accordingly, scientists interested in marijuana—or swans—must be careful to sample systematically and observe carefully, to understand the full universe of observable phenomena.

Empirical science can take many forms and can be employed in a variety of ways, but there are certain principles of the scientific process that undergird all good science. Science often begins with observations or questions about how things (usually called variables) in the world are related. These questions lead to hypotheses or predictions about the nature of a relationship between two variables. The scientific process requires that hypotheses can be tested, usually through experimentation or observation, but this cannot take place until there are valid and reliable ways to gather data and measure variables. Following experimentation and observation, data are analyzed and summarized. Finally, conclusions are communicated to other researchers and contribute to the formation of theories.

Evidence presented in this book is largely the product of "peer-reviewed" or "refereed" scientific research. Peer-reviewed evidence is that which has been evaluated, scrutinized, and reviewed by peer scientists. Scientific evidence is generally considered most valid once it has been peer-reviewed and replicated. It is very important to remember that no single experiment, or conclusion, or statistic—even if it has been peer-reviewed—is ever enough to prove absolutely that something is true. Instead, it is only when several lines of evidence converge that scientists are able to develop a consensus about how the world works.

Many scientific disciplines conduct research on marijuana, and these disciplines utilize a variety of research methods. Each research method has strengths and weaknesses that must be taken into account when interpreting the results. Most people are familiar with basic experimental research designs in which researchers expose research subjects (or cases) to an intervention in order to assess the impact of that intervention. When experimental conditions are tightly controlled and when research subjects are randomly assigned to various exposure groups (i.e., experimental and control groups), researchers can isolate the effects of an independent variable on a dependent variable (see Creswell 2009). Because well-designed experiments are able to systematically control and manipulate the research conditions they are often seen as the optimal way to test causal hypotheses (Singleton and Straits 2010).

While experimental research designs can be very useful in helping to establish causation, some research questions do not lend themselves to human experimentation. For example, if researchers are interested in determining the effect of long-term marijuana smoking on lung cancer, it would not be ethical to randomly assign adolescent human subjects to prolonged marijuana exposure. However, other types of experimental studies can be used. For example, researchers might choose to experiment on animals, or they might choose to utilize laboratory studies that test cellular and molecular processes outside of the human body. These types of experimental studies are very good at establishing a certain type of causation, but they are limited in their relevance to actual human disease. Even if a particular experimental exposure causes cancer in monkeys, for example, this evidence is not sufficient to conclude that the same result would occur in humans.

In experimental research, scientists are able to systematically control and manipulate the research conditions. However, humans do not live in controlled circumstances, and some research questions simply cannot be tested within an experimental paradigm. Accordingly, some forms of research—aptly named observational research—rely on the careful observation of humans in their natural environment. Observational research has more direct relevance to the human condition than does experimental research, but it has its own weaknesses. The primary weakness of observational research lies in the inability of researchers to control the research conditions in such a way that all causal processes can be positively identified. While experiments rely on random assignment in order to isolate the effects of an independent variable on a dependent variable, random assignment does not exist in the real world. For example, many marijuana smokers also smoke tobacco, making it challenging to isolate the effects of marijuana smoke versus the effects of tobacco smoke on pulmonary health outcomes. Therefore, observational researchers often utilize statistical methods that take into account (or control for) other relevant variables in order to understand how one variable affects another.

In order to make strong causal inferences using observational research, three general conditions or criteria must be met (see sidebar below). The first criterion requires that a statistical *association* (or correlation) exist between two variables. Logically, two variables must be associated or correlated for it to be possible that one variable causes the other. The second criterion relates to the observed temporal association or *direction of influence*. This criterion requires that the cause precede the effect. For example, if conduct problems precede marijuana use, it would not make sense to infer that marijuana use is the cause of the conduct problems. Finally, causal inferences can be made only in the *absence of other explanations*. This criterion requires that the observed relationship between two variables must not be due to a third (or confounding) variable. Put another way, *correlation does not mean causation*. For example, there is consistent evidence that marijuana use is associated with criminal activity (see Q19; Caulkins et al. 2015). However, this association is not necessarily causal. There is some research showing that individuals who use marijuana at a young age already belong to a high-risk group, and that a predisposition to use marijuana and commit crime may be rooted in common risk factors like childhood adversity, social disadvantage, or genetic disposition (e.g., Fergusson and Horwood 1997).

THE THREE NECESSARY CONDITIONS FOR ESTABLISHING CAUSALITY

1. **Association**
   Variable A and Variable B are related or associated with each other.
2. **Direction of Influence**
   For Variable A to cause Variable B, Variable A must occur before Variable B.
3. **Absence of Other Explanations**
   The association between Variable A and Variable B must not be due to a third or confounding variable.

There are two additional forms of scientific evidence that are worth noting. The first type are *case studies*, in which individual cases (e.g., patients, events, programs) are observed or analyzed in order to understand them better. Case studies allow researchers to make very detailed observations that can help uncover complex or nuanced phenomena. Sometimes atypical or extreme cases are chosen for in-depth case-studies because researchers want to focus closely on the unique aspects of the case. In some instances, a single case study can help answer very important questions. Using the previous example, a single case consisting of a black swan definitively disproves the proposition that "all swans are white" (Ryan 2013). However, for other research questions, the results of case studies may not be generalizable to the larger population.

In contrast to case studies, which focus on single cases or incidents, there are other types of research that systematically combine data or synthesize results from other studies in order to summarize the full breadth of existing research. This type of research includes *meta-analyses* and *systematic review* articles, both of which summarize scientific research on a particular topic. Meta-analyses combine data from previous studies into a single new dataset, which subsequently increases statistical precision and power (Porta 2014). Systematic reviews use a comprehensive, predetermined search strategy to find all relevant studies on a particular topic in order to synthesize the findings and present the reader with the scientific consensus, or lack thereof, on a particular topic. Meta-analyses and systematic reviews are particularly useful because they summarize data and research to the extent that strong causal inferences can be made. Whenever possible, this book utilizes both meta-analyses and systematic reviews in order to present the reader with the most up-to-date scientific consensus.

Individuals interested in accessing scientific research on marijuana should direct their attention to academic articles and books. These sources can be found in libraries and library databases, or by consulting with librarians and teachers. For those individuals who do not have access to library databases, an emerging source of peer-reviewed research can be found online, using Google Scholar. One of the most interesting and exciting aspects of marijuana research is that it spans many academic disciplines. Students of medicine, biology, chemistry, psychology, sociology, criminal justice, public health, history, and law are all likely to find research on marijuana in their discipline. Each entry in this volume draws heavily on scientific evidence and points readers toward relevant sources of information in the Further Reading section. Regardless of how these scientific books and articles are accessed, they are the leading source of evidence-based information on the risks and benefits of marijuana.

FURTHER READING

Caulkins, Jonathan P., Beau Kilmer, Mark A. R. Kleiman, Robert J. MacCoun, Gregory Midgette, Pat Oglesby, Rosalie Liccardo Pacula, and Peter H. Reuter. "Considering marijuana legalization." Santa Monica, CA: RAND, 2015.

Creswell, John. *Research design: qualitative, quantitative, and mixed methods approaches*. 3rd ed. Thousand Oaks, CA: Sage Publications, 2009.

Fergusson, David M., and L. Horwood. "Early onset cannabis use and psychosocial adjustment in young adults." *Addiction* 92, no. 3 (1997): 279–296.

Porta, Miquel, ed. *A dictionary of epidemiology*. 6th ed. New York: Oxford University Press, 2014.

Ryan, Alan. Introduction to *The open society and its enemies*, edited by Karl Popper. Princeton, NJ: Princeton University Press, 2013.

Singleton, Royce A., and Bruce C. Straits. *Approaches to social research*. 5th ed. New York: Oxford University Press, 2010.

Q9. DOES MARIJUANA USE OR MISUSE INCREASE RISK FOR PHYSICAL HEALTH PROBLEMS?

Answer: Yes. While most occasional or infrequent marijuana users are unlikely to develop serious physical health problems related to their marijuana use, regular or heavy marijuana users may be at an increased risk for some serious health problems. Long-term marijuana users who choose smoking as their primary route of administration and marijuana users with underlying health conditions may be particularly at risk.

The Facts: Among Americans ages 12 and older, there are an estimated 22 million past-month users of marijuana, and an estimated 118 million Americans have used marijuana in their lifetime (CBHSQ 2016). The federal government designates marijuana as a Schedule I substance, suggesting that it has no accepted medical use, a lack of accepted safety for use under medical supervision, and a high potential for abuse (see introduction to view the controlled substance use schedules). Considering the federal prohibition of marijuana, it might seem contradictory that more than half of U.S. states permit the use of marijuana for medical purposes. However, it is not unusual for some of the most dangerous controlled substances to be used as medicines.

While some substances such as alcohol, tobacco, cocaine, and opioids are widely recognized as potentially dangerous, the health risks of marijuana are less well understood. This is the case, in part, because misinformation has followed marijuana since its introduction to the United States in the early 1900s (see Q16). However, the risks and benefits of marijuana are also misunderstood because they are difficult to study. Most long-term studies on the health risks of marijuana follow marijuana users over many years and observe how likely they are to develop diseases or to die prematurely. The challenge with these types of studies is that people who use marijuana are often the same people who use other substances such as alcohol and cigarettes, and who engage in other risky lifestyle behaviors. As a result, it can be difficult to know if observed negative health outcomes are the result of marijuana use or if they are the result of other risk factors. Laboratory evidence using non-human models can be useful in helping to answer these questions, but laboratory research has limited generalizability to humans. Due to these challenges, there is a considerable amount of conflicting evidence in the scientific literature. This conflicting evidence has been used by both marijuana protagonists and marijuana prohibitionists to support their respective arguments.

As is the case with all drugs, the risks associated with using marijuana vary depending on how the drug is administered, and it can be difficult to parcel out which health risks are due to the drug and which are due to the various methods of exposure. This is especially true for marijuana. Marijuana is commonly smoked in joints, pipes, or water pipes, and the majority of research on the long-term health effects of marijuana has focused on individuals who choose smoking as their primary route of administration. Smoking marijuana allows for rapid onset of desired effects and flexible dosing, but it also involves the inhalation of known carcinogens (Grotenhermen 2001; Huang et al. 2015). Although some people believe that marijuana smoked in a water pipe (bong) is less harmful than other methods, there is some research indicating that this is not the case (see Caulkins et al. 2012). On the other hand, vaporizers, which are specialized devices that heat marijuana to the point of vaporization, may provide a healthier alternative to smoking, but more research is needed to understand better the long-term effects of inhaling marijuana vapor (Gieringer et al. 2004). Marijuana can also be baked or cooked into "edibles," extracted into oils, or made into marijuana "tea"—each of which offers a route of administration that bypasses the lungs, but may affect other parts of the body. Marijuana edibles can also be harder to dose and might increase the risk for accidental consumption. While there is little doubt that the chronic inhalation of combusted marijuana flowers is risky, less is known about how other routes of administration affect health in the long term.

ASSESSING RISK

Epidemiologists use specific terms to express the various ways that substances can be risky to individuals and to the population. Researchers interested in the relationship between marijuana use and lung cancer, for example, would first want to know the total number of lung cancer cases in a population at a specified point in time (the prevalence), as well as the number of new lung cancer cases within a specified time period (the incidence). The risks related to marijuana use can then be assessed at both the individual level and population level (Hall et al. 1995). At the individual level, various methods are used to compare the risk of lung cancer among people who smoke marijuana with the risk of lung cancer among people who do not smoke marijuana. For example, researchers could calculate measures of *relative risk* to express the increase in the odds of lung cancer among individuals who smoke marijuana compared to those who do not smoke marijuana (Hall et al. 1995). On a broader scale, a variety of methods are also used to make population risk assessments to estimate the public health impact of marijuana smoking. For example, researchers could calculate measures of *attributable risk* to estimate the proportion of cases of lung cancer in the population that are attributable to marijuana smoking (Hall 1995).

SHORT-TERM HEALTH RISKS

While many people who use marijuana experience a feeling of euphoria or "high," some users report less pleasant experiences and sensations. Anxiety and panic reactions are commonly reported, especially among less experienced users (Hall 2014). Less experienced users may also experience decrements in attention, concentration, memory, and decision-making speed (Crean et al. 2011). Short-term physical side effects can also include reddening of the conjunctivae (red eyes), dry mouth, and increased heart rate (Pujazon-Zazik and Park 2009). Research generally suggests that the increased heart rate associated with marijuana use represents only a mild cardiovascular stress for healthy individuals (Hall 2009). However, people with hypertension (high blood pressure) and cerebrovascular disease may be at more risk, and patients with heart disease may experience angina (Hall 2009; Hall and Degenhardt 2009). Some research has also shown that smoking marijuana can be a rare trigger of acute myocardial infarction (heart attack), but the evidence linking acute marijuana intoxication and heart attack is mixed (Mittleman et al. 2001; National Academies of Science, Engineering and Medicine 2017).

Toxicity

There are few reports of fatal poisonings due to marijuana use, and it is unclear if marijuana was directly responsible for these deaths (Room et al. 2008). Accordingly, a 2017 report from the National Academies of Sciences concludes that "there is insufficient evidence to support or refute a statistical association between cannabis use and death due to cannabis overdose" (National Academies of Sciences, Engineering, and Medicine 2017: 9–15). Animal studies using dogs, mice, and monkeys have established that marijuana can be acutely toxic at high enough doses; however, there is very little human evidence that can be used to estimate the lethal dose of marijuana for people (Hall et al. 2001). In the absence of human evidence, the risk of dying from marijuana poisoning must be estimated.

In an article published in the journal *Addiction*, Robert S. Gable (2004) estimated that the typical recreational dose of marijuana is about 15 mg (or 0.0005 ounces), while the estimated lethal dose of marijuana is greater than 15 g (just over one-half of an ounce). Thus, it is estimated that an individual would need to consume more than 1,000 times the typical dose of marijuana to risk fatal poisoning. A comparable study published in the journal *Scientific Reports* used a similar method to calculate the ratio of the *estimated lethal dose* to the *estimated human intake dose* for various substances (Lachenmeier and Rehm 2015). Estimations were made for both licit (legal) and illicit (illegal) substances for both the individual and the population. For individuals, tetrahydrocannabinol (THC) presented the lowest risk compared to other substances. Taken together, these studies support the scientific consensus that it is very unlikely that marijuana users will suffer acute overdose poisoning death strictly from using marijuana.

Limited case studies have suggested that marijuana use may be a very rare risk factor for sudden cardiac (heart-related) death. A 2013 article published in the journal *Forensic Science International* described two cases of young, healthy men who died unexpectedly under the influence of marijuana (Hartung et al. 2014). After a full postmortem investigation, the researchers ruled out other causes of death and assumed that marijuana use led to fatal cardiovascular complications. Similar cases were also reported in a 2001 research study published in the same journal (Bachs and Mørland 2001). The researchers describe six cases of acute cardiovascular death in young adults, wherein recent marijuana ingestion was indicated in blood samples. No other drugs were identified in the blood samples. These case studies are suggestive of a need to understand better how marijuana affects the cardiovascular system, but they do not provide evidence that marijuana intoxication was the cause of death. Because case studies do not select cases randomly, the potential exists that these cardiovascular events occurred at random among marijuana users. Nevertheless, these case studies provide some indication that marijuana could be a rare trigger of cardiovascular death in people with undiagnosed cardiovascular disease (see Hall 2014).

Overdose

While the relative risk of fatal marijuana poisoning is extremely low, there is population-level evidence that marijuana use may be a contributing factor in some deaths. This evidence comes from official mortality data compiled by the Centers for Disease Control and Prevention's (CDC's) National Center for Health Statistics which are publicly available through the CDC WONDER online database. Mortality statistics are based on data from all death certificates filed in the United States. Each death certificate contains a single underlying cause of death and up to 20 multiple causes. If a poisoning death involves more than one drug, then all drugs are counted as (multiple) causes of death. As a result, marijuana is listed a (multiple) cause of death even in poisoning deaths that involve more dangerous substances such as heroin, other opioids, alcohol, or cocaine.

Between 2000 and 2015, the number of annual poisoning deaths that involved marijuana as a multiple cause of death increased from 40 to 409; however, the vast majority of those deaths involved other substances as well (CDC WONDER 2016). In every year between 2000 and 2015, for example, the majority of deaths that involved marijuana as a multiple cause of death also involved opioids. Thus, the extent that marijuana contributed to these poisoning deaths is not clear. However, as described earlier, a 2017 review by the National Academies of Sciences could identify no study in which marijuana was determined to be the direct cause of overdose death.

LONG-TERM HEALTH RISKS

All-Cause Mortality

Illicit substance use can lead to death in many ways other than lethal poisoning, including motor vehicle crashes, other types of accidents, diseases, suicide, homicide, and infection. Little evidence exists indicating the extent to which marijuana use contributes to an increased risk of all-cause mortality. For example, a systematic review of epidemiological evidence published in the journal *Drug and Alcohol Review* examined whether marijuana users were at an increased risk of premature death and found that there were too few studies to make an assessment (Calabria et al. 2010). While other studies have found that users of opioids and cocaine are at an increased risk of mortality, there remains insufficient evidence to determine if all-cause mortality is elevated among marijuana users (see Degenhardt et al. 2010, 2011).

There is some evidence that chronic marijuana smoking may be associated with a higher risk of mortality among those individuals who experience heart attacks (myocardial infarction). In a 2008 study published in the *American Heart Journal*, researchers found that marijuana smoking was associated with threefold higher mortality following heart attack (Mukamal et al. 2008). They also found that the highest risk was among those who smoked marijuana most frequently. The researchers concluded that marijuana does not appear to increase mortality in the general population, but it may present certain risks for those with cardiovascular disease. This study provides further indication that marijuana use may be associated with cardiovascular risks, particularly for vulnerable people and for people with underlying conditions.

Marijuana misuse (abuse and dependence) may also be a contributing factor in some deaths. Between 2000 and 2015, data from the CDC WONDER database show that there were 61 deaths (between 1 and 13 deaths per year) classified with an underlying cause of death resulting from "mental and behavioral disorders due to use of cannabinoids." The specific mechanisms leading to these deaths remain unclear; however, 1 death in that period was coded as "acute intoxication," 11 were coded as "harmful use," and 14 were coded as "dependence syndrome" (see also Caulkins et al. 2012).

Morbidity

Chronic, regular, or heavy substance use can lead to morbidity, disease, and other adverse health outcomes. Several expert reviews have evaluated the physical health risks associated with marijuana use, and there is evidence that there are some underappreciated ways that chronic marijuana use can be dangerous (Gordon et al. 2013; Hall 2009; Room et al. 2008). For example, there is relatively strong evidence from systematic reviews and meta-analyses that heavy marijuana use is associated with cardiovascular effects and that marijuana use is also associated with liver damage among patients with Hepatitis C infections (Gordon 2010). In addition, there is some evidence linking marijuana use to respiratory problems (ibid.). The link between marijuana use and the development of cancer is reviewed in Q14.

Considerable evidence suggests that the endocannabinoid system (the part of the central nervous system that allows for marijuana to affect the human body) plays a key role in the function of the cardiovascular system (Montecucco and Di Marzo 2012; Gordon 2010). It is therefore not surprising that marijuana affects the cardiovascular system in several ways. Researchers have observed, for example, several acute cardiovascular effects related to marijuana use, including increased heart rate, changes in blood pressure, palpitations, cardiac arrhythmia, and decreased exercise tolerance (Gordon 2010; Gordon et al. 2013).

There is also some evidence indicating that chronic marijuana use results in long-term cardiovascular consequences. There is evidence, for example, that marijuana use is associated with cannabis arteritis, which is an inflammation in the arteries due to the inhalation of marijuana smoke (Gordon 2010). According to a literature review published in the *Journal of the European Academy of Dermatology and Venerology*, around 50 cases of cannabis arteritis have been reported in the literature since it was first described in 1960 (Peyrot et al. 2007). Whereas tobacco is a leading cause of thromboangiitis obliterans (Buerger disease), case studies on cannabis arteritis suggest that a parallel disorder could occur among marijuana smokers (Combemale et al. 2005). Abstinence from marijuana and tobacco smoking is key to treatment. Continued smoking can lead to amputation (Peyrot et al. 2007).

The evidence linking marijuana intoxication to an increased risk of heart attack (acute myocardial infarction) is mixed (Gordon et al. 2013; National Academies of Science, Engineering, and Medicine 2017). However, research published in the journal *Circulation* suggests that marijuana use may be a rare trigger of heart attack among high-risk patients (Mittleman et al. 2001; see also Gordon et al. 2010). Researchers used a case-crossover design to assess the risk of heart attack in the one hour following marijuana use. Of the 3,882 heart attack patients who were interviewed, 9 patients smoked marijuana in the hour prior to heart attack symptoms. Marijuana users in the study were more likely to be male, current cigarette users, and obese. However, even after controlling for differences between patients, the researchers found that the risk of heart attack was elevated 4.8 fold in the hour following marijuana consumption. A sensitivity analysis that eliminated three patients who also engaged in other known triggers suggested that the risk of heart attack was elevated 3.2 fold compared to periods of nonuse. The three- to fivefold increase in the risk of heart attack following marijuana use compares to a 4.3-fold increase in the risk of heart attack after strenuous exercise, a 3.1-fold increase after alcohol exposure, and a 23.7-fold increase in the risk of heart attack in the hour following cocaine use (Nawrot et al. 2011).

Various lines of laboratory evidence indicate that cannabinoids can decrease immune function and affect resistance to both bacteria and viruses (Friedman et al. 2006). The strongest clinical evidence showing that marijuana might increase susceptibility to infection in humans comes from research involving patients with chronic hepatitis C infection (see Gordon 2010). In a study published in *Gastroenterology*, researchers found that marijuana use was associated with steatosis (fatty liver) among patients with chronic hepatitis C infection, and that daily marijuana use predicted steatosis even after taking into account virus genotype and alcohol intake (Hézode et al. 2008). Moreover, a study published in *Clinical Gastroenterology and Hepatology* found that daily marijuana use was associated with moderate to severe fibrosis (liver scarring) among a sample of 204 persons with chronic hepatitis C infection (Ishida et al. 2008).

As described earlier, many of the risks associated with using marijuana can be traced back to the harmful effects of smoking—the primary method of exposure. Not surprisingly, there is some evidence that chronic marijuana smoking is associated with increased risks for respiratory symptoms, adverse respiratory function, and respiratory damage.

There is consistent evidence that long-term marijuana smoking is associated with increased respiratory *symptoms*. A 2007 review published in the *Archives of Internal Medicine* found that long-term smoking was associated with increased cough, sputum production, and wheeze (Tetrault et al. 2007). The association between marijuana smoking and respiratory symptoms persisted after researchers accounted for tobacco smoking. A 2011 review published in the journal *Expert Review of Respiratory Medicine* found that marijuana use was also associated with symptoms of chronic bronchitis, increased airway resistance, and airway inflammation (Lee and Hancox 2011). Other studies have found that marijuana smokers are also at an increased risk for shortness of breath, chest tightness, pharyngitis, and worsening asthma symptoms (Owen et al. 2014).

The evidence linking marijuana use to *impairment* in respiratory function is more mixed (see Owen et al. 2014; Tetrault et al. 2007). Some studies, for example, have found links between marijuana smoking and decreases in respiratory function (e.g., Taylor et al. 2000). A review published in *Clinical Reviews in Allergy & Immunology*, however, found more evidence supporting a lack of effect of marijuana smoking on pulmonary (lung) function (Owen et al. 2014). Moreover, a review published in the *Archives of Internal Medicine* assessed studies on the long-term consequences of marijuana smoking on pulmonary (lung) function and was unable to identify a consistent association between long-term marijuana smoking and pulmonary function (Tetrault et al. 2007). Moreover, while some research has shown a link between marijuana use and airway obstruction, a review published in the *Canadian Medical Association Journal* found that marijuana smoking, by itself, was an unlikely cause of chronic obstructive pulmonary disease (COPD; Tashkin 2009).

While the evidence linking marijuana smoke to impaired respiratory function is mixed, there is consistent evidence that chronic exposure to marijuana smoke can lead to physiologic changes in the respiratory tract. For example, a review published in the *Monaldi Archives for Chest Disease* found that both marijuana smokers and tobacco smokers exhibited visual evidence of airway injury (Tashkin 2005). Moreover, a 1998 study examined bronchial mucosa biopsy specimens from smokers of marijuana, cocaine, and tobacco and found that smokers of any substance exhibited more alterations in the bronchial epithelium (Barsky et al. 1998). These alterations are significant in that they may be a risk factor for the development of lung cancer. These observations are consistent with evidence from an experiment in which 24 rhesus monkeys were exposed to varying doses of marijuana smoke, sham smoke, or placebo for 12 months (Fligiel et al. 1991). Pathological alterations were found in all smoking groups, but bronchiolitis/peribronchiolitis (viral infection/inflammation) were found most frequently in the high-dose marijuana group. Finally, some evidence suggests that smoking marijuana may impair the immunological abilities of the respiratory system and increase susceptibility to infections (Room et al. 2008).

FURTHER READING

Bachs, Liliana, and Henning Mørland. "Acute cardiovascular fatalities following cannabis use." *Forensic Science International* 124, no. 2 (2001): 200–203.

Barsky, Sanford H., Michael D. Roth, Eric C. Kleerup, Michael Simmons, and Donald P. Tashkin. "Histopathologic and molecular alterations in bronchial epithelium in habitual smokers of marijuana, cocaine, and/ or tobacco." *Journal of the National Cancer Institute* 90, no. 16 (1998): 1198–1205.

Calabria, Bianca, Louisa Degenhardt, Wayne Hall, and Michael Lynskey. "Does cannabis use increase the risk of death? Systematic review of epidemiological evidence on adverse effects of cannabis use." *Drug and Alcohol Review* 29, no. 3 (2010): 318–330.

Caulkins, Jonathan P., Angela Hawken, Beau Kilmer, and Mark A. R. Kleiman. *Marijuana legalization: what everyone needs to know.* New York: Oxford University Press, 2012.

Center for Behavioral Health Statistics and Quality. *2015 National Survey on Drug Use and Health: detailed tables.* Rockville, MD: Substance Abuse and Mental Health Services Administration, 2016.

Centers for Disease Control and Prevention, National Center for Health Statistics. Multiple Cause of Death 1999–2014 on CDC WONDER Online Database, released 2015. Data are from the Multiple Cause of Death Files, 1999–2014, as compiled from data provided by the 57 vital statistics jurisdictions through the Vital Statistics Cooperative Program. Accessed October 16, 2016. http://wonder.cdc.gov/mcd-icd10.html

Combemale, P., T. Consort, L. Denis-Thelis, J.-L. Estival, M. Dupin, and J. Kanitakis. "Cannabis arteritis." *British Journal of Dermatology* 152, no. 1 (2005): 166–169.

Crean, Rebecca D., Natania A. Crane, and Barbara J. Mason. "An evidence based review of acute and long-term effects of cannabis use on executive cognitive functions." *Journal of Addiction Medicine* 5, no. 1 (2011): 1.

Degenhardt, Louisa, Chiara Bucello, Bradley Mathers, Christina Briegleb, Hammad Ali, Matt Hickman, and Jennifer McLaren. "Mortality among regular or dependent users of heroin and other opioids: a systematic review and meta-analysis of cohort studies." *Addiction* 106, no. 1 (2010): 32–51.

Degenhardt, Louisa, Jessica Singleton, Bianca Calabria, Jennifer McLaren, Thomas Kerr, Shruti Mehta, Gregory Kirk, and Wayne D. Hall. "Mortality among cocaine users: a systematic review of cohort studies." *Drug and Alcohol Dependence* 113, no. 2 (2011): 88–95.

Fligiel, Suzanne E. G., Ted F. Beals, Donald P. Tashkin, Merle G. Paule, Andrew C. Scallet, Syed F. Ali, John R. Bailey, and William Slikker. "Marijuana exposure and pulmonary alterations in primates." *Pharmacology Biochemistry and Behavior* 40, no. 3 (1991): 637–642.

Friedman, Herman, Susan Pross, and Thomas W. Klein. "Addictive drugs and their relationship with infectious diseases." *FEMS Immunology & Medical Microbiology* 47, no. 3 (2006): 330–342.

Gable, Robert S. "Comparison of acute lethal toxicity of commonly abused psychoactive substances." *Addiction* 99, no. 6 (2004): 686–696.

Gieringer, Dale, Joseph St. Laurent, and Scott Goodrich. "Cannabis vaporizer combines efficient delivery of THC with effective suppression of pyrolytic compounds." *Journal of Cannabis Therapeutics* 4, no. 1 (2004): 7–27.

Gordon, Adam J. *Physical illness and drugs of abuse: a review of the evidence.* Cambridge University Press, 2010.

Gordon, Adam J., James W. Conley, and Joanne M. Gordon. "Medical consequences of marijuana use: a review of current literature." *Current Psychiatry Reports* 15, no. 12 (2013): 1–11.

Grotenhermen, Franjo. "Harm reduction associated with inhalation and oral administration of cannabis and THC." *Journal of Cannabis Therapeutics* 1, no. 3–4 (2001): 133–152.

Hall, Wayne. "The adverse health effects of cannabis use: what are they, and what are their implications for policy?" *International Journal of Drug Policy* 20, no. 6 (2009): 458–466.

Hall, Wayne, and Louisa Degenhardt. "Adverse health effects of non-medical cannabis use." *The Lancet* 374, no. 9698 (2009): 1383–1391.

Hall, Wayne, Louisa Degenhardt, and Michael Lynskey. "The health and psychological effects of cannabis use." Monograph series No. 44. National Drug and Alcohol Research Centre, University of New South Wales, 2001.

Hall, Wayne, Robin Room, and Susan Bondy. *A comparative appraisal of the health and psychological consequences of alcohol, cannabis, nicotine and opiate use.* Addiction Research Foundation, 1995.

Hartung, Benno, Silke Kauferstein, Stefanie Ritz-Timme, and Thomas Daldrup. "Sudden unexpected death under acute influence of cannabis." *Forensic Science International* 237 (2014): e11–e13.

Hézode, Christophe, Elie Serge Zafrani, Françoise Roudot-Thoraval, Charlotte Costentin, Ali Hessami, Magali Bouvier-Alias, Fatiha Medkour, Jean-Michel Pawlostky, Sophie Lotersztajn, and Ariane Mallat. "Daily cannabis use: a novel risk factor of steatosis severity in patients with chronic hepatitis C." *Gastroenterology* 134, no. 2 (2008): 432–439.

Huang, Yu-Hui Jenny, Zuo-Feng Zhang, Donald P. Tashkin, Bingjian Feng, Kurt Straif, and Mia Hashibe. "An epidemiologic review of marijuana and cancer: an update." *Cancer Epidemiology Biomarkers & Prevention* 24, no. 1 (2015): 15–31.

Ishida, Julie H., Marion G. Peters, Chengshi Jin, Karly Louie, Vivian Tan, Peter Bacchetti, and Norah A. Terrault. "Influence of cannabis use on severity of hepatitis C disease." *Clinical Gastroenterology and Hepatology* 6, no. 1 (2008): 69–75.

Lachenmeier, Dirk W., and Jürgen Rehm. "Comparative risk assessment of alcohol, tobacco, cannabis and other illicit drugs using the margin of exposure approach." *Scientific Reports* 5 (2015): 1–7.

Lee, Marcus H. S., and Robert J. Hancox. "Effects of smoking cannabis on lung function." *Expert Review of Respiratory Medicine* 5, no. 4 (2011): 537–547.

Mittleman, Murray A., Rebecca A. Lewis, Malcolm Maclure, Jane B. Sherwood, and James E. Muller. "Triggering myocardial infarction by marijuana." *Circulation* 103, no. 23 (2001): 2805–2809.

Montecucco, Fabrizio, and Vincenzo Di Marzo. "At the heart of the matter: the endocannabinoid system in cardiovascular function and dysfunction." *Trends in Pharmacological Sciences* 33, no. 6 (2012): 331–340.

Mukamal, Kenneth J., Malcolm Maclure, James E. Muller, and Murray A. Mittleman. "An exploratory prospective study of marijuana use and mortality following acute myocardial infarction." *American Heart Journal* 155, no. 3 (2008): 465–470.

National Academies of Sciences, Engineering, and Medicine. *The health effects of cannabis and cannabinoids: the current state of evidence and recommendations for research.* Washington, DC: The National Academies Press, 2017.

Nawrot, Tim S., Laura Perez, Nino Künzli, Elke Munters, and Benoit Nemery. "Public health importance of triggers of myocardial infarction: a comparative risk assessment." *The Lancet* 377, no. 9767 (2011): 732–740.

Owen, Kelly P., Mark E. Sutter, and Timothy E. Albertson. "Marijuana: respiratory tract effects." *Clinical Reviews in Allergy & Immunology* 46, no. 1 (2014): 65–81.

Peyrot, I., A.-M. Garsaud, I. Saint-Cyr, O. Quitman, B. Sanchez, and D. Quist. "Cannabis arteritis: a new case report and a review of literature." *Journal of the European Academy of Dermatology and Venereology* 21, no. 3 (2007): 388–391.

Porta, Miquel, ed. *A dictionary of epidemiology.* New York: Oxford University Press, 2014.

Pujazon-Zazik, Melissa, and M. Jane Park. "Marijuana: use among young males and health outcomes." *American Journal of Men's Health* 3, no. 3 (2009): 265–274.

Room, Robin, Benedikt Fischer, Wayne Hall, Simon Lenton, and Peter Reuter. *The global cannabis commission report.* Oxford: The Beckley Foundation, 2008.

Tashkin, D. P. "Smoked marijuana as a cause of lung injury." *Monaldi Archives for Chest Disease* 63, no. 2 (2005): 93–100.

Tashkin, Donald P. "Does smoking marijuana increase the risk of chronic obstructive pulmonary disease?" *Canadian Medical Association Journal* 180, no. 8 (2009): 797–798.

Taylor, D. Robin, Richie Poulton, Terrie E. Moffitt, Padmaja Ramankutty, and Malcolm R. Sears. "The respiratory effects of cannabis dependence in young adults." *Addiction* 95, no. 11 (2000): 1669–1677.

Tetrault, Jeanette M., Kristina Crothers, Brent A. Moore, Reena Mehra, John Concato, and David A. Fiellin. "Effects of marijuana smoking on pulmonary function and respiratory complications: a systematic review." *Archives of Internal Medicine* 167, no. 3 (2007): 221–228.

Q10. DOES MARIJUANA POSE MORE OF A HEALTH RISK THAN TOBACCO OR ALCOHOL?

Answer: No. The adverse health outcomes associated with heavy marijuana use, while very real and important to understand, are generally not as severe as the adverse health outcomes associated with heavy alcohol use or heavy tobacco use.

The Facts: Alcohol, tobacco, and marijuana are the three most commonly used psychoactive substances in the United States. As Figure 2.1 shows, among the population ages 12 and older, there were roughly 138 million past-month users of alcohol, 64 million past-month users of tobacco, and 22 million past-month users of marijuana in 2015 (CBHSQ 2016). While the adverse health effects of alcohol and tobacco are fairly well known, the harms and risks of marijuana are less well understood. Like alcohol, marijuana is a popular intoxicant that alters perception and mood. Like tobacco, marijuana is often smoked. All three substances are commonly used recreationally, and all can be dangerous when used heavily or irresponsibly.

Comparing the risks and harms related to alcohol, tobacco, and marijuana is challenging. The task is complicated by the fact that many of the most dangerous substances are also potent remedies. In fact, as Robin M. Murray and colleagues point out, the Greek term *pharmakon* includes both remedies and poisons, and illustrates that many substances contain within them the power to both harm and heal (Murray et al. 2007). In the United States and elsewhere, law makers aim to balance the risks and benefits of each drug in such a way that maximizes a given drug's therapeutic

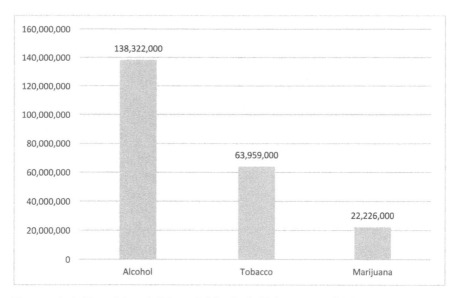

Figure 2.1 Past-Month Use of Alcohol, Tobacco, and Marijuana among Individuals Ages 12 and Older: 2015.
Source: CBHSQ 2016.

value while minimizing its potential for abuse. Critics of the federal drug scheduling laws suggest, however, that these laws do not always accurately acknowledge the potential risks and benefits of particular substances.

Comparing the risks of alcohol, tobacco, and marijuana is further complicated by the fact that they are used at such vastly different rates. Certain toxic substances are very risky for individuals, but present a low population risk because they are not commonly used. On the other hand, moderately toxic substances may not be tremendously risky for an individual to use, but these substances might present a high population risk if they are used at a high rate. For example, at the individual level, cyanide is more toxic than ethanol (drinking alcohol), and even very small doses of cyanide can be fatal. At the population level, however, ethanol use and misuse is a much larger public health concern than cyanide because ethanol is consumed at a much higher rate (see CDC 2015; Desai and Su 2016; U.S. Department of Health and Human Services 2006).

As discussed in Q9, epidemiologists use a variety of calculations to make individual-level and population-level risk assessments (see Hall et al. 1995). To begin, researchers need to estimate the *incidence* and *prevalence* of a given disease (or other health-related outcome) in order to understand how widespread the disease is in the population. To calculate individual-level risks, various measures of *relative risk* can be used to compare the risk of a given disease (or other outcome) among people who use marijuana with the risk of the disease among people who do not use marijuana. To understand the public health impact of marijuana use, measures of *attributable risk* can be used to express the proportion of cases of the disease in the population which are attributable to marijuana use.

The existence of these various forms of risk helps to illustrate that the pharmacological and toxicological characteristics of substances are only part of what makes a drug risky or dangerous. The "set" (the attitude and personality of each drug user) and the "setting" (the physical and social setting within which substance use occurs) also influence how substances affect individuals (Zinberg 1984). Consider, for instance, how the dangers of alcohol use change when it is consumed rapidly and in excess (binge drinking), or when an intoxicated person decides to drive an automobile. In short, the pharmacological characteristics of a substance interact with the set and setting in ways that determine the risks of use. In total, a thorough evaluation of the risks and benefits of particular substances must take into account social, cultural, environmental, chemical, and legal variables—all of which can make it very difficult to know exactly how specific substances affect individuals and society.

SHORT-TERM HEALTH RISKS

Some psychoactive substances are acutely toxic and can lead to fatal overdose. For individuals and for the population, alcohol poses a higher risk of acute toxic overdose than does tobacco or marijuana. This is the case because alcohol is chemically toxic, because alcohol use is widespread, and because binge drinking is widespread. Over 60 million Americans ages 12 and older report binge alcohol use in the past-month, which is nearly one-quarter of people ages 12 and older (CBHSQ 2016). Due in part to these factors, there are 2,200 alcohol-attributed poisoning deaths each year (CDC Factsheet 2015). As discussed in Q9, CDC data from 2015 showed that marijuana is listed as a multiple cause of death in 409 poisoning deaths, the majority of which also involved more dangerous substances.

Considering its legal status and how frequently it is used, alcohol is a surprisingly toxic substance. Binge drinkers are at particularly high risk of acute toxic overdose because the lethal dose of alcohol is relatively close to the normal recreational dose (effective dose). Robert S. Gable's 2004 article in the journal *Addiction* estimated that the median lethal dose of alcohol (the dose that leads to fatal overdose in 50 percent of the population) is only about 10 times greater than the median effective dose of alcohol. The same research showed that the lethal dose of marijuana is over 1,000 times greater than the median effective dose.

Nicotine and tobacco are also toxic. They pose less risk of toxic overdose than alcohol, but present a greater risk of toxic overdose than marijuana. Historically, many cases of documented nicotine poisonings have been related to methods of exposure other than smoking, such as nicotine pesticide exposure, and intentional exposure (Mayer 2014). In recent years there has been an increase in nicotine poisonings attributed to the expansion of the electronic cigarette market. Electronic cigarettes vaporize concentrated liquid nicotine, some of which is pleasantly flavored. Liquid nicotine solutions present a unique toxic risk since a strong concentration of nicotine is available in a very small amount of liquid. In 2014, more than half of poison control center calls involving electronic cigarettes involved children under five years old (Chatham-Stephens et al. 2014). In a 2014 article published in the journal *Scientific Reports*, researchers compared the median lethal dose of various substances with the estimated human intake dose of the same substance. They found that for both individuals and for the population, nicotine exposure presented a risk lower than that of alcohol exposure but greater than that of tetrahydrocannabinol /cannabis exposure (Lachenmeier and Rehm 2015).

LONG-TERM HEALTH RISKS

Mortality

Acute toxic overdose is only one way that substance use can lead to death. In fact, for many substances the risk of acute lethal overdose is much lower than the risk of dying from other factors related to the chronic and heavy use of that substance. For example, because of the long-term health risks associated with tobacco use, chronic (long-term) tobacco use is much more dangerous than acute (short-term) tobacco use. This section investigates the number of overall deaths that are attributed to alcohol, tobacco, and marijuana each year in the United States. This section also examines whether the risk of early death is increased among those individuals who use alcohol, tobacco, and/or marijuana.

Public health data clearly show that tobacco use, and in particular cigarette smoking, is responsible for more deaths each year than either alcohol use or marijuana use. The CDC estimates that smoking is responsible for over 480,000 deaths per year, more than 41,000 of which are related to secondhand smoke exposure (CDC 2016a). The 2009 Global Health Risks report from the World Health Organization determined that tobacco use was the second leading global risk for mortality behind high blood pressure (WHO 2009). Alcohol use also contributes to a substantial number of deaths. The CDC estimates that 1 in 10 deaths among adults ages 20 to 64 are related to excessive drinking, and alcohol contributes to about 88,000 deaths annually (CDC 2016b). Alcohol liver disease is the most common chronic cause of alcohol-attributed deaths, while automobile crashes are the most common acute cause of alcohol-attributed deaths (Stahre et al. 2014). Comparable data on marijuana-attributed deaths are not available; however, CDC data indicate that marijuana use and marijuana misuse may play a contributing role in some deaths (see Q9).

The relationship between alcohol use and mortality is complex. On the one hand, there is consistent evidence that heavy, long-term alcohol use is associated with increased mortality. On the other hand, there is also evidence that regular, low-dose alcohol use is associated with decreased mortality. For many years, observational research has shown that the association between alcohol and mortality follows a J-shaped curve (U.S. Department of Health and Human Services 2000; Stockwell et al. 2016). That is, low levels of alcohol intake are associated with a decreased mortality risk compared to abstaining, while heavy or long-term use is associated with an increased mortality risk. There is ongoing debate, however, as to whether low-level alcohol use actually protects against mortality, or if other explanations could account for why low-dose drinkers have a lower mortality risk compared to abstainers (Stockwell et al. 2016). Aside from this debate, there is consistent evidence that high-volume drinkers and individuals with alcohol use disorder are at an increased risk for mortality (U.S. DHHS 2000; Stockwell et al. 2016; Roerecke and Rehm 2013).

There is also consistent evidence from several large studies that cigarette smoking is associated with an increased risk of mortality (U.S. DHHS 2014; Jha et al. 2013). A study published in the *New England Journal of Medicine* that drew on a sample of over 200,000 individuals from the United States found that the mortality rate among current smokers was about three times higher than among those who never smoked (Jha et al. 2013). Other evidence shows that cigarette smokers lose about 10 years of life expectancy compared to individuals who never smoke (Jha et al. 2013; U.S. DHHS 2014). Although smokers have substantially higher mortality risks than never-smokers, research has shown that quitting smoking prior to the age of 40 reduces the risk of smoking-related death by about 90 percent (Jha et al. 2013; U.S. DHHS 2014). On the other hand, simply reducing the number of cigarettes per day is much less effective in reducing mortality risk than quitting smoking (U.S. DHHS 2014).

There is less evidence indicating how marijuana use affects mortality risk. A 2010 study published in the *Drug and Alcohol Review* surveyed the existing literature to investigate whether marijuana use is associated with an increased mortality risk (Calabria et al. 2010). The researchers used a systematic peer-reviewed literature search to assess evidence of increased mortality risk among marijuana smokers in population studies published between 1990 and 2008. They concluded that there is insufficient evidence to assess whether all-cause mortality rates are elevated among cannabis users in the general population. However, the review did find that fatal motor vehicle accidents, and possibly respiratory and brain cancers, are elevated among heavy cannabis users.

Morbidity

There are many health risks associated with chronic or heavy alcohol use. In fact, the *International Classification of Diseases*, 10th edition (ICD-10), lists 30 conditions that include the term alcohol in their name or definition (Rehm 2011). Additionally, the 2009 Global Health Risks report determined that alcohol use was the third leading risk for burden of disease, behind childhood underweight status and unsafe sex (WHO 2009). Alcohol consumption is the leading cause of liver disease in the United States, and heavy alcohol use is associated with both short-term and long-term liver damage (Penny 2013; Lucey et al. 2009). Evidence does not indicate that marijuana affects the liver in a way that is equivalent to alcohol; however, there is evidence that daily marijuana use is related to steatosis (fatty liver) and moderate to severe fibrosis (first-stage liver scarring) among patients with chronic Hepatitis C infections (see Q9). A strong causal link has also been established between alcohol consumption and cancer of the oral cavity, pharynx, larynx, esophagus, liver, colorectum, and female breast (Rehm 2011). As will be described in more detail in Q14, the evidence linking heavy marijuana use with the development of various cancers is equivocal or inconclusive (see Q14).

Chronic heavy alcohol use is also a risk factor for several cardiovascular complications, including cardiomyopathy (degenerative disease of heart muscle), hypertension, dangerous heart rhythms, and stroke (U.S. DHHS 2000). Moreover, binge drinking, which can contribute acutely to alcohol poisoning, has been linked to an increased risk for major coronary events, heart attack, and coronary heart disease (U.S. DHHS 2000). On the other hand, some studies show that light-to-moderate alcohol consumption may have a beneficial effect on the cardiovascular system. For example, compared to abstinence, low to moderate drinking (fewer than two drinks per day) is associated with lower coronary heart disease incidence (Room et al. 2005). Once again, there is ongoing debate as to whether low-level alcohol use actually confers protective benefits. Evidence indicates that marijuana use also affects the cardiovascular system, although not necessarily in ways that are equivalent to alcohol. As discussed in Q9, increased heart rate is a common acute side effect of marijuana use, but is generally not considered a significant cardiovascular stress for healthy individuals (Hall 2009). However, marijuana use may be risky for users with coronary risk factors, and mixed evidence shows that marijuana may be a rare trigger of heart attack (Mittleman 2001).

Considering the high mortality burden associated with cigarette and tobacco use, it is not surprising that regular tobacco use can also lead to disease. A comprehensive 2014 report from the U.S. Department of Health and Human Services (U.S. DHHS 2014) indicated that cigarette smoking constitutes "an enormous avoidable public health tragedy" (7). The report confirms what many people already know, namely that cigarette smoking causes several diseases and has contributed to millions of premature deaths. Indeed, the CDC estimates that smoking increases the risk of developing lung cancer by 25 times, and can cause cancer in sites throughout the body (CDC 2016a). The evidence linking marijuana smoke to cancer, on the other hand, is mixed (see Q14).

It is also well established that cigarettes cause damage to the airways and lungs in ways that impair lung function and lead to disease (see U.S. DHHS 2014 for review). For example, cigarette smoking is the dominant cause of COPD. Cigarettes have also been identified as a cause of coronary heart disease and stroke (U.S. DHHS 2014; CDC 2016a). Similarly, there is evidence that exposure to secondhand smoke increases the risk of stroke by 20–30 percent, and that the implementation of smoke-free laws reduces coronary events in people younger than 65 years of age. There is also evidence that cigarette smoking increases the risk of tuberculosis, and that the risk of developing diabetes is 30–40 percent higher among active smokers than among nonsmokers (U.S. DHHS 2014). Additionally, smoking has been causally linked to macular degeneration, diabetes, erectile dysfunction, suppression of the immune system, and rheumatoid arthritis (U.S. DHHS 2014). Given that marijuana smoke contains known carcinogens, including many of the same carcinogens found in tobacco, there is good reason to be concerned about how marijuana smoke affects respiratory health and function (Huang et al. 2015). As described in Q9, there is consistent evidence that heavy marijuana use is associated with an increase in respiratory symptoms, and that chronic exposure to marijuana smoke can lead to physiologic changes in the respiratory tract. The evidence linking marijuana smoke to impaired respiratory function is more mixed.

MULTIPLE CRITERIA COMPARISONS

Most distinct indicators of risk and harm show that alcohol use, tobacco use, and marijuana use can each increase the risk of some adverse health outcomes. However, comparing these adverse outcomes in isolation can inadvertently be a bit like missing the forest for the trees. In recognition of this, it can be helpful to look at the big picture and see how the combined risks of marijuana compare to the combined risks of alcohol and tobacco. Indeed, federal drug classifications endeavor to do this very thing—take into account all potential risks, harms, and medical benefits to make a single decision regarding how best to control each drug. In an effort to bring evidence to bear on how various substances compare across a variety of harm indicators, members of the Independent Scientific Committee on Drugs convened an expert panel to compare substances using multiple empirical criteria of drug harm (Nutt et al. 2010). They combined data on 16 separate measures of physical, psychological, and social harm to produce scores that could be compared and rank-ordered. Each drug's harms were scored out of 100 points, with higher scores representing greater harm.

The results of the multiple criteria comparison indicated that alcohol presented the most harms, even when compared to illicit substances. Marijuana was rated as only slightly less harmful than tobacco. This research validates the evidence in this volume showing that marijuana is not at all a harmless drug, but that the individual and social harms associated with alcohol use and tobacco use are generally greater than the individual and social harms associated with marijuana use.

FURTHER READING

Calabria, Bianca, Louisa Degenhardt, Wayne Hall, and Michael Lynskey. "Does cannabis use increase the risk of death? Systematic review of epidemiological evidence on adverse effects of cannabis use." *Drug and Alcohol Review* 29, no. 3 (2010): 318–330.

Center for Behavioral Health Statistics and Quality. *2015 National Survey on Drug Use and Health: detailed tables*. Rockville, MD: Substance Abuse and Mental Health Services Administration, 2016.

Centers for Disease Control and Prevention. "Alcohol poisoning deaths." 2015. http://www.cdc.gov/vitalsigns/alcohol-poisoning-deaths/index .html

Centers for Disease Control and Prevention. "Health effects of cigarette smoking." 2016a. Accessed July 12, 2016. https://www.cdc.gov/tobacco/ data_statistics/fact_sheets/health_effects/effects_cig_smoking/

Centers for Disease Control and Prevention. "Fact sheets—alcohol use and your health." 2016b. https://www.cdc.gov/alcohol/fact-sheets/alcohol-use.htm

Chatham-Stephens, Kevin, Royal Law, Ethel Taylor, Paul Melstrom, Rebecca Bunnell, Baoguang Wang, Benjamin Apelberg, and Joshua G. Schier. "Notes from the field: calls to poison centers for exposures to electronic cigarettes—United States, September 2010–February 2014." *Morbidity and Mortality Weekly* 63, no. 13 (2014): 292–293.

Desai, Shoma, and Mark Su. "Cyanide poisoning." UpToDate. 2016 https://www.uptodate.com/contents/cyanide-poisoning

Gable, Robert S. "Comparison of acute lethal toxicity of commonly abused psychoactive substances." *Addiction* 99, no. 6 (2004): 686–696.

Hall, Wayne. "The adverse health effects of cannabis use: what are they, and what are their implications for policy?" *International Journal of Drug Policy* 20, no. 6 (2009): 458–466.

Hall, Wayne, Robin Room, and Susan Bondy. *A comparative appraisal of the health and psychological consequences of alcohol, cannabis, nicotine and opiate use.* WHO Project on Health Implications of Cannabis Use, 1995.

Huang, Yu-Hui Jenny, Zuo-Feng Zhang, Donald P. Tashkin, Bingjian Feng, Kurt Straif, and Mia Hashibe. "An epidemiologic review of marijuana and cancer: an update." *Cancer Epidemiology Biomarkers & Prevention* 24, no. 1 (2015): 15–31.

Jha, Prabhat, Chinthanie Ramasundarahettige, Victoria Landsman, Brian Rostron, Michael Thun, Robert N. Anderson, Tim McAfee, and Richard Peto. "21st-century hazards of smoking and benefits of cessation in the United States." *New England Journal of Medicine* 368, no. 4 (2013): 341–350.

Lachenmeier, Dirk W., and Jürgen Rehm. "Comparative risk assessment of alcohol, tobacco, cannabis and other illicit drugs using the margin of exposure approach." *Scientific Reports* 5 (2015): 1–7.

Lucey, Michael R., Philippe Mathurin, and Timothy R. Morgan. "Alcoholic hepatitis." *New England Journal of Medicine* 360, no. 26 (2009): 2758–2769.

Mayer, Bernd. "How much nicotine kills a human? Tracing back the generally accepted lethal dose to dubious self-experiments in the nineteenth century." *Archives of Toxicology*. 88, no. 1 (2014): 5–7.

Mittleman, Murray A., Rebecca A. Lewis, Malcolm Maclure, Jane B. Sherwood, and James E. Muller. "Triggering myocardial infarction by marijuana." *Circulation* 103, no. 23 (2001): 2805–2809.

Murray, Robin M., Paul D. Morrison, Cécile Henquet, and Marta Di Forti. "Cannabis, the mind and society: the hash realities." *Nature Reviews Neuroscience* 8, no. 11 (2007): 885–895.

Nutt, David J., Leslie A. King, and Lawrence D. Phillips. "Drug harms in the UK: a multicriteria decision analysis." *The Lancet* 376 (2010): 1558–1565.

Penny, Steven M. "Alcoholic liver disease." *Radiologic Technology* 84, no. 6 (2013): 577–592.

Rehm, Jürgen. "The risks associated with alcohol use and alcoholism." *Alcohol Research & Health: The Journal of the National Institute on Alcohol Abuse and Alcoholism* 34, no. 2 (2011): 135.

Roerecke, Michael, and Jürgen Rehm. "Alcohol use disorders and mortality: a systematic review and meta-analysis." *Addiction* 108, no. 9 (2013): 1562–1578.

Room, Robin, Thomas Babor, and Jürgen Rehm. "Alcohol and public health." *Lancet* 365 (2005): 519–530.

Stahre, Mandy, Jim Roeber, Dafna Kanny, Robert D. Brewer, and Xingyou Zhang. "Contribution of excessive alcohol consumption to deaths and years of potential life lost in the United States." *Preventing Chronic Disease* 11 (2014): 1–12.

Stockwell, Tim, Jinhui Zhao, Sapna Panwar, Audra Roemer, Timothy Naimi, and Tanya Chikritzhs. "Do 'moderate' drinkers have reduced mortality risk? A systematic review and meta-analysis of alcohol consumption and all-cause mortality." *Journal of Studies on Alcohol and Drugs* 77, no. 2 (2016): 185–198.

U.S. Department of Health and Human Services. *The health consequences of smoking—50 years of progress: a report of the Surgeon General*. Atlanta, GA: US Department of Health and Human Services, Centers for Disease Control and Prevention, National Center for Chronic Disease Prevention and Health Promotion, Office on Smoking and Health, 2014.

U.S. Department of Health and Human Services. *Tenth Special Report to the U.S. Congress on Alcohol and Health*. Public Health Service. National Institutes of Health. National Institute on Alcohol Abuse and Alcoholism, 2000.

U.S. Department of Health and Human Services. *Toxicological Profile for Cyanide.* Atlanta, GA: Public Health Services. Agency for Toxic Substances and Disease Registry, 2006.

World Health Organization. *Global health risks: mortality and burden of disease attributable to selected major risks.* World Health Organization, 2009.

Zinberg, Norman E. *Drug, set and setting.* New Haven, CT: Yale University Press, 1984.

Q11. DOES MARIJUANA POSE LESS OF A HEALTH RISK THAN OTHER ILLICIT DRUGS?

Answer: It depends, but generally the physical health risks associated with using marijuana are less severe than those associated with the nonmedical use of other illicit substances.

The Facts: Marijuana is designated as a Schedule I substance, suggesting that it is among the most harmful of substances because it has a high potential for abuse, has no accepted medical use, and lacks an acceptable

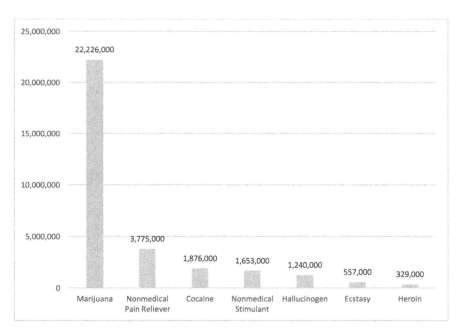

Figure 2.2 Past-Month Use of Illicit Substances among Individuals Ages 12 and Older: 2015.
Source: CBHSQ 2016.

level of safety for use under medical supervision (U.S. Department of Justice 2016). As illustrated in Figure 2.2, marijuana is the most commonly used illicit substance, with an estimated 22.2 million past-month users. Other illicit substances are used at lower rates. It is estimated that 3.8 million people are past-month nonmedical users of prescription pain relievers, 1.9 million people are past-month users of cocaine, 1.7 million people are past-month nonmedical users of prescription stimulants, 1.2 million people are past-month users of hallucinogens, 557,000 people are past-month users of Ecstasy (MDMA), and 329,000 people are past-month users of heroin (CBHSQ 2016).

Many people use illicit substances without developing physical illnesses or other problems. However, a number of people who use illicit substances develop physical, emotional, psychological, cognitive, legal, and/or psychosocial problems related to substance use. This chapter compares the adverse physical effects associated with using marijuana with the harms and risks associated with the nonmedical use of opioids, amphetamine-type stimulants, cocaine, MDMA (Ecstasy), and hallucinogens.

ILLICIT SUBSTANCE DESCRIPTIONS

Marijuana	
	Preparations derived from the cannabis plant typically composed of the flowering tops and dried leaves
Opioids	
	Natural derivatives of the opium poppy as well as synthetic and semi-synthetic analogues
	morphine, codeine, methadone, fentanyl, oxycodone (OxyContin), hydromorphone (Dilaudid)
Amphetamine-Type Stimulants	
	Class of synthetic drugs with central nervous system stimulant properties
	amphetamine, methamphetamine, dextroamphetamine (Dexedrine), methylphenidate (Ritalin)

(Continued)

Cocaine	
	Central nervous system stimulant derived from the coca plant
Ecstasy	
	Street name for drugs that contain 3,4-methylenedioxymethamphetamine (MDMA) as the primary ingredient, but may also contain other amphetamine-type drugs
Hallucinogens	
	Diverse group of drugs that includes LSD (lysergic acid diethylamide) and psilocybin ("magic mushrooms")

Source: Merck Manual (2017).

As discussed in Q10, comparing the risks and harms of marijuana to the risk and harms of alcohol and tobacco is challenging, and the same is true for comparing the risks and harms of marijuana to those of other illicit substances. Research has shown that many users of illicit substances participate in other behaviors—including alcohol use, tobacco use, risky sexual behavior, and poly-substance use—which can influence health risks. As a result, it can be difficult to parcel out the independent contribution that any particular substance or behavior makes in the development of health problems. Even when individuals use only one type of drug, it can take years for health problems to develop, during which time environmental factors, genetic factors, and the natural course of aging can affect health.

Illicit substances also differ in how they are used, which further complicates head-to-head comparisons. Some substances are smoked, some are injected intravenously, some are taken nasally, and some are taken orally in pill form or liquid form. Different routes of administration pose risks that are sometimes above and beyond the risks of the substance itself. For example, intravenous (IV) drug users are at an increased risk for infection from using dirty or shared needles; yet, this risk exists regardless of the type of substance being injected. As discussed in Q10, the "set" (the attitude and personality of each drug user) and the "setting" (the physical and social environment within which substance use occurs) also affect how substances affect individuals (Zinberg 1984). For example, "party drugs" like MDMA (Ecstasy) are often taken in conjunction with physical exertion (dancing) in warm ambient environments (clubs), increasing the risk of hyperthermia and dehydration. Pharmacological characteristics, the route of administration, and the set and setting all contribute to the various ways that illicit substances can be dangerous to those that use them.

In an attempt to account for such methodological challenges, the harms and risks of particular substances are assessed through multiple dimensions of harm and risk. Marijuana, opioids, amphetamine-type stimulants, cocaine, Ecstasy, and hallucinogens are assessed according to measures of toxicity, overdose risk, mortality, emergency department (ED) visits, and morbidity (disease). The goal of this chapter is to determine if, after consideration of multiple dimensions of risk, empirical evidence can help shed light on the harms and risks associated with different substances—especially in cases where serious risks have been obscured or when unlikely risks have been exaggerated or mythologized.

SHORT-TERM HEALTH RISKS

Toxicity

In a 2004 article published in the journal *Addiction*, Robert S. Gable estimated "safety ratios" for 20 substances. Safety ratios are expressed as the ratio of *the median lethal dose* to *the median effective dose* for a 70-kg (154-pound) adult. When the numerator of the ratio is divided by the denominator, the result is a number representing the factor by which the median effective dose would need to be multiplied in order for the dose to be potentially lethal. The results from this study are presented in Table 2.1 and show that heroin and methamphetamine have very dangerous safety ratios. The usual lethal dose of heroin is only 6 times greater than the usual effective dose, and the usual lethal dose of methamphetamine is only 10 times greater than the usual effective dose. Cocaine, MDMA, and codeine are slightly safer, with ratios of 15, 16, and 20, respectively. Psilocybin mushrooms, LSD, and marijuana are each estimated to have safety ratios of 1000 or greater.

A comparable study published in the journal *Scientific Reports* used a similar method but took a "margin of exposure" (MOE) approach (Lachenmeier and Rehm 2015). The MOE was expressed as a ratio of *the estimated lethal dose* to *the estimated human intake dose*. Margins of exposure were estimated for licit and illicit substances at the individual and population levels. Substances with a lower MOE are those that present a greater

Table 2.1 Safety Ratios for Commonly Used Illicit Substances

Substance Name	Safety Ratio (Lethal Dose/ Effective Dose)
Heroin	6
Methamphetamine	10
Cocaine	15
MDMA	16
Codeine	20
Psilocybin	1000*
LSD	1000*
Marijuana	>1000*

*Fewer than three reports of human fatalities were located by the author; lethal doses were estimated using animal studies.

Source: Gable (2004).

risk for humans. At the individual level, alcohol, nicotine, cocaine, and heroin were considered "high risk," with a MOE of less than 10. With the exception of THC, the other substances considered fell into the "risk" category; THC was determined to have the lowest individual risk, with a MOE greater than 100.

Overdose

As described in Q9, data from the CDC WONDER online database provides mortality statistics from all registered death certificates in the United States. Each death certificate contains a single underlying cause of death and up to 20 multiple causes. This allows for drug poisoning deaths to be compared across substances. However, if a poisoning death involves more than one substance, both substances are counted as (multiple) causes of death. This presents a substantial methodological challenge insofar as drug poisoning deaths that implicate multiple substances do not indicate which substance was most likely to have contributed to the death. As a result, marijuana is listed as a (multiple) cause of death even in poisoning deaths that involve more dangerous substances such as alcohol, cocaine, heroin, and other opioids.

The total number of overdose deaths in the United States increased dramatically in the period from the year 2000 to 2015—from 17,415 to 52,404 (NIH 2017). This increase has been driven overwhelmingly by prescription drug deaths, especially opioid analgesic deaths (Paulozzi 2012). This dramatic increase in opioid analgesic drug poisoning deaths has been labeled an "epidemic" by many experts, and unlike some "drug scares" in American history (see Q16), the term "epidemic" may not be an overstatement of the problem. In 2000, there were 4,400 documented drug poisoning deaths due to opioid analgesics; this number grew to 22,598 by 2015. During this same period, deaths involving cannabis also increased from 40 to just over 400. These data depict a disquieting trend in overdose fatalities in the United States, and point toward opioids as a primary contributor. However, these data have limitations. As described, when a poisoning death involves more than one drug, each drug is counted as a (multiple) cause of death. In every year between 2000 and 2015, for example, the majority of deaths that involved marijuana as a multiple cause of death also involved opioids. Thus, the extent to which marijuana contributed to these poisoning deaths is not clear.

Emergency Department Visits

Drug risks can also be assessed according to how often particular drugs are implicated in emergency department (ED) visits. Through the year 2011, the U.S. Department of Health and Human Services published nationally representative data on drug-related emergency department visits. The data, known as the Drug Abuse Warning Network (DAWN), documented the instances in which specific drugs were involved in ED visits. For a drug to be captured in DAWN data, it needed to be explicitly named in the medical record as having been involved in the visit. Importantly, however, the link between the drug use and the visit need not be causal. A drug may be implicated without having caused or directly led to the visit.

The most recent DAWN data estimates that there were over 5.1 million drug-related ED visits in 2011, with 2.5 million visits associated with drug misuse or abuse. Between 2004 and 2011, ED visits attributable to drug misuse or abuse increased 52 percent, by about 844,000 visits. During this time, ED visits related to the use of pharmaceuticals with no other drug involvement rose substantially, by 148 percent. Similarly, ED visits involving pharmaceuticals with illicit drugs rose 137 percent during this time, while visits involving pharmaceuticals with alcohol rose 84 percent.

Over half of the 2.5 million ED visits that involved drug misuse or abuse involved illicit drugs, and over half of illicit drug ED visits involved multiple drugs. Cocaine was the most commonly involved drug in ED visits, with over 505,000 visits. Marijuana was the second most commonly involved drug in ED visits, with over 455,000 visits. Heroin was involved in over 258,000 visits, and amphetamine-type stimulants were involved in over 159,000 visits. MDMA was involved in over 22,000 visits, LSD was involved in over 4,000 visits, and other hallucinogens were involved in over 8,000 visits. One challenge in interpreting DAWN data has to do with attribution. Over half of illicit drug ED visits in 2011 involved multiple drugs, and DAWN data do not indicate which drug or drugs directly contributed to the ED visit. These limitations make it difficult to determine the number of ED visits precipitated by marijuana use in relation to other substances.

LONG-TERM HEALTH RISKS

All-Cause Mortality

Illicit substance use can lead to death in many ways other than toxic overdose, including motor vehicle crashes and other types of accidents, disease, suicide, homicide, and infection. Standardized mortality ratios (SMRs), which are measures of all-cause mortality risk, compare the observed deaths among a sample of particular substance users with the expected deaths among a comparable sample of nonusers. SMRs above 1 indicate an increased mortality risk, while SMRs below 1 indicate a decreased mortality risk.

Several recent meta-analyses have combined data from other studies in order to estimate SMRs for particular illicit substance users. Based on data pooled from 27 studies, for example, researchers found that mortality was 14 times higher among opioid users than among counterparts in the general population (Degenhardt et al. 2010). Data from four samples of cocaine users were pooled to reveal that mortality was 4–8 times higher among cocaine users than among peers in the general population (Degenhardt et al. 2011). The data on amphetamine users are less reliable since the researchers could identify only one existing study that calculated SMRs among amphetamine users. Compared to counterparts in the general population, mortality was over six times higher in the sample of amphetamine users (Singleton et al. 2009). Insufficient evidence existed for researchers to estimate all-cause SMRs among marijuana users, although there was some evidence that marijuana users were at an increased risk of death due to motor vehicle crashes (Calabria et al. 2010).

Morbidity

The use of opioids can lead to respiratory depression and fatal overdose. Acute reactions to opioids can also result in drowsiness, sedation, nausea, vomiting, constipation, and apnea (Merck Manual 2017). Opioid use can also lead to chronic health problems. A 2010 review indicated that opioids are associated with many complications (Gordon 2010). The strongest evidence indicates that opioid use is linked to rhabdomyolysis, renal disease, and neonatal abstinence disorder, and that methadone use is linked to ventricular tachycardia. When opioids are administered intravenously, users are at additional risk of HIV infection as well as Hepatitis B or C (Merck Manual 2017).

Cocaine use, like opioid use, carries an increased risk of acute toxic overdose, and this risk distinguishes both drugs from marijuana. Chronic cocaine use is also dangerous and can lead to adverse health outcomes. This is true whether cocaine is taken nasally, injected, or smoked. There is evidence, for example, that individuals who snort cocaine are more likely to have sniffling, sinus problems, diminished olfaction, nasal crust, recurrent epistaxis, and midline nasal lesions (Gordon 2010). There is also evidence that cocaine use is associated with myocardial infarction (heart attack), strokes, digestive problems, seizures, asthma, respiratory symptoms, renal dysfunction, and nutritional disorders (Gordon 2010).

While amphetamine-type stimulants present less risk of overdose compared to opioids, researchers have found evidence that psychostimulant use can lead to overdose and death, primarily by way of seizures, cardiac arrhythmias, respiratory failure, and cardiovascular complications (Darke et al. 2007, 2008). The same researchers found that toxic reactions to amphetamines can occur across a range of doses, even at small doses and on the first occasion of use. In addition to posing an overdose risk, the misuse of both legally prescribed and illicit forms of amphetamine-type stimulants can have other serious health consequences, including rhabdomyolysis, brain damage, and neurotransmission disruption (Gordon 2010).

Case reports and laboratory experiments suggest a host of adverse health outcomes for which MDMA likely plays a role. There is some evidence, for example, linking MDMA with hepatoxicity, tooth wear, brain damage, neurotransmission disruption, valvular heart disease, and fetal abnormalities (Gordon 2010). Researchers from the National Institute for Health Research in the United Kingdom found that it is uncommon for MDMA to be reported as a cause of death in cases that do not involve other drugs. When fatalities related to MDMA do occur, they commonly involve hyperthermia (high body temperature) or hyponatraemia (decrease in serum sodium concentration) as the immediate cause of death (Rogers et al. 2009). Both of these syndromes may be related to the "rave" setting in which MDMA is commonly consumed.

The long-term use of hallucinogens does not appear to increase the risk of physical illness, but it can be risky for other reasons. Hallucinogens are unpredictable, and intoxication can last up to 12 hours. Perceptions become distorted during intoxication, and users may experience any number of emotions, including elation, depression, arousal, paranoia, and panic (Gordon 2010). Users of hallucinogens have reported experiencing "bad trips," wherein paranoia and depression can become overwhelming. While lethal intoxication due to hallucinogens is unlikely, deaths due to suicide or trauma during intoxication have been reported.

The harms and risks of marijuana use are outlined in Q9. Some of the long-term consequences of marijuana use overlap with those of other substances, while some do not. For example, respiratory depression—one of the very serious risks associated with opioid use—has been reported in young children following the accidental ingestion of marijuana products (National Academies of Science, Engineering, and Medicine 2017). However, opioid use presents a very serious overdose risk, while marijuana does not. Like cocaine and amphetamine-type stimulants, marijuana use has been linked to sudden cardiac events. However, most evidence suggests that marijuana users with underlying conditions are most at risk. As is the case with opioids and cocaine, the risks associated with using marijuana may depend on how it is administered. It is clear, for instance, that marijuana smoke can cause respiratory symptoms and damage. Although many people believe that vaporizers and "edibles" provide a healthier route of administration for marijuana users, there is little evidence indicating their long-term impacts.

MULTIPLE CRITERIA COMPARISONS

The multiple criteria drug harm analysis conducted by members of the Independent Scientific Committee on Drugs was described in detail in Q10 (Nutt et al. 2010). The researchers created a summary of drug harm scores based on 16 separate measures of physical, psychological, and social harm. Each drug's harms were scored out of 100 points, with higher scores indicating greater harm. Compared to all drugs included

Table 2.2 Drugs Ordered by Their Overall Harm Scores

Alcohol	72	Ketamine	15
Heroin	55	Methadone	14
Crack cocaine	54	Mephedrone	13
Methamphetamine	33	Butane	11
Cocaine	27	Anabolic steroids	10
Tobacco	26	Khat	9
Amphetamine	23	Ecstasy	9
Cannabis	20	LSD	7
GHB	19	Buprenorphine	7
Benzodiazepines	15	Magic mushrooms	6

Presented are overall harm scores (0–100), normalized and weighted according to 16 criteria of harm to self and others.
Source: Nutt et al. (2010).

in the analysis, alcohol was rated as being the most harmful, followed by heroin, crack cocaine, and methamphetamine. The results are presented in Table 2.2, and show that marijuana (cannabis) was rated as less harmful than cocaine, tobacco, and amphetamine. However, this analysis determined marijuana was more harmful than Ecstasy, LSD, and "magic mushrooms."

FURTHER READING

Calabria, Bianca, Louisa Degenhardt, Wayne Hall, and Michael Lynskey. "Does cannabis use increase the risk of death? Systematic review of epidemiological evidence on adverse effects of cannabis use." *Drug and Alcohol Review* 29, no. 3 (2010): 318–330.

Center for Behavioral Health Statistics and Quality. *2015 National Survey on Drug Use and Health: detailed tables.* Rockville, MD: Substance Abuse and Mental Health Services Administration, 2016.

Centers for Disease Control and Prevention, National Center for Health Statistics. Multiple Cause of Death 1999–2015 on CDC WONDER Online Database, released 2015. Data are from the Multiple Cause of Death Files, 1999–2015, as compiled from data provided by the 57 vital statistics jurisdictions through the Vital Statistics Cooperative Program. http://wonder.cdc.gov/mcd-icd10.html

Darke, Shane, Sharlene Kaye, Rebecca McKetin, and Johan Duflou. "Major physical and psychological harms of methamphetamine use." *Drug and Alcohol Review* 27, no. 3 (2008): 253–262.

Darke, Shane, Sharlene Kaye, Rebecca McKetin, and Johan Duflou. *Physical and psychological harms of psychostimulant use*. Sydney: National Drug and Alcohol Research Centre, 2007.

Degenhardt, Louisa, Chiara Bucello, Bradley Mathers, Christina Briegleb, Hammad Ali, Matt Hickman, and Jennifer McLaren. "Mortality among regular or dependent users of heroin and other opioids: a systematic review and meta-analysis of cohort studies." *Addiction* 106, no. 1 (2010): 32–51.

Degenhardt, Louisa, Jessica Singleton, Bianca Calabria, Jennifer McLaren, Thomas Kerr, Shruti Mehta, Gregory Kirk, and Wayne D. Hall. "Mortality among cocaine users: a systematic review of cohort studies." *Drug and Alcohol Dependence* 113, no. 2 (2011): 88–95.

Gable, Robert S. "Comparison of acute lethal toxicity of commonly abused psychoactive substances." *Addiction* 99, no. 6 (2004): 686–696.

Gordon, Adam J. *Physical illness and drugs of abuse: a review of the evidence*. Cambridge University Press, 2010.

Lachenmeier, Dirk W., and Jürgen Rehm. "Comparative risk assessment of alcohol, tobacco, cannabis and other illicit drugs using the margin of exposure approach." *Scientific Reports* 5 (2015): 1–7.

Merck Manual. 2017. http://www.merckmanuals.com

National Academies of Sciences, Engineering, and Medicine. *The health effects of cannabis and cannabinoids: the current state of evidence and recommendations for research*. Washington, DC: The National Academies Press, 2017.

National Institute of Health. "Overdose Death Rates." *National Institute on Drug Abuse*. 2017.

Nutt, David J., Leslie A. King, and Lawrence D. Phillips. "Drug harms in the UK: a multicriteria decision analysis." *The Lancet* 376, no. 9752 (2010): 1558–1565.

Paulozzi, Leonard J. "Prescription drug overdoses: a review." *Journal of Safety Research* 43, no. 4 (2012): 283–289.

Rogers, G., J. Elston, R. Garside, C. Roome, R. Taylor, P. Younger, A. Zawada, and M. Somerville. "The harmful health effects of recreational ecstasy: a systematic review of observational evidence." *Health Technology Assessment* 13, no. 6 (2009): xii–338.

Singleton, Jessica, Louisa Degenhardt, Wayne Hall, and Tomas Zabransky. "Mortality among amphetamine users: a systematic review of cohort studies." *Drug and Alcohol Dependence* 105, no. 1 (2009): 1–8.

Substance Abuse and Mental Health Services Administration, *Drug Abuse Warning Network, 2011: National Estimates of Drug-Related Emergency Department Visits.* HHS Publication No. (SMA) 13–4760, DAWN Series D-39. Rockville, MD: Substance Abuse and Mental Health Services Administration, 2013.

U.S. Department of Justice. "Definitions of Controlled Substances Schedules." 2016. Accessed July 12, 2016. http://www.deadiversion.usdoj.gov/schedules/

Zinberg, Norman E. *Drug, set and setting.* New Haven, CT: Yale University Press, 1984.

Q12. IS MARIJUANA SAFE AND EFFECTIVE FOR TREATING MEDICAL DISORDERS?

Answer: Yes. Scientific evidence supports the use of marijuana and cannabinoids in the treatment of some medical disorders. A consistent body of anecdotal, observational, and clinical research strongly suggests that marijuana, THC, and other cannabinoids have therapeutic potential in the treatment of pain, spasticity due to multiple sclerosis, nausea and vomiting due to chemotherapy, and weight loss in patients with debilitating diseases.

The Facts: Marijuana preparations are among the oldest drugs in medicine. Marijuana extracts have been used as medicine for thousands of years in China, India, and other countries of the Far East. Descriptions of marijuana's use in Chinese medicine date back to early editions of the Pen-Ts'ao in the first or second century AD (Iversen 2008). This herbal pharmacopeia outlined medical uses of many medicines, including marijuana—which was known by the name "ma"—a pun for "chaotic" (Iversen 2008). The use of marijuana in ancient India is thought to date back to the Atharva Veda (ca. 1600), wherein bhanga (or *bhang*) is one of five herbs indicated to treat anxiety or grief (Russo 2007). It is believed that cannabis was used in the ancient ayurvedic medical system by 300–400 BC (Russo 2007). Medieval ayurvedic texts indicate that cannabis was used as a sleep medication, appetite stimulant, digestive aid, aphrodisiac, and anesthetic (Iversen 2008).

The introduction of medical cannabis in Western medicine dates back only to the middle of the nineteenth century, and is often attributed to an Irish physician named W. B. O'Shaughnessy. While working in India, O'Shaughnessy conducted animal experiments on the safety and efficacy of "Indian Hemp" and wrote a paper indicating the drug's usefulness in alleviating pain, vomiting, convulsions, and spasticity (Bostwick 2012). By 1854, cannabis was listed along with other medicines in the U.S. Dispensatory (Iversen 2008). Two decades after O'Shaughnessy's work, the first American clinical conference on medical marijuana was held by the Ohio State Medical Society in 1860 (Mack and Joy 2000). At the conference, marijuana was indicated as a treatment for chronic cough, gonorrhea, pain, and other conditions.

In the 1930s, the Federal Bureau of Narcotics was established, and law enforcement grew increasingly concerned over marijuana and its association with crime. Under pressure from the Federal Bureau of Narcotics, the U.S. government passed the Marihuana Tax Act in 1937 (see Q16 for more information on marijuana laws). Marijuana was removed from the U.S. pharmacopeia in 1942 (Aggarawal 2012). In spite of federal laws prohibiting the use of medical marijuana, states began legalizing medical marijuana in the 1990s (NCSL 2016). Following the U.S. election in November 2016, comprehensive medical marijuana laws have been enacted in 29 states, the District of Columbia, Guam, and Puerto Rico.

THE ENDOCANNABINOID SYSTEM

Although various forms of marijuana have been used to treat medical conditions for millennia, only recently have researchers begun to understand the biological and chemical mechanisms that are responsible for its therapeutic and psychoactive effects. Delta-9-tetrahydrocannabinol (THC), the main psychoactive component in marijuana, belongs to a class of compounds known as cannabinoids. THC was first isolated in the 1960s by Yechiel Gaoni and Raphael Mechoulam, and it took decades longer for researchers to identify cannabinoid receptors in the human body through which THC and other cannabinoids act (see Mechoulam and Parker 2012). The elucidation of these cannabinoid receptors along with identification of endogenously produced cannabinoids led to the characterization of the endogenous cannabinoid system—which can be thought of as "the body's own cannabinoid system" (Grotenhermen and Müller-Vahl 2012).

Marijuana contains more than one hundred cannabinoids in addition to THC, including cannabidiol (CBD) and cannabinol (CBN) (National Academies of Science, Engineering, and Medicine 2017). The cannabinoids contained in marijuana are known as *exogenous phytocannabinoids.* The term "exogenous" indicates that these compounds originate outside the human body, and the term "phyto" indicates that they come from plants. Some cannabinoids also originate from within the human body and are known as *endogenous cannabinoids.* When THC or other exogenous cannabinoids enter the human body, they bind to cannabinoid receptors. The binding of THC or other cannabinoids to cannabinoid receptors activates a series of events that are responsible for some of their psychoactive and therapeutic effects.

There are currently two FDA-approved synthetic cannabinoid pharmaceuticals. Dronabinol (Marinol) is a synthetic cannabinoid approved for nausea and vomiting associated with chemotherapy and for the treatment of anorexia associated with weight loss in patients with AIDS. Nabilone (Cesamet) is a synthetic cannabinoid approved only for the treatment of nausea and vomiting associated with chemotherapy. Phytocannabinoids, including botanical marijuana and its extracts, are not approved by the FDA, but other countries have approved nabiximols (Sativex), an oromucosal (oral) spray containing extracts of THC and cannabidiol (CBD). Nabiximols is approved in several countries for the relief of spasticity in adults with multiple sclerosis (MS), for neuropathic pain in patients with MS, and for intractable cancer pain (Borgelt et al. 2013).

TYPES OF CANNABINOIDS

CANNABINOIDS	
Phytocannabinoids—exogenous cannabinoids derived from cannabis plants	
	delta-9-tetrahydrocannabinol (Δ^9-THC, THC), cannabidiol (CBD), cannabinol (CBN), nabiximols (Sativex)
Synthetic cannabinoids—pharmaceutically produced exogenous cannabinoids	
	dronabinol (Marinol), nabilone (Cesamet)
Endocannabinoids—endogenous compounds produced within the human body	
	anandamide, 2-arachidonoylglycerol (2-AG)

Source: Bostwick (2012), Mechoulam and Parker (2012), and Stout and Cimino (2014).

CONCERNS OVER MEDICAL MARIJUANA

Although both synthetic cannabinoids and botanical marijuana have therapeutic applications, some physicians, legislators, and people in the general public view them very differently. Specifically, some people endorse the medical use of synthetic cannabinoids, but disapprove of the medical use of botanical marijuana. There are fears, for instance, that botanical medical marijuana will be diverted for recreational use, and there is some evidence that this occurs (e.g., Thurstone et al. 2011). There are also concerns that medical marijuana laws will lead to increases in the recreational use of botanical marijuana (see Q24). Additionally, whereas synthetic cannabinoids are often administered in capsule form, botanical marijuana is often smoked; and there are currently no FDA-approved medications that involve smoking. Furthermore, unlike most prescription medications, botanical marijuana is not a uniform substance—it contains over one hundred cannabinoids. This introduces challenges related to potency, dosage, drug interactions, and purity. There is also limited research on the long-term health risks associated with the medical use of botanical marijuana.

EVALUATING THE SAFETY AND EFFICACY OF MEDICAL MARIJUANA AND CANNABINOIDS

In order to understand the role of marijuana and cannabinoids in the treatment of medical disorders, various evaluations can be made, but the most stringent evidence required for FDA approval comes from several phases of clinical trials. Clinical trials evaluate how cannabinoids compare to placebos (or inactive substitutes used as controls in drug testing) or an already-available medicine for treating medical disorders. Medicines should outperform placebos in order to be considered for approval. Observational evidence, case studies, and anecdotal reports can help identify potential risks and benefits of marijuana, but they are not sufficient evidence for FDA approval. However, these latter forms of evidence are often helpful in initiating the clinical trial process. Finally, as with all medications, evidence of therapeutic efficacy must be balanced against evidence of safety and tolerability.

THE THERAPEUTIC USE OF CANNABINOIDS

Multiple reviews of clinical evidence have come to the consistent conclusion that marijuana and cannabinoids have medical and therapeutic potential. In a systematic review and meta-analysis published in the *Journal of the American Medical Association*, researchers reviewed randomized clinical trials on the medical uses of cannabinoids and found that there was "moderate-quality evidence to support the use of cannabinoids for the treatment of chronic pain and spasticity" (Whiting et al. 2015, 2456). They also found "low-quality evidence" that cannabinoids are associated with improvements in the two FDA-approved indications: nausea and vomiting due to chemotherapy and weight gain in HIV infection. In a clinical review article also published in the *Journal of the American Medical Association*, 28 randomized clinical trials on the use of cannabinoids were examined and the results indicated that the "use of marijuana for chronic pain, neuropathic pain, and spasticity due to multiple sclerosis is supported by high quality evidence" (Hill 2015: 2474). This review did not evaluate the evidence supporting the use of cannabinoids in the treatment of nausea and vomiting associated with chemotherapy and appetite stimulation in wasting illnesses—both of which are indications with FDA-approved cannabinoid medicines.

Two complementary review articles corroborate the conclusions published in the *Journal of the American Medical Association* and further suggest that marijuana and cannabinoids can be used to relieve pain, to treat symptoms of multiple sclerosis, as appetite stimulants, and as antiemetics (drugs that reduce vomiting and nausea). The first study, a 2006 review published in the *Journal of Ethnopharmacology*, reviewed 72 controlled studies on the therapeutic potential of cannabinoids published prior to July 1, 2005 (Ben Amar 2006). The second study, a 2010 review published in the journal *Cannabinoids*, reviewed studies published from 2005 to 2009 (Hazekamp and Grotenhermen 2010). Together, these reviews cover clinical studies performed between 1975 and 2009, and confirm that botanical marijuana and other cannabinoids have potential as analgesics, as appetite stimulants and antiemetics, and in the symptomatic treatment of multiple sclerosis (see Hazekamp and Pappas 2014).

Pain Management

Marijuana has well known analgesic properties, and there is considerable research documenting the use of marijuana and cannabinoids in the management of chronic pain. Both review articles published in the *Journal of the American Medical Association*, for example, found evidence supporting the use of cannabinoids for the treatment of chronic pain (Hill 2015; Whiting et al. 2015). A 2017 review published by the National Academies of Sciences, Engineering, and Medicine further supports the conclusion that cannabis is an effective treatment for chronic pain in adults.

Research suggests that medical marijuana in botanical form can be used successfully to help alleviate certain types of pain. A 2015 review published in the journal *Canadian Family Physician* analyzed evidence from randomized controlled trials to investigate the role of smoked or vaporized botanical marijuana for the alleviation of chronic non-cancer pain (Deshpande et al. 2015). All articles that met the inclusion criteria showed that medical marijuana reduced non-cancer pain, and half the experiments found a "clinically relevant" improvement in pain intensity (measured as 30 percent improvement or better). The authors of the review conclude that there is scientific evidence supporting the use of very low-dose medical marijuana to treat neuropathic pain in patients concurrently using analgesics.

Several other studies show that botanical marijuana can be used effectively to treat pain. A 2013 review published in the journal *Pharmacotherapy* documented evidence from multiple studies showing that smoked medical marijuana led to significant pain relief (Borgelt et al. 2013). These studies showed that smoked marijuana consistently outperformed placebo and indicated that marijuana with higher THC content (up to 9.4 percent THC) appeared to be most effective for pain relief. There is also evidence that smoked marijuana can help reduce neuropathic pain. A 2015 review published in the journal *Current Pain and Headache Reports* detailed several studies, each of which showed that botanical cannabis outperformed placebos as an effective treatment for neuropathic pain (Jensen et al. 2015).

There is also extensive evidence that other cannabinoid treatments are effective in the treatment of various types of pain, especially neuropathic pain (see Grotenhermen and Muller-Vahl 2012; Jensen et al. 2015). A 2010 systematic review published in the *British Journal of Clinical Pharmacology* found evidence that oromucosal extracts, nabilone, and dronabinol each demonstrated a positive analgesic effect on non-cancer pain (Lynch and Campbell 2010). Another review found that oral THC and nabiximols were effective in reducing cancer pain (Jensen et al. 2015). Finally, there is evidence from several studies that nabiximols, dronabinol, and nabilone are also effective in reducing chronic pain (Hill 2015; Borgelt et al. 2013; Grant et al. 2012).

Spasticity in Multiple Sclerosis

Multiple sclerosis is a potentially disabling disease of the central nervous system that affects over two million people worldwide (National Multiple Sclerosis Society 2016). Spasticity is a common symptom of MS and refers to feelings of stiffness and involuntary muscle spasms in the legs and other extremities (ibid.). Spasticity can also be accompanied by pain, immobility, and sleep disturbances (Beard et al. 2003). While there are several medications indicated to treat spasticity in patients with MS, there is only limited evidence that these medications are effective (Syed et al. 2014).

Some patients with MS report using marijuana for the treatment of symptoms, and many find that marijuana helps relieve or reduce symptoms (Hazekamp et al. 2013). For example, in a survey of 112 people with MS who used marijuana to relieve symptoms, over 70 percent of people found that marijuana helped reduce spasticity, chronic pain of extremities, tremor, and emotional dysfunction (Consroe et al. 1997). While many patients with MS find that marijuana helps to reduce symptoms of spasticity and pain, cannabinoid-based treatments of MS are not approved in the United States.

Few clinical studies have investigated the role of smoked cannabis in reducing spasticity in patients with MS, and the results are mixed. For example, in a 2012 trial published in the *Canadian Medical Association Journal,* MS patients treated with smoked cannabis showed a significant reduction in spasticity based on patient scores on the modified Ashworth scale (Corey-Bloom et al. 2012). Additionally, the marijuana treatment resulted in a reduction of pain scores. On the other hand, a study published in *Clinical Pharmacology and Therapeutics* found that MS patients with spasticity who smoked marijuana demonstrated worsened posture and balance (Greenberg et al. 1994). The latter study conducted a functional assessment of how patients responded to "balance perturbations" (disturbing the platform they were standing on), and did not evaluate spasticity symptoms, per se. Nevertheless, this research warrants consideration alongside the limited other research on how smoked marijuana may affect patients with MS.

Other cannabinoid medications have shown promise in the treatment of MS symptoms (see Whiting et al. 2015; Zajicek and Apostu 2011). For example, nabiximols is approved as an add-on treatment for spasticity in patients with MS in some countries and has been documented in several studies for its ability to improve subjective assessments of MS symptoms (Syed et al. 2014; Zajicek and Apostu 2011). Other research has shown that Cannador, a cannabis extract capsule containing THC and cannabidiol, is also effective for improving patients' perceptions of spasticity (Zajicek et al. 2003). Although many patients in both the real-world and in experimental settings report that cannabinoids provide subjective relief from MS symptoms, these subjective improvements do not always translate to significant improvements in clinical measurements of spasticity (see Zajicek et al. 2003). Nevertheless, the evidence showing that cannabinoids provide symptomatic benefits to patients has led several researchers and federal governments to endorse the use of cannabinoids as an add-on treatment for spasticity in patients with MS (Zajicek and Apostu 2011).

Nausea and Vomiting

Although unpleasant, nausea and vomiting (emesis) are defensive responses that help protect humans and other animals from ingesting harmful or dangerous substances (Sharkey et al. 2014). Nausea and vomiting are also common side effects of many medications used in the treatment of pain and cancer (e.g., opioids and chemotherapy). It is medically necessary that patients undergoing medical treatments for pain and cancer manage their nausea and vomiting so that they are able to meet their nutritional needs and adhere to treatment protocols. The FDA has approved several medications for the treatment of chemotherapy-induced nausea and vomiting (CINV), including the synthetic cannabinoids dronabinol and nabilone. Botanical cannabis and THC are also frequently used as defenses against nausea and vomiting in states that have legalized medical marijuana.

Two studies from the same research team examined the antiemetic properties of oral and smoked THC in cancer patients receiving chemotherapy (Chang et al. 1979, 1981). In the first study, the researchers examined the effects of oral and smoked THC in 15 patients with osteogenic sarcoma (bone cancer) receiving high-dose methotrexate chemotherapy. Patients received placebo and oral THC three times each over the course of three paired trials during six hospitalizations. If vomiting occurred under a given treatment, the patient was switched to either placebo or THC cigarette. The results showed that increased THC blood concentrations resulted in decreased episodes of vomiting. The authors concluded that the combination of oral and smoked THC was a highly effective anti-emetic compared to placebo. On the other hand, a subsequent study compared the anti-emetic effects of oral and smoked THC in eight cancer patients being treated with Adriamycin and Cytoxan chemotherapy. Compared to placebo, oral and smoked THC did not reduce the incidence of nausea and vomiting among these patients. The authors infer that lower THC concentrations in the latter study may explain mixed results, and that the anti-emetic effects of THC may be effective only against specific types of chemotherapy drugs.

Additional studies have compared smoked botanical marijuana to other anti-emetic treatments. For example, results from several state-run clinical trials were summarized in a 2001 review and the researchers concluded that the inhalation of smoked cannabis appeared to be equal to or better than the oral route in the treatment of nausea and emesis (Musty and Rossi 2001). More research is needed comparing smoked cannabis to conventional anti-emetics. One study, conducted by the Michigan Cancer Foundation, compared smoked cannabis with thiethylperazine in the treatment of CINV, and showed only marginal differences between the two treatments (Musty and Rossi 2001).

Appetite Stimulation

Cannabis has been used as an appetite stimulant for centuries, and the "munchies" are a popularly known side effect of recreational marijuana use. Appetite stimulation is also an important component of treatment for patients with both HIV/AIDS and cancer. Research has shown that malnutrition negatively affects immune function, increases the risk of infection, diminishes tolerance and response to therapy, and affects overall survival (Von Roenn and Knopf 1996). Accordingly, it is important to find safe and efficacious treatments that can help increase appetite, preserve and increase body mass, counter metabolic abnormalities, and treat other nutritional disorders in patients experiencing disease-related wasting and weight loss. Dronabinol is FDA approved for anorexia related to weight loss in patients with AIDS, and other cannabinoids are being investigated as appetite stimulants for patients with advanced HIV and for patients with cancer-related anorexia cachexia syndrome.

The first systematic study to show that smoked cannabis increased appetite and led to weight gain was conducted by Isaac Greenberg and colleagues (1976), who studied the effects of smoked cannabis on body weight and caloric intake among a sample of experienced cannabis users (see also Pagotto et al. 2006). Caloric intake and body weight increased after only a few days of treatment. As the study went on, caloric intake stabilized, but body weight continued to increase. Subsequent research has similarly shown that smoked marijuana increases appetite and food intake among healthy subjects (Foltin et al. 1988). Researchers continue to explore how cannabinoids and cannabinoid receptor antagonists might affect metabolic processes beyond their impact on food intake.

Smoked marijuana has also been shown to increase food intake and lead to weight gain in patients with HIV. However, there is ongoing controversy regarding the use of smoked cannabis among patients with HIV. A 2003 article published in *Annals of Internal Medicine* evaluated weight gain among 62 subjects with HIV infection and found that both oral THC and smoked THC led to statistically greater weight gain than placebo (Abrams et al. 2003). A 2005 study published in *Psychopharmacology* found that both smoked cannabis and dronabinol increased food intake in a sample of HIV-positive experienced marijuana users (Haney et al. 2005). Similarly, a 2007 study published in the *Journal of Acquired Immune Deficiency Syndromes* found that smoked cannabis and dronabinol both dose-dependently increased caloric intake and body weight among HIV-positive marijuana smokers (Haney et al. 2007).

ADVERSE EVENTS AND CONTRAINDICATIONS

In many clinical trials, patients receiving cannabis and cannabinoids also experience adverse events. Side effects are common in many medical treatments, and there is a critical need to understand the adverse events associated with all medications, including cannabinoids. A 2008 systematic review published in the *Canadian Medical Association Journal* drew on 23 randomized controlled studies and 8 observational studies to evaluate the adverse effects of medical cannabinoids (Wang et al. 2008). In the controlled trials, the median duration of cannabinoid exposure was two weeks. A total of 4,779 adverse events were reported, 96.6 percent of which were not serious. The most common serious adverse events were relapse to multiple sclerosis, vomiting, and urinary tract infection. Dizziness was the most commonly reported non-serious event. More research is needed in order to understand better the long-term consequences associated with the medical use of botanical marijuana.

FURTHER READING

Abrams, Donald I., Joan F. Hilton, Roslyn J. Leiser, Starley B. Shade, Tarek A. Elbeik, Francesca T. Aweeka, Neal L. Benowitz et al. "Short-term effects of cannabinoids in patients with HIV-1 infection: a randomized, placebo-controlled clinical trial." *Annals of Internal Medicine* 139, no. 4 (2003): 258–266.

Aggarwal, Sunil K. "Cannabinergic pain medicine: a concise clinical primer and survey of randomized-controlled trial results." *The Clinical Journal of Pain* 29, no. 2 (2013): 162–171.

Amar, Mohamed Ben. "Cannabinoids in medicine: a review of their therapeutic potential." *Journal of Ethnopharmacology* 105, no. 1 (2006): 1–25.

Beard, S. M., Amanda Hunn, and Jeremy Wight. "Treatments for spasticity and pain in multiple sclerosis: a systematic review." *Health Technology Assessment* 7, no. 40 (2003): 1–121.

Borgelt, Laura M., Kari L. Franson, Abraham M. Nussbaum, and George S. Wang. "The pharmacologic and clinical effects of medical cannabis." *Pharmacotherapy: The Journal of Human Pharmacology and Drug Therapy* 33, no. 2 (2013): 195–209.

Bostwick, J. Michael. "Blurred boundaries: the therapeutics and politics of medical marijuana." *Mayo Clinic Proceedings* 87, no. 2 (2012): 172–186.

Chang, Alfred E., David J. Shiling, Richard C. Stillman, Nelson H. Goldberg, Claudia A. Seipp, Ivan Barofsky, and Steven A. Rosenberg. "A prospective evaluation of delta-9-tetrahydrocannabinol as an antiemetic in patients receiving adriamycin and cytoxan chemotherapy." *Cancer* 47 (1981): 1746–1751.

Chang, Alfred E., David J. Shiling, Richard C. Stillman, Nelson H. Goldberg, Claudia A. Seipp, Ivan Barofsky, Richard M. Simon, Steven A. Rosenberg. "Delta-9-tetrahydrocannabinol as an antiemetic in cancer patients receiving high-dose methotrexate: a prospective, randomized evaluation." *Annals of Internal Medicine* 91, no. 6 (1979): 819–824.

Consroe, Paul, Rik Musty, Judith Rein, Whitney Tillery, and Roger Pertwee. "The perceived effects of smoked cannabis on patients with multiple sclerosis." *European Neurology* 38, no. 1 (1997): 44–48.

Corey-Bloom, Jody, Tanya Wolfson, Anthony Gamst, Shelia Jin, Thomas D. Marcotte, Heather Bentley, and Ben Gouaux. "Smoked cannabis for spasticity in multiple sclerosis: a randomized, placebo-controlled trial." *Canadian Medical Association Journal* 184, no. 10 (2012): 1143–1150.

Deshpande, Amol, Angela Mailis-Gagnon, Nivan Zoheiry, and Shehnaz Fatima Lakha. "Efficacy and adverse effects of medical marijuana for chronic noncancer pain. Systematic review of randomized controlled trials." *Canadian Family Physician* 61, no. 8 (2015): e372–e381.

Foltin, Richard W., Marian W. Fischman, and Maryanne F. Byrne. "Effects of smoked marijuana on food intake and body weight of humans living in a residential laboratory." *Appetite* 11, no. 1 (1988): 1–14.

Gaoni, Yechiel, and R. Mechoulam. "Isolation, structure, and partial synthesis of an active constituent of hashish." *Journal of the American Chemical Society* 86, no. 8 (1964): 1646–1647.

Greenberg, Harry S., Susan A. S. Werness, James E. Pugh, Robert O. Andrus, David J. Anderson, and Edward F. Domino. "Short-term effects of smoking marijuana on balance in patients with multiple sclerosis and normal volunteers." *Clinical Pharmacology & Therapeutics* 55, no. 3 (1994): 324–328.

Greenberg, Isaac, John Kuehnle, Jack H. Mendelson, and Jerrold G. Bernstein. "Effects of marihuana use on body weight and caloric intake in humans." *Psychopharmacology* 49, no. 1 (1976): 79–84.

Grotenhermen, Franjo, and Kirsten Müller-Vahl. "The therapeutic potential of cannabis and cannabinoids." *Deutsches Ärzteblatt International* 109, no. 29–30 (2012): 495–501.

Haney, Margaret, Erik W. Gunderson, Judith Rabkin, Carl L. Hart, Suzanne K. Vosburg, Sandra D. Comer, and Richard W. Foltin. "Dronabinol and marijuana in HIV-positive marijuana smokers: caloric intake, mood, and sleep." *JAIDS: Journal of Acquired Immune Deficiency Syndromes* 45, no. 5 (2007): 545–554.

Haney, Margaret, Judith Rabkin, Erik Gunderson, and Richard W. Foltin. "Dronabinol and marijuana in HIV+ marijuana smokers: acute effects on caloric intake and mood." *Psychopharmacology* 181, no. 1 (2005): 170–178.

Hazekamp, Arno, and Franjo Grotenhermen. "Review on clinical studies with cannabis and cannabinoids 2005–2009." *Cannabinoids* 5, no. special issue (2010): 1–21.

Hazekamp, Arno, and George Pappas. "Self-medication with cannabis." In *Handbook of cannabis*, edited by Roger G. Pertwee, 319–338. New York: Oxford University Press, 2014.

Hazekamp, Arno, Mark A. Ware, Kirsten R. Muller-Vahl, Donald Abrams, and Franjo Grotenhermen. "The medicinal use of cannabis and cannabinoids—an international cross-sectional survey on administration forms." *Journal of Psychoactive Drugs* 45, no. 3 (2013): 199–210.

Hill, Kevin P. "Medical marijuana for treatment of chronic pain and other medical and psychiatric problems: a clinical review." *JAMA* 313, no. 24 (2015): 2474–2483.

Iversen, Leslie L. *The science of marijuana*. New York: Oxford University Press, 2008.

Jensen, Bjorn, Jeffrey Chen, Tim Furnish, and Mark Wallace. "Medical marijuana and chronic pain: a review of basic science and clinical evidence." *Current Pain and Headache Reports* 19, no. 10 (2015): 1–9.

Lynch, Mary E., and Fiona Campbell. "Cannabinoids for treatment of chronic non-cancer pain: a systematic review of randomized trials." *British Journal of Clinical Pharmacology* 72, no. 5 (2011): 735–744.

Mack, Alison, and Janet Joy. *Marijuana as medicine?: the science beyond the controversy*. National Academies Press, 2000.

Mechoulam, Raphael, and Linda A. Parker. "The endocannabinoid system and the brain." *Annual Review of Psychology* 64 (2012): 21–47.

Musty, Richard E., and Rita Rossi. "Effects of smoked cannabis and oral Δ9-tetrahydrocannabinol on nausea and emesis after cancer chemotherapy: a review of state clinical trials." *Journal of Cannabis Therapeutics* 1, no. 1 (2001): 29–56.

National Academies of Sciences, Engineering, and Medicine. *The health effects of cannabis and cannabinoids: the current state of evidence and recommendations for research*. Washington, DC: The National Academies Press. 2017.

National Conference of State Legislators (NCSL). "State medical marijuana laws." 2016. Accessed December 8, 2016. http://www.ncsl.org/research/health/state-medical-marijuana-laws.aspx.

National Multiple Sclerosis Society. http://www.nationalmssociety.org/

Pagotto, Uberto, Giovanni Marsicano, Daniela Cota, Beat Lutz, and Renato Pasquali. "The emerging role of the endocannabinoid system in endocrine regulation and energy balance." *Endocrine Reviews* 27, no. 1 (2006): 73–100.

Russo, Ethan B. "History of cannabis and its preparations in saga, science, and sobriquet." *Chemistry & Biodiversity* 4, no. 8 (2007): 1614–1648.

Sharkey, Keith A., Nissar A. Darmani, and Linda A. Parker. "Regulation of nausea and vomiting by cannabinoids and the endocannabinoid system." *European Journal of Pharmacology* 722 (2014): 134–146.

Stout, Stephen M., and Nina M. Cimino. "Exogenous cannabinoids as substrates, inhibitors, and inducers of human drug metabolizing enzymes: a systematic review." *Drug Metabolism Reviews* 46, no. 1 (2014): 86–95.

Syed, Yahiya Y., Kate McKeage, and Lesley J. Scott. "Delta-9-tetrahydro-cannabinol/cannabidiol (Sativex®): a review of its use in patients with moderate to severe spasticity due to multiple sclerosis." *Drugs* 74, no. 5 (2014): 563–578.

Thurstone, Christian, Shane A. Lieberman, and Sarah J. Schmiege. "Medical marijuana diversion and associated problems in adolescent substance treatment." *Drug and Alcohol Dependence* 118, no. 2 (2011): 489–492.

Unimed Pharmaceuticals, Inc. NDA 18–651/S-021. Marinol (dronabinol) Capsules. http://www.fda.gov/ohrms/dockets/dockets/05n0479/05N-0479-emc0004-04.pdf

Valeant Pharmaceuticals International. NDA 18–677/S-011. Cesament (nabilone) Capsules. http://www.accessdata.fda.gov/drugsatfda_docs/label/2006/018677s011lbl.pdf

Von Roenn, J. H., and Kevin Knopf. "Anorexia/cachexia in patients with HIV: lessons for the oncologist." *Oncology (Williston Park, NY)* 10, no. 7 (1996): 1049–56.

Wang, Tongtong, Jean-Paul Collet, Stan Shapiro, and Mark A. Ware. "Adverse effects of medical cannabinoids: a systematic review." *Canadian Medical Association Journal* 178, no. 13 (2008): 1669–1678.

Whiting, Penny F., Robert F. Wolff, Sohan Deshpande, Marcello Di
     Nisio, Steven Duffy, Adrian V. Hernandez, J. Christiaan Keurentjes
     et al. "Cannabinoids for medical use: a systematic review and meta-
     analysis." *JAMA* 313, no. 24 (2015): 2456–2473.
Zajicek, John P., and Vicentiu I. Apostu. "Role of cannabinoids in multi-
     ple sclerosis." *CNS Drugs* 25, no. 3 (2011): 187–201.
Zajicek, John P., Patrick Fox, Hilary Sanders, David Wright, Jane
     Vickery, Andrew Nunn, Alan Thompson, and UK MS research group.
     "Cannabinoids for treatment of spasticity and other symptoms related
     to multiple sclerosis (CAMS study): multicentre randomised placebo-
     controlled trial." *The Lancet* 362, no. 9395 (2003): 1517–1526.

Q13. ARE ALL MEDICAL USES FOR MARIJUANA SUBSTANTIATED BY RESEARCH?

Answer: No. It is generally accepted that randomized clinical trials are
necessary in order to assess the safety and efficacy of medications; however,
marijuana is currently used to treat some conditions for which this type
of evidence does not exist. Based on evidence from randomized clinical
trials, the strongest scientific evidence supports the use of marijuana and
cannabinoids in the treatment of pain, spasticity due to multiple sclerosis,
nausea and vomiting due to chemotherapy, and in weight loss in patients
with HIV (see Q12). The evidence supporting the use of marijuana and
cannabinoids for the treatment of other medical disorders is based primarily on observational and anecdotal evidence. An accumulation of observational and anecdotal evidence may be the basis for future clinical studies
on the therapeutic effects of various cannabinoids. Yet there is *currently*
insufficient clinical evidence to support the use of cannabinoids to treat
all indications for which medical marijuana has been used.

The Facts: Given that the federal government prohibits the use of
marijuana for medical purposes, U.S. states have exercised considerable
discretion in passing medical marijuana laws and in deciding which medical conditions qualify patients for a medical marijuana license. Doctors
who recommend marijuana to patients do so in the absence of support
from the American Medical Association (AMA), which has stated its
position on medical marijuana in this way:

> Our AMA urges that marijuana's status as a federal Schedule I con-
> trolled substance be reviewed with the goal of facilitating the conduct

of clinical research and development of cannabinoid-based medicines, and alternate delivery methods. This should not be viewed as an endorsement of state-based medical cannabis programs, the legalization of marijuana, or that scientific evidence on the therapeutic use of cannabis meets the current standards for a prescription drug product. (American Medical Association 2017)

People who use marijuana for medical purposes report using it to address a wide variety of medical conditions and to alleviate a wide variety of symptoms. In an international survey of 953 medical marijuana patients, researchers found that each of the 47 medical conditions listed in the survey was selected at least once as the primary medical condition for which cannabinoid medications were used (Hazekamp et al. 2013). The medical conditions most commonly selected were back pain, sleeping disorder, depression, pain resulting from injury or accident, and multiple sclerosis. Similarly, in a study of 1,746 medical marijuana patients in California, researchers found that patients most commonly used medical marijuana to relieve pain, muscle spasms, headaches, anxiety, and nausea/vomiting (Reinarman et al. 2011). A smaller study of medical marijuana patients from Washington State found that intractable pain, nausea/vomiting/appetite loss, spasticity disorder, HIV, and multiple sclerosis were the most commonly cited medical conditions reported by patients (Aggarwal et al. 2012).

The medical conditions that qualify patients for medical marijuana programs vary by state, but there is considerable overlap. For example, in addition to the treatment of pain, spasticity, nausea and vomiting, and weight loss in patients with HIV, many states grant participation in medical marijuana programs based on the following diagnoses: cancer, glaucoma, Parkinson's disease, Huntington's disease, epilepsy, Crohn's disease, PTSD, Tourette's syndrome, Alzheimer's disease, amyotrophic lateral sclerosis, and hepatitis C virus (Belendiuk et al. 2015; Hill 2015). Some states also require that the diagnosis of a qualifying condition is accompanied by a "complicating condition," such as cachexia (wasting syndrome), chronic pain, nausea, seizures, or muscle spasms (e.g., New York State Medical Marijuana Program 2017).

As discussed in Q12, the most robust scientific evidence supports the medical use of marijuana and cannabinoids in the treatment of chronic pain, spasticity due to multiple sclerosis, nausea and vomiting due to chemotherapy, and weight loss in patients with HIV. These conclusions are based on evidence from randomized clinical trials that have been reviewed and evaluated by multiple expert reviewers (Hill 2015; Whiting et al. 2015; Ben Amar 2006; Hazekamp and Grotenhermen 2010). There is less evidence or lower-quality evidence supporting the use of marijuana and cannabinoids in the treatment of other medical conditions, including sleep disorders, Tourette's syndrome, inflammatory bowel disease, Parkinson's disease, epilepsy, glaucoma, mental health disorders, and substance use disorders. There is also insufficient evidence supporting the use of marijuana in the treatment of cancer (see Q14).

Clearly there is some divergence between the clinically supported indications for medicinal marijuana and the many conditions and symptoms that patients report treating with marijuana. This divergence can be understood as either an opportunity or problem. On the one hand, many of the therapeutic benefits of medicinal marijuana were first described in anecdotal reports of patients who self-medicated using marijuana (Hazekamp and Pappas 2014). As a result, providing broad access to medical marijuana may lead to the identification of additional symptoms that could be treated with marijuana. Additionally, proponents of medical marijuana cite the acceptable safety profile of marijuana and the concept of "compassionate care" as reasons to provide patients with relatively broad access to marijuana and cannabinoids—even in the absence of consistent clinical evidence.

On the other hand, all substances have both risks and benefits, and citizens in the United States and elsewhere have relied on clinical studies, medical researchers, and medical doctors to guide various pharmacotherapies. However, the AMA does not endorse state-level marijuana laws and a substantial number of surveyed physicians report concerns over the safety and efficacy of using marijuana for medical purposes. In a survey of 520 family physicians from Colorado, for example, researchers found that 46 percent thought that physicians should not recommend medical marijuana, 19 percent thought that physicians should recommend it, and the majority believed that marijuana posed mental and physical health risks (Kondrad and Reid 2013). Other surveys have similarly shown that physicians are divided when it comes to the safety and efficacy of medical marijuana (e.g., Charuvastra et al. 2005).

SLEEP DISORDERS

Medical marijuana patients frequently report using marijuana to treat sleep disorders (Reinarman et al. 2011; Hazekamp et al. 2013). While some sleep problems may improve with the use marijuana and cannabinoids, there is currently insufficient clinical evidence to conclusively determine the effects of cannabinoids on sleep disorders. A 2014 review published in *Sleep Medicine Reviews* found mixed evidence regarding the ways that marijuana affects sleep (Gates et al. 2014). Based on their review of 39 studies, the researchers found that marijuana use may lead to a decrease in slow wave sleep and an increase in stage 2 sleep, but they found no consistent effect on total sleep time. Other studies show that the analgesic properties of cannabinoids may help improve sleep for patients who are in pain (see Gates et al. 2014). For example, in a 2010 study published in the *Canadian Medical Association Journal*, patients with neuropathic pain who smoked marijuana (9.4 percent THC) reported significantly more drowsiness and reported getting to sleep more easily, faster, and with fewer periods of wakefulness (Ware et al. 2010). Nevertheless, more research is needed on medical marijuana and sleep.

TOURETTE'S SYNDROME

Tourette's syndrome (TS) is a neurological disorder characterized by chronic motor (e.g., eye blinking) and phonic (e.g., sniffling) tics (Curtis et al. 2009). It is estimated that 200,000 Americans have the most severe form of TS, and as many as 1 in 100 exhibit milder and less complex symptoms (National Institute of Neurological Disorders and Stroke 2017). Many patients with TS also have symptoms of attention deficit hyperactivity disorder (ADHD) and obsessive compulsive disorder (OCD), both of which can detract from overall quality of life (Leckman 2002). The medical treatment of TS is individualized and often involves medications, including pimozide, haloperidol, and clonidine. Yet many patients do not benefit from these drugs (Müller-Vahl 2003).

Some patients report using cannabinoids to treat TS (Hazekamp et al. 2013). However, limited clinical research has examined the role of cannabinoids in the treatment of Tourette's syndrome, and most has focused on the use of oral THC. In a 2002 study published in *Pharmacopsychiatry*, researchers performed a randomized double-blind placebo trial to evaluate the effects of THC on adults with TS (Müller-Vahl et al. 2002). Results from this study indicated that a single dose treatment with THC was effective and safe in treating tics and obsessive compulsive behaviors. Similarly, a 2003 study published in the *Journal of Clinical Psychiatry* utilized a comparable design to test the effects of THC on symptomatic tics in a sample of 24 adult patients with TS (Müller-Vahl et al. 2003). This research showed that THC was safe and effective in the treatment of tics. More research among larger samples is necessary to better asses the role of cannabinoids, and specifically marijuana, in the treatment of TS.

INFLAMMATORY BOWEL DISEASE

Inflammatory bowel disease (IBD), which includes Crohn's disease and ulcerative colitis, is a medical disorder that involves inflammation in the gastrointestinal tract. Symptoms vary, but can include diarrhea, abdominal pain, and abdominal cramps (Merck Manual 2017). Studies have shown that patients with IBD utilize medical marijuana; however, there is limited clinical evidence indicating the efficacy of marijuana in the treatment of IBD. Some research has demonstrated that marijuana can have anti-inflammatory effects, and that cannabinoids can reduce experimentally induced colitis in mice (see Klein 2005; Massa et al. 2004). It has therefore been suggested that cannabinoids play a likely role in regulating inflammation in the colon (Klein 2005). In a 2013 placebo-controlled study of 21 adult patients with Crohn's disease, researchers observed that the group assigned to the experimental marijuana group showed greater clinical improvements than the placebo group; however, marijuana was not superior to placebo in induction of remission (Naftali et al. 2013). More clinical research on medical marijuana and IBD is needed.

PARKINSON'S DISEASE

Parkinson's disease (PD) is a progressive degenerative disorder that affects about one in 250 people over the age of 40. Symptoms include tremors, increased stiffness or rigidity, slowed movements, impaired balance, and in some cases, dementia (Merck Manual 2017). Some medical marijuana patients report using marijuana or cannabinoids to treat Parkinson's disease (Hazekamp et al. 2013). However, there is inconsistent evidence that cannabinoids can reduce PD symptoms. A 2014 open-label observational study published in the journal *Clinical Neuropharmacology* found that smoked marijuana helped improve tremor, rigidity, pain, and sleep among Parkinson's patients (Lotan et al. 2014). Some research has shown that nabilone (a synthetic cannabinoid) significantly reduces levodopa-induced dyskinesia (involuntary movements) in PD patients (Sieradzan et al. 2001). However, other research has shown that oral cannabis has no effect on dyskinesia or other PD outcomes (Carroll et al. 2004). A 2014 review published by the American Academy of Neurology found that oral cannabis extract was likely not effective for treating levodopa-induced dyskinesia in patients with PD (Koppel et al. 2014).

EPILEPSY

Epilepsy, also known as epileptic seizure disorder, is a chronic brain disorder marked by recurrent seizures (Merck Manual 2017). About 1 percent of the world's population is affected by epilepsy, and it is estimated that up to 30 percent of people with epilepsy are not able to control their symptoms with conventional drugs (Robson 2001). Surveys of medical marijuana patients show that marijuana and cannabinoids are used to treat epilepsy and control symptomatic seizures. However, there have been limited trials to verify the safety and efficacy of cannabinoid treatments for epilepsy (see Maa and Figi 2014). Some animal models have demonstrated that cannabis and cannabinoids can have an anticonvulsant effect, but other evidence suggests that cannabinoids can lower the threshold for seizures (Belendiuk et al. 2015). In spite of some positive evidence, literature reviews have concluded that there is currently insufficient clinical evidence to support or refute the use of cannabinoids for the treatment of epilepsy (Koppel et al. 2014).

GLAUCOMA

Glaucomas are a group of eye disorders, sometimes associated with increased intraocular pressure (IOP), characterized by progressive optic nerve damage (Merck Manual 2017). Glaucoma affects millions of people worldwide and is a leading cause of blindness. Anecdotal reports and studies on small samples have reported reductions in IOP following the administration of marijuana (see Ben Amar 2006; Belendiuk 2015). However, few controlled studies have evaluated the effects of THC on patients with glaucoma, and the results are mixed. In a 1980 study, marijuana inhalation was associated with decreased intraocular pressure in patients with glaucoma (Merritt et al. 1980). However, side effects were common. More recently, a study published in the *Journal of Glaucoma* evaluated the effects of THC and CBD on six patients with ocular hypertension or early primary open angle glaucoma (Tomida et al. 2006). A 5 mg sublingual dose (under the tongue) of THC reduced IOP temporarily, 20 mg CBD did not reduce IOP, and 40 mg CBD led to a short term increase in IOP. The American Glaucoma Society and the American Academy of Ophthalmology Complementary Therapies Task Force have found insufficient evidence that marijuana is safer or more effective than existing therapies for reducing IOP (Belendiuk 2015).

MENTAL HEALTH

While patients report the use of medical marijuana to treat mental health symptoms and disorders, evidence from randomized controlled trials has yet to substantiate the use of medical marijuana in the treatment of mental health disorders. As of 2013, the American Psychiatric Association (APA) found no evidence that marijuana is beneficial for the treatment of any psychiatric disorder (APA 2013). One of the primary concerns related to the use of marijuana in the treatment of mental health disorders relates to the association between recreational marijuana use and the increased risk of psychiatric disorders (see Hall and Degenhardt 2009). For example, in a 2007 meta-analysis published in the *Lancet*, researchers found that marijuana users were at a 40 percent increased risk for developing psychosis (Moore et al. 2007). More frequent marijuana users were at even greater risk. However, the authors could not rule out alternative explanations for this association.

While surveys show that some medical marijuana patients use marijuana or cannabinoids to alleviate depressive symptoms, a review published in the *Journal of the American Medical Association* could not identify any randomized controlled trials that evaluated the effects of cannabinoids on depression (Whiting et al. 2015). While there have been few examinations of medical marijuana as a treatment for depression, there is mixed evidence documenting an association between marijuana use and depression (Hall and Degenhardt 2010). In a 2007 review, for example, researchers found that 5 out of 10 observational studies observed a link between marijuana use and the diagnosis of depression (Moore et al. 2007).

There is also very limited evidence indicating that marijuana should be used in the treatment of anxiety. The 2015 review published in *The Journal of the American Medical Association* identified only one randomized controlled trial that assessed the use of cannabinoids to treat anxiety (Whiting et al. 2015). The study found that among patients with generalized social anxiety disorder, cannabidiol was associated with a reduction in anxiety during a simulated public speaking test (Bergamaschi et al. 2011). Other studies have also reported that cannabinoids may reduce anxiety, but these studies were not assessing patients with anxiety disorders (see Whiting et al. 2015).

Medical marijuana patients also report using marijuana and cannabinoids to treat the symptoms of post-traumatic stress disorder (PTSD) and to cope with the consequences of stress exposure (Hazekamp et al. 2013). While some individuals find that cannabinoids can be helpful in this regard, few trials have assessed the efficacy of cannabinoids in the treatment of symptoms related to stress and PTSD. However, a small double-blind trial found that the synthetic cannabinoid, nabilone, provided a reduction in PTSD nightmares among military personnel with PTSD (Jetley et al. 2015). In spite of some positive results, there have been too few randomized controlled trials to support the use of marijuana or cannabinoids in treating PTSD.

Finally, there is some evidence that medical marijuana patients use marijuana as a substitute for other substances or to directly address dependency on alcohol, opiates, or other substances (Hazekamp et al. 2013; Reinarman et al. 2011). For example, in a study of 350 medical marijuana patients, 40 percent had used marijuana as a substitute for alcohol, 26 percent as a substitute for illicit drugs, and 66 percent as a substitute for prescription drugs (Reiman 2009). Comparable substitution rates were identified in samples of medical marijuana patients in Canada (Lucas et al. 2013). Naturally, there are concerns over the use of marijuana to treat drug addiction, since marijuana itself can be misused. However, from a harm-reduction perspective, using marijuana as a substitute for other drugs may be beneficial for patients who would otherwise be using substances with more dangerous safety profiles.

FURTHER READING

Aggarwal, S. K., G. T. Carter, Mark D. Sullivan, C. Zumbrunnen, R. Morrill, and J. D. Mayer. "Prospectively surveying health-related quality of life and symptom relief in a lot-based sample of medical cannabis-using patients in urban Washington State reveals managed chronic illness and debility." *American Journal of Hospice and Palliative Medicine* 30, no. 6 (2012): 523–531.

American Academy of Neurology. "Position statement: use of medical marijuana for neurologic disorders." 2014. https://www.aan.com/uploadedFiles/Website_Library_Assets/Documents/6.Public_Policy/1.Stay_Informed/2.Position_Statements/3.PDFs_of_all_Position_Statements/Final%20Medical%20Marijuana%20Position%20Statement.pdf

American Medical Association. "AMA policy: medical marijuana." *South Dakota State Medical Association*. Accessed May 5, 2017. https://www.sdsma.org/docs/pdfs-new_site/Advocacy/AMA%20Policy%20on%20Medical%20Marijuana%20-%2020150610.pdf

American Psychiatric Association. "Position statement on marijuana as medicine." 2013. https://www.psychiatry.org/

Belendiuk, Katherine A., Lisa L. Baldini, and Marcel O. Bonn-Miller. "Narrative review of the safety and efficacy of marijuana for the treatment of commonly state-approved medical and psychiatric disorders." *Addiction Science & Clinical Practice* 10, no. 1 (2015): 1.

Ben Amar, Mohamed. "Cannabinoids in medicine: a review of their therapeutic potential." *Journal of Ethnopharmacology* 105, no. 1 (2006): 1–25.

Bergamaschi, Mateus M., Regina Helena Costa Queiroz, Marcos Hortes Nisihara Chagas, Danielle Chaves Gomes de Oliveira, Bruno Spinosa De Martinis, Flávio Kapczinski, Joao Quevedo et al. "Cannabidiol reduces the anxiety induced by simulated public speaking in treatment-naive social phobia patients." *Neuropsychopharmacology* 36, no. 6 (2011): 1219–1226.

Carroll, C. B., P. G. Bain, L. Teare, X. Liu, C. Joint, C. Wroath, S. G. Parkin et al. "Cannabis for dyskinesia in Parkinson disease. A randomized double-blind crossover study." *Neurology* 63, no. 7 (2004): 1245–1250.

Charuvastra, Anthony, Peter D. Friedmann, and Michael D. Stein. "Physician attitudes regarding the prescription of medical marijuana." *Journal of Addictive Diseases* 24, no. 3 (2005): 87–93.

Curtis, Adrienne, Carl E. Clarke, and Hugh E. Rickards. "Cannabinoids for Tourette's syndrome." *The Cochrane Library* (2009): 1–13.

Gates, Peter J., Lucy Albertella, and Jan Copeland. "The effects of cannabinoid administration on sleep: a systematic review of human studies." *Sleep Medicine Reviews* 18, no. 6 (2014): 477–487.

Hall, Wayne, and Louisa Degenhardt. "Adverse health effects of non-medical cannabis use." *The Lancet* 374, no. 9698 (2009): 1383–1391.

Hazekamp, Arno, and Franjo Grotenhermen. "Review on clinical studies with cannabis and cannabinoids 2005–2009." *Cannabinoids* 5, special issue (2010): 1–21.

Hazekamp, Arno, and George Pappas. "Self-medication with cannabis." *Handbook of Cannabis* (2014): 319.

Hazekamp, Arno, Mark A. Ware, Kirsten R. Muller-Vahl, Donald Abrams, and Franjo Grotenhermen. "The medicinal use of cannabis and cannabinoids—an international cross-sectional survey on administration forms." *Journal of Psychoactive Drugs* 45, no. 3 (2013): 199–210.

Hill, Kevin P. "Medical marijuana for treatment of chronic pain and other medical and psychiatric problems: a clinical review." *JAMA* 313, no. 24 (2015): 2474–2483.

Jetly, Rakesh, Alexandra Heber, George Fraser, and Denis Boisvert. "The efficacy of nabilone, a synthetic cannabinoid, in the treatment of PTSD-associated nightmares: a preliminary randomized, double-blind, placebo-controlled cross-over design study." *Psychoneuroendocrinology* 51 (2015): 585–588.

Klein, Thomas W. "Cannabinoid-based drugs as anti-inflammatory therapeutics." *Nature Reviews Immunology* 5, no. 5 (2005): 400–411.

Kondrad, Elin, and Alfred Reid. "Colorado family physicians' attitudes toward medical marijuana." *The Journal of the American Board of Family Medicine* 26, no. 1 (2013): 52–60.

Koppel, Barbara S., John C. M. Brust, Terry Fife, Jeff Bronstein, Sarah Youssof, Gary Gronseth, and David Gloss. "Systematic review: efficacy and safety of medical marijuana in selected neurologic disorders. Report of the Guideline Development Subcommittee of the American Academy of Neurology." *Neurology* 82, no. 17 (2014): 1556–1563.

Leckman, James F. "Tourette's syndrome." *The Lancet* 360, no. 9345 (2002): 1577.

Lotan, Itay, Therese A. Treves, Yaniv Roditi, and Ruth Djaldetti. "Cannabis (medical marijuana) treatment for motor and non–motor symptoms of Parkinson disease: an open-label observational study." *Clinical Neuropharmacology* 37, no. 2 (2014): 41–44.

Lucas, Philippe, Amanda Reiman, Mitch Earleywine, Stephanie K. McGowan, Megan Oleson, Michael P. Coward, and Brian Thomas. "Cannabis as a substitute for alcohol and other drugs: a dispensary-based survey of substitution effect in Canadian medical cannabis patients." *Addiction Research & Theory* 21, no. 5 (2013): 435–442.

Maa, Edward, and Paige Figi. "The case for medical marijuana in epilepsy." *Epilepsia* 55, no. 6 (2014): 783–786.

Massa, Federico, Giovanni Marsicano, Heike Hermann, Astrid Cannich, Krisztina Monory, Benjamin F. Cravatt, Gian-Luca Ferri, Andrei Sibaev, Martin Storr, and Beat Lutz. "The endogenous cannabinoid system protects against colonic inflammation." *The Journal of Clinical Investigation* 113, no. 8 (2004): 1202–1209.

Merck Manual. 2017. http://www.merckmanuals.com

Merritt, John C., William J. Crawford, Paul C. Alexander, Alfred L. Anduze, and Solomon S. Gelbart. "Effect of marihuana on intraocular and blood pressure in glaucoma." *Ophthalmology* 87, no. 3 (1980): 222–228.

Moore, Theresa H. M., Stanley Zammit, Anne Lingford-Hughes, Thomas R. E. Barnes, Peter B. Jones, Margaret Burke, and Glyn Lewis. "Cannabis use and risk of psychotic or affective mental health outcomes: a systematic review." *The Lancet* 370, no. 9584 (2007): 319–328.

Müller-Vahl, Kirsten R. "Cannabinoids reduce symptoms of Tourette's syndrome." *Expert Opinion on Psychotherapy* 4, no. 10 (2003): 1717–1725.

Müller-Vahl, Kirsten R., Udo Schneider, A. Koblenz, M. Jöbges, H. Kolbe, T. Daldrup, and H.M. Emrich. "Treatment of Tourette's syndrome with Δ9-tetrahydrocannabinol (THC): a randomized cross-over trial." *Pharmacopsychiatry* 35, no. 02 (2002): 57–61.

Müller-Vahl, Kirsten R., Udo Schneider, Heidrun Prevedel, Karen Theloe, Hans Kolbe, Thomas Daldrup, and Hinderk M. Emrich. "Δ9-tetrahydrocannabinol (THC) is effective in the treatment of tics in Tourette syndrome: a 6-week randomized trial." *The Journal of Clinical Psychiatry* (2003): 1–7.

Naftali, Timna, Lihi Bar-Lev Schleider, Iris Dotan, Ephraim Philip Lansky, Fabiana Sklerovsky Benjaminov, and Fred Meir Konikoff. "Cannabis induces a clinical response in patients with Crohn's disease: a prospective placebo-controlled study." *Clinical Gastroenterology and Hepatology* 11, no. 10 (2013): 1276–1280.

National Institute of Neurological Disorders and Stroke. "Tourette Syndrome Information Page." Accessed May 5, 2017. https://www.ninds.nih .gov/Disorders/All-Disorders/Tourette-Syndrome-Information-Page

New York State Medical Marijuana Program. "Frequently asked questions." 2017. https://www.health.ny.gov/regulations/medical_marijuana/ faq.htm

Reiman, Amanda. "Cannabis as a substitute for alcohol and other drugs." *Harm Reduction Journal* 6, no. 1 (2009): 35.

Reinarman, Craig, Helen Nunberg, Fran Lanthier, and Tom Heddleston. "Who are medical marijuana patients? Population characteristics from nine California assessment clinics." *Journal of Psychoactive Drugs* 43, no. 2 (2011): 128–135.

Robson, Philip. "Therapeutic aspects of cannabis and cannabinoids." *The British Journal of Psychiatry* 178, no. 2 (2001): 107–115.

Sieradzan, K.A., S.H. Fox, M. Hill, J.P.R. Dick, A.R. Crossman, and J.M. Brotchie. "Cannabinoids reduce levodopa-induced dyskinesia in Parkinson's disease: a pilot study." *Neurology* 57, no. 11 (2001): 2108–2111.

Tomida, Ileana, Augusto Azuara-Blanco, Heather House, Maggie Flint, Roger G. Pertwee, and Philip J. Robson. "Effect of sublingual application of cannabinoids on intraocular pressure: a pilot study." *Journal of Glaucoma* 15, no. 5 (2006): 349–353.

Ware, Mark A., Tongtong Wang, Stan Shapiro, Ann Robinson, Thierry Ducruet, Thao Huynh, Ann Gamsa, Gary J. Bennett, and Jean-Paul Collet. "Smoked cannabis for chronic neuropathic pain: a randomized controlled trial." *Canadian Medical Association Journal* 182, no. 14 (2010): E694–E701.

Whiting, Penny F., Robert F. Wolff, Sohan Deshpande, Marcello Di Nisio, Steven Duffy, Adrian V. Hernandez, J. Christiaan Keurentjes et al. "Cannabinoids for medical use: a systematic review and meta-analysis." *JAMA* 313, no. 24 (2015): 2456–2473.

Q14. DOES MARIJUANA CAUSE CANCER?

Answer: The evidence is inconclusive. More research is needed to understand the associations between marijuana and cancer. Several lines of laboratory research suggest that marijuana smoke may be carcinogenic (potentially cancer-causing), and there is mixed observational evidence that marijuana smokers may be at an increased risk for developing some cancers. At the same time, research has shown that cannabinoids can inhibit the growth of certain tumor cells in laboratory and animal models. Other research has shown that cannabinoids can promote the growth of some cancer cells.

The Facts: Cancer is a group of diseases characterized by the rapid creation of abnormal cells (WHO 2017). Cancer is the second leading cause of death in the United States, with over 591,000 deaths in 2014 (CDC 2017). Each year there are millions of new cancer cases diagnosed in the United States, and it is estimated that nearly 40 percent of Americans will be diagnosed with cancer at some point in their lives (NIH 2017). Cancer is a genetic disease, but environmental factors—including substance use—can trigger the genetic changes that cause cancer. For example, a strong causal link has been identified between alcohol use and the development of various cancers, and cigarette smoking increases the risk of lung cancer by roughly 25 times (see Q10).

Researchers from diverse fields use a variety of methods to assess the link between marijuana and cancer. For example, experimental and laboratory researchers have investigated whether there are plausible mechanisms that could link marijuana or THC to cancer. These experiments sometimes involve exposing healthy organisms or cells to marijuana smoke or THC to see how they react. Observational researchers and epidemiologists explore links between marijuana use and cancer in the population. These studies help determine whether cancer rates are elevated among marijuana users. Finally, some researchers examine whether cannabinoids play a role in the treatment of cancer. This research primarily takes place in laboratory settings and involves observing how tumors or tumor cells respond to cannabinoid treatments.

PLAUSIBLE LINKS BETWEEN MARIJUANA AND CANCER

Multiple lines of evidence provide reason to suspect that marijuana smoke could play a role in the development of some human cancers. For example, marijuana smoke contains known carcinogens, including many of the same carcinogens found in tobacco smoke (Huang et al. 2015). Moreover, marijuana smokers often use a deeper inhalation technique to inhale a larger volume of smoke per inhalation than do tobacco smokers (Mehra et al. 2006). Research has also shown that, compared to cigarette smoking, marijuana smoking results in a greater deposition of tar in the respiratory tract (see Huang et al. 2015). Additionally, there is evidence that heavy marijuana smokers exhibit bronchial abnormalities, some of which may be associated with a pre-cancerous progression (Barsky et al. 1998).

Laboratory studies provide further evidence that marijuana smoke could be carcinogenic. For example, studies have shown that marijuana smoke can cause cellular mutations in the Ames test, which is a laboratory test that uses bacteria to assess whether chemicals are mutagenic (able to change genetic material like DNA) (see Owen et al. 2014; Hall and McPhee 2002). While the Ames test is not a direct test of carcinogenicity, a positive mutagenic response in the Ames test is predictive of carcinogenicity in rodents (Mortelmans and Zeiger 2000). Evidence also exists showing that marijuana smoke is mutagenic in rodent skin tests, and that marijuana tar has cancerous effects on mouse skin (see Hall et al. 2005; Owen et al. 2014). While marijuana smoke is implicated in both mutagenesis and carcinogenesis, research has shown that THC itself is not mutagenic in the Ames test and is not carcinogenic in rats or mice (Hall and MacPhee 2002; Chan et al. 1996).

OBSERVATIONAL EVIDENCE

While experimental and laboratory research can help determine whether a link between marijuana and cancer is plausible, it does not examine the link between marijuana use and cancer in the real world. Observational evidence is necessary to determine if marijuana users are at an increased risk for cancer. Since observational researchers do not manipulate or control research conditions, they face unique challenges related to inferring the existence of a causal relationship between two variables. As discussed in Q8, causation can be inferred from observational evidence only (1) when two variables are statistically associated, (2) when the causal variable temporally precedes the outcome variable, and (3) when alternative explanations for the observed association have been ruled out. In observational research, the final criterion of "nonspuriousness" is the most difficult to meet because marijuana use and tobacco smoking are often correlated. As a result, it can be difficult to parcel out the independent contribution that each behavior makes in the development of cancer.

Given that many people smoke marijuana, there are obvious concerns that it could, like smoked tobacco, lead to lung cancer. Despite these concerns, evidence indicates that a causal link does not exist between marijuana use and lung cancer (National Academies of Sciences, Engineering and Medicine 2017). There is no question that some studies have found that smoking marijuana increases the risk of lung cancer (e.g., Berthiller et al. 2008). However, when the accumulated evidence is combined in meta-analyses or review articles, the results generally indicate a lack of association between marijuana use and lung cancer or that the evidence is equivocal, inconclusive, or insufficient (e.g., Zhang et al. 2015; Huang et al. 2015; Bowles 2012; Owen et al. 2014).

Observational researchers have also explored the link between marijuana use and the development of head and neck cancers, which are additional sites in the human body that come into direct contact with marijuana smoke. Again, there is some evidence suggesting that heavy marijuana use is associated with an increased risk of cancer in the head and neck (e.g., Feng et al. 2009). However, the weight of evidence suggests a lack of association between marijuana use and incidence of head and neck cancer (National Academies of Science, Engineering and Medicine 2017). This conclusion is further supported by evidence from meta-analyses and review articles, which indicate that a causal link between marijuana use and the development of upper aerodigestive cancers has not been established or that the evidence is equivocal or inconclusive (de Carvalho et al. 2015; Huang et al. 2015; Bowles et al. 2012; Owen et al. 2014).

While there is reason to suspect that marijuana could have a carcinogenic effect in sites of the human body that come into direct contact with marijuana smoke, there is some evidence that marijuana use could increase the risk of cancer in other sites, as well. For example, several studies have shown a possible link between marijuana use and testicular germ cell tumors (Daling et al. 2009; Trabert et al. 2011; Lacson et al. 2012). In one study, a case-control design was used to compare 369 men with testicular germ cell tumors (TGCTs) with 979 aged-match controls (Daling et al. 2009). Even after controlling for possible confounders (age, alcohol use, and current smoking), current marijuana use was associated with a 70 percent increased risk of TGCT. In a meta-analysis published in

Cancer, Epidemiology, Biomarkers & Prevention, evidence from these three studies was combined to show that ever using marijuana was not associated with an increased risk for TGCT (Huang et al. 2015). However, smoking marijuana more than once per week and smoking for more than 10 years was associated with an increased risk for TGCT.

Research on the role of marijuana in the development of other cancers is mixed. For example, in a large study that examined the link between marijuana use and all cancers, researchers statistically controlled for sociodemographic factors, cigarette smoking, and alcohol use and found that marijuana use (ever used or current use) was not associated with increased risk of cancer of all sites (Sidney et al. 1997). However, among marijuana users who did not use tobacco, ever having used marijuana was associated with an increased risk of prostate cancer and possibly cervical cancer. Another large cohort study found an increased risk of malignant primary glioma among those individuals who reported smoking marijuana one or more times per month (Efird et al. 2004). In a case-control study of 52 men with transitional cell carcinoma, researchers found that smoking marijuana might increase the risk of bladder cancer (Chacko et al. 2006). These studies provide further evidence that heavy marijuana use might be a risk for certain cancers. However, it remains that more evidence is needed in order to support or refute a relationship between marijuana use and prostate cancer, cervical cancer, malignant gliomas, penile cancer, anal cancer, and bladder cancer (National Academies of Sciences, Engineering and Medicine 2017).

ANTITUMOR EFFECTS OF CANNABINOIDS

Over half of the states in the United States have laws allowing some form of medical marijuana, and cancer is a common qualifying condition for medical marijuana use. As discussed in Q12, two FDA-approved pharmaceuticals, dronabinol and nabilone, are used to treat nausea and vomiting associated with chemotherapy, and there is evidence that smoked marijuana may also relieve these symptoms in some patients. Moreover, physician surveys have demonstrated that some internists and oncologists are interested in having the ability to recommend botanical marijuana to cancer patients for symptom management (see Bowles et al. 2012).

In addition to providing symptomatic relief for cancer patients, cannabinoids may eventually play a role in the treatment of cancer. While results from this line of research have been promising, there is currently no evidence that marijuana or cannabinoids are an effective treatment for cancer (National Academies of Sciences, Engineering and Medicine

2017). Rather, there is initial evidence from cellular and molecular experiments that cannabinoids may have clinically relevant antitumoral properties. These studies generally examine the effects of cannabinoids on tumor-bearing laboratory animals or on tumor cells. Results indicate that cannabinoids play a role in inducing tumor cell death, inhibiting tumor cell growth, reducing tumor size, and inhibiting metastasis (see Guzman 2003; Rocha et al. 2013). On the other hand, there is also evidence that THC can have a pro-cancerous effect in certain cancer cell lines (Cridge and Rosenberg 2013).

A seminal study by Manuel Guzman and colleagues (2006) published in the *British Journal of Cancer* examined the antitumoral actions of cannabinoids in human patients. Nine patients with terminal malignant brain tumors for whom surgery and radiotherapy had not been successful were chosen for the study. The medical team used a specialized catheter to administer a solution of THC directly into a surgically created cavity in the tumor. The primary goal of this research was to assess the safety of intracranial THC administration in humans. The researchers concluded that the intracranial administration of THC was safely achieved without overt psychoactive effects. The researchers also observed that THC inhibited tumor cell proliferation in biopsied tumor cell cultures. This early research may open the door for additional human trials wherein cannabinoids, or a combination of cannabinoids and other drugs, could be directly administered into tumor sites.

As shown in Q12, marijuana has low toxicity and is currently used by cancer patients receiving chemotherapy to treat nausea and vomiting. As a result, researchers are optimistic that the antitumoral effects of cannabinoids can continue to be assessed in humans without putting patients at risk. While marijuana, THC, and other cannabinoids may or may not turn out to be effective cancer treatments in humans, research investigating the role of cannabinoids in cancer treatment has contributed to a growing knowledge of how the endocannabinoid system plays an important role in cell proliferation, cell death, and cell signaling (see Guzman 2003). Cancer treatment has been notoriously difficult, and researchers are hopeful that additional research will help clarify the potential role of cannabinoids in the treatment of cancer.

FURTHER READING

Barsky, Sanford H., Michael D. Roth, Eric C. Kleerup, Michael Simmons, and Donald P. Tashkin. "Histopathologic and molecular alterations in bronchial epithelium in habitual smokers of marijuana, cocaine, and/or tobacco." *Journal of the National Cancer Institute* 90, no. 16 (1998): 1198–1205.

Berthiller, Julien, Kurt Straif, Mathieu Boniol, Nicolas Voirin, Veronique Benhaïm-Luzon, Wided Ben Ayoub, Iman Dari et al. "Cannabis smoking and risk of lung cancer in men: a pooled analysis of three studies in Maghreb." *Journal of Thoracic Oncology* 3, no. 12 (2008): 1398–1403.

Bowles, Daniel W., Cindy L. O'Bryant, D. Ross Camidge, and Antonio Jimeno. "The intersection between cannabis and cancer in the United States." *Critical Reviews in Oncology/Hematology* 83, no. 1 (2012): 1–10.

Centers for Disease Control and Prevention. "Deaths and Mortality." *National Center for Health Statistics.* 2017. https://www.cdc.gov/nchs/fastats/deaths.htm

Chacko, Julie A., Jared G. Heiner, Wendy Siu, Marie Macy, and Martha K. Terris. "Association between marijuana use and transitional cell carcinoma." *Urology* 67, no. 1 (2006): 100–104.

Chan, P.C., R.C. Sills, A.G. Braun, J.K. Haseman, and J.R. Bucher. "Toxicity and carcinogenicity of Δ9-tetrahydrocannabinol in Fischer rats and B6C3F1 mice." *Toxicological Sciences* 30, no. 1 (1996): 109–117.

Cridge, Belinda J., and Rhonda J. Rosengren. "Critical appraisal of the potential use of cannabinoids in cancer management." *Cancer Manag Res* 5 (2013): 301–313.

Daling, Janet R., David R. Doody, Xiaofei Sun, Britton L. Trabert, Noel S. Weiss, Chu Chen, Mary L. Biggs, Jacqueline R. Starr, Sudhansu K. Dey, and Stephen M. Schwartz. "Association of marijuana use and the incidence of testicular germ cell tumors." *Cancer* 115, no. 6 (2009): 1215–1223.

de Carvalho, M. F. F., M. R. Dourado, I. B. Fernandes, C. T. P. Araújo, A. T. Mesquita, and M. L. Ramos-Jorge. "Head and neck cancer among marijuana users: A meta-analysis of matched case–control studies." *Archives of Oral Biology* 60, no. 12 (2015): 1750–1755.

Efird, Jimmy T., Gary D. Friedman, Stephen Sidney, Arthur Klatsky, Laurel A. Habel, Natalia V. Udaltsova, Stephen Van Den Eeden, and Lorene M. Nelson. "The risk for malignant primary adult-onset glioma in a large, multiethnic, managed-care cohort: cigarette smoking and other lifestyle behaviors." *Journal of Neuro-Oncology* 68, no. 1 (2004): 57–69.

Feng, B.J., M. Khyatti, W. Ben-Ayoub, S. Dahmoul, M. Ayad, F. Maachi, W. Bedadra, et al. "Cannabis, tobacco and domestic fumes intake are associated with nasopharyngeal carcinoma in North Africa." *British Journal of Cancer* 101, no. 7 (2009): 1207–1212.

Guzman, Manuel. "Cannabinoids: potential anticancer agents." *Nature Reviews Cancer* 3, no. 10 (2003): 745–755.

Guzman, Manuel, M.J. Duarte, C. Blazquez, J. Ravina, M.C. Rosa, I. Galve-Roperh, C. Sanchez, G. Velasco, and L. Gonzalez-Feria. "A pilot clinical study of Δ9-tetrahydrocannabinol in patients with recurrent glioblastoma multiforme." *British Journal of Cancer* 95, no. 2 (2006): 197–203.

Hall, Wayne, MacDonald Christie, and David Currow. "Cannabinoids and cancer: causation, remediation, and palliation." *The Lancet Oncology* 6, no. 1 (2005): 35–42.

Hall, Wayne, and Donald MacPhee. "Cannabis use and cancer." *Addiction* 97, no. 3 (2002): 243–247.

Hashibe, Mia, Hal Morgenstern, Yan Cui, Donald P. Tashkin, Zuo-Feng Zhang, Wendy Cozen, Thomas M. Mack, and Sander Greenland. "Marijuana use and the risk of lung and upper aerodigestive tract cancers: results of a population-based case-control study." *Cancer Epidemiology and Prevention Biomarkers* 15, no. 10 (2006): 1829–1834.

Huang, Yu-Hui Jenny, Zuo-Feng Zhang, Donald P. Tashkin, Bingjian Feng, Kurt Straif, and Mia Hashibe. "An epidemiologic review of marijuana and cancer: an update." *Cancer Epidemiology Biomarkers & Prevention* 24, no. 1 (2015): 15–31.

Lacson, John Charles A., Joshua D. Carroll, Ellenie Tuazon, Esteban J. Castelao, Leslie Bernstein, and Victoria K. Cortessis. "Population-based case-control study of recreational drug use and testis cancer risk confirms an association between marijuana use and nonseminoma risk." *Cancer* 118, no. 21 (2012): 5374–5383.

Mehra, Reena, Brent A. Moore, Kristina Crothers, Jeanette Tetrault, and David A. Fiellin. "The association between marijuana smoking and lung cancer: a systematic review." *Archives of Internal Medicine* 166, no. 13 (2006): 1359–1367.

Mortelmans, Kristien, and Errol Zeiger. "The Ames Salmonella/microsome mutagenicity assay." *Mutation Research/Fundamental and Molecular Mechanisms of Mutagenesis* 455, no. 1 (2000): 29–60.

National Academies of Sciences, Engineering, and Medicine. *The health effects of cannabis and cannabinoids: the current state of evidence and recommendations for research.* Washington, DC: The National Academies Press, 2017.

National Cancer Institute. "Cancer Statistics." *National Institutes of Health.* 2017. https://www.cancer.gov/about-cancer/understanding/statistics

Owen, Kelly P., Mark E. Sutter, and Timothy E. Albertson. "Marijuana: respiratory tract effects." *Clinical Reviews in Allergy & Immunology* 46, no. 1 (2014): 65–81.

Rocha, Francisco Carlos Machado, Jair Guilherme dos Santos Júnior, Sergio Carlos Stefano, and Dartiu Xavier da Silveira. "Systematic review of the literature on clinical and experimental trials on the antitumor effects of cannabinoids in gliomas." *Journal of Neuro-Oncology* 116, no. 1 (2014): 11–24.

Sidney, Stephen, Charles P. Quesenberry Jr., Gary D. Friedman, and Irene S. Tekawa. "Marijuana use and cancer incidence (California, United States)." *Cancer Causes & Control* 8, no. 5 (1997): 722–728.

Trabert, Britton, Alice J. Sigurdson, Anne M. Sweeney, Sara S. Strom, and Katherine A. McGlynn. "Marijuana use and testicular germ cell tumors." *Cancer* 117, no. 4 (2011): 848–853.

World Health Organization. "Cancer." 2017. http://www.who.int/mediacentre/factsheets/fs297/en/

Zhang, Li Rita, Hal Morgenstern, Sander Greenland, Shen-Chih Chang, Philip Lazarus, M. Dawn Teare, Penella J. Woll, et al. "Cannabis smoking and lung cancer risk: pooled analysis in the International Lung Cancer Consortium." *International Journal of Cancer* 136, no. 4 (2015): 894–903.

Q15. IS MARIJUANA ADDICTIVE?

Answer: It depends on how addiction is defined. Empirical evidence from diverse fields shows that some marijuana users have trouble controlling their use, continue to use marijuana despite persistent problems related to that use, experience unpleasant symptoms during abstinence following heavy use, and have trouble maintaining abstinence. Additionally, there is a growing body of neurobiological research highlighting some important ways that marijuana mirrors other addictive substances in how it affects neural and biological processes. However, in addition to this evidence there is likewise a compelling body of research suggesting that marijuana should not be considered alongside other more addictive substances such as opiates, stimulants, nicotine, and alcohol. For example, unlike other forms of addiction, problematic marijuana use rarely involves severe physical dependence, and marijuana withdrawal is characterized by fewer severe symptoms compared to withdrawal from other substances. In addition, the dependence liability of marijuana is much lower than the dependence liability of other substances—meaning that marijuana users are less likely than users of other drugs to transition from recreational use to problematic use.

The Facts: In the debate over the addictiveness of marijuana, it is often compared to other addictive drugs, such as alcohol, tobacco, stimulants, and opioids. Marijuana protagonists and marijuana prohibitionists both draw heavily on these comparisons in their respective claims about the addictiveness of marijuana. Prohibitionists cite evidence that marijuana—like alcohol, tobacco, stimulants, and opioids—can lead to symptoms of addiction, dependence, and withdrawal. Protagonists cite evidence showing that addictive liability of marijuana is less severe than that of other substances. Implicit in these types of comparisons is a common notion of addiction that can be applied in all instances of compulsive and problematic substance use.

Most researchers and clinicians think of addiction in terms of the specific diagnostic criteria outlined by the American Psychiatric Association (APA) in the *Diagnostic and Statistical Manual of Mental Disorders* (DSM). Significant changes were made between the fourth and fifth editions of the DSM with regard to how problematic substance use is defined and diagnosed. In the fourth edition (DSM-IV), a distinction was made between *substance dependence* and *substance abuse*—each diagnosed according to separate criteria (see Q1 for those criteria). In the fifth edition (DSM-5), a distinction is no longer made between *substance dependence* and *substance abuse*. Instead the diagnosis of *substance use disorder* (i.e., cannabis use disorder) is made according to 11 criteria relating to impaired control, social impairment, risky use, and pharmacologic criteria. While the DSM-5 diagnosis of substance use disorder is increasingly used by clinicians, some researchers continue to use the DSM-IV criteria and definitions in order to make comparisons with historical data.

DSM-5 DIAGNOSTIC CRITERIA FOR MARIJUANA (CANNABIS) USE DISORDER

Impaired Control	
	There is a persistent desire or unsuccessful effort to cut down or control use of marijuana.
	Marijuana is often taken in larger amounts or over a longer period than was intended.

(Continued)

	A great deal of time is spent in activities necessary to obtain, use, or recover from marijuana.
	Craving, or a strong desire to use marijuana.
Social Impairment	
	Recurrent use of marijuana resulting in a failure to fulfill major role obligations at work, school, or home.
	Continued use of marijuana despite having persistent or recurrent social or interpersonal problems caused or exacerbated by the effects of its use.
	Important social, occupational, or recreational activities are given up or reduced because of marijuana use.
Risky Use	
	Recurrent use of marijuana in situations in which it is physically hazardous.
	Use of marijuana is continued despite knowledge of having a persistent or recurrent physical or psychological problem that is likely to have been caused or exacerbated by the substance.
Pharmacological Criteria	
	Tolerance, as defined by either a need for markedly increased amounts of marijuana to achieve intoxication or desired effect, or a markedly diminished effect with continued use of the same amount of marijuana.
	Withdrawal, as manifested by either the characteristic withdrawal syndrome for marijuana or the substance is taken to relieve or avoid withdrawal symptoms.

Source: DSM-5, NIDA https://www.drugabuse.gov/publications/media-guide/science-drug-abuse-addiction-basics

HUMAN EVIDENCE

A key issue related to marijuana's addictive liability is whether or not it causes physical dependence and withdrawal in humans. Dependence and withdrawal occur when the human body adapts to the prolonged exposure to particular drugs—including legal drugs. In basic terms, these adaptations are the body's attempt to maintain balance. When heavy substance use disrupts the body's balance, the organism adjusts in order to restore balance. When a person is dependent on drugs or alcohol it means that his or her body has found ways of adapting to the chronic use of that substance, and his or her body now depends on the substance in order to maintain this newly found balance. In the abrupt absence of alcohol or certain drugs, the body is thrown out of balance. The result is known as withdrawal.

A central argument made by those who believe that marijuana is not addictive is that marijuana dependence and withdrawal have a psychological—but not a physiological—basis. The suggestion is that marijuana withdrawal may be uncomfortable or upsetting, but it does not cause clinically relevant medical, physical, or somatic symptoms comparable to the symptoms that accompany the withdrawal from more addictive substances. For example, serious flu-like symptoms, abdominal cramps, vomiting, and diarrhea can accompany withdrawal from opiates; seizures have been reported during withdrawal from benzodiazepines; and hypertension, tremors, fever, headache, and seizures can accompany withdrawal from alcohol (Hu 2011; Hyman et al. 2006; Mckeon et al. 2008; Kosten and O'Connor 2003). These types of medical problems are indicative of dependence and are rarely seen following abstinence from marijuana. However, there is evidence from both humans and animals that marijuana withdrawal can produce a host of unpleasant symptoms, and that these symptoms likely have a neural and physiological basis. Moreover, there is emerging evidence that the processes that underlie marijuana dependence and withdrawal are indeed similar to those observed with other substances (see Maldonado and de Fonseco 2002 for review).

Cannabis Dependence and Withdrawal

It was long believed that marijuana did not produce clinically significant withdrawal symptoms. This view was reflected in the fact that the DSM-IV did not include a cannabis withdrawal disorder diagnosis (Budney 2011). However, recent research has challenged this view, and the DSM-5 now recognizes a cannabis withdrawal syndrome with defined criteria (Hesse and Thylstrup 2013). Multiple research studies have shown that some heavy users of marijuana experience emotional, behavioral, and some physical symptoms during periods of abstinence. These symptoms include nervousness, irritability, depression, craving, tension, restlessness, sleep disturbances, and appetite change (e.g., Budney et al. 2004; Cornelius et al. 2008; Arendt et al. 2007). For example, a 2008 study examined the prevalence of cannabis withdrawal symptoms among a nationally representative sample and found that over 40 percent of frequent marijuana users reported experiencing two or more cannabis withdrawal symptoms following cessation (Hasin et al. 2008). In another 2008 study, 29 percent of past-year marijuana users reported experiencing at least two withdrawal symptoms (Agrawal et al. 2008). For those users who experience cannabis withdrawal, symptoms generally begin one to three days after cessation, and last one to two weeks (Budney et al. 2004).

The symptoms of marijuana dependence are generally considered less severe than those associated with other substance use disorders, and research has shown that cannabis withdrawal symptoms are primarily emotional and behavioral (Budney 2007; Budney et al. 2004). Moreover, cannabis withdrawal symptoms generally do not include medical or physical symptoms comparable to those observed in opioid, sedative, or alcohol withdrawal (Budney and Hughes 2006). While cannabis withdrawal symptoms are generally less severe than withdrawal symptoms from other substances, many researchers believe that the symptoms have clear clinical significance. For example, research has shown that cannabis withdrawal symptoms are associated with the rapid reinstatement of dependence symptoms (Cornelius et al. 2008). However, other research has also shown that cannabis withdrawal symptoms do not predict relapse to cannabis use (Arendt et al. 2007).

The preceding evidence indicates that some marijuana users experience emotional and behavioral withdrawal symptoms. In addition to this evidence, there is a growing body of neurobiological research that is helping researchers understand more about marijuana addiction, dependence, and withdrawal. For example, there is converging evidence that "natural rewards and addictive drugs alike influence behavior as a result of their ability to increase synaptic dopamine in the nucleus accumbens (NAc), the major component of the ventral striatum" (Hyman et al. 2006, 571). Research has shown, for instance, that amphetamine, cocaine, alcohol, and nicotine use are all associated with increased dopamine levels in the human striatum. A 2009 study was the first of its kind to demonstrate that THC also induces dopamine release in the human striatum (Bossong et al. 2009).

This provides some evidence that marijuana use affects brain reward pathways in ways that mirror other substances.

Human Self-Administration

Arguably, the rewarding and reinforcing effects of marijuana are demonstrated by the fact that many people use and misuse marijuana. In 2015, for example, there were an estimated 22.2 million Americans ages 12 and older who used marijuana in the past month, and there were an estimated 4 million Americans ages 12 and older who met the clinical criteria for marijuana use disorder (CBHSQ 2016). Laboratory research with human subjects confirms the commonsense notion that marijuana and THC can be rewarding and are self-administered by some human subjects (see Cooper and Haney 2008 for review). Moreover, human self-administration studies frequently show that research participants prefer higher THC concentrations (ibid.).

Observational research provides further evidence that marijuana, and other drugs, are misused by a subset of drug users. Data from the 1990s, for example, indicated that about 9 percent of people who ever smoked cannabis developed dependence (Anthony et al. 1994). The same data showed that about 32 percent of tobacco users developed dependence, while 23 percent of heroin users, 17 percent of cocaine users, 15 percent of alcohol users, and 11 percent of stimulant users developed dependence. These findings are confirmed by more recent evidence. Drawing on data from the National Epidemiologic Survey on Alcohol and Related Conditions, researchers found that the probability of transitioning from first use to dependence was lower for marijuana than for nicotine, alcohol, and cocaine (Lopez-Quintero et al. 2011). The researchers estimated that about 9 percent of marijuana users would become dependent at some point. Other substance users had higher probabilities of transitioning from first use to dependence. It was estimated that 68 percent of nicotine users, 23 percent of alcohol users, and 21 percent of cocaine users would become dependent at some point.

ANIMAL MODELS

Research using laboratory animals is also used to examine how various substances can lead to symptoms of dependence or withdrawal. These experimental paradigms allow researchers to manipulate experimental conditions in such a way that would not be possible in research using human subjects. As a result, there are many questions regarding the effects of cannabinoids that are best investigated using animal models. Critics of this research believe that neither the animals nor the manipulated experimental conditions to which they are exposed accurately mirror the real-world conditions of humans.

Animal Self-Administration

One way to evaluate the rewarding properties of drugs is to observe whether laboratory animals self-administer drugs under varied research conditions. In these paradigms, animals are given opportunities to self-administer a drug by pressing a lever or inserting their nose into a specific hole. Extensive scientific evidence shows that laboratory animals will self-administer psychostimulants, narcotics, ethanol, and nicotine (Panagis and Nomikos 2008; Tanda and Goldberg 2003). There is only mixed evidence that laboratory animals will self-administer THC and other cannabinoids.

Many early studies did not observe cannabinoid self-administration among laboratory animals, and until relatively recently, there were only a few studies showing that animals would self-administer THC or synthetic cannabinoids (see Cooper and Haney 2008). For example, whereas earlier studies found that rhesus monkeys would not consistently self-administer intravenous THC, recent reports have shown that low-dose THC is intravenously self-administered by cocaine-experienced and drug-naïve monkeys (Justinova et al. 2003; Tanda et al. 2000; see Cooper and Haney 2008). Similarly, early studies observed THC self-administration among food-deprived rats, but there was less evidence of rodent self-administration under other research conditions. However, a 2005 study observed the self-administration of low-dose THC in fed and watered Wistar rats (Braida et al. 2004).

Some of the evidence showing that animals will self-administer cannabinoids has been gathered under experimental conditions which might limit the generalizability of the findings (see Justinova et al. 2003; Cooper and Haney 2009). For example, THC self-administration has been observed in experiments using physically restrained mice and food-deprived rats (see Justinova et al. 2003). Under such conditions, animals may have an increased appetite for the analgesic properties of THC (ibid.). Similarly, early evidence demonstrating the self-administration of THC among primates was observed in monkeys which had previously been given cocaine (Tanda et al. 2000). However, animals with a history of cocaine administration may differ in important ways from drug-naïve animals. Nevertheless, there is recent evidence that drug-naïve squirrel monkeys and rodents will intravenously self-administer THC (Justinova et al. 2003).

Conditioned Place Preference

Another way to evaluate the reinforcing properties of drugs is in the *conditioned place preference* paradigm. These procedures test whether animals have a preference for, or an aversion to, environments that have been paired with certain drugs. Most drugs of abuse have been shown to increase the time animals spend in the drug-paired environment (see Panagis and Nomikos 2008). Conditioned place preference experiments with THC and other cannabinoids have yielded inconsistent results (see Tanda and Goldberg 2003). Indeed, several reviews have found that THC can produce both conditioned place preferences and aversions in rats and mice, depending on the experimental parameters (Fattore et al. 2008; Murray and Bevins 2010). In addition, there is some evidence that high doses of cannabinoids can have an aversive effect, while lower doses can have a rewarding effect (Murray and Bevins 2010; Cooper and Haney 2008).

Dependence and Withdrawal in Animal Models

Two research paradigms are commonly used to examine substance dependence and withdrawal in animals. The first method involves a spontaneous *abstinence withdrawal* procedure, while the second method involves an *antagonist-precipitated withdrawal* procedure (Panagis et al. 2008). The *abstinence withdrawal* procedure mimics a 'cold turkey' approach to abstinence. Animals are given repeated doses of a particular drug, and researchers observe the animals while the drug is abruptly discontinued. Rodents, pigeons, dogs, and monkeys do not generally exhibit physical withdrawal symptoms during periods of spontaneous abstinence from THC (Maldonado 2002; Panagis et al. 2008). The absence of spontaneous withdrawal symptoms after the discontinuation of chronic THC exposure may be due to the slow elimination of THC from the body (Panagis et al. 2008).

While *abstinence withdrawal* symptoms do not generally follow the abrupt discontinuation of THC, there is evidence from research using the *antagonist-precipitated withdrawal* paradigm that THC dependency and withdrawal may involve biochemical processes similar to those involved in other forms of dependency and withdrawal. In pharmacologic terms, *agonists* bind to receptors and initiate a response, while *antagonists* prevent agonists from binding to receptors, thereby limiting receptor activation. In everyday terms, when THC or other cannabinoid agonists are administered, they can be thought of as keys that fit into cannabinoid receptors, activating a chain of events leading to the psychoactive effects of THC. Cannabinoid receptor antagonists, on the other hand, block the keyhole and dampen the actions of the agonist (Bradley 2014). The *antagonist-precipitated withdrawal* paradigm involves chronically exposing animals to cannabinoid agonists (e.g., THC) and then suddenly exposing them to cannabinoid antagonists (e.g., CB1 antagonist SR 141716A). Under these conditions, the chronic activation of cannabinoid receptors is suddenly interrupted with the introduction of the antagonist. Research using cannabinoid agonists and antagonists in this paradigm have observed that rodents display a host of somatic symptoms including wet dog shakes, head shakes, facial rubbing, front paw tremor, and body tremor (Maldonado and Fonseca 2002). Because THC is eliminated slowly from the body under normal abstinence conditions, the symptoms of withdrawal demonstrated using the *antagonist-precipitated withdrawal* paradigm are unlikely under everyday circumstances. Nevertheless, this research lends additional credence to the notion that cannabinoid dependence and withdrawal likely have a physiological basis.

FURTHER READING

Agrawal, Arpana, Michele L. Pergadia, and Michael T. Lynskey. "Is there evidence for symptoms of cannabis withdrawal in the national epidemiologic survey of alcohol and related conditions?" *American Journal on Addictions* 17, no. 3 (2008): 199–208.

American Psychiatric Association. *Diagnostic and statistical manual of mental disorders (DSM-5®).* Arlington, VA: American Psychiatric Publishing, 2013.

American Psychiatric Association. *Diagnostic criteria from DSM-IV-tr.* American Psychiatric Publications, 2000.

Anthony, James C., Lynn A. Warner, and Ronald C. Kessler. "Comparative epidemiology of dependence on tobacco, alcohol, controlled substances, and inhalants: basic findings from the National Comorbidity Survey." *Experimental and Clinical Psychopharmacology* 2, no. 3 (1994): 244.

Arendt, Mikkel, Raben Rosenberg, Leslie Foldager, Leo Sher, and Povl Munk-Jørgensen. "Withdrawal symptoms do not predict relapse among subjects treated for cannabis dependence." *American Journal on Addictions* 16, no. 6 (2007): 461–467.

Bossong, Matthijs G., Bart NM van Berckel, Ronald Boellaard, Lineke Zuurman, Robert C. Schuit, Albert D. Windhorst, Joop MA van Gerven, Nick F. Ramsey, Adriaan A. Lammertsma, and René S. Kahn. "Δ9-tetrahydrocannabinol induces dopamine release in the human striatum." *Neuropsychopharmacology* 34, no. 3 (2009): 759–766.

Bradley, Joseph J. *Addiction: from suffering to solution.* Breaux Press International, 2014.

Braida, Daniela, Stefania Iosue, Simona Pegorini, and Mariaelvina Sala. "Δ9-tetrahydrocannabinol-induced conditioned place preference and intracerebroventricular self-administration in rats." *European Journal of Pharmacology* 506, no. 1 (2004): 63–69.

Budney, Alan J. "Should cannabis withdrawal disorder be included in DSM-5? New studies call for more research on helping patients quit marijuana." *Psychiatric Times* 28, no. 2 (2011): 48–48.

Budney, Alan J., and John R. Hughes. "The cannabis withdrawal syndrome." *Current Opinion in Psychiatry* 19, no. 3 (2006): 233–238.

Budney, Alan J., John R. Hughes, Brent A. Moore, and Ryan Vandrey. "Review of the validity and significance of cannabis withdrawal syndrome." *American Journal of Psychiatry* 161, no. 11 (2004): 1967–1977.

Budney, Alan J., Roger Roffman, Robert S. Stephens, and Denise Walker. "Marijuana dependence and its treatment." *Addiction Science & Clinical Practice* 4, no. 1 (2007): 4.

Center for Behavioral Health Statistics and Quality. *2015 National Survey on Drug Use and Health: detailed tables.* Rockville, MD: Substance Abuse and Mental Health Services Administration, 2016.

Cooper, Ziva D., and Margaret Haney. "Cannabis reinforcement and dependence: role of the cannabinoid CB1 receptor." *Addiction Biology* 13, no. 2 (2008): 188–195.

Cornelius, Jack R., Tammy Chung, Christopher Martin, D. Scott Wood, and Duncan B. Clark. "Cannabis withdrawal is common among treatment-seeking adolescents with cannabis dependence and major depression, and is associated with rapid relapse to dependence." *Addictive Behaviors* 33, no. 11 (2008): 1500–1505.

Fattore, L., P. Fadda, M. S. Spano, M. Pistis, and W. Fratta. "Neurobiological mechanisms of cannabinoid addiction." *Molecular and Cellular Endocrinology* 286, no. 1 (2008): S97–S107.

Gardner, Eliot L. "Endocannabinoid signaling system and brain reward: emphasis on dopamine." *Pharmacology Biochemistry and Behavior* 81, no. 2 (2005): 263–284.

Hasin, Deborah S., Katherine M. Keyes, Donald Alderson, Shuang Wang, Efrat Aharonovich, and Bridget F. Grant. "Cannabis withdrawal in the United States: a general population study." *The Journal of Clinical Psychiatry* 69, no. 9 (2008): 1354.

Hesse, Morten, and Birgitte Thylstrup. "Time-course of the DSM-5 cannabis withdrawal symptoms in poly-substance abusers." *BMC Psychiatry* 13, no. 1 (2013): 258.

Hu, Xiaohong. "Benzodiazepine withdrawal seizures and management." *The Journal of the Oklahoma State Medical Association* 104, no. 2 (2011): 62–65.

Hyman, Steven E., Robert C. Malenka, and Eric J. Nestler. "Neural mechanisms of addiction: the role of reward-related learning and memory." *Annual Review of Neuroscience* 29 (2006): 565–598.

Justinova Z., G. Tanda, G. H. Redhi, S. R. Goldberg. Self-administration of Delta (9)-tetrahydrocannabinol (THC) by drug naive squirrel monkeys. *Psychopharmacology* (Berl) 169 (2003): 135–140. [PubMed:12827345]

Kosten, Thomas R., and Patrick G. O'Connor. "Management of drug and alcohol withdrawal." *New England Journal of Medicine* 348, no. 18 (2003): 1786–1795.

Lopez-Quintero, Catalina, José Pérez de los Cobos, Deborah S. Hasin, Mayumi Okuda, Shuai Wang, Bridget F. Grant, and Carlos Blanco. "Probability and predictors of transition from first use to dependence on nicotine, alcohol, cannabis, and cocaine: results of the National Epidemiologic Survey on Alcohol and Related Conditions (NESARC)." *Drug and Alcohol Dependence* 115, no. 1 (2011): 120–130.

Maldonado, Rafael. "Study of cannabinoid dependence in animals." *Pharmacology & Therapeutics* 95, no. 2 (2002): 153–164.

Maldonado, Rafael, and Fernando Rodriguez de Fonseca. "Cannabinoid addiction: behavioral models and neural correlates." *The Journal of Neuroscience* 22, no. 9 (2002): 3326–3331.

McKeon, Andrew, Mark A. Frye, and Norman Delanty. "The alcohol withdrawal syndrome." *Journal of Neurology, Neurosurgery & Psychiatry* 79, no. 8 (2008): 854–862.

Murray, Jennifer E., and Rick A. Bevins. "Cannabinoid conditioned reward and aversion: behavioral and neural processes." *ACS Chemical Neuroscience* 1, no. 4 (2010): 265–278.

National Institute on Drug Abuse. "The science of drug abuse and addiction: the basics." 2016. https://www.drugabuse.gov/publications/media-guide/science-drug-abuse-addiction-basics

Panagis, George, Styliani Vlachou, and George G. Nomikos. "Behavioral pharmacology of cannabinoids with a focus on preclinical models for studying reinforcing and dependence-producing properties." *Current Drug Abuse Reviews* 1, no. 3 (2008): 350–374.

Sussman, Steve, Nadra Lisha, and Mark Griffiths. "Prevalence of the addictions: a problem of the majority or the minority?" *Evaluation & the Health Professions* 34, no. 1 (2011): 3–56.

Tanda, Gianluigi, and Steven R. Goldberg. "Cannabinoids: reward, dependence, and underlying neurochemical mechanisms—a review of recent preclinical data." *Psychopharmacology* 169, no. 2 (2003): 115–134.

Tanda, Gianluigi, Patrik Munzar, and Steven R. Goldberg. "Self-administration behavior is maintained by the psychoactive ingredient of marijuana in squirrel monkeys." *Nature Neuroscience* 3, no. 11 (2000): 1073–1074.

3

❖

Policy Considerations

Q16. WAS MARIJUANA CRIMINALIZED TO PROTECT PUBLIC HEALTH AND SAFETY?

Answer: Yes, but the first marijuana prohibitions were enacted during a period when the dangers of the drug were misrepresented or misunderstood. Marijuana is not a harmless drug, and even modern-day marijuana protagonists generally acknowledge that heavy marijuana use can be risky. However, during the time when the first marijuana laws were passed, the dangers related to the drug were greatly exaggerated, and these exaggerations played an important role in the formation of early marijuana laws. In the early part of the twentieth century marijuana gained a reputation as a drug that caused violence, crime, escalation to other drug use, insanity, debauchery, depravity, and addiction. While many of these sensationalized claims have been debunked, enduring fears about marijuana continue to affect public opinion and public policy.

The Facts: The Marihuana Tax Act of 1937 was the first federal law restricting the possession of marijuana, and was passed amid exaggerated concerns over marijuana and the people who used it. In the first part of the twentieth century, the practice of smoking marijuana was not widespread, and the use of the drug was primarily associated with Spanish-speakers, African Americans, and lower-strata social groups. Marijuana (or "marihuana") also became associated with violence, crime, insanity, and debauchery, and was accordingly labeled the "marihuana menace," the "killer weed," the "assassin of youth," and the "jazz weed." The years surrounding the passage of the Marihuana Tax Act are sometimes referred to as the Reefer Madness era, because news reports, movies, law enforcement officials, and government testimonies made exaggerated claims about marijuana and marijuana users. The Federal Bureau of Narcotics and its first commissioner, Harry J. Anslinger, played a key role in the campaign against marijuana. However, fears over marijuana existed well before the Bureau was established in 1930. Marijuana's image as the "killer weed" persisted until the 1960s when new fears emerged that marijuana was a "dropout drug" that destroyed ambition among America's youth.

DRUG SCARES IN AMERICAN HISTORY

Historical accounts from the early twentieth century show that reactions to marijuana were out of proportion to the objective threats posed by the drug and those who smoked it. Historians and social scientists have pointed out that it is not uncommon for a social problem to be depicted by the media, law enforcement, politicians, and the public in such a way that is "above and beyond what a sober empirical assessment of its concrete danger would sustain" (Goode and Ben-Yehuda 1994, 156). These inflated concerns have been called "moral panics" (ibid.). When a moral panic is in reaction to fears over a psychoactive substance, the phenomenon is known as a "drug scare" or "drug panic" (see Reinarman 2011). Drug scares can, and sometimes do, emerge independent of any actual changes in problematic drug use.

To understand drug scares, a key question must be asked: if a drug scare occurs in the absence of substantial drug problems, what is the cause of the drug scare? This question is relevant to the heightened alarm over marijuana during the Reefer Madness era, since marijuana use did not become widespread in the United States until the 1960s (Dennis et al. 2002). While each drug scare emerges within unique historical circumstances, Craig Reinarman (2011) proposes that many drug scares in the United States have shared common characteristics. For example, many drug scares contain *a kernel of truth* that becomes the basis for exaggerated fears; and these fears are often aggravated by a process of *media magnification*. Powerful individuals or groups also play a key role in drug scares. *Politico-moral entrepreneurs* create or magnify the drug problem, and *professional interest groups* lobby to control or influence the drug problem. Oftentimes, there is an *historical context of conflict* that provides fertile soil for the drug scare to grow; and in many cases, a *dangerous class* of people who are perceived as disreputable or threatening are *scapegoated* or blamed—along with the drug—for existing social problems.

An unfortunate legacy of many drug scares lives on in the codification of policies and practices that disproportionately affect certain social groups. In some cases, responses to drug-related problems have been described as the basis for minority oppression and mass incarceration (Helmer 1975; Alexander 2012). Even in the absence of overt racism, history has shown that drugs often become a social problem when they are associated with social groups already believed to be dangerous or threatening (Musto 1999). It has been argued, for example, that the temperance movement was partially based on existing tensions between native-born Protestants and Catholic immigrants during industrialization (Reinarman 2011); that the campaign against opium in late nineteenth-century California was rooted in fears that Chinese workers represented surplus labor following a decline in railroad jobs (Musto 1999; Helmer 1975); that the cocaine problem around the turn of the 20th century was based on fears that the drug caused violence among southern blacks (Bonnie and Whitebread 1999); and that the problem of crack cocaine in the 1980s gained attention largely because crack use was linked to existing urban decay in minority neighborhoods (Reinarman and Levine 1997).

The extent to which racism, nativism, and xenophobia contributed to the prohibition of marijuana has been debated; however, evidence strongly indicates that racial and ethnic tensions played a significant role in marijuana's initial prohibition. Marijuana smoking first became associated with Mexican immigrants and was later linked to Caribbean sailors, African Americans, jazz musicians, and other lower-strata social groups (see Himmelstein 1983b; Bonnie and Whitebread 1999). Accounts from the time document an historical context of cultural conflict, some of which presaged the scapegoating of marijuana and its users. For example, the willingness of some Mexican immigrants to work for low wages around the turn of the century, and again during the Depression, was an independent source of conflict between Mexican immigrants and American workers (Abel 1980; Helmer 1975). Further, it has been suggested that perceptions of Mexicans were made worse in 1916, when Pancho Villa and his followers attacked Columbus, New Mexico (Abel 1980). As marijuana smoking became associated with Caribbean sailors and blacks in the South, and with jazz musicians in large cities, it is not surprising that perceptions of the drug came to reflect existing cultural sentiments related to these already-marginalized groups.

THE EARLY HISTORY OF MARIJUANA
AND HEMP IN THE UNITED STATES

The history of marijuana and hemp in the United States has been punctuated by periods of veneration and condemnation. As a cash crop, hemp was cultivated widely in the early American colonies, primarily for its fiber which was used to produce rope and fabric (Grinspoon 1994). In fact, it is reported that both George Washington and Thomas Jefferson cultivated hemp on their farms (Booth 2004; Abel 1980). When the use of hemp in the production of rope and canvas declined in the middle of the 1800s, it was subsequently used in the production of fine paper and in birdseed (Grinspoon 1994). By the late 1800s, hemp production in the United States had declined substantially, owing in part to the growth of the cotton industry (Bonnie and Whitebread 1999).

By the second half of the nineteenth century marijuana was one of many drugs listed in the United States Pharmacopoeia (Cohen 2009). At the time, the use of marijuana in the United States was mostly limited to medical applications; however, the recreational use of the drug was not unheard of. For example, in the mid-1850s, Bayard Taylor wrote about his experiences with hashish during a journey to Egypt, and Fitz Hugh Ludlow documented his vast experimentations with marijuana in *The Hasheesh Eater* in 1857 (Booth 2004). Additionally, Martin Booth (2004) tells of a Turkish hashish stand at the American Centennial Exposition in 1876, and documents the availability of cannabis candies around 1864. The first candy of this sort, the *Arabian Gunje of Enchantment confectionised—A most pleasurable and harmless stimulant*, was apparently available for years in 25-cent and one-dollar boxes.

America's relationship with psychoactive substances shifted around the turn of the century. Addiction had been a problem since the end of the Civil War, during which time many soldiers returned home suffering from opiate withdrawal—a disorder which came to be known as "army disease" (Abel 1980). An unregulated patent medicine industry also contributed to accidental addiction, as did the indiscriminate use of narcotic medicines (Bonnie and Whitebread 1999). At the time, patent medicines containing morphine, cocaine, or heroin were available to the public, and Coca-Cola still contained cocaine (Musto 1999). The Pure Food and Drug Act of 1906 began to address these problems by requiring that food and drug labels list dangerous or addictive ingredients, including marijuana (Musto 1991, 1999). Fourteen years later, alcohol prohibition was adopted nationally when the Eighteenth Amendment went into effect on January 16, 1920.

MARIJUANA PROHIBITION PRIOR TO 1937

By most accounts, the practice of smoking marijuana entered the United States around 1900 along the Mexican border, and then a decade later along the Gulf Coast (Bonnie and Whitebread 1999). In the southwest border states, marijuana was first introduced by Mexican immigrants. In New Orleans and other port cities on the Gulf of Mexico, the use of marijuana originated with Caribbean sailors and West Indian immigrants and eventually spread to other lower-strata groups (Himmelstein 1983b; Bonnie and Whitebread 1999).

As the practice of smoking marijuana spread, local law enforcement and newspapers took notice. Evidence from the time demonstrates that misperceptions and exaggerations developed soon after the practice arrived in the Southwest. A *Fort Worth Star-Telegram* article from March 8, 1913, appearing under the headline, "Evil Mexican Plants That Drive You Insane," provides an early example of how marijuana was seen as both a Mexican drug and a drug that caused violence and insanity. In time, the claim that marijuana led to violence and aggression would come to dominate the discourse.

> The dry leaves of marihuana, alone or mixed with tobacco, make the smoker wilder than a wild beast. . . . The next stage of intoxication is full of terrors. Troops of ferocious wild animals march before the vision of the smoker. Lions, tigers, panthers, and other wild beasts occupy his vision. These wild animals are then attacked by hosts of devils and monsters of unheard-of shapes. The smoker becomes brave and possessed of superhuman strength. It is at this stage of the debauch that murders are committed by smokers of the marijuana weed. (*Fort Worth Star-Telegram* 1913)

The possession and sale of marijuana were banned in El Paso in 1914, and a marijuana prohibition was enacted in Texas in 1919 (Bonnie and Whitebread 1999).

Around the same time, concerns over marijuana were taking hold in New Orleans, Houston, Galveston, and other port cities along the Gulf of Mexico. Although the practice of smoking marijuana was introduced to the Gulf coast by Caribbean and West Indian sailors, it apparently became widespread among local segments of the underworld (see Bonnie and Whitebread 1999). A *Washington Post* story, appearing in the magazine section on August 24, 1924 (the same year that marijuana prohibition was passed in Louisiana), highlights some of the prevailing concerns in New Orleans. Under the headline, "Mystery of the Strange Mexican Weed," the article read:

> Imported into Mexico from India and Egypt, it has been the scourge of the lower classes. Into the cities of Texas and other Southern States, the dread dope has followed the Mexican element, caus-ing untold death and trouble. . . . Recently a strange state of affairs held sway in New Orleans. The young Americans, tiring of petting-parties and seeking a super-thrill, cast about for other pleasures. . . . Hundreds of school children were becoming drug addicts and mari-huana parties were of daily occurrence. (*The Washington Post* 1924)

The idea that marijuana use was spreading to school children proved to be an alarming narrative that fostered concerns in New Orleans and else-where (Morgan 1981). A *Chicago Daily Tribune* article from June 3, 1929, printed under the headline "Ban on Hashish Blocked Despite Ravages of Drug," illustrates that marijuana was feared not only because it was used by Mexicans, but also because the practice was believed to be spreading to American youth.

> The sale of the drug flourishes in and around Chicago in the form of cigarettes known as "muggles" or "loco weed." It is also known by its Mexican name, "marijuana" and as "moota" and "grifa". . . . The habit was introduced a dozen years ago or so by Mexican laborers, it is stated, but it has become widespread among American youths and girls, and even among school children. (*Chicago Daily Tribune* 1929)

Marijuana prohibition was enacted in Illinois in 1931. By 1933, 33 states prohibited the use of marijuana for nonmedical purposes (Bonnie and Whitebread 1999).

Marijuana was also popular among black jazz musicians in New Orle-ans, and both traveled up the Mississippi River to northern cities. Jazz musicians who embraced marijuana were known as "vipers," and none was more famous than Louis Armstrong (Lee 2012). Born in New Orleans in 1901, Armstrong made his way to Chicago and embraced viper music. Like other famous jazz artists, Armstrong referenced marijuana in his music—most famously and explicitly in the song "muggles" (Booth 2004). Before long, marijuana use among white and black jazz musicians became widespread in many American cities, and jazz musicians were portrayed as rebels whose music was likely to sully America's youth (Booth 2004).

The media and law enforcement took notice of marijuana use among jazz musicians. A *Duluth News-Tribune* article from October 17, 1921, printed under the headline "Jazz Weed, Used by Dopes, Is Cause of Crime in the Southwest," demonstrates how jazz musicians, many of whom were black, were implicated along with Mexicans as part of the dangerous class of drug users:

> Marihuana, a weird "Jazz weed" frequently used by Mexican drug addicts is the source of much crime in the southwest, according to Inspector Fred C. Boden, of the Board of Pharmacy of California, who has started an unrelenting fight to curb the use of the narcotic. "Eliminate marihuana and crime among the laboring class of Mexicans will be appreciably reduced," said Boden. "Prevent persons from planting and growing the weed and much wickedness will be spared the world." (*Duluth News-Tribune* 1921)

Louis Armstrong was arrested for marijuana possession in Los Angeles in the early 1930s, and in the following decades federal law enforcement efforts specifically targeted marijuana use among jazz musicians (Bonnie and Whitebread 1999; Booth 2004).

THE FEDERAL BUREAU OF NARCOTICS AND THE MARIHUANA TAX ACT

The Federal Bureau of Narcotics was formed in 1930, and Harry J. Anslinger was named its first commissioner. As commissioner, Anslinger made exaggerated claims about marijuana and was a key figure in the passage of the Marihuana Tax Act in 1937. He oversaw a public educational campaign that, with the help of several newspapers and magazines, depicted marijuana as a cause of horrific violence and aggression (see Bonnie and Whitebread 1999). While there is little doubt that Anslinger's moral entrepreneurship ultimately influenced public opinion and federal legislation, it is inaccurate to attribute the nation's fears over marijuana solely to his efforts (see Bonnie and Whitebread 1999; Musto 1999). As shown earlier, local newspapers had been linking marijuana use with minority populations and crime for some time; and 24 states already prohibited marijuana prior to the creation of the Bureau in 1930 (Bonnie and Whitebread 1999).

In its early years, the Bureau did not express concerns about marijuana. Drawing on evidence from official reports, researchers have shown that the Bureau tended to minimize the marijuana problem in the early 1930s (see Himmelstein 1983a). In fact, from 1931 to 1934 the Bureau officially reported that the marijuana problem was being exaggerated by the media and that federal action was not necessary (Himmelstein 1983a; Musto 1999). However, by the middle of the 1930s, the Bureau reversed its stance on marijuana, and began its antimarijuana campaign (Himmelstein 1983a). In a 1935 report, the Bureau stated:

> A problem which has proved most disquieting to the Bureau during the year is the rapid development of a widespread traffic in Indian Hemp, or marihuana, throughout the country. (see Himmelstein 1983a, 58)

Scholars of federal narcotics policy have suggested a host of moralistic, budgetary, legislative, and bureaucratic motivations that may have undergirded the Bureau's change in attitude toward marijuana in the mid-1930s. Motivations aside, the ensuing public information campaign highlights the role of Anslinger and the Bureau in steering the discourse on marijuana. In contrast to the claims put forth by local media that linked marijuana with marginalized groups, the Bureau's campaign focused primarily on the manifold ways that marijuana corrupted individuals and society. Moreover, the Bureau was able to use the news media, both directly and indirectly, to link marijuana use with gruesome acts of violence and aggression (Himmelstein 1983a; Bonnie and Whitebread 1999).

Beyond the sensationalized stories that were published in newspapers and magazines, several antimarijuana films were produced in the 1930s. The film *Marihuana—Weed with Roots in Hell* was made in 1935 and featured the tagline "Weird Orgies! Wild Parties! Unleashed Passions!" The movie poster showed a man injecting drugs into a woman's arm with a hypodermic needle and depicted a devilish hand grasping at marijuana cigarettes labeled "lust," "crime," "sorrow," "hate," "shame," and "despair" (Library of Congress 2016). Perhaps the most famous antimarijuana movie of the time was the 1936 film *Reefer Madness*. Intended as a cautionary tale, *Reefer Madness* later became a "cult humor classic" among college students (Lee 2012). The foreword to the movie warns viewers:

> The motion picture you are about to witness may startle you. It would not have been possible, otherwise, to sufficiently emphasize the frightful toll of the new drug menace which is destroying the youth of America in alarmingly increasing numbers. Marihuana is that drug—a violent narcotic—an unspeakable scourge—The Real

Public Enemy Number One! Its first effect is sudden, violent uncontrollable laughter, then come dangerous hallucinations—space expands—time slows down, almost stands still . . . fixed ideas come next, conjuring up monstrous extravagances—followed by emotional disturbances, the total inability to direct thoughts, the loss of all power to resist physical emotions . . . leading finally to acts of shocking violence . . . ending often in incurable insanity. In picturing its soul-destroying effect no attempt was made to equivocate. The scenes and incidents, while fictionized for the purpose of this story, are based upon actual research into the results of Marihuana addiction. (excerpted from Markert 2013)

A year after *Reefer Madness* was released, Harry J. Anslinger and Courtney Ryley Cooper authored an article entitled "Marijuana: Assassin of Youth" that appeared in *American Magazine* (1937). Like the depictions that appeared in film, Anslinger and Cooper sketched a gruesome picture of marijuana that portrayed the drug as a cause of violence and depravity. The article was published in July 1937, just prior to the passage of the Marihuana Tax Act. Excerpts from the article highlight the tone of the campaign against marijuana and the manifold ways that marijuana was blamed for existing social problems:

The sprawled body of a young girl lay crushed on the sidewalk the other day after a plunge from the fifth story of a Chicago apartment house. Everyone called it suicide, but actually it was murder. The killer was a narcotic known to America as marijuana, and to history as hashish. It is a narcotic used in the form of cigarettes, comparatively new to the United States and as dangerous as a coiled rattlesnake.

A Chicago mother, watching her daughter die as an indirect result of marijuana addiction, told officers that at least fifty of the girl's young friends were slaves to the narcotic. This means fifty unpredictables. They may cease its use; that is not so difficult as with some narcotics. They may continue addiction until they deteriorate mentally and become insane. Or they may turn to violent forms of crime, to suicide or to murder.

It would be well for law-enforcement officers everywhere to search for marijuana behind cases of criminal and sex assault. During the last year a young male addict was hanged in Baltimore for criminal assault on a ten-year-old girl. His defense was that he was temporarily insane from smoking marijuana. In Alamosa, Colo., a degenerate brutally attacked a young girl while under the influence of the drug. In Chicago, two marijuana smoking boys murdered a policeman.

In at least two dozen other comparatively recent cases of murder or degenerate sex attacks, many of them committed by youths, marijuana proved to be a contributing cause. Perhaps you remember the young desperado in Michigan who, a few months ago, caused a reign of terror by his career of burglaries and holdups, finally to be sent to prison for life after kidnapping a Michigan state policeman, killing him, then handcuffing him to the post of a rural mailbox. This young bandit was a marijuana fiend.

One of the first places in which marijuana found a ready welcome was in a closely congested section of New York. Among those who first introduced it there were musicians, who had brought the habit northward with the surge of "hot" music demanding players of exceptional ability, especially in improvisation. Along the Mexican border and in seaport cities it had been known for some time that the musician who desired to get the "hottest" effects from his playing often turned to marijuana for aid. (excerpted from Inciardi and McElrath 2011)

In the 1937 Marihuana Tax Act hearings, Anslinger recounted similar gruesome stories. He also made the case that marijuana was more dangerous than opium.

Here we have a drug that is not like opium. Opium has all the good of Dr. Jekyll and all the evil of Mr. Hyde. This drug is entirely the monster Hyde, the harmful effect of which cannot be measured. (cited from Ferraiolo 2007)

Dr. William C. Woodward, legislative counsel for the American Medical Association (AMA), appeared at the hearings in opposition to the Marihuana Tax Act, and called into question the claims being made about marijuana (Grinspoon 1994). Woodward represented a powerful professional interest group, the AMA, which primarily opposed the act on the basis of how it would restrict physicians (Armstrong and Parascandola 1972). Nonetheless, Woodward's arguments were largely ignored (Musto 1999). Other voices of dissent and moderation existed at the time, but none were sufficient to hinder the passage of the Marihuana Tax Act (see Loue 2007).

The Marihuana Tax Act was passed by Congress and took effect in October 1937 (Musto 1999). It outlawed the nonmedical, untaxed possession or sale of marijuana (Ferraiolo 2007). Framed as a revenue bill, the Marihuana Tax Act controlled the drug by requiring a license and transfer tax on transactions involving marijuana (Musto 1991). Stamps or licenses were not made available to private citizens. Marijuana was subsequently removed from the United States Pharmacopoeia in 1942 (Morgan 1981). Until the Comprehensive Drug Abuse Prevention and Control Act of 1970, marijuana continued to be controlled through a transfer tax (Musto 1991).

THE LA GUARDIA REPORT (1944)

Shortly after the Marihuana Tax Act was passed, the sensationalized claims that were used to support the bill came under scientific scrutiny. In September 1938, the mayor of New York City, Fiorello La Guardia, requested assistance from the New York Academy of Medicine to assess the social and clinical effects of marijuana (Bonnie and Whitebread 1999). Thirty-one scientists were enlisted in the effort to better understand the pharmacological, clinical, and sociological effects of marijuana (Lee 2012). The La Guardia Report was published in 1944 and debunked many of the claims made about marijuana (Lee 2012). In the foreword of the report, La Guardia writes,

> When rumors were recently circulated concerning the smoking of marihuana by large segments of our population and even by school children, I sought advice from The New York Academy of Medicine, as is my custom when confronted with problems of medical import. . . . I am glad that the sociological, psychological, and medical ills commonly attributed to marihuana have been found to be exaggerated insofar as the City of New York is concerned. I hasten to point out, however, that the findings are to be interpreted only as a reassuring report of progress and not as encouragement to indulgence, for I shall continue to enforce the laws prohibiting the use of marihuana until and if complete findings may justify an amendment to existing laws. The scientific part of the research will be continued in the hope that the drug may prove to possess therapeutic value for the control of drug addiction. (Schaffer Library of Drug Policy 2016)

In respect to the "stepping-stone" hypothesis, which later became known as the gateway hypothesis, the report concluded:

> We have been unable to confirm the opinion expressed by some investigators that marihuana smoking is the first step in the use of

such drugs as cocaine, morphine, and heroin. The instances are extremely rare where the habit of marihuana smoking is associated with addiction to these other substances. (Grinspoon 1994, p. 238)

As might be expected, the conclusions drawn by the La Guardia Report were not well received by Anslinger. In 1956, along with William F. Tompkins, Anslinger wrote *The Traffic in Narcotics* in which the scientific basis of the La Guardia Report was called into doubt.

There has also been a climate of public opinion which has favored the spread of narcotic addiction. Contributing to this was a very unfortunate report released some years ago by the so-called LaGuardia committee on marihuana. The Bureau immediately detected the superficiality and hollowness of its findings and denounced it. (Anslinger and Tompkins 1956)

1950s: THE BOGGS ACT AND THE NARCOTIC CONTROL ACT

During the late 1940s and early 1950s, a growing concern over opiate addiction in the United States provided the backdrop for new drug legislation (Bonnie and Whitebread 1999). Under the Marihuana Tax Act, marijuana violations had been punishable by up to five years in prison and/or a $2,000 fine (McBride and Terry-McElrath 2015). However, the actual penalties were left to the discretion of the court (Abel 1980). Following the passage of Boggs Act in 1951 and the Narcotic Control Act in 1956, penalties for marijuana violations were increased, and minimum sentences were imposed (Bonnie and Whitebread 1999). Although the concern at the time was primarily over narcotics, marijuana figured in this new legislation in several ways.

Earlier in the century, marijuana had been labeled a narcotic; however, a distinction was eventually made between marijuana and opiates (Bonnie and Whitebread 1999). The Boggs Act, however, created uniform penalties for violations of both narcotic laws and marijuana laws (Sloman 1998). The rationale for strict marijuana penalties was no longer based on its misclassification as a narcotic, but rather it rested primarily on the belief that marijuana acted as a "stepping-stone" to more serious drug use (see Q18 for more information about the gateway hypothesis). Commissioner Anslinger once again played a key role in the passage of this legislation. Although Anslinger had denied the stepping-stone hypothesis during the Marihuana Tax Act hearings in 1937 (see Bonnie and

Whitebread 1999; Himmelstein 1983a), his testimony during the Boggs Act hearings emphasized that marijuana users were likely to transition to the use of harder drugs. Anslinger stated:

> The danger is this: Over 50 percent of these young addicts started on marihuana smoking. They started there and graduated to heroin; they took the needle when the thrill of marihuana was gone. (Bonnie and Whitebread 1999, 213)

By the end of the 1950s, first offenses for narcotic or marijuana possession violations were punishable by a minimum sentence of 2 years, second offenses by a minimum sentence of 5 years, third and subsequent offenses by a minimum sentence of 10 years (Bonnie and Whitebread 1999).

1960s: THE DROP-OUT DRUG

The prevalence of marijuana use increased in the 1960s (Dennis et al. 2002), and its cultural significance shifted dramatically. From Haight-Ashbury to Woodstock, from Ginsberg to the Beatles, from Vietnam protests to hippie love-ins, many of the iconic people, places, and ideas from the 1960s were influenced by, or were under the influence of, marijuana (see Booth 2004; Lee 2012). The face of marijuana users changed as well. In the 1930s, marijuana users were primarily identified as Spanish-speakers, African Americans, musicians, and members of lower-strata groups. However, in the 1960s, marijuana use became more widespread among middle-class American youth (Himmelstein 1983a). As the face of marijuana users changed, so too did prevailing fears. Earlier in the century, fears over marijuana centered around its purported ability to induce insanity, crime, and violence. In the 1960s, however, fears over marijuana were based on a growing belief that marijuana destroyed motivation and stifled ambition—that it was a "drop-out drug."

By the end of the 1960s, this phenomenon was known as "amotivational syndrome," and it was receiving a good deal of media attention. Jerome Himmelstein (1983a, 1983b) documented this shift by comparing how marijuana was portrayed in samples of articles indexed in the *Readers Guide to Periodical Literature* during the Reefer Madness era and in the 1960s–1970s. He found that the portrayal of marijuana as the "killer weed" during the Reefer Madness era gave way in the 1960s and 1970s to new claims that marijuana use led to amotivational syndrome. The claim that marijuana was a drop-out drug did not dominate the headlines the way the violence claim had during the Reefer Madness era, largely because the Bureau did not monopolize the conversation the way it had in the 1930s (Himmelstein 1983a). Nonetheless, the characterization of marijuana had shifted dramatically in just a few decades. What was once a drug that allegedly induced violence and aggression was now a drug said to do quite the opposite—it bred passivity and deadened ambition.

1970s: THE COMPREHENSIVE DRUG ABUSE PREVENTION AND CONTROL ACT

Marijuana use continued to increase into the 1970s, and peaked at the end of the decade (Miech et al. 2016; CBHSQ 2016). In October 1970, Congress passed the Comprehensive Drug Abuse Prevention and Control Act, which replaced the Marihuana Tax Act by consolidating federal drug legislation (Peterson 1985). Under the act, all illegal substances were categorized according to their abuse potential, known effect, harmfulness, and level of accepted medical uses (Bonnie and Whitebread 1999; Musto 1999). Marijuana was given a Schedule I designation—alongside heroin and LSD—making it unlawful to use or possess marijuana for recreational or medical purposes. Morphine and cocaine were designated Schedule II substances, which was reserved for the most dangerous prescription drugs (Musto 1999). Critics of the act questioned the placement of marijuana in the most restrictive category and criticized the preclusion of its use in medicine.

On the other hand, the act removed mandatory minimum sentences and reduced the penalties for marijuana possession (Booth 2004; Peterson 1985). This new act also called for the creation of the National Commission on Marijuana and Drug Abuse (later known as the Shafer Commission) to report on marijuana use and drug abuse in general (Booth 2004). The commission recommended that possession of marijuana for personal use be decriminalized (Shafer 1999; Musto 1999); however, President Nixon did not support the commission's recommendation, and he remained opposed to marijuana decriminalization (Musto 1999; Musto and Korsmeyer 2008). Four decades after the passage of the Marihuana Tax Act, President Carter endorsed the decriminalization of marijuana, but his efforts were thwarted by a host of obstacles (Musto 1999). Nevertheless, several states relaxed marijuana penalties in the 1970s (Pacula et al. 2003).

THE TWENTY-FIRST CENTURY

As of 2017, a total of eight states plus the District of Columbia have passed laws allowing the recreational use of marijuana, and over half the states have passed laws allowing the use of marijuana for medical purposes (National Conference of State Legislatures 2016a, 2016b). Despite state-level initiatives to legalize marijuana, the Drug Enforcement Administration (DEA) denied a 2016 petition to reschedule marijuana. In doing so, the DEA reaffirmed the federal government's position that marijuana has a high potential for abuse, that marijuana has no currently accepted medical use, and that marijuana lacks accepted safety for use under medical supervision (DEA 2016). While marijuana remains federally prohibited as a Schedule I substance, public acceptance of marijuana has been growing (see Q17 on public opinion regarding marijuana criminalization). Nonetheless, doctors, politicians, and the public remain divided over marijuana. The tension between state marijuana laws, federal marijuana laws, and the growing public acceptance of marijuana represents the latest chapter in the complex and colorful history of marijuana prohibition in the United States.

FURTHER READING

Abel, Ernest L. *Marihuana: the first twelve thousand years*. New York: Plenum Press, 1980.

Alexander, Michelle. *The new Jim Crow: mass incarceration in the age of colorblindness*. New York: The New Press, 2012.

Anslinger, Harry J., and Courtney Ryley Cooper. "Marihuana: assassin of youth." *American Magazine* 124, 1937.

Anslinger, Harry J., and William F. Tompkins. *The traffic in narcotics*. New York: Funk and Wagnall's, 1953.

Armstrong, William D., and John Parascandola. "American concern over marihuana in the 1930's." *Pharmacy in History* 14, no. 1 (1972): 25–35.

Bonnie, Richard J., and Charles H. Whitebread II. *The marihuana conviction: a history of marihuana prohibition in the United States*. New York: The Lindesmith Center, 1999.

Booth, Martin. *Cannabis: a history*. New York: Picador, 2004.

Center for Behavioral Health Statistics and Quality. *2015 National Survey on Drug Use and Health: detailed tables*. Rockville, MD: Substance Abuse and Mental Health Services Administration, 2016.

Chicago Daily Tribune. "Ban on hashish blocked despite ravages of drug." Chicago, Illinois, June 3, 1929.

Cohen, Peter J. "Medical marijuana: the conflict between scientific evidence and political ideology." *Utah Law Review* 35, (2009): 35–104.

Dennis, Michael, Thomas F. Babor, M. Christopher Roebuck, and Jean Donaldson. "Changing the focus: the case for recognizing and treating cannabis use disorders." *Addiction* 97, no. s1 (2002): 4–15.

Drug Enforcement Agency. *Denial of petition to initiate proceedings to reschedule marijuana.* Document Citation: 81 FR 53687, Page: 53687–53766; Agency/Docket Number: Docket No. DEA-426; Document Number: 2016–17954. August 12, 2016.

Duluth News-Tribune. "Jazz weed, used by dopes, is cause of crime in southwest." Duluth, Minnesota, October 17, 1921.

Ferraiolo, Kathleen. "From killer weed to popular medicine: the evolution of American drug control policy, 1937–2000." *Journal of Policy History* 19, no. 2 (2007): 147–179.

Fort Worth Star-Telegram. "Evil Mexican plants that drive you insane." Fort-Worth, Texas, March 8, 1913.

Goode, Erich, and Nachman Ben-Yehuda. "Moral panics: culture, politics, and social construction." *Annual Review of Sociology* (1994): 149–171.

Grinspoon, Lester. *Marihuana reconsidered.* San Francisco: Quick American Archives, 1994.

Helmer, John. *Drugs and minority oppression.* New York: Seabury Press, 1975.

Himmelstein, Jerome L. "From killer weed to drop-out drug: the changing ideology of marihuana." *Contemporary Crises* 7, no. 1 (1983b): 13–38.

Himmelstein, Jerome L. *The strange career of marihuana: politics and ideology of drug control in the United States.* Westport, Connecticut: Greenwood Press, 1983a.

Inciardi, James A., and Karen McElrath. *The American drug scene: an anthology.* New York: Oxford University Press, 2011.

Lee, Martin A. *Smoke signals: a social history of marijuana—medical, recreational and scientific.* New York: Simon and Schuster, 2012.

Library of Congress. "Marihuana." Prints & Photographs Online Catalog. Accessed December 8, 2016. http://www.loc.gov/pictures/item/2013648139/

Loue, Sana. *Case studies in forensic epidemiology.* Springer Science & Business Media, 2007.

Markert, John. *Hooked in film: substance abuse on the big screen.* Lanham, MD: Scarecrow Press, 2013.

McBride, Duane C., and Yvonne Terry-McElrath. "Drug policy in the United States." In *The handbook of drugs and society,* edited by Henry H. Brownstein, 574–593. Malden, MA: Wiley Blackwell, 2015.

Miech, Richard. A., Lloyd. D. Johnston, Patrick. M. O'Malley, Jerald. G. Bachman, and John. E. Schulenberg. *Monitoring the Future national survey results on drug use, 1975–2015: Volume I, Secondary school students*. Ann Arbor: Institute for Social Research, The University of Michigan. 2016.

Morgan, Howard Wayne. *Drugs in America: a social history, 1800–1980*. Vol. 1017. Syracuse University Press, 1981.

Musto, David F. *The American disease: origins of narcotic control*. New York: Oxford University Press, 1999.

Musto, David F. "Opium, cocaine and marijuana in American history." *Scientific American* 265, no. 1 (1991): 40–47.

Musto, David F., and Pamela Korsmeyer. *The quest for drug control: politics and federal policy in a period of increasing substance abuse, 1963–1981*. Yale University Press, 2008.

National Conference of State Legislatures (NCSLa). "Marijuana overview." 2016. Accessed December 8, 2016a. http://www.ncsl.org/research/civil-and-criminal-justice/marijuana-overview.aspx

National Conference of State Legislatures (NCSLb). "State medical marijuana laws." 2016. Accessed December 8, 2016b. http://www.ncsl.org/research/health/state-medical-marijuana-laws.aspx#3

Pacula, Rosalie Liccardo, Jamie F. Chriqui, and Joanna King. *Marijuana decriminalization: what does it mean in the United States?* No. w9690. National Bureau of Economic Research, 2003.

Peterson, Ruth D. "Discriminatory decision making at the legislative level: an analysis of the Comprehensive Drug Abuse Prevention and Control Act of 1970." *Law and Human Behavior* 9, no. 3 (1985): 243.

Reinarman, Craig. "The social impact of drugs and the war on drugs: the social construction of drug scares." In *The American drug scene: an anthology*, edited by James A. Inciardi and Karen McElrath, 6th ed., 80–89. New York: Oxford University Press, 2011.

Reinarman, Craig, and Harry Levine. "The crack attack." In *Crack in America: demon drugs and social justice*, edited by Craig Reinarman and Harry G. Levine, 18–51. Berkeley and Los Angeles: University of California Press, 1997.

Schaffer Library of Drug Policy. "The La Guardia Committee Report." Accessed December 8, 2016. http://www.druglibrary.org/schaffer/library/studies/lag/lagmenu.htm

Shafer, Raymond P. Foreword to *The Marihuana Conviction*, edited by Richard J. Bonnie and Charles H. Whitebread II. New York: The Lindesmith Center, 1999.

Sloman, Larry. *Reefer madness: a history of marijuana*. New York: St. Martin's Press, 1998.

Washington Post Magazine Section. "Mystery of the Strange Mexican Weed." Washington, DC, August 24, 1924.

Q17. DO MOST AMERICANS SUPPORT THE CRIMINALIZATION OF MARIJUANA?

Answer: No. As of 2016, over half of the U.S. population favored the legalization of marijuana and more than 80 percent of Americans believed that medical marijuana should be legal. Historically, public support for the legalization of marijuana has waxed and waned, but support has been increasing since the early 1990s. As recently as 2009, a majority of Americans still believed that marijuana should be illegal. However, since 2013 most Americans have supported the legalization of marijuana.

The Facts: Data from the leading public opinion polls show that a majority of Americans favor the legalization of marijuana. Depending on the data source, surveys show that between 50 percent and 60 percent of Americans support the legalization of marijuana, and over 80 percent of Americans believe that medical marijuana should be legal. As shown in Figure 3.1, historical data from Gallup indicate that support for marijuana legalization has increased over time, and reached roughly 60 percent in 2016 (Gallup 2016). The most recent 2016 data from the Pew Research Center show that about 57 percent of Americans support the legalization of marijuana (Geiger 2016). Similarly, a 2016 Quinnipiac University Poll found that 54 percent of Americans think that the use of marijuana should be made legal, and 89 percent believe medical marijuana should be legal (Quinnipiac 2016).

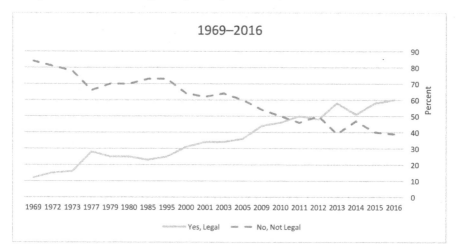

Figure 3.1 Gallup Polls: Do You Think the Use of Marijuana Should Be Made Legal, or Not?

Source: Gallup 2016.

PUBLIC OPINION AND HISTORICAL CONTEXT

In 1969, when Gallup first surveyed Americans about marijuana legalization, only about 12 percent of the population favored marijuana legalization, and 84 percent believed that marijuana should be illegal (Gallup 2016). The historic Woodstock music festival was held that year, and both marijuana and Woodstock were regarded as symbols of the counterculture. This was a period when marijuana use became more widespread among middle-class youth, and it was increasingly seen as a "drop-out" drug (see Q16). To some, marijuana users and members of the counterculture lacked ambition and initiative; however, others saw a culture of inspired rebellion that opposed mainstream values and questioned established authority (Andreas 2013). The year 1969 is also noteworthy because it was the first year of the Nixon administration (1969–1974), and the year that President Nixon announced a national "war on drugs" (Musto and Korsmeyer 2008).

Marijuana use among teenagers increased throughout the 1970s and peaked at the end of the decade when marijuana legalization was favored by about 25 percent of Americans (Johnston et al. 2014; CBHSQ 2016; Gallup 2016). Drug laws also changed in the 1970s. The Controlled Substances Act, passed early in the Nixon administration as part of the Comprehensive Drug Abuse Prevention and Control Act, replaced the Marihuana Tax Act by categorizing all illicit substances according to abuse potential, known effect, harmfulness, and level of accepted medical uses (Bonnie and Whitebread 1999). With this new legislation, marijuana was given the most restrictive, Schedule I designation.

The Comprehensive Drug Abuse Prevention and Control Act also removed mandatory minimum sentences, reduced the penalties for marijuana possession, and called for the establishment of the National Commission on Marijuana and Drug Abuse (Bonnie and Whitebread 1999). The first report by the Commission, *Marihuana: A Signal of Misunderstanding*, recommended that possession of small quantities be decriminalized. However, President Nixon did not support decriminalization (Musto 1999). During the Carter administration (1977–1981), there were again indications that marijuana might be decriminalized at the federal level, but there were no legislative changes (Musto and Korsmeyer 2008). While marijuana prohibition was ultimately sustained at the federal level, several states decriminalized or relaxed marijuana penalties in the 1970s (Pacula et al. 2003).

Marijuana use decreased throughout the 1980s as did support for the notion that marijuana should be made legal (see Q1; CBHSQ 2016; General Social Survey 2016). The war on drugs, which was renewed during the Reagan administration (1981–1989), may have affected public attitudes toward marijuana and other drugs. At the beginning of the decade about 25 percent of Americans favored the legalization of marijuana and fewer than 5 percent believed that drugs were the most important problem facing the country (GSS 2016; Jones 2016). By the end of the decade, only about 16 percent of Americans favored marijuana legalization and Americans increasingly believed that drugs were the most important problem in the United States (GSS 2016; Jones 2016).

Although Americans were already concerned about the drug problem at the outset of the George H. W. Bush administration (1989–1993), concern over drugs spiked dramatically in September 1989 following the president's first nationally televised address in which he outlined his national drug control agenda (Boyum and Reuter 2005; Jones 2016). Other factors related to the war on drugs may also have contributed to the decrease in public support for marijuana legalization that took place through the 1980s. For example, tough new drug laws passed in 1986 and 1988, fears over crack cocaine, the "Just Say No" campaign, the establishment of the DARE program, and an increase in federal drug control spending may have added to public concern over drugs and led to the concomitant decrease in support for the legalization of marijuana (see Boyum and Reuter 2005; National Research Council 2014).

In the early 1990s, public support for the legalization of marijuana began to increase and continued to increase throughout the decade (GSS 2016). During this time, marijuana use among teenagers increased, while marijuana use remained relatively stable in the general population (Johnston et al. 2014; CBHSQ 2016). An emphasis on drug enforcement continued during the Clinton administration (1993–2001), despite the fact that during the 1992 presidential primary, then-Arkansas governor Bill Clinton famously went on record saying, "I experimented with marijuana a time or two, and didn't like it. I didn't inhale and I didn't try it again" (*New York Times* 1992). During the Clinton years the number of federal prisoners serving time for drug offenses increased from 48,554 to 78,501, and marijuana arrests nearly doubled (Beck and Gilliard 1995; Harrison and Beck 2003; Dorsey and James 2009). At the same time, marijuana policies began to change at the state level. Beginning with California, several states legalized medical marijuana in the 1990s (National Conference of State Legislatures 2016a). At the beginning of the 1990s about 16 percent of Americans supported the legalization of marijuana. By the year 2000, support for legalization had roughly doubled to 31 percent (GSS 2016).

During the first decade of the twenty-first century, support for marijuana legalization continued to increase while concerns over drugs as a national problem decreased slightly (GSS 2016; Jones 2016). Marijuana use increased somewhat in the general population over the course of the decade, but use remained steady among 12- to 17-year-olds (see Q1; CBHSQ 2016). Drug control and prevention remained a priority during the George W. Bush administration (2001–2009). The number of federal prisoners sentenced for drug offenses increased from 78,501 to 96,735 between 2001 and 2009, and the number of annual marijuana arrests increased from 723,600 to 858,400 (Federal Bureau of Investigation 2016; Harrison and Beck 2003; Guerino et al. 2011). Substantial resources were also dedicated to marijuana prevention. For example, the National Youth Anti-Drug Media Campaign, which began in the late 1990s, continued into the 2000s, and introduced the Marijuana Initiative in 2002 (Hornik et al. 2008). Nevertheless, by the year 2010, 44 percent of Americans favored the legalization of marijuana (GSS 2016).

Support for marijuana legalization continued to grow throughout the Obama administration (2009–2016), during which time marijuana use increased slightly (CBHSQ 2016; Johnston et al. 2014). The number of federal prisoners sentenced for drug offenses decreased from 96,735 in 2009 to 92,000 in 2015, while annual marijuana arrests decreased from 858,400 to 643,100 during the same period (Federal Bureau of Investigation 2016; Guerino et al. 2011; Carson and Anderson 2016). Beginning with Colorado and Washington in 2012, several states legalized marijuana, and the Obama administration expressed tolerance toward state-level marijuana legalization (see Cole 2013; Weiner 2012). The president himself acknowledged his own past marijuana use, saying, "I smoked pot as a kid, and I view it as a bad habit and a vice. . . . I don't think it is more dangerous than alcohol" (Remnick 2014). As President Trump entered office, a majority of Americans supported the legalization of marijuana, and eight states along with the District of Columbia had passed legislation making the possession of small amounts of marijuana legal (National Conference of State Legislatures 2016b).

CHANGING VIEWS ON THE RISKS OF MARIJUANA

Increased support for marijuana legalization is likely related to a concomitant shift in how Americans view the risks related to marijuana use (see Q9 on risks). For example, it is increasingly less common for Americans to see marijuana as a gateway drug (see Q18 on the gateway hypothesis). Data from the Pew Research Center show that about 60 percent of

Americans in 1977 believed that using marijuana led to the use of hard drugs, whereas only 38 percent thought so in 2013 (Pew 2013). Gallup data from 2016 also show that the public is less concerned about marijuana than about other drugs. Compared to heroin, painkillers, cigarettes, alcohol, and cocaine, marijuana is the substance least likely to be considered a "crisis" or a "very serious problem," and it is the substance most likely to be considered "not much of a problem" (Gallup 2016) (see Q10 and Q11 on drug risk comparisons).

Perceptions of risk are also important because they are a "leading indicator" of marijuana use among teenagers (Johnston et al. 2014). Since the 1970s, teen marijuana use has generally been highest at times when perceptions of risk were low, and teen marijuana use has generally been lowest at times when perceptions of risk were high. While it is very difficult to know whether perceptions of risk lead to marijuana use or vice versa, many people believe that the growing acceptability of medical marijuana may lead to decreased perceptions of risk and increased use. On the other hand, others have argued that decades' worth of overstated risks (i.e., Reefer Madness) may have had the unintended consequence of steering youth toward marijuana and perhaps leading some to dismiss actual marijuana-related health risks.

While perceptions of risk have decreased among high school seniors since 2005, a substantial portion of the larger population still believes that marijuana is a dangerous drug. Pew data from 2015 show that many people who do not favor legalization cite marijuana-related dangers as the main reasons why they believe marijuana should be prohibited (Pew 2015). Among the roughly 44 percent of Americans who did not favor legalization, 43 percent said that main reason why they think marijuana should be illegal is because it hurts society and is bad for individuals, and 30 percent said that marijuana is a dangerous or addictive drug. About 11 percent said marijuana should be illegal because it is a gateway drug, while eight percent thought marijuana is "bad for young people."

WHO FAVORS MARIJUANA LEGALIZATION?

While a majority of Americans believe that marijuana should be legal, some social groups favor legalization more than others. For example, men are more likely than women to favor marijuana legalization (Quinnipiac 2016). Additionally, younger people are more likely than older people to favor legalization (Geiger 2016; Quinnipiac 2016). Pew data from 2016 show that 71 percent of millennials (born 1981–1998) favor legalization, compared to 57 percent of people in Generation X (born 1965–1980), and 56 percent of baby boomers (born 1946–1964). The Silent generation (born 1928–1945) is the least likely to support the legalization of marijuana, with only about 33 percent in favor.

Attitudes toward marijuana legalization also vary by political party affiliation. Yet a substantial portion of people across the political spectrum favor legalization. Data from both Quinnipiac University and the Pew Research Center show that Democrats and Independents are more likely than Republicans to favor legalization. Sixty-six percent of people who identify as Democrats support legalizing marijuana, compared to 41 percent of Republicans, and 63 percent of Independents (Geiger 2016). Within each political party there is some variation in who favors legalization. For example, Pew data show that marijuana legalization is supported by 78 percent of liberal Democrats and by 55 percent of moderate Democrats. However, moderate Republicans are more likely than moderate Democrats to favor legalization. Conservative Republicans are least likely to support marijuana legalization (33 percent).

One way to understand the growing acceptability of marijuana is in the context of a national trend toward the acceptance of controversial behaviors. Research from Pew shows that about 50 percent of Americans in 2006 thought smoking marijuana was morally wrong, whereas only 32 percent thought so in 2013 (Pew 2013). Similarly, the percentage of Americans who thought that smoking marijuana was not a moral issue increased from 35 percent in 2006 to 50 percent in 2013. Research on other controversial issues similarly shows a trend toward acceptability. According to research published in 2016 by Gallup, Americans were more likely in 2015 than in 2001 to find many controversial issues morally acceptable, including divorce, suicide, abortion, and sex outside of marriage (Newport 2016). Most notably, about 40 percent of Americans found gay or lesbian relations morally acceptable in 2001, whereas 63 percent did so in 2015. Additionally, the percentage of Americans who viewed having a child outside of marriage as morally acceptable increased from 45 percent in 2001 to 61 percent in 2015. Using this lens, the growing support for marijuana legalization might be expected given that other controversial issues have become increasingly accepted.

MEDICAL MARIJUANA VIEWS

The Drug Enforcement Administration (DEA) denied a 2016 petition to reschedule marijuana, which affirmed the federal stance on marijuana that was established under the Controlled Substances Act. While the use of marijuana for medical purposes remains prohibited under federal law, over half the states permit the use of marijuana as medicine (NCSL 2016b). Medical and recreational marijuana policies represent an interesting divide between state and federal laws. The Department of Justice, representing the federal government, indicated in 2013 that it would not interfere with state marijuana laws provided that states "implement strong and effective regulatory and enforcement systems that will address the threat those state laws could pose to public safety, public health, and other law enforcement interests" (Cole 2013).

Opinion polls and results from state referenda have demonstrated widespread public support for medical marijuana. For example, the 2016 Quinnipiac University Poll found that 89 percent of Americans support allowing adults to legally use marijuana for medical purposes if prescribed by a doctor. A 2013 poll from the Pew Research Center found that 77 percent of Americans believed that marijuana has legitimate medical uses, including 76 percent of Democrats, 72 percent of Republicans, and 82 percent of Independents. Interestingly, trend data from Gallup show that 73 percent of Americans in 1999 favored making marijuana "legally available for doctors to prescribe in order to reduce pain and suffering," which climbed to 78 percent in 2005, and decreased to 70 percent by 2010 (Gallup 2016).

Compared to the strong public support for medical marijuana, there appears to be less consensus among medical practitioners. Drawing on 960 responses from family physicians, internists, obstetrician-gynecologists, psychiatrists, and addiction specialists (66 percent adjusted response rate), researchers found that 36 percent of surveyed doctors thought prescribed marijuana should be legal and 38 percent believed prescribed marijuana should not be legal (Charuvastra et al. 2005). Other surveys similarly show mixed support for medical marijuana among health care providers. In a survey of Colorado family physicians, 46 percent did not support medical marijuana, while 19 percent supported it (Kondrad and Reid 2013). Notably, 64 percent of the Colorado physicians surveyed agreed that marijuana poses serious mental health risks, and 61 percent agreed that marijuana poses serious physical health risks. Due to a low response rate (30 percent), however, results from this survey must be interpreted with caution, since the views of those doctors who responded may be different from the views of those doctors who did not respond.

There is also evidence that medical practitioners' views on medical marijuana vary according to medical specialty. For example, in a survey of hospice professionals, including doctors, nurses, social workers, and other professionals (response rate 49 percent), researchers found that 90 percent believed that medical marijuana should be legal (Uritsky et al. 2011).

On the other hand, a survey conducted by the *Psychiatric Times* showed that the mental health practitioners who responded were divided on the issue of medical marijuana (Kweskin 2013). About 40 percent of respondents said they would consider prescribing marijuana in some circumstances, and 11 percent would consider prescribing it only in pill form. The generalizability of these studies remains unclear, however, since it is unknown if those practitioners who chose to respond share similar opinions with those who did not choose to respond.

FURTHER READING

Andreas, Peter. *Smuggler nation: how illicit trade made America*. New York: Oxford University Press, 2013.

Beck, Allen J., and K. Darrell Gilliard. *Prisoners in 1994*. Washington, DC: Bureau of Justice Statistics, NCJ-11654, 1995.

Bonnie, Richard J., and Charles H. Whitebread II. *The marihuana conviction: a history of marihuana prohibition in the United States*. New York: The Lindesmith Center, 1999.

Boyum, David, and Peter Reuter. *An analytic assessment of U.S. drug policy*. Washington, DC: The AEI Press, 2005.

Carson, E. Ann, and Elizabeth Anderson. *Prisoners in 2015*. Washington, DC: Bureau of Justice Statistics, NCJ 250229, 2016.

Center for Behavioral Health Statistics and Quality. *2015 National Survey on Drug Use and Health: detailed tables*. Substance Abuse and Mental Health Services Administration, Rockville, MD, 2016.

Charuvastra, Anthony, Peter D. Friedmann, and Michael D. Stein. "Physician attitudes regarding the prescription of medical marijuana." *Journal of Addictive Diseases* 24, no. 3 (2005): 87–93.

Cole, James M. *Memorandum for all United States Attorneys: Guidance regarding marijuana enforcement*. U.S. Department of Justice. Office of the Deputy Attorney General. August 29, 2013.

Dorsey, Tina, and Doris James. *Drugs and crime facts*. Washington, DC: U.S. Department of Justice, NCJ 165148, Washington, 2009. Accessed December 10, 2016. https://www.bjs.gov/content/pub/pdf/dcf.pdf

Drug Enforcement Administration. *Denial of petition to initiate proceedings to reschedule marijuana*. Document Citation: 81 FR 53687, Page: 53687–53766; Agency/Docket Number: Docket No. DEA-426; Document Number: 2016–17954. August 12, 2016.

Federal Bureau of Investigation. "Crime in the United States." 1995–2015. Arrest Tables. Accessed December 10, 2016. https://ucr.fbi.gov/crime-in-the-u.s

Gallup. "Illegal drugs." 2016. Accessed December 8, 2016. http://www
    .gallup.com/poll/1657/illegal-drugs.aspx

Geiger, Abigail. "Support for marijuana legalization continues to rise."
    Pew Research Center, Factank, News in Numbers. 2016. Accessed
    December 8, 2016. http://www.pewresearch.org/fact-tank/2016/10/12/
    support-for-marijuana-legalization-continues-to-rise/

General Social Survey (GSS). "GSS data explorer." 2016. Accessed
    December 8, 2016. https://gssdataexplorer.norc.org/

Guerino, Paul, Paige M. Harrison, and William J. Sabol. *Prisoners in
    2010*. Washington, DC: Bureau of Justice Statistics, NCJ 236096, 2011.

Harrison, Paige M., and Allen J. Beck. *Prisoners in 2002*. Washington,
    DC: Bureau of Justice Statistics, NCJ 200248, 2003.

Hornik, Robert, Lela Jacobsohn, Robert Orwin, Andrea Piesse, and Graham
    Kalton. "Effects of the national youth anti-drug media campaign on
    youths." *American Journal of Public Health* 98, no. 12 (2008): 2229–2236.

Johnston, L. D., P.M. O'Malley, R. A. Miech, J.G. Bachman, and J. E.
    Schulenberg. *Monitoring the Future national results on drug use: 1975–2013:
    Overview, key findings on adolescent drug use*. Ann Arbor: Institute for
    Social Research, The University of Michigan, 2014.

Jones, Jeffrey M. "In U.S., 65% say drug problem 'extremely' or 'very serious.'".
    Gallup Social Issues. October 28, 2016. http://www.gallup.com/poll/
    196826/say-drug-problem-extremelyserious.aspx?g_source=CATE
    GORY_SOCIAL_ISSUES&g_medium=topic&g_campaign=tiles

Kondrad, Elin, and Alfred Reid. "Colorado family physicians' attitudes
    toward medical marijuana." *The Journal of the American Board of Family
    Medicine* 26, no. 1 (2013): 52–60.

Kweskin, Susan. "The dope on medical cannabis: results of a survey of
    psychiatrists." *Psychiatric Times* 30, no. 7 (2013): 11–11.

Musto, David F. *The American disease: origins of narcotic control*. New York:
    Oxford University Press, 1999.

Musto, David F., and Pamela Korsmeyer. *The quest for drug control: politics
    and federal policy in a period of increasing substance abuse, 1963–1981*.
    Yale University Press, 2008.

National Conference of State Legislatures (NCSLa). "Marijuana overview."
    2016b. Accessed December 8, 2016b. http://www.ncsl.org/research/
    civil-and-criminal-justice/marijuana-overview.aspx

National Conference of State Legislatures (NCSLb). "State medical
    marijuana laws." 2016a. Accessed December 8, 2016. http://www.ncsl
    .org/research/health/state-medical-marijuana-laws.aspx#3

National Research Council. *The growth of incarceration in the united states:
    exploring causes and consequences*. Committee on causes and conse-
    quences of high rates of incarceration, edited by J. Travis, B. Western,

and S. Redburn. Washington, DC: Committee on Law and Justice, Division of Behavioral and Social Sciences and Education, The National Academies Press, 2014.

Newport, Frank. "Americans continue to shift left on key moral issues." *Gallup Social Issues. 2016.* Accessed December 8, 2016. http://www.gallup .com/poll/183413/americans-continue-shift-left-key-moral-issues.aspx

New York Times. "Clinton tried marijuana as a student, he says." 1992. Accessed December 8, 2016. http://www.nytimes.com/1992/03/30/ news/30iht-bill_1.html

Pacula, Rosalie Liccardo, Jamie F. Chriqui, and Joanna King. *Marijuana decriminalization: what does it mean in the United States?* No. w9690. National Bureau of Economic Research, 2003.

Pew Research Center. "Majority now supports legalizing marijuana." 2013. Accessed on December 8, 2016. http://www.people-press.org/2013/ 04/04/majority-now-supports-legalizing-marijuana/

Pew Research Center. "In debate over legalizing marijuana, disagreement over drug's dangers." 2015. Accessed on December 8, 2016. http://www.people-press.org/2015/04/14/in-debate-over-legalizing-marijuana-disagreement-over-drugs-dangers/

Quinnipiac University Poll. Release Detail. June 6, 2016. Accessed December 8, 2016. https://poll.qu.edu/national/release-detail?ReleaseID=2354

Remnick, David. "Going the distance. On and off the road with Barack Obama." *The New Yorker.* January 27, 2014. Accessed December 8, 2016. http://www.newyorker.com/magazine/2014/01/27/going-the-distance-david-remnick

Uritsky, Tanya J., Mary Lynn McPherson, and Françoise Pradel. "Assessment of hospice health professionals' knowledge, views, and experience with medical marijuana." *Journal of Palliative Medicine* 14, no. 12 (2011): 1291–1295.

Weiner, Rachel. "Obama: I've got 'bigger fish to fry' than pot smokers." *The Washington Post. Post Politics.* December 14, 2012. Accessed December 8, 2016. https://www.washingtonpost.com/news/post-politics/ wp/2012/12/14/obama-ive-got-bigger-fish-to-fry-than-pot-smokers/? utm_term=.ddf6302b8b05

Q18. IS MARIJUANA USE A "GATEWAY" TO OTHER ILLICIT DRUG USE OR MISUSE?

Answer: Yes and no. The gateway hypothesis subsumes three related propositions regarding the relationship between early marijuana use and the subsequent use of more serious drugs, but only two of those propositions are supported by scholarly research. The first proposition, relating to the *temporal sequence* of drug initiation, suggests that individuals rarely use hard drugs without first using "gateway" substances such as marijuana. Extensive evidence supports this proposition, although research has shown that some populations follow alternative drug initiation sequences. The second proposition, relating to *statistical association*, suggests that the use of marijuana is associated or correlated with an increased risk of progressing to the use of more serious drugs. Substantial research demonstrates a strong and consistent statistical association between marijuana use and the subsequent progression to more serious drugs. The third proposition, relating to *causation*, posits that marijuana use actually causes individuals to progress to the use of more serious substances. This third proposition is difficult to empirically validate, and the evidence supporting this hypothesis is mixed. In the sense that marijuana use commonly precedes the use of more serious drugs and in the sense that marijuana use is statistically associated with the use of more serious drugs, it could be called a gateway drug. However, marijuana's role in causing individuals to progress in the sequence of drug initiation remains controversial.

The Facts: Since the 1970s, extensive research has shown that most young people who use substances follow a consistent pattern of progressive drug use that begins with alcohol or tobacco and is potentially followed in sequence by the use of marijuana and then more serious drugs (Kandel 1975, 2003; Golub and Johnson 2002). Very few individuals who try alcohol or tobacco will go on to use hard drugs; however, it is uncommon for individuals to skip directly to hard drugs without first using lower-stage drugs (Kandel 1975; Kandel and Kandel 2015). Likewise, not all marijuana users will progress to using harder drugs, but an estimated 45 percent of Americans who ever use marijuana will progress to other illicit drug use at some point in their lives (Secades-Villa et al. 2015). As a result, marijuana is often labeled a "gateway" drug, with the assumption that the use of marijuana causes individuals to progress to more serious drugs. It is further assumed that delaying or preventing the use of marijuana will help prevent the progression to more serious drug use.

Although alcohol, tobacco, and marijuana can each be seen as gateway drugs, a preponderance of attention has been given to marijuana, which is often viewed as the bridge that links alcohol and tobacco with more serious drugs like cocaine and heroin. Although alcohol use and tobacco use are more prevalent than marijuana use, public concern over gateway drugs is heavily focused on marijuana. The marijuana gateway hypothesis is often invoked in debates related to marijuana legalization, medical marijuana, public policy, and substance use prevention. Considering the widespread concern over marijuana's role as a gateway drug, it is important to evaluate the marijuana gateway hypothesis using empirical evidence. Such an evaluation necessarily begins with the understanding that the gateway hypothesis is actually not a single hypothesis. Rather, the gateway hypothesis contains three distinct propositions related to the role of marijuana in the progression of substance use initiation (Kandel and Jessor 2002).

THE FIRST GATEWAY PROPOSITION

The first gateway proposition, relating to the *temporal sequence* of drug initiation, suggests the existence of a consistent developmental progression of drug use that regularly begins with alcohol or tobacco and is potentially followed in sequence by the use of marijuana and then more serious drugs. This proposition is supported by extensive evidence (Kandel 2003; Kandel and Jessor 2002). In a seminal article published in *Science* in 1975, Denise Kandel (1975) observed the prototypical sequence of substance use initiation among high school students in New York, and subsequent research has affirmed that substance use generally progresses from alcohol or tobacco, to marijuana, to hard drugs such as cocaine or heroin. For example, nationally representative data from the 1990s showed that 68 percent of cigarette/marijuana users used cigarettes first, 94 percent of alcohol/cocaine users used alcohol first, and 89 percent of marijuana/cocaine users used marijuana first (Kandel and Yamaguchi 2002). Similarly, in 2012, nearly all cocaine users (96.9 percent) in a nationally representative sample reported smoking or drinking prior to initiating cocaine use, and most marijuana users (64.6 percent) initiated smoking or drinking prior to using marijuana (Kandel and Kandel 2015).

While most research shows that the use of alcohol or tobacco generally precedes the use of marijuana, and that marijuana use generally precedes the use of harder drugs, some variation in this pattern has been observed. For example, the gateway sequence is somewhat less common among racial minorities and among younger birth cohorts (see Kandel and Jessor 2002). Additionally, research has shown that serious drug users sometimes follow alternative drug initiation sequences. For instance, in a study of 60 "delinquent" boys, researchers found that only 57 percent initiated substance use by using either alcohol or tobacco (Young et al. 1995). Drawing on a sample of 285 serious drug users, other researchers observed that about 40 percent of the sample used other illicit drugs prior to using marijuana, and only 33 percent followed the typical gateway sequence (Mackesy-Amiti et al. 1997).

THE SECOND GATEWAY PROPOSITION

The second gateway proposition, relating to *statistical association*, suggests that the use of a lower-stage drug is statistically associated with an increased risk of using a higher-stage drug (Kandel and Jessor 2002). This proposition is generally well supported. For example, individuals who have used alcohol or tobacco are at increased risk of progressing to marijuana use, and the regular use of marijuana is associated with an increased risk of using more serious illicit substances (Kandel and Jessor 2002; Hall and Lynskey 2005).

The hypothesized association between marijuana use and the subsequent use of more serious drugs is further supported by evidence showing that early and heavy marijuana use are consistently associated with the progression to more serious substances (Kandel and Yamaguchi 2002). For example, using data from a sample of 1,265 children from New Zealand, researchers found that younger heavy users of marijuana were more susceptible than older heavy users to other illicit substance use (Fergusson et al. 2002). Moreover, in a study of same-sex twin pairs in which only one had used marijuana prior to the age of 17, researchers found that the early initiation of marijuana use was associated with an increased risk of other drug use (Lynskey et al. 2003). Additional evidence from the New Zealand sample further showed that frequent or heavy marijuana use was associated with an increased risk of using other illicit substances (Fergusson, Boden, and Horwood 2006; Fergusson and Horwood 2000).

THE THIRD GATEWAY PROPOSITION

The third gateway proposition, relating to *causation*, posits that the use of lower-stage substances actually causes the progression to more serious, or higher-stage, substance use. This proposition is often invoked in policy debates when it is suggested that preventing the use of marijuana (or other lower-stage substances) will keep adolescents from escalating to harder drugs like cocaine and heroin. The logic of such claims is based on an assumption of causality. However, it remains unclear whether or not the use of marijuana (or other lower-stage drugs) actually causes individuals to progress to more serious drugs (Kandel and Jessor 2002; Kandel 2003).

It is intuitively tempting to take the strong evidence supporting the first two gateway propositions as evidence that marijuana causes individuals to escalate to more serious drugs. However, as John Morgan and colleagues (1993) have aptly noted, driving a car slowly and safely cannot be legitimately viewed as the cause of speeding recklessly, even though the former generally precedes the latter. Almost all reckless speeding is preceded by safe driving, just as the majority of hard drug use is preceded by the use of marijuana. The temporal sequencing alone in these scenarios is insufficient to establish a causal relation. Similarly, it is often suggested that a statistical correlation exists between ice cream sales and incidents of drowning. Ice cream sales and drownings are directly correlated, just as marijuana use and hard drug use are directly correlated. Yet the associations in both scenarios may be due to an unmeasured third variable—such as the effect of warm weather on both ice cream sales and the number of people who go swimming.

The consistency with which the first two gateway propositions have been observed makes it very unlikely that the link between early marijuana use and the subsequent use of more serious drugs is due to chance. Accordingly, researchers have extensively investigated this relationship in order to understand the mechanisms and processes that might link early marijuana use with the subsequent use of more serious drugs. While a causal process may be at play, other explanations have been explored as well. The potential explanations that could account for the observed associations between early marijuana use and the subsequent use of more serious drugs fall into one of three broad hypotheses (see Hall and Lynskey 2005).

The first hypothesis, known as the *sociological* or *environmental* explanation, postulates that the link between marijuana use and the use of more serious drugs exists because marijuana and other illicit substances are bought and sold in the same black markets. The second hypothesis, sometimes called the *common-cause* or the *common liability* explanation, posits that individuals with certain characteristics are at an increased risk for both marijuana use and the use of other more serious drugs. That is, environmental, interpersonal, or genetic factors that influenced the use of marijuana may also be responsible for the use of higher-stage, or more serious, drugs (see Kandel and Jessor 2002). The third hypothesis, known as the *causal* explanation, suggests that there is something about marijuana, perhaps its pharmacology, that makes marijuana users more likely to progress in the sequence of substance initiation. The three hypotheses are not mutually exclusive.

The Sociological or Environmental Explanation

The first hypothesis outlined earlier suggests that some marijuana users progress to more serious drugs because they have increased access to black markets in which both marijuana and other illicit substances are available. Whereas the causal gateway hypothesis suggests that marijuana, itself, causes individuals to progress to hard drugs, this hypothesis suggests that the social and environmental context of marijuana use provides users more opportunities to try other substances. Because marijuana users are exposed to illicit drug markets, illicit drug dealers, and drug-using peers, they likely have increased access to purchase or use other illicit substances and are exposed to social norms that support drug use.

There is some evidence supporting the sociological explanation of the gateway sequence. Drawing on nationally representative samples of young adults in the United States, researchers found that young people who use gateway drugs have increased opportunities to use other drugs and are more likely to use them given the opportunity (Wagner and Anthony 2002). For example, young people who had used tobacco or alcohol were about three times more likely than nonusers to have an opportunity to try marijuana. Moreover, among those who never used alcohol, tobacco, or marijuana, about 13 percent had an opportunity to use cocaine by the age of 25. In contrast, among those young people who had already used marijuana and either alcohol or tobacco, 75 percent had an opportunity to use cocaine by the age of 25.

Cross-national evidence also provides some support for the sociological explanation. Drawing on data from 17 countries, researchers explored how drug use initiation varies between countries (Degenhardt et al. 2010). While it was generally observed that lower-stage substances in the gateway sequence predicted the use of higher-stage substances, the strength of the associations varied between countries. Moreover, "violations" to the gateway sequence were observed in some countries. In Japan, for example, the use of other illicit substances by young people was more prevalent than the use of marijuana, and 83 percent of other illicit drug users did not use marijuana prior to using other illicit substances. Given that marijuana was rarely used before other illicit substances in countries where marijuana use was uncommon, this research indicates that access or exposure to certain drugs plays a part in the sequence of substance use initiation. This and other evidence showing that the gateway sequence is not universal suggests that social or environmental factors likely influence the order of substance use initiation.

The Common-Cause Explanation

The second hypothesis outlined earlier proposes that marijuana use and the use of other illicit drugs are associated because both behaviors are caused by common factors (Hall and Lynskey 2005). That is, it is hypothesized that the factors that influence the use of marijuana also influence the use of higher-stage, or more serious, drugs (see Kandel and Jessor 2002). Following this hypothesis, it is possible for marijuana use to both precede and predict more serious drug use without being the cause of more serious drug use. This theory is also referred to as the *common liability* hypothesis because it is proposed that the factors that make a person liable to use marijuana are similar to those that make him or her liable to use other substances.

Controlled laboratory experiments would be the ideal method for determining marijuana's causal role in substance use progression and for ruling out common causes. However, it is neither feasible nor ethical to randomly assign some adolescents to take marijuana and compare their subsequent illicit drug use with a control group of adolescents who were not assigned the marijuana condition. Researchers are therefore left to observe the effects of early marijuana use among only those adolescents who select to use marijuana. The unavoidable methodological problem with this procedure is that those adolescents who select to use marijuana are not randomly assigned. To the contrary, early marijuana users are more likely to display other nonconforming and antisocial behaviors (Hall and Lynskey 2005). Therefore, it may be that early marijuana use and the use of other illicit substances are simply behaviors exhibited by those individuals with a penchant for risk-taking and nonconformity.

While observational researchers cannot randomly assign some adolescents to use marijuana, there are statistical procedures which help to isolate the effects of early marijuana use on the subsequent use of more serious drugs. These methods, which can be varied and complex, generally follow the same basic procedures. First, researchers gather individual-level data on marijuana use, illicit drug use, and the factors that could be common causes of both marijuana use and the use of more serious drugs. In gateway models, common causes might include measures of family life, age, gender, deviant behavior, peer associations, adversity, socioeconomic status, traumatic experiences, psychological health, and other psychosocial factors that could make individuals vulnerable to all forms of illicit drug use. Second, researchers identify whether marijuana use precedes other illicit substance use and whether a statistical association exists between early marijuana use and subsequent illicit drug use. Third, researchers statistically "control" for these common causes and assess if the statistical association between early marijuana use and later illicit drug use remains after taking into account the influence of these factors.

This method has been applied widely to test gateway causation, and results suggest that common causes explain some of the documented temporal and statistical associations between early marijuana use and the subsequent use of more serious drugs. For example, using data from a sample of young adults from South Florida, researchers documented the existence of a statistical association between early marijuana use and the subsequent use of more serious drugs (Van Gundy and Rebellon 2010). They also found that this association remained statistically significant, even after controlling for variables related to age, life course roles, and adolescent stress exposure. However, the statistical association between early marijuana use and later illicit drug *abuse or dependence* was no longer statistically significant after taking into account teen stress exposure and life course variables. In addition, they found that early marijuana use did not elevate the risk for other illicit substance use among young adults who were employed or among individuals over 20 years of age.

A study from New Zealand similarly found some evidence that other factors help explain the link between marijuana use and illicit substance use (Fergusson and Horwood 1997). As expected, early onset marijuana users had higher rates of later substance use. However, the association between early marijuana use and later illicit substance use decreased substantially after the researchers accounted for the fact that early marijuana users already belonged to a high-risk population. Specifically, early marijuana users were characterized by social disadvantage, childhood adversity, behavioral difficulties, and affiliations with substance-using or delinquent peers. While the association between early marijuana use and other substance use was substantially reduced after taking into account these risk factors, these common causes did not fully explain the observed relationship between early marijuana use and the subsequent use of more serious drugs.

An interesting research design that helps to test whether genetic or environmental factors are causes of both marijuana use and the use of other illicit substances involves the observation of twins (see Lynskey et al. 2003). Specifically, this type of research helps to parcel out the relative contributions of environmental and genetic factors as common causes of both marijuana use and other illicit substance use. If it is assumed that twins who were raised in the same household shared a common environment, then differences between twin siblings in respect to substance use progression would presumably not be the result of environmental factors.

Genetic factors are also hypothesized as a common cause of both marijuana use and the use of more serious drugs. Twin studies that observe both monozygotic (identical) and dizygotic (fraternal) twin siblings can therefore observe the risks of progressing from marijuana to more serious drugs among genetically similar and genetically different siblings who shared a common environment (see Cleveland and Wiebe 2008).

Several studies have examined differences in substance use between twin siblings, and there is consistent evidence that genetic and environmental risk factors account for some, but not necessarily all, of the link between early marijuana use and the subsequent use of more serious substances. A review of this research identified four studies that used samples of twins to explicitly test the marijuana gateway model (Agrawal and Lynskey 2006). Each study found significant evidence supporting the common-cause hypothesis as a possible explanation of the link between marijuana use and the subsequent use of other hard drugs. However, two of the studies could not rule out the possibility that early marijuana use had a causal influence on the subsequent use of hard drugs.

The Causal Explanation

There is also evidence supporting the third hypothesis that the relationship between early marijuana use and the subsequent use of more serious drugs may be causal (see Hall and Lynskey 2005 for review). Some of this evidence comes from longitudinal studies that observe an association between early marijuana use and the subsequent use of more serious drugs that persists even after statistically controlling for the factors that could influence both behaviors.

In an article published in the *Journal of Drug Issues*, researchers used longitudinal data from a sample of 1,725 youth to assess whether variables derived from the leading criminological theories help explain the link between early marijuana use and later illicit drug use (Rebellon and Van Gundy 2006). They found that even after statistically controlling for potential common causes, marijuana users were between three and five times more likely than counterparts to use other illicit substances. Similar results were reported in a series of studies from New Zealand (Fergusson et al. 2000, 2006). In an article published in the journal *Addiction*, researchers found that marijuana use remained strongly correlated with other forms of illicit drug use even after controlling for common factors (Fergusson et al. 2000). These results provide some evidence that marijuana has a causal influence on subsequent illicit substance use. However, the possibility that unmeasured common causes account for the association between marijuana use and more serious substance use limits the extent that these types of studies can definitively establish causation.

Research on twins also provides evidence that the link between early marijuana use and subsequent illicit substance use cannot be fully explained by genetic or environmental factors (see Hall and Lynskey 2005). For example, Michael T. Lynskey and colleagues (2003) examined the relationship between early marijuana use and other illicit substance use in pairs of twin siblings in which only one of the twins had used marijuana prior to the age of 17. They found that the twin who used marijuana by the age of 17 had higher odds of other drug use compared to their twin sibling who had not used marijuana prior to the age of 17. The researchers further found that early marijuana use was strongly associated with later illicit drug use even after statistically controlling for correlated risk factors such as early-onset alcohol or tobacco use, parental conflict, childhood sexual abuse, conduct disorder, and depression.

It has also been hypothesized that the pharmacological characteristics of marijuana may cause the progression from marijuana use to the use of more serious drugs (see Hall and Lynskey 2005; Fergusson and Horwood 2015). There is some evidence supporting this hypothesis. In a 2009 article published in the journal *Pharmacological Research*, researchers reviewed animal studies related to the gateway hypothesis and found evidence that the gateway progression may have a neurobiological basis (Realini et al. 2009). In an article published in the journal *Neuropsychopharmacology*, for instance, researchers found that THC exposure in male adolescent rats increased opiate self-administration (Ellgren et al. 2007). Similarly, an article published in the same journal found that chronic exposure to a synthetic cannabinoid agonist increased susceptibility to cocaine self-administration in female but not male adolescent rats (Higuera-Matas et al. 2008). On the other hand, an article published in the *European Journal of Pharmacology* found that cannabinoid exposure in adolescent rats did not affect subsequent responses to amphetamines (Ellgren et al. 2004). While more research is necessary, it is likely that advancements in neurological and pharmacological research will help answer important questions about the gateway hypothesis.

NATURAL EXPERIMENTS

Marijuana's gateway effects can also be indirectly assessed by looking at illicit substance use in states where marijuana has been legalized for either recreational or medical use. If medical or recreational marijuana laws increase the prevalence of marijuana use in these states, the gateway causation hypothesis would predict a concomitant increase in the use of more serious drugs. Very few studies have investigated the link between marijuana legalization and other illicit substance use, and more research is necessary to make strong causal inferences. The limited existing evidence suggests that the implementation of medical marijuana laws is not associated with increases in the use of other psychoactive substances. For example, research published in the *Journal of Health Economics* found that state medical marijuana laws were associated with an increase in marijuana use, but they did not affect the use of other substances (Wen et al. 2015). Moreover, an article published in *JAMA Internal Medicine* found that state-level medical marijuana laws were associated with reductions in opioid overdose mortality rates (Bachhuber et al. 2014). While this research neither establishes a causal link between marijuana use and overdose deaths nor speaks directly to gateway patterns of substance use, it nevertheless introduces the possibility that access to medical marijuana may reduce opioid use and related problems.

FURTHER READING

Agrawal, Arpana, and Michael T. Lynskey. "The genetic epidemiology of marijuana use, abuse and dependence." *Addiction* 101, no. 6 (2006): 801–812.

Agrawal, Arpana, Michael C. Neale, Carol A. Prescott, and Kenneth S. Kendler. "Marijuana and other illicit drugs: comorbid use and abuse/dependence in males and females." *Behavior Genetics* 34, no. 3 (2004): 217–228.

Bachhuber, Marcus A., Brendan Saloner, Chinazo O. Cunningham, and Colleen L. Barry. "Medical marijuana laws and opioid analgesic overdose mortality in the United States, 1999–2010." *JAMA Internal Medicine* 174, no. 10 (2014): 1668–1673.

Cleveland, H. Harrington, and Richard P. Wiebe. "Understanding the association between adolescent marijuana use and later serious drug use: gateway effect or developmental trajectory?" *Development and Psychopathology* 20, no. 02 (2008): 615–632.

Degenhardt, Louisa, Lisa Dierker, Wai Tat Chiu, Maria Elena Medina-Mora, Yehuda Neumark, Nancy Sampson, Jordi Alonso, et al. "Evaluating the drug use 'gateway' theory using cross-national data: consistency and associations of the order of initiation of drug use among participants in the WHO World Mental Health Surveys." *Drug and Alcohol Dependence* 108, no. 1 (2010): 84–97.

Ellgren, Maria, Yasmin L. Hurd, and Johan Franck. "Amphetamine effects on dopamine levels and behavior following cannabinoid exposure during adolescence." *European Journal of Pharmacology* 497, no. 2 (2004): 205–213.

Ellgren, Maria, Sabrina M. Spano, and Yasmin L. Hurd. "Adolescent cannabis exposure alters opiate intake and opioid limbic neuronal populations in adult rats." *Neuropsychopharmacology* 32, no. 3 (2007): 607–615.

Fergusson, David M., Joseph M. Boden, and L. John Horwood. "Marijuana use and other illicit drug use: testing the marijuana gateway hypothesis." *Addiction* 101, no. 4 (2006): 556–569.

Fergusson, David M., Joseph M. Boden, and L. John Horwood. "Psychosocial sequelae of marijuana use and implications for policy: findings from the Christchurch Health and Development Study." *Social Psychiatry and Psychiatric Epidemiology* 50, no. 9 (2015): 1317–1326.

Fergusson, David M., and L. John Horwood. "Does marijuana use encourage other forms of illicit drug use?" *Addiction* 95, no. 4 (2000): 505–520.

Fergusson, David M., and L. John Horwood. "Early onset marijuana use and psychosocial adjustment in young adults." *Addiction* 92, no. 3 (1997): 279–296.

Fergusson, David M., L. John Horwood, and Nicola Swain-Campbell. "Marijuana use and psychosocial adjustment in adolescence and young adulthood." *Addiction* 97, no. 9 (2002): 1123–1135.

Golub, Andrew, and Bruce D. Johnson. "Substance use progression and hard drug use in inner-city New York." In *Stages and pathways of drug involvement: examining the gateway hypothesis*, edited by Denise B. Kandel, 90–112. Cambridge: Cambridge University Press, 2002.

Hall, Wayne D., and Michael Lynskey. "Is marijuana a gateway drug? Testing hypotheses about the relationship between marijuana use and the use of other illicit drugs." *Drug and Alcohol Review* 24, no. 1 (2005): 39–48.

Higuera-Matas, Alejandro, María Luisa Soto-Montenegro, Nuria Del Olmo, Miguel Miguéns, Isabel Torres, Juan José Vaquero, Javier Sánchez, Carmen García-Lecumberri, Manuel Desco, and Emilio Ambrosio. "Augmented acquisition of cocaine self-administration and altered brain glucose metabolism in adult female but not male rats exposed to a cannabinoid agonist during adolescence." *Neuropsychopharmacology* 33, no. 4 (2008): 806–813.

Kandel, Denise B. "Does marijuana use cause the use of other drugs?" *JAMA* 289, no. 4 (2003): 482–483.

Kandel, Denise B. "Stages in adolescent involvement in drug use." *Science* 190, no. 4217 (1975): 912–914.

Kandel, Denise B., and Richard Jessor. "The gateway hypothesis revisited." In *Stages and pathways of drug involvement. examining the gateway hypothesis*, edited by Denise B. Kandel, 365–373. Cambridge: Cambridge University Press, 2002.

Kandel, Denise B., and Eric Kandel. "The gateway hypothesis of substance abuse: developmental, biological and societal perspectives." *Acta Paediatrica* 104, no. 2 (2015): 130–137.

Kandel, Denise B., and Kazuo Yamaguchi. "Stages of drug involvement in the U.S. population." In *Stages and pathways of drug involvement: examining the gateway hypothesis*, edited by Denise B. Kandel, 65–89. Cambridge: Cambridge University Press, 2002.

Kandel, Denise B., Kazuo Yamaguchi, and K. Chen. Stages of progression in drug involvement from adolescence to adulthood: further evidence for the gateway theory. *Journal of Studies on Alcohol* 53, no. 5 (1992): 447–457.

Lynskey, Michael T., Andrew C. Heath, Kathleen K. Bucholz, Wendy S. Slutske, Pamela A. F. Madden, Elliot C. Nelson, Dixie J. Statham, and Nicholas G. Martin. "Escalation of drug use in early-onset marijuana users vs co-twin controls." *JAMA* 289, no. 4 (2003): 427–433.

Lynskey, Michael T., Jacqueline M. Vink, and Dorret I. Boomsma. "Early onset marijuana use and progression to other drug use in a sample of Dutch twins." *Behavior Genetics* 36, no. 2 (2006): 195–200.

Mackesy-Amiti, Mary Ellen, Michael Fendrich, and Paul J. Goldstein. "Sequence of drug use among serious drug users: typical vs atypical progression." *Drug and Alcohol Dependence* 45, no. 3 (1997): 185–196.

Morgan, John P., Diane Riley, and Gregory B. Chesher. "Marijuana: legal reform, medicinal use and harm reduction." In *Psychoactive drugs and harm reduction: from faith to science*, edited by Nick Heather, Alex Wodak, Ethan Nadelmann, and Pat O'Hare, 211–229. London: Whurr, 1993.

Realini, N., T. Rubino, and D. Parolaro. "Neurobiological alterations at adult age triggered by adolescent exposure to cannabinoids." *Pharmacological Research* 60, no. 2 (2009): 132–138.

Rebellon, Cesar J., and Karen Van Gundy. "Can social psychological delinquency theory explain the link between marijuana and other illicit drug use? A longitudinal analysis of the gateway hypothesis." *Journal of Drug Issues* 36, no. 3 (2006): 515–539.

Secades-Villa, Roberto, Olaya Garcia-Rodríguez, Chelsea J. Jin, Shuai Wang, and Carlos Blanco. "Probability and predictors of the cannabis gateway effect: a national study." *International Journal of Drug Policy* 26, no. 2 (2015): 135–142.

Van Gundy, Karen, and Cesar J. Rebellon. "A life-course perspective
on the 'gateway hypothesis.'" *Journal of Health and Social Behavior* 51,
no. 3 (2010): 244–259.

Wagner, Fernando A., and James C. Anthony. "Into the world of illegal
drug use: exposure opportunity and other mechanisms linking the
use of alcohol, tobacco, marijuana, and cocaine." *American Journal of
Epidemiology* 155, no. 10 (2002): 918–925.

Wen, Hefei, Jason M. Hockenberry, and Janet R. Cummings. "The effect
of medical marijuana laws on adolescent and adult use of marijuana,
alcohol, and other substances." *Journal of Health Economics* 42 (2015):
64–80.

Young, Susan E., Susan K. Mikulich, Matthew B. Goodwin, John Hardy,
Cheryl L. Martin, Mark S. Zoccolillo, and Thomas J. Crowley. "Treated
delinquent boys' substance use: onset, pattern, relationship to conduct
and mood disorders." *Drug and Alcohol Dependence* 37, no. 2 (1995):
149–162.

Q19. DOES MARIJUANA USE OR MISUSE INCREASE CRIMINAL BEHAVIOR?

Answer: The evidence is mixed. However, there is no overwhelming
evidence that the use of marijuana increases engagement in criminal
behavior.

The Facts: Most research confirms that marijuana users are more likely
than non-users to engage in criminal or deviant behavior. In spite of this
consistent evidence, the exact nature of this relationship remains unclear.
Certainly, marijuana use causes an increase in crimes related to the possession and sale of the drug. However, there is inconsistent evidence that
marijuana use leads to an increase in other criminal behavior. While
there is some evidence of a causal relationship between marijuana use
and crime, there is also evidence indicating that marijuana use and other
problem behaviors share common causes.

HISTORY

Soon after marijuana arrived in the United States it developed a reputation as a very dangerous drug. Marijuana was initially believed to be a
narcotic, and was viewed alongside other narcotics (opioids) as a pow-
erfully addictive drug. Marijuana was said to cause insanity, mania, and

psychosis – sometimes irreversibly. There was also widespread belief that marijuana acted as a "stepping-stone" (or gateway) to other drug use. As described in Q16, the Reefer Madness era played host to many fears over marijuana and the people who used it, but few were more enduring than the assertion that marijuana led to crime, violence, and aggression.

In the decades leading up to the 1937 Marihuana Tax Act, many Americans learned about marijuana and marijuana users from sensationalized portrayals in newspapers, magazines, and movies. Decades later, some of this media content was rediscovered by a generation of young Americans who could not help but see a bit of humor and irony in the caricature of marijuana users. The 1936 film *Reefer Madness*, for example, warned viewers that "marihuana is that drug—a frightful narcotic—an unspeakable scourge—The Real Public Enemy Number One!" (Markert 2013). Government officials, law enforcement personnel, and medical doctors also contributed to the prevailing fears over marijuana. In July 1937, just prior to the passage of the Marihuana Tax Act, Harry J. Anslinger, the first commissioner of the Federal Bureau of Narcotics, coauthored "Marijuana: Assassin of Youth" which depicted the scourge in gruesome detail:

> It was an unprovoked crime some years ago which brought the first realization that the age-old drug had gained a foothold in America. An entire family was murdered by a youthful addict in Florida. When officers arrived at the home they found the youth staggering about in a human slaughterhouse. With an ax he had killed his father, his mother, two brothers, and a sister. He seemed to be in a daze.
>
> In at least two dozen other comparatively recent cases of murder or degenerate sex attacks, many of them committed by youths, marijuana proved to be a contributing cause. Perhaps you remember the young desperado in Michigan who, a few months ago, caused a reign of terror by his career of burglaries and holdups, finally to be sent to prison for life after kidnapping a Michigan state policeman, killing him, then handcuffing him to the post of a rural mailbox. This young bandit was a marijuana fiend. (Anslinger and Cooper 1937)

THEORIES OF DRUG USE AND CRIME

Although fears over marijuana have tempered and changed with time, there are still concerns that marijuana causes crime and violence. In fact, this belief is one of the reasons why marijuana and other drugs are prohibited. The most obvious link between marijuana use and crime relates to its prohibition. In jurisdictions that prohibit marijuana possession, for example, individuals who possess marijuana are, by default, committing crimes. In this sense, nearly 45 percent of Americans ages 12 and older have committed the crime of marijuana possession at some point in their lives.

Several theories that could help explain the link between drug use and crime have been advanced, some of which could also help explain the association between marijuana use and crime. Paul Goldstein (2011), for example, proposed a three-part framework to explain the relationship between drugs and violence. First, the intoxicating effects of some drugs can cause excitement and irrationality, leading to a form of *psychophar-macological* violence. Second, some drug users may engage in *economically compulsive* violence in order to support an expensive drug habit. Finally, *systemic* violence can occur within the context of illegal drug markets wherein violence or aggression may be used to control territory, settle disputes, or enforce rules. While Goldstein's framework was proposed as a basis for understanding connections between drugs and violence, a broader application of the theory is suggestive of the various ways that drugs might be linked to crime more generally.

There are reasons to suspect that marijuana use might increase the likelihood of crime. For example, marijuana use can affect memory, cognition, and attention (Moore and Stuart 2005). As a result, marijuana users may find it difficult to interpret social cues during interpersonal conflicts. Additionally, marijuana intoxication is sometimes accompanied by feelings of paranoia and panic, which could lead to aggression or violence if an individual feels threatened or provoked. Given that marijuana is illegal in most places, marijuana users might develop a certain level of comfort participating in other deviant or illegal behaviors. On the other hand, there are also reasons to suspect that marijuana use might lead to decreases in violence, aggression, and crime. For example, some marijuana users report feeling relaxed, sedated, empathic, euphoric, and tolerant, none of which would seem likely to promote violent or aggressive behavior (see Ashton 2001; Ostrowsky 2011; Agrawal et al. 2014).

Another possibility is that marijuana use and crime are not causally related—that the association between the two is spurious. That is, even if marijuana use and crime are statistically related, they both may be the result of something else. As discussed in Q8, in observational research, causation can be inferred only (1) when two variables are statistically associated, (2) when the causal variable precedes the outcome variable, and (3) when alternative explanations for the association have been ruled out. The final criterion, known as "nonspuriousness," is perhaps the most challenging criterion to meet. This is true because of the possibility that both marijuana use and criminal behavior share some of the same risk factors. The same genetic, environmental, or personal factors that make some individuals liable to use marijuana may also make them liable to participate in other deviant or problem behaviors.

EXPERIMENTAL EVIDENCE

Experimental researchers have developed novel ways to investigate whether marijuana and THC affect human aggression. These experiments generally put research participants and research confederates into competitive situations wherein the participant is antagonized by the confederate. Observations are then made to determine whether marijuana use affects how the participants respond to being antagonized. Because these experiments take place under controlled experimental conditions, the results may indicate whether marijuana itself induces aggression. An early review of this literature found evidence indicating that marijuana and THC decreased aggressive and violent behavior in humans (Miczek et al. 1994). However, a more recent review concluded that laboratory studies on marijuana and aggression were mixed and that the evidence was insufficient to support or refute a direct relationship between marijuana and violence (Moore and Stuart 2005)

In an early experimental study of marijuana and aggression, 30 male college students were treated with low-dose, medium-dose, or high-dose THC and then competed against an increasingly provocative opponent in a reaction-time competition (Myerscough and Taylor 1985). The winner of each task would administer an electric shock to his competitor at an intensity of his choosing. The researchers observed which shock intensity the participants chose and documented if aggression varied on account of the marijuana dose. The research did not include a placebo control group, but the results showed that the subjects in the low-dose group were most aggressive, whereas the subjects in the high-dose group remained relatively nonaggressive. In a related study that used a Point Subtraction Aggression Paradigm, participants were given variable doses of marijuana or placebo and were paired with fictitious partners who had the ability to remove monetary points from the participants (Cherek et al. 1993). The researchers found that aggressive responding was increased in the first hour after smoking marijuana and that aggression was highest following the use of the high concentration marijuana cigarette. However, in a second study, the same research team found that marijuana use was associated with a decrease in aggressive responding, compared to placebo, under the high provocation condition but not under the low provocation condition (Cherek and Dougherty 1995).

Given the evidence demonstrating the existence of a marijuana withdrawal syndrome, some researchers have examined whether the sudden discontinuation of heavy marijuana use is associated with aggression (see Budney et al. 2004; Q15). Limited research indicates that chronic marijuana users exhibit increased aggression during the first week of abstinence. For example, using a variation of the Point Subtraction Aggression Paradigm, researchers found that heavy marijuana users exhibited more aggressive behavior on days 3 and 7 of a 28-day abstinence period (Kouri et al. 1999). Increases in aggressive responding returned to pre-abstinence levels by the end of the study.

OBSERVATIONAL EVIDENCE

Relatively consistent observational evidence shows that marijuana use is common among arrestees and incarcerated individuals. For example, 1990s data from the International Arrestee Drug Abuse Monitoring (I-ADAM) program showed that 40.6 percent of detained arrestees in the United States tested positive for marijuana, and almost 65 percent of arrestees ages 15–20 tested positive for marijuana (Taylor and Bennett 1999). Likewise, drawing on data from the 2004 Survey of Inmates in State and Federal Correctional Facilities, researchers found that over 78 percent of state prisoners had used marijuana in their lifetime, 40 percent had used marijuana in the month before their offense, and 15 percent used marijuana at the time of their offense (Mumola and Karberg 2006).

Evidence from outside the criminal justice system also shows that individuals who use marijuana are more likely than nonusers to participate in deviant or criminal acts. For example, a meta-analysis that combined data from 30 studies found that marijuana use was positively associated with delinquent and problem behaviors (Derzon and Lipsey 1999). However, there was also some evidence that problem behaviors preceded marijuana use. A 2005 review of the literature that covered 25 years of studies found that cross-sectional and longitudinal evidence supported the existence of an association between marijuana use and violence (Moore and Stuart 2005). Similarly, a meta-analysis that combined data from multiple studies found that marijuana users were 1.5 times more likely than nonmarijuana users to criminally offend (Bennett et al. 2008). This research also showed that the odds of heroin users offending were over 3 times higher than the odds of non-heroin users offending, while cocaine users were about 2.5 times more likely than non-cocaine users to offend.

While the preceding observational evidence suggests that marijuana use is associated with delinquent or violent behavior, additional forms of evidence are needed to better characterize this documented association. Specifically, evidence is needed to clarify whether the relationship between marijuana use and problem behaviors reflects causal processes or if both behaviors result from the same common causes. This type of evidence comes from longitudinal studies that are able to examine temporal associations between marijuana use and problem behaviors, as well as determine if alternative explanations might account for observed associations between the two behaviors. Evidence from longitudinal research, however, has resulted in conflicting evidence.

Some longitudinal evidence suggests that marijuana use leads to an increase in crime. For example, a study published in the journal, *Psychological Medicine* utilized longitudinal data from a sample of 411 young males from a working-class neighborhood in London to track the association between marijuana use and violence (Schoeler et al. 2016). The researchers found that marijuana use was associated with an increased risk of subsequent violent offending, even after controlling for potential confounders such as family history of criminality, other substance use, childhood antisocial behavior, and mental health history. Moreover, the researchers observed a dose-response relationship between marijuana use and violence, wherein the continued use of marijuana had a particularly strong effect on violence. There was also evidence of a reciprocal (bi-directional) relationship between marijuana use and violence in early adulthood, indicating that violence also predicted marijuana use at that life stage. In late life, though, violence was not associated with subsequent marijuana use. While observational data of this sort cannot be used to confirm a causal link, these authors conclude that this evidence supports the existence of a causal relationship between marijuana use and subsequent violent outcomes.

Other research has shown that a substantial portion of the association between marijuana use and delinquent behaviors can be explained by the existence of confounding or covarying variables. Using longitudinal data from a sample of young people from New Zealand, researchers found that marijuana use before the age of 16, and particularly frequent marijuana use, was associated with an increased risk for juvenile offending later in life (Fergusson and Horwood 1997). They also found that early onset marijuana users were a high-risk population characterized by social disadvantage and childhood adversity. When the researchers statistically adjusted for these early-life risk factors, the relationship between marijuana use and juvenile offending was reduced substantially. Nevertheless, early marijuana users were still at an increased risk for juvenile offending even after adjusting for early-life risk factors. Thus, this research provides suggestive evidence that social disadvantage and childhood adversity put some individuals at an increased risk for both early onset marijuana use and juvenile offending. However, because only a portion of the link between early onset marijuana use and delinquent behavior was explained by these childhood and family factors, this research also provides some evidence of a cause and effect association between early marijuana use and problem behaviors.

Whereas the preceding evidence indicates the possible existence of a causal link between early marijuana use and subsequent problem behaviors, other studies have inferred the absence of a causal link. For example, drawing on a sample of youth from Pittsburgh, researchers found consistent longitudinal associations between frequent marijuana use and violence; however, they also found that the relationship between frequent marijuana use and violence was spurious (Wei et al. 2004). That is, the association between early marijuana use and subsequent violence was no longer significant when common risk factors, such as hard drug use, property crime, academic achievement, and race/ethnicity, were taken into account. Moreover, in a longitudinal study of a youth sample from Norway, researchers observed a link between early marijuana use and later criminal involvement that persisted even after controlling for confounding variables (Pedersen and Skardhamar 2009). However, when drug charges were excluded from the model, the researchers no longer observed a significant association between early marijuana use and subsequent criminal charges.

NATURAL EXPERIMENTS

A separate body of research examines how medical marijuana laws might affect crime rates. The existing research, however, has produced mixed results. For example, two studies examining medical marijuana laws and FBI crime data utilized different methods and came to conflicting conclusions. In a 2014 study, researchers examined data from 1990 to 2006 and found that state medical marijuana laws did not predict higher crime rates (Morris et al. 2014). Another study from 2014 used comparable data from 1995 to 2012 and observed contrasting patterns (Alford 2014). The results of this study showed that allowing for medical marijuana dispensaries increased property crime by 8.1 percent and increased robbery rates by just under 11 percent. On the other hand, policies allowing for the home cultivation of medical marijuana did not affect property crime rates and decreased the robbery rate by about 10 percent.

There are some reasons to suspect that medical marijuana dispensaries may uniquely affect crime rates (see Alford 2014). For example, if a lag exists between the time medical marijuana laws are passed and the time dispensaries open, there may be an unmet demand for marijuana that could affect robbery and assault rates. Also, once dispensaries are open, many operate as cash-only businesses, which could make the dispensaries or their employees targets for crime. Other evidence on the link between dispensaries and crime has been mixed, and more research is necessary to better understand how specific medical marijuana policy dimensions affect local communities (see Freisthler et al. 2013, 2016).

FURTHER READING

Agrawal, Arpana, Pamela A. F. Madden, Kathleen K. Bucholz, Andrew C. Heath, and Michael T. Lynskey. "Initial reactions to tobacco and cannabis smoking: a twin study." *Addiction* 109, no. 4 (2014): 663–671.

Alford, Catherine. *How medical marijuana laws affect crime rates*. University of Virginia, 2014.

Anslinger, Harry J., and Courtney Ryley Cooper. "Marihuana: assassin of youth." *American Magazine* 124 (1937): 19.

Ashton, C. Heather. "Pharmacology and effects of cannabis: a brief review." *The British Journal of Psychiatry* 178, no. 2 (2001): 101–106.

Bennett, Trevor, Katy Holloway, and David Farrington. "The statistical association between drug misuse and crime: a meta-analysis." *Aggression and Violent Behavior* 13, no. 2 (2008): 107–118.

Budney, Alan J., John R. Hughes, Brent A. Moore, and Ryan Vandrey. "Review of the validity and significance of cannabis withdrawal syndrome." *American Journal of Psychiatry* 161, no. 11 (2004): 1967–1977.

Cherek, Don R., and D. M. Dougherty. "Provocation frequency and its role in determining the effects of smoked marijuana on human aggressive responding." *Behavioural Pharmacology* 6, no. 4 (1995): 405–412.

Cherek, Don R., John D. Roache, Mark Egli, Chester Davis, Ralph Spiga, and Katherine Cowan. "Acute effects of marijuana smoking on aggressive, escape and point-maintained responding of male drug users." *Psychopharmacology* 111, no. 2 (1993): 163–168.

Derzon, James H., and Mark W. Lipsey. "A synthesis of the relationship of marijuana use with delinquent and problem behaviors." *School Psychology International* 20, no. 1 (1999): 57–68.

Fergusson, David M., and L. Horwood. "Early onset cannabis use and psychosocial adjustment in young adults." *Addiction* 92, no. 3 (1997): 279–296.

Freisthler, Bridget, Nancy J. Kepple, Revel Sims, and Scott E. Martin. "Evaluating medical marijuana dispensary policies: spatial methods for the study of environmentally based interventions." *American Journal of Community Psychology* 51, (2013): 278–288.

Freisthler, Bridget, William R. Ponicki, Andrew Gaidus, and Paul J. Gruenewald. "A micro-temporal geospatial analysis of medical marijuana dispensaries and crime in Long Beach, California." *Addiction* 111, (2016): 1027–1035.

Goldstein, Paul J. "The drugs/violence nexus: a tripartite conceptual framework." In *The American drug scene: an anthology*, edited by James A. Inciardi, and Karen McElrath, 6th ed., 374–384. New York: Oxford University Press, 2011.

Kouri, Elena M., Harrison G. Pope Jr., and Scott E. Lukas. "Changes in aggressive behavior during withdrawal from long-term marijuana use." *Psychopharmacology* 143, no. 3 (1999): 302–308.

Markert, John. *Hooked in film: substance abuse on the big screen.* Scarecrow Press, 2013.

Miczek, Klaus A., Joseph F. DeBold, Margaret Haney, Jennifer Tidey, Jeffrey Vivian, and Elise M. Weerts. "Alcohol, drugs of abuse, aggression, and violence." *Understanding and Preventing Violence* 3 (1994).

Moore, Todd M., and Gregory L. Stuart. "A review of the literature on marijuana and interpersonal violence." *Aggression and Violent Behavior* 10, no. 2 (2005): 171–192.

Morris, Robert G., Michael TenEyck, James C. Barnes, and Tomislav V. Kovandzic. "The effect of medical marijuana laws on crime: evidence from state panel data, 1990–2006." *PloS One* 9, no. 3 (2014): e92816.

Mumola, Christopher J., and Jennifer C. Karberg. *Drug use and dependence, state and federal prisoners, 2004.* Washington, DC: U.S. Department of Justice, Office of Justice Programs, Bureau of Justice Statistics, NCJ 213530, 2006.

Myerscough, Rodney, and Stuart P. Taylor. "The effects of marijuana on human physical aggression." *Journal of Personality and Social Psychology* 49, no. 6 (1985): 1541.

Ostrowsky, Michael K. "Does marijuana use lead to aggression and violent behavior?" *Journal of Drug Education* 41, no. 4 (2011): 369–389.

Pedersen, Willy, and Torbjørn Skardhamar. "Cannabis and crime: findings from a longitudinal study." *Addiction* 105, no. 1 (2009): 109–118.

Schoeler, Tabea, Delphine Theobald, J.-B. Pingault, David P. Farrington, Wesley G. Jennings, Alex R. Piquero, Jeremy W. Coid, and Sagnik

Bhattacharyya. "Continuity of cannabis use and violent offending over the life course." *Psychological Medicine* 46, no. 8 (2016): 1663–1677.

Taylor, Bruce, and Trevor Bennett. *Comparing drug use rates of detained arrestees in the United States and England.* Collingdale, PA: DIANE Publishing, 1999.

Wei, Evelyn H., Rolf Loeber, and Helene Raskin White. "Teasing apart the developmental associations between alcohol and marijuana use and violence." *Journal of Contemporary Criminal Justice* 20, no. 2 (2004): 166–183.

Q20. IS DRIVING UNDER THE INFLUENCE OF MARIJUANA SAFE?

Answer: No. Although the evidence is not definitive, research from diverse fields suggests that driving under the influence of marijuana is not safe. Cognitive and psychomotor research studies strongly indicate that many of the important skills necessary for safe driving are negatively affected by acute marijuana intoxication. Interactive driving simulators and closed-course driving tests generally, but not always, show that marijuana intoxication negatively affects driving performance. However, the performance decrements observed in cognitive and psychomotor research do not always translate to performance impairments in driving simulations and in closed-course driving tests. Observational research that investigates automobile accidents in the real world generally shows that marijuana intoxication increases the risk of crash.

The Facts: Motor vehicle-related deaths decreased by 15 percent between 2007 and 2015; however, over 32,000 Americans still die each year in traffic accidents (CDC 2016). Although traffic accidents affect people of all ages, they are the leading cause of death for Americans under 30 years of age (CDC 2016). National data from 2014 indicate that 12.4 percent of Americans drove under the influence of alcohol in the past year, and 9,957 people were killed in alcohol-impaired driving crashes (Azofeifa et al. 2015; CDC 2017). It is further estimated that about 3.2 percent of Americans drove under the influence of marijuana in the past year, and there has been a substantial increase in the number of weekend nighttime drivers who test positive for THC (Azofeifa et al. 2015; Berning et al. 2015). Given the increase in the number of states with medical and recreational marijuana laws, there is heightened concern that marijuana-impaired individuals will take to the roads and put themselves and others at risk.

METHODOLOGICAL CONSIDERATIONS

Researchers from several disciplines use a variety of methods to investigate the link between marijuana and traffic safety. Some researchers focus on the cognitive and psychomotor skills necessary for safe driving and use laboratory experiments to test the effects of marijuana intoxication on cognition, attention, coordination, and reaction time. Other researchers compare marijuana-impaired drivers with sober drivers as they navigate obstacles and scenarios on closed courses or on computer simulators. While the results of these investigations lend themselves to some inferences regarding how marijuana intoxication might affect driving, they do not directly test what happens in the real world.

It is possible to investigate the link between marijuana use and traffic safety in the real world; however, this research presents its own set of challenges. For example, some observational studies use blood or urine samples to test for THC-COOH, an inactive metabolite, which has a long detection window and is not always a reliable indicator of impairment or intoxication (see Gjerde and Mørland 2016; Hartman and Huestis 2013). Even when studies examine THC blood concentrations as an indicator of recent marijuana use, there is ongoing debate regarding the THC levels that are associated with impairment (see National Academies of Sciences, Engineering, and Medicine 2017). Moreover, real-world links between marijuana use and motor vehicle accidents are confounded by the demographics of risky drivers. Young, risk-taking males are more likely to participate in many problem behaviors, including both marijuana use and dangerous driving (Hartman and Huestis 2013). As a result, marijuana is likely to be detected among risky or dangerous drivers regardless of its effect on driving (Smiley 1999).

COGNITIVE AND PSYCHOMOTOR
LABORATORY RESEARCH

Given the ubiquity of automobiles, it can be easy to underestimate how many complex skills and abilities are necessary in order to drive safely. Safe driving requires sustained attention, focus, quick decisions and reactions, coordination, task prioritization, and ongoing risk assessments. Accordingly, one method used to evaluate whether marijuana and other substances affect automobile operation involves testing how specific cognitive functions and psychomotor skills are affected by drug use. These experiments generally take place in laboratories and assess how marijuana or THC affects the skills necessary for safe driving.

Laboratory research investigating how marijuana affects cognitive functioning and psychomotor skills uses a variety of research designs. Some tests evaluate how marijuana affects "free recall" of previously learned information. Other tests measure how the perception of time and distance is affected by marijuana use. Others measure how balance and coordination are affected by marijuana use. Some tests are quite novel. For example, the *Wisconsin Card Sorting Task*—used to evaluate executive function—tests the subjects' ability to match cards according to color, form, and number based on rules that are discovered through trial and error. The *Tower of London* test is also used to assess executive function by evaluating the speed and accuracy with which subjects can guess how many single moves are required to rearrange a set of colored balls to match a desired end arrangement. Various *gambling tasks* are also used to assess risk-taking behavior by evaluating the speed and accuracy with which subjects can choose the most likely outcome in a low-stakes gambling paradigm.

Most laboratory-based experiments show that marijuana and THC cause performance decrements in tasks measuring memory, divided and sustained attention, reaction time, recall of learned information, and motor control (Ramaekers et al. 2004; Laberge and Ward 2004). While marijuana does not necessarily affect all cognitive functions and psychomotor abilities, the weight of evidence suggests that many of the important skills necessary for safe driving are negatively affected by acute marijuana intoxication. A 2013 review published in *Clinical Chemistry* summarized the existing research and showed that many, but not all, cognitive and psychomotor experiments indicate that marijuana and THC can cause impairments in perception, reaction time, risk taking, coordination, and divided attention (Hartman and Huestis 2013).

In order to drive safely, drivers must be able to react to unexpected circumstances, and there is relatively strong evidence that marijuana intoxication negatively affects reaction time. For example, in a 2009 study published in the *Journal of Psychopharmacology*, researchers found that THC intoxication led to increased stop reaction time in both occasional and frequent marijuana users (Ramaekers et al. 2009). Similarly, in a 2006 study published in the journal *Neuropsychopharmacology*, the same research team found that high-potency marijuana increased stop reaction time in a sample of recreational marijuana users (Ramaekers et al. 2006).

However, a 2011 study found that THC did not affect stop reaction time in a sample of 21 heavy marijuana users (Ramaekers et al. 2011).

Drivers must also be able to pay close attention to their surroundings and accurately respond to changes in their environment. In a 2008 study published in the *Journal of Psychopharmacology*, researchers evaluated how 13 mg and 17 mg THC cigarettes affected these skills in a sample of regular marijuana users (Weinstein et al. 2008). In general, the researchers found that smoking the high-dose THC cigarette consistently resulted in cognitive-motor impairments, whereas the lower-dose cigarettes caused less impairment. In a virtual maze test, for example, participants collided with the walls more often after smoking the 17 mg THC cigarette, but not after the 13 mg THC cigarette. Results from *the Wisconsin Card Sorting Task* indicated performance impairments with both the 13 mg and 17 mg THC cigarettes, but a more pronounced impairment was observed with the higher-dose THC. In a gambling task, only the 17 mg THC treatment was associated with an increase in risk taking.

Researchers also employ novel experimental paradigms to test the effects of marijuana on tasks requiring divided attention. For example, a study published in *Accident Analysis and Prevention* tested the effects of THC on the ability of occasional marijuana users to complete arithmetic calculations while simultaneously performing a target-detection task (Ronen et al. 2010). The results showed that THC cigarettes reduced success in the arithmetic exercises. Other research examining the effects of marijuana on divided attention tasks indicates that marijuana may affect experienced users differently. For example, in a study of experienced marijuana users that required subjects to track a moving circle while also signaling when a dot appeared on a video screen, performance on the tracking task improved following the administration of a high-dose marijuana cigarette (Hart et al. 2001). Other studies that investigate how THC affects divided attention tasks also show that heavy marijuana users may be less susceptible to marijuana-related impairments than are occasional smokers (Desrosiers et al. 2015; Ramaekers et al. 2009).

Although some research has shown that frequent or heavy marijuana users exhibit fewer performance impairments compared to less experienced users, there is also research showing that marijuana use can lead to cognitive and psychomotor impairments even among experienced users (see Hartman and Huestis 2013). It may be that frequent users of marijuana develop tolerance to the undesirable effects of marijuana or that they learn to alter their behavior in order to compensate for their impairments (Theunissen et al. 2012). However, there is substantial evidence from multiple studies indicating that marijuana can impair cognitive and psychomotor functioning regardless of marijuana use history.

SIMULATED AND ON-ROAD DRIVING ASSESSMENTS

Interactive driving simulators, closed-course driving tests, and even on-the-road driving evaluations have all been used to test the effects of marijuana intoxication on driving performance. Results from these types of studies frequently demonstrate that driving performance is affected by marijuana use. However, there is also evidence showing that the cognitive and psychomotor impairments commonly observed in laboratory experiments do not always translate to comparable impairments in simulated and on-road driving scenarios (Neavyn et al. 2014).

A 2013 literature review published in the journal *Clinical Chemistry* documents the manifold ways that marijuana and THC affect driving performance in simulated and on-road assessments (Hartman and Huestis 2013). Driving and simulator studies have, for example, confirmed results from cognitive and psychomotor experiments by consistently showing that the use of marijuana or THC leads to impairments in reaction time (Sewell et al. 2009; Hartman and Huestis 2013). There is also some evidence that marijuana- or THC-impaired drivers have more trouble maintaining their headway and speed, weave more often, and have difficulty using information acquired while intoxicated (Ronen et al. 2008, 2010; Lenné et al. 2010; Anderson et al. 2010). Drivers under the influence of marijuana have also reported an increase in perceived driving effort (Lamers and Ramaekers 2001). Although simulated and on-road driving tests do not directly assess how marijuana affects drivers in the real world, they provide very useful evidence that drivers under the influence of marijuana or THC have more trouble reacting to unexpected events, maintaining continuous attention, and dividing attention between multiple demands (Hartman and Huestis 2013; Sewell et al. 2009; Smiley 1999).

Simulated and on-road driving assessments have also consistently observed that marijuana and THC can cause research subjects to drive more conservatively (see Ramaekers et al. 2004). It has been proposed that marijuana-intoxicated drivers may be aware of their impairment and drive more cautiously in order to compensate (Lamers and Ramaekers 2001; Lenné et al. 2010). Whereas alcohol-impaired drivers often increase their speed, several studies have observed that marijuana- or THC-impaired drivers drive more slowly (Sewell et al. 2009; Ronen et al. 2008; Lenné et al. 2010; Anderson et al. 2010). Other evidence has shown that marijuana and THC cause subjects to maintain an increased distance between their car and the car in front of them, refuse opportunities to pass, and allow more distance when passing (Ramaekers et al. 2004; Sewell et al. 2009; Earleywine 2002). While these compensatory behaviors may reduce some of the risks associated with driving under the influence of marijuana, the weight of evidence from driving and simulator studies suggests that compensatory behaviors are not sufficient to allay the overall risks associated with driving under the influence of marijuana (Ramaekers et al. 2004; Sewell et al. 2009; Hartman and Huestis 2013).

OBSERVATIONAL EVIDENCE

While experimental research designs help to elucidate how marijuana use affects driving skills in controlled research settings, observational research is necessary to examine marijuana's impact on automobile accidents that occur in the real world. Given that observational researchers do not manipulate or control research conditions, there are challenges inherent in observational research that are not necessarily present in experimental research. As described in Q8, causation can be inferred from observational evidence only (1) when two variables are statistically associated, (2) when the causal variable temporally precedes the outcome variable, and (3) when alternative explanations for the observed association have been ruled out. In the case of observational evidence regarding marijuana's role in automobile accidents, the final criterion of "nonspuriousness" is the most difficult to meet. This is primarily the case because marijuana smokers share characteristics with other groups at a high risk for automobile accidents, making it difficult to identify the specific factors that contribute to a given automobile accident.

Observational researchers face additional challenges related to the accurate measurement of marijuana exposure among injured or culpable drivers. To test for marijuana use among drivers, researchers have generally relied on either self-reported marijuana use or the analysis of biological samples. While biological samples provide more concrete evidence, they do not necessarily provide direct evidence of impairment. For example, urine tests generally assess the presence of THC-COOH, an inactive metabolite that can be detected for a week or more after marijuana use (Wille et al. 2014). Therefore, blood samples are generally used to test for acute intoxication (Gjerde and Mørland 2016). However, THC concentrations in blood peak prior to when the psychomotor effects of marijuana peak, and psychomotor impairments can remain even after THC concentrations have decreased (Neavyn et al. 2014). Moreover, THC levels decline more quickly in occasional marijuana users than in frequent users, and it remains a matter of debate which THC concentrations are indicative of intoxication (National Academies of Sciences, Engineering, and Medicine 2017).

Historically, observational research on the link between marijuana intoxication and car crash risk produced mixed results; however, recent observational evidence more consistently indicates an increased risk of accident among marijuana-impaired drivers (Hall 2014; National Academies of Sciences, Engineering, and Medicine 2017). This emerging consensus is based on evidence from multiple meta-analyses and literature reviews. For example, in a 2016 meta-analysis published in the journal *Addiction*, researchers combined data from 21 observational studies and found that acute marijuana intoxication is related to a statistically significant increase in crash risk (Rogeberg and Elvik 2016). A 2012 meta-analysis published in the *BMJ* combined data from nine studies and found that acute marijuana consumption was associated with a near-doubling of risk for an automobile accident resulting in serious injury or death (Asbridge et al. 2012). Likewise, a 2012 meta-analysis published in *Epidemiologic Reviews* similarly concluded that drivers who use marijuana are more than twice as likely as other drivers to be involved in crashes (Li et al. 2012).

ROADSIDE TESTING

In consideration of the preceding evidence, preventing or limiting marijuana-impaired driving is a key public health issue. In the United States, driving under the influence of alcohol is prohibited at blood alcohol concentrations (BAC) above 0.08 grams per deciliter (Lacey et al. 2010). This type of prohibition, known as a *per se* limit, makes it illegal to operate a motor vehicle at or above the legal BAC threshold, regardless of whether the driver shows signs of intoxication or impairment (Rodriguez-Iglesias et al. 2001). The strictest per se laws employ a zero-limit (or zero-tolerance) approach which prohibits drivers from operating a motor vehicle with any detectable amount of a given substance in their system (Grotenhermen et al. 2007). However, the enforcement of *per se* laws for driving under the influence of marijuana is potentially fraught with the same measurement challenges faced by observational researchers. That is, even when biological specimens are collected in a timely manner and are used to assess THC concentrations (rather than inactive metabolites), there remains significant controversy over the specific THC concentrations that indicate impairment.

An alternative approach is the establishment of an *impairment* or *effect-based* approach which penalizes drivers who are assessed as being unfit to drive or whose driving is impaired. Once a driver is suspected of being impaired, police officers can use the standardized field sobriety test (SFST) to further assess whether the driver is under the influence of drugs or alcohol. Whereas biological samples are used to detect *per se* limit violations, a battery of SFST tests can help detect psychomotor impairment. These tests include the Horizontal Gaze Nystagmus (an eye examination), the Walk and Turn, and the One Leg Stand (Downey et al. 2015). However, there is only mixed evidence that SFSTs can help officers detect impairment among drivers who recently used marijuana (see Bondallaz et al. 2016).

Given the limitations of other roadside testing procedures, there is hope that oral fluid testing devices may provide law enforcement personnel with a roadside screening device that can detect recent marijuana use. However, several large-scale evaluations have assessed the ability of oral fluid testing devices to detect recent exposure to THC, and the results generally indicate that these devices do not yet meet standards related to sensitivity, specificity, and accuracy (Vanstechelman et al. 2012; Blencowe et al. 2011; Wille et al. 2014). Assuming that these devices continue to improve, they may prove useful in the enforcement of *per se* limits. However, controversies surrounding which THC concentrations correlate with driver impairment will still need to be resolved.

MARIJUANA LAWS AND PUBLIC SAFETY

In light of existing evidence, there is sufficient reason to be concerned about the effects of marijuana impairment on individual drivers. Less is known, however, about the potential effects of marijuana laws on highway safety. The limited evidence that does exist is mixed, and more research is necessary in order to better understand how marijuana laws affect traffic safety.

Some evidence suggests that medical marijuana laws do not lead to an increase in traffic fatalities. A 2014 study investigated changes in driver cannabinoid prevalence among fatal-crash-involved drivers in 12 states following the implementation of medical marijuana laws (Masten and Guenzburger 2014). The authors found increased driver cannabinoid prevalence in California, Hawaii, and Washington between 1992 and 2009, but not in the other nine states. In a 2013 study, researchers examined the effect of medical marijuana laws on traffic fatalities between 1990 and 2010 (Anderson et al. 2013). The authors found that, in the first full year after coming into effect, legalization of medical marijuana was associated with an 8–11 percent decrease in traffic fatalities. They further found that medical marijuana laws were associated with decreased alcohol consumption, and a 13 percent decrease in fatalities involving alcohol.

Other evidence suggests that the legalization of medical marijuana might increase traffic fatalities. For example, a 2014 study used data from the Fatality Analysis Reporting System to examine traffic fatalities in Colorado and in nonmedical marijuana states before and after the legalization of medical marijuana in Colorado (Salomonsen-Sautel et al. 2014). The researchers found that the proportion of drivers in a fatal crash who tested positive for marijuana was decreasing in Colorado in the period prior to when medical marijuana became commercially available. However, the proportion of drivers in a fatal crash who tested positive for marijuana increased after medical marijuana became commercially available. Comparable changes were not observed in nonmedical marijuana states, nor were changes observed in the proportion of drivers in a fatal crash who were under the influence of alcohol.

FURTHER READING

Anderson, Mark D., Benjamin Hansen, and Daniel I. Rees. "Medical marijuana laws, traffic fatalities, and alcohol consumption." *The Journal of Law and Economics* 56, no. 2 (2013): 333–369.

Anderson, Beth M., Matthew Rizzo, Robert I. Block, Godfrey D. Pearlson, and Daniel S. O'Leary. "Sex differences in the effects of marijuana on simulated driving performance." *Journal of Psychoactive Drugs* 42, no. 1 (2010): 19–30.

Asbridge, Mark, Jill A. Hayden, and Jennifer L. Cartwright. "Acute cannabis consumption and motor vehicle collision risk: systematic review of observational studies and meta-analysis." *BMJ* 344 (2012): 1–9.

Azofeifa, Alejandro, Margaret E. Mattson, and Rob Lyerla. "Driving under the influence of alcohol, marijuana, and alcohol and marijuana combined among persons aged 16–25 years—United States, 2002–2014." *MMWR* 64, no. 48 (2015): 1325–1329.

Berning, Amy, Richard Compton, and Kathryn Wochinger. *Results of the 2013–2014 National Roadside Survey of Alcohol and Drug Use by Drivers.* Washington, DC: U.S. Department of Transportation, National Highway Safety Administration, Report No. DOT HS 812 118, 2015.

Blencowe, Tom, Anna Pehrsson, Pirjo Lillsunde, Kari Vimpari, Sjoerd Houwing, Beitske Smink, René Mathijssen, et al. "An analytical evaluation of eight on-site oral fluid drug screening devices using laboratory confirmation results from oral fluid." *Forensic Science International* 208, no. 1 (2011): 173–179.

Bondallaz, Percy, Bernard Favrat, Haïthem Chtioui, Eleonora Fornari, Philippe Maeder, and Christian Giroud. "Cannabis and its effects on driving skills." *Forensic Science International* 268 (2016): 92–102.

Centers for Disease Control and Prevention. "CDC Winnable Battles Final Report: motor vehicle injuries." 2016. https://www.cdc.gov/winnablebattles/report/docs/wb-motor-vehicles.pdf

Centers for Disease Control and Prevention. "Impaired driving: get the facts." 2017. https://www.cdc.gov/motorvehiclesafety/impaired_driving/impaired-drv_factsheet.html

Desrosiers, Nathalie A., Johannes G. Ramaekers, Emeline Chauchard, David A. Gorelick, and Marilyn A. Huestis. "Smoked cannabis' psycho-motor and neurocognitive effects in occasional and frequent smokers." *Journal of Analytical Toxicology* 39, no. 4 (2015): 251–261.

Downey, Luke A., Amie C. Hayley, Amy J. Porath-Waller, Martin Boorman, and Con Stough. "The standardized field sobriety tests (SFST) and measures of cognitive functioning." *Accident Analysis & Prevention* 86 (2016): 90–98.

Earleywine, Mitch. *Understanding marijuana: a new look at the scientific evidence.* Oxford University Press, 2002.

Gjerde, Hallvard, and Jørg Mørland. "Risk for involvement in road traffic crash during acute cannabis intoxication." *Addiction* 111, no. 8 (2016): 1492–1495.

Grotenhermen, Franjo, Gero Leson, Günter Berghaus, Olaf H. Drummer, Hans-Peter Krüger, Marie Longo, Herbert Moskowitz, et al. "Developing limits for driving under cannabis." *Addiction* 102, no. 12 (2007): 1910–1917.

Hall, Wayne. "What has research over the past two decades revealed about the adverse health effects of recreational cannabis use?" *Addiction* 110, no. 1 (2014): 19–35.

Hart, Carl L., Wilfred Van Gorp, Margaret Haney, Richard W. Foltin, and Marian W. Fischman. "Effects of acute smoked marijuana on complex cognitive performance." *Neuropsychopharmacology* 25, no. 5 (2001): 757–765.

Hartman, Rebecca L., and Marilyn A. Huestis. "Cannabis effects on driving skills." *Clinical Chemistry* 59, no. 3 (2013): 478–492.

Laberge, Jason C., and Nicholas J. Ward. "Research note: cannabis and driving—research needs and issues for transportation policy." *Journal of Drug Issues* 34, no. 4 (2004): 971–990.

Lacey, John, Katharine Brainard, and Samantha Snitow. *Drug per se laws: a review of their use in States.* Report No. HS-811 317. Washington, DC: National Highway Traffic Safety Administration, Report No. DOT HS 811 317, 2010.

Lamers, Caroline T. J., and Johannes Gerardus Ramaekers. "Visual search and urban driving under the influence of marijuana and alcohol." *Human Psychopharmacology: Clinical and Experimental* 16, no. 5 (2001): 393–401.

Lenné, Michael G., Paul M. Dietze, Thomas J. Triggs, Susan Walmsley, Brendan Murphy, and Jennifer R. Redman. "The effects of cannabis and alcohol on simulated arterial driving: influences of driving experience and task demand." *Accident Analysis & Prevention* 42, no. 3 (2010): 859–866.

Li, Mu-Chen, Joanne E. Brady, Charles J. DiMaggio, Arielle R. Lusardi, Keane Y. Tzong, and Guohua Li. "Marijuana use and motor vehicle crashes." *Epidemiologic Reviews* 34, no. 1 (2012): 65–72.

Masten, Scott V., and Gloriam Vanine Guenzburger. "Changes in driver cannabinoid prevalence in 12 US states after implementing medical marijuana laws." *Journal of Safety Research* 50 (2014): 35–52.

National Academies of Sciences, Engineering, and Medicine. *The health effects of cannabis and cannabinoids: the current state of evidence and recommendations for research.* Washington, DC: The National Academies Press. 2017.

Neavyn, Mark J., Eike Blohm, Kavita M. Babu, and Steven B. Bird. "Medical marijuana and driving: a review." *Journal of Medical Toxicology* 10, no. 3 (2014): 269–279.

Ramaekers, Johannes G., Günter Berghaus, Margriet van Laar, and Olaf H. Drummer. "Dose related risk of motor vehicle crashes after cannabis use." *Drug and Alcohol Dependence* 73, no. 2 (2004): 109–119.

Ramaekers, Johannes G., Gerhold Kauert, Peter van Ruitenbeek, Eef L. Theunissen, Erhard Schneider, and Manfred R. Moeller. "High-potency marijuana impairs executive function and inhibitory motor control." *Neuropsychopharmacology* 31, no. 10 (2006): 2296–2303.

Ramaekers, Johannes Gerardus, Gerhold Kauert, E. L. Theunissen, Stefan W. Toennes, and M. R. Moeller. "Neurocognitive performance during acute THC intoxication in heavy and occasional cannabis users." *Journal of Psychopharmacology* 23, no. 3 (2009): 266–277.

Ramaekers, Johannes G., Eef L. Theunissen, Marjolein De Brouwer, Stefan W. Toennes, Manfred R. Moeller, and Gerhold Kauert. "Tolerance and cross-tolerance to neurocognitive effects of THC and alcohol in heavy cannabis users." *Psychopharmacology* 214, no. 2 (2011): 391–401.

Rodriguez-Iglesias, C., C. H. Wiliszowski, and J. H. Lacey. *Legislative history of .08 laws.* Washington, DC: National Highway Traffic Safety Administration, Report No. DOT HS 809 286, 2001.

Rogeberg, Ole, and Rune Elvik. "The effects of cannabis intoxication on motor vehicle collision revisited and revised." *Addiction* 111, no. 8 (2016): 1348–1359.

Ronen, Adi, Pnina Gershon, Hanan Drobiner, Alex Rabinovich, Rachel Bar-Hamburger, Raphael Mechoulam, Yair Cassuto, and David Shinar. "Effects of THC on driving performance, physiological state and subjective feelings relative to alcohol." *Accident Analysis & Prevention* 40, no. 3 (2008): 926–934.

Ronen, Adi, Hadas Schwartz Chassidim, Pnina Gershon, Yisrael Parmet, Alex Rabinovich, Rachel Bar-Hamburger, Yair Cassuto, and David Shinar. "The effect of alcohol, THC and their combination on perceived effects, willingness to drive and performance of driving and non-driving tasks." *Accident Analysis & Prevention* 42, no. 6 (2010): 1855–1865.

Salomonsen-Sautel, Stacy, Sung-Joon Min, Joseph T. Sakai, Christian Thurstone, and Christian Hopfer. "Trends in fatal motor vehicle crashes before and after marijuana commercialization in Colorado." *Drug and Alcohol Dependence* 140 (2014): 137–144.

Sewell, R. Andrew, James Poling, and Mehmet Sofuoglu. "The effect of cannabis compared with alcohol on driving." *American Journal on Addictions* 18, no. 3 (2009): 185–193.

Smiley, Alison M. "Marijuana: on-road and driving simulator studies." In *The health effects of cannabis*, edited by Harold Kalant, William Corrigall, Wayne Hall, and Reginald Smart. Toronto: Centre for Addiction and Mental Health, 1999.

Theunissen, Eef L., Gerold F. Kauert, Stefan W. Toennes, Manfred R. Moeller, Anke Sambeth, Mathieu M. Blanchard, and Johannes G. Ramaekers. "Neurophysiological functioning of occasional and heavy cannabis users during THC intoxication." *Psychopharmacology* 220, no. 2 (2012): 341–350.

Vanstechelman, Sylvie, Cristina Isalberti, Trudy Van der Linden, Kristof Pil, Sara-Ann Legrand, and Alain G. Verstraete. "Analytical evaluation of four on-site oral fluid drug testing devices." *Journal of Analytical Toxicology* 36, no. 2 (2012): 136–140.

Weinstein, A., O. Brickner, H. Lerman, M. Greemland, Miki Bloch, H. Lester, R. Chisin, et al. "A study investigating the acute dose—response effects of 13 mg and 17 mg Δ 9-tetrahydrocannabinol on cognitive—motor skills, subjective and autonomic measures in regular users of marijuana." *Journal of Psychopharmacology* 22, no. 4 (2008): 441–451.

Wille, Sarah M. R., Vincent Di Fazio, Stefan W. Toennes, Janelle H. P. Wel, Johannes G. Ramaekers, and Nele Samyn. "Evaluation of

Δ9-tetrahydrocannabinol detection using DrugWipe5S® screening and oral fluid quantification after Quantisal™ collection for roadside drug detection via a controlled study with chronic cannabis users." *Drug Testing and Analysis* 7, no. 3 (2014): 178–186.

Q21. ARE MARIJUANA INFRACTIONS FAIRLY PUNISHED?

Answer: No. The likelihood of being caught and punished for a marijuana violation varies across social status groups. Most evidence suggests that African Americans, Hispanic Americans, and males are overrepresented among those arrested or incarcerated for marijuana violations.

The Facts: While some states and municipalities have legalized or decriminalized recreational marijuana use, federal laws still prohibit marijuana possession. In 2015, there were over 640,000 marijuana arrests in the United States, 89 percent of which were for possession (Federal Bureau of Investigation 2016). Given that over 36 million Americans use marijuana each year, it is evident that relatively few marijuana users are arrested. However, the likelihood of being arrested or incarcerated for a marijuana violation varies across social status groups, with most evidence indicating that males and minorities are overrepresented among those caught and punished for marijuana violations.

The criminal justice system in the United States has changed dramatically over the past 50 years. As illustrated in Figure 3.2, the number of prisoners in state and federal correctional facilities increased from just over 300,000 in 1978 to over 1.6 million in 2009 (Carson and Mulako-Wangota 2016). By 2015, the number of prisoners had decreased to around 1.5 million. The total number of incarcerated individuals in the United States, which includes the roughly 700,000 people who are held in local jails, was over 2.1 million in 2015 (Kaeble and Glaze 2016). For comparison, it is estimated that there are about 1.7 million prisoners in China (plus an unknown number in detention), roughly 640,000 in the Russian Federation, and only about 38,000 in Canada (Walmsley 2016). Moreover, the United States regularly ranks among the countries with the highest prison population rates, with 698 prisoners per 100,000 persons (Walmsley 2016). In 2015 the incarceration rate in the United States was second only to Seychelles (799 per 100,000), and ranked above all other countries, including Cuba (510 per 100,000), the Russian Federation (445 per 100,000), and Rwanda (434 per 100,000).

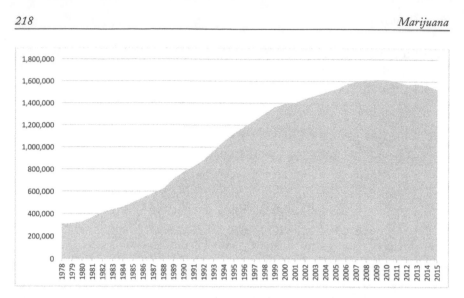

Figure 3.2 Prisoners under the Jurisdiction of State or Federal Correctional Authorities from 1978 to 2015

Source: National Prisoner Statistics Program.

It would be naïve to think that arrests and incarcerations increase and decrease in direct proportion to rates of criminal offending without regard to other factors. Certainly, the number of people who commit crimes affects the number of people who might be arrested and incarcerated, but other factors also contribute to how many people enter the criminal justice system. Law enforcement procedures, sentencing policies, and the political climate also contribute to how, why, and how many people become involved in the criminal justice system. In the United States, crime increased from the early 1960s until the 1980s, and this period of increasing crime roughly coincided with the expansion of the prison population (National Research Council 2014; Kearney et al. 2014). However, between 1990 and 2012 both the violent crime rate and the property crime rate decreased substantially, while the prison population doubled (Kearney et al. 2014; Carson and Mulako-Wangota 2016).

THE WAR ON DRUGS

President Nixon declared a "war on drugs" in 1969, with a focus on international crop controls and drug treatment (Boyum and Reuter 2005). President Reagan launched another drug war in the early 1980s, but it

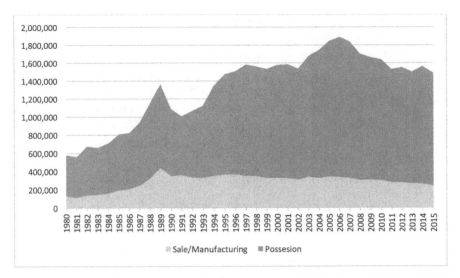

Figure 3.3 Total Drug Arrests by Possession and Sales from 1980 to 2015
Source: Dorsey and James (2009) and Federal Bureau of Investigation (2016).

was a renewed effort in 1986, against a backdrop of increasing fears over crack cocaine, that led to significant policy changes (Reinarman and Levine 1997; Mitchell and Caudy 2015). The drug war launched in the late 1980s had an expanded focus that included lower-level drug dealers and drug users, and an emphasis on street-level enforcement (Mitchell and Caudy 2015; see ONDCP 1989). These changes contributed significantly to an increase in arrests and incarcerations for drug use and possession (National Research Council 2014). For example, between 1980 and 2006, total annual drug arrests increased from 580,900 to 1.89 million (Snyder and Mulako-Wangota 2016). As Figure 3.3 shows, most of this increase was due to the rise in arrests for drug possession. From 1980 to 2006, for example, arrests for drug sales or manufacturing increased from 129,700 arrests per year to 336,800 arrests per year. During the same period, possession arrests increased from 451,200 per year to over 1.5 million arrests per year (Snyder and Mulako-Wangota 2016).

RACE, SUBSTANCE USE, AND SALES

Despite perceptions that racial and ethnic minorities use illicit substances at rates higher than whites, data from multiple sources fail to support that assumption. Data from the 2015 Monitoring the Future study, for example, show that rates of past 12-month illicit substance use and rates of past 12-month marijuana use were very similar for Hispanic and white 12th-graders, while rates were slightly lower for African American 12th-graders (Johnston et al. 2016). Data from the 2015 National Survey on Drug Use and Health (NSDUH) show some variation in past 12-month marijuana use between white, black, and Hispanic Americans ages 12 and older. An estimated 13.6 percent of whites, 16.8 percent of blacks, and 11.9 percent of Hispanics used marijuana in the past year (CBHSQ 2016). As described in Q2, marijuana use is highest among young adults ages 18 to 25, and evidence from this age group does not support the notion that minorities use marijuana at levels higher than their non-minority counterparts. Prior to 2012, for example, rates of past 12-month marijuana use among young white adults were significantly higher than such rates among both African Americans and Hispanics. However, in 2012 and 2014, white and African American young adults reported using marijuana at essentially equivalent rates. The NSDUH also periodically collects data on drug sales. Data from 2006 show that 1.6 percent of whites and 2.8 percent of African Americans reported selling drugs in the past year (Fellner 2014). However, given that whites make up a larger proportion of the population, there were far more white than black drug dealers. More recently, an analysis of the 2008 NSDUH found no racial/ethnic differences in drug sales among youth ages 12 to 17 (Vaughn et al. 2011).

ARRESTS

Marijuana Arrests

While overall drug arrests increased from the early 1980s to the mid-2000s, marijuana arrests followed a different pattern. Marijuana arrests decreased through the 1980s and increased sharply in the 1990s (FBI 2016). The increase in marijuana arrests during the 1990s has been significant. Total drug arrests grew from just over 1 million in 1990 to over 1.5 million in 1999, an increase of 442,600 total drug arrests. Over 85 percent of this increase was due to the rise in marijuana arrests. As shown in Figure 3.4, the number of marijuana arrests more than doubled between 1990 and 1999. Marijuana arrests peaked at 872,700 in 2007, and dropped to 643,100 by 2015. Marijuana possession arrests decreased during that time as well. In 2015 there were 574,600 marijuana possession arrests, accounting for 89 percent of all marijuana arrests and 39 percent of all drug violation arrests.

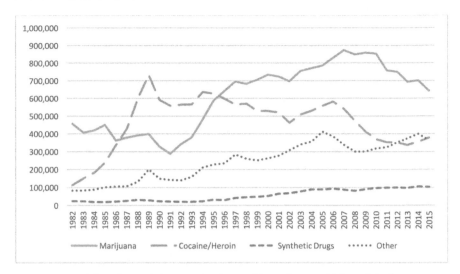

Figure 3.4 Number of Arrests by Drug Type from 1982 to 2015
Source: Federal Bureau of Investigation (2016).

Drug Arrests and Social Status

African Americans are arrested for drug crimes at a rate considerably higher than whites. Racial disparities in arrests existed prior to the war on drugs. However, as Figure 3.5 shows, racial disparities in drug arrests increased dramatically in the 1980s. Between 1980 and 2006, the national drug arrest rate among whites increased from about 226 per 100,000 to 501 per 100,000 (Snyder and Mulako-Wangota 2016). During the same period, the national drug arrest rate among African Americans increased from about 505 arrests per 100,000 to 1663 per 100,000. At the peak of the disparity in 1991, the drug violation arrest rate for African Americans was over 4.5 times higher than the rate for white Americans. Drug arrest rates for both races have decreased since the mid-2000s, as has the racial disparity. However, in 2012, African Americans were still arrested for drug violations at a rate over 2.5 times higher than the drug violation arrest rate for white Americans.

Drug possession arrest rates also vary by sex/gender. Although males use illicit substances at higher rates than females, they are disproportionately arrested for drug possession violations. In 2012, an estimated 11.6 percent of males used illicit substances in the past month, whereas an estimated 6.9 percent of females used illicit substances in the past month (Substance Abuse and Mental Health Services Administration 2013). Arrest data from 2012

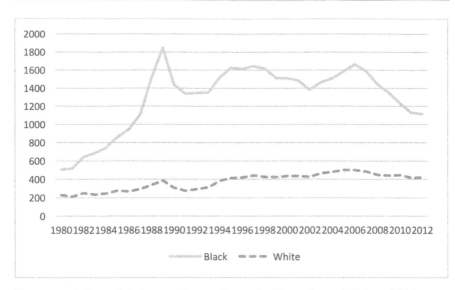

Figure 3.5 Drug Violation Arrest Rates by Race from 1980 to 2012
Source: Snyder and Mulako-Wangota (2017).

show that there were just over one million males arrested for drug posses-sion violations, compared to 263,530 female arrests (Snyder and Mulako-Wangota 2016). Thus, the elevated rate at which males are arrested for drug possession violations is indicative of a sex/gender disparity in drug arrests that exceeds the elevated rate of drug use among males.

Marijuana Arrests and Social Status

For many years, researchers have observed that certain social groups are disproportionately arrested for marijuana possession violations. For exam-ple, males are consistently overrepresented among marijuana possession arrestees (Golub et al. 2007; Nguyen and Reuter 2012; Gettman 2009). African Americans are also more likely than whites to be arrested for mar-ijuana possession (Golub et al. 2007; Nguyen and Reuter 2012; Reuter et al. 2001; Gettman 2009; Levine et al. 2010; Edwards et al. 2013). Taken together, there is strong evidence that males and minority Americans are arrested for marijuana violations at rates disproportionate to the relative size of those populations, as well as at rates disproportionate to violation prevalence.

Several researchers have documented racial disparities in marijuana arrests at the state-level (e.g., Levine et al. 2010; Reuter et al. 2001).

Disparities have also been observed at the city-level. For example, in a 2007 article, researchers found substantial racial disparities in New York City marijuana arrests during the period from 1980 to 2003 (Golub et al. 2007). Specifically, the researchers looked at misdemeanor arrests for smoking marijuana in public view (MPV), and found that in 2000, African American adults represented 23 percent of the population in New York City, but accounted for 52 percent of MPV arrests. Whites, on the other hand, represented 38 percent of the population and only 15 percent of MPV arrests. Moreover, African Americans and Hispanics made up 74 percent to 91 percent of MPV arrests in every year from 1980 to 2003. While both African Americans and Hispanics were overrepresented in MPV arrests according to population size, this research did not assess the extent to which these disparities might be based on racial differences in the prevalence of MPV.

Racial disparities in marijuana arrests have also been observed at the national level (e.g., Gettman 2007). In a 2012 article, researchers examined national-level data and found that white and black marijuana users did not share the same probability of being arrested for marijuana possession (Nguyen and Reuter 2012). In 2000, for example, the rate of arrest for black adolescent marijuana users was nearly double that of their white counterparts. The discrepancy decreased somewhat by the year 2008, when the rate of arrest for white juvenile marijuana users was two-thirds of the rate for black juveniles. Even greater disparities were observed among adult marijuana users. In 2000, the rate of arrest for black adult marijuana users was four times that of whites. By 2008, the discrepancy had narrowed, but the rate of arrest was still three times higher for black adults than for whites.

A 2013 report published by the American Civil Liberties Union similarly found that African Americans were more likely than whites to be arrested for marijuana possession (Edwards et al. 2013). Using FBI data, Census data, and substance use data from the NSDUH, the researchers calculated marijuana possession arrest rates by race. The analysis showed that in 2010 the African American arrest rate for marijuana possession was 716 per 100,000 while the white arrest rate was 192 per 100,000. In that year, 11.6 percent of whites reported past 12-month marijuana use, while 14.0 percent of African Americans reported past 12-month marijuana use. However, as described in Q2, among 18- to 25-year-olds in 2010, past 12-month marijuana use was higher among whites than blacks. Therefore, despite relatively similar rates of use, African Americans were 3.7 times more likely than whites to be arrested for marijuana possession.

DETENTION, CONVICTION, AND INCARCERATION

Bias in Detentions

Courts sometimes hold individuals in detention during court proceedings in order to protect the community, to ensure appearance at court hearings, or to evaluate the individual (Hockenberry and Puzzanchera 2015). Several lines of research have shown that minorities are more likely than whites to be detained before trial, and that pre-trial detention increases the probability of a prison sentence (National Research Council 2014). Juvenile court statistics show that the number of delinquency drug cases resulting in detention increased from 1985 to 1999, and then decreased from 1999 to 2013 (Hockenberry and Puzzanchera 2015). African American youth accounted for 29 percent of all drug offense cases between 1985 and 2013, but represented 44 percent of cases detained (ibid.). In the analysis of New York City marijuana arrests described earlier, arrestees for MPV and misdemeanor marijuana sale were less likely than other arrestees to be detained (Golub et al. 2007). However, among MPV arrestees, African American were more than twice as likely as whites to be detained.

Marijuana Incarcerations—All Races

The consequences that follow a marijuana possession arrest depend on several factors, including the amount of marijuana involved, the criminal history of the person arrested, and where the arrest occurs. In some states, possession of less than an ounce carries no penalty; in other states, possession of less than one ounce is considered a civil infraction and is accompanied by a fine; still, in other states, it is possible that possession of less than an ounce could lead to time in jail or prison (Caulkins et al. 2012; NORML 2017). In most cases, possession of larger quantities is a more serious offense, as is the distribution of marijuana. Other considerations, such as whether the arrestee is on parole or probation and how close the arrest occurred to a school zone, can also influence what happens to a person after being arrested for possession of marijuana. There are also extralegal factors, such as the race and sex/gender of the arrestee, which can also influence what happens to a person after being arrested.

The number of annual marijuana arrests more than doubled between 1990 and 2000. However, felony marijuana convictions did not grow nearly as rapidly. In a 2006 article published in the *Harm Reduction Journal*, researchers analyzed National Judicial Reporting Program data and found that the substantial increase in marijuana arrests in the 1990s did not translate to a concomitant increase in state court felony convictions for marijuana violations (King and Mauer 2006). Whereas the marijuana arrest rate increased by 124 percent from 1990 to 2000, the proportion of all persons sentenced for a marijuana felony in state courts increased by only 39 percent (King and Mauer 2006; Dorsey and James 2009). Moreover, national and local data show that only a fraction of marijuana arrests actually result in a felony conviction. In the year 2000, for example, there were 734,000 marijuana arrests in the United States, of which 41,000 resulted in felony convictions—about 1 in 18 (King and Mauer 2006). In New York City from 1992 to 2003, most (80 percent) of the 360,000 MPV arrests were dismissed, and only 45 people arrested for MPV went to prison (Golub et al. 2007).

While relatively few marijuana arrestees are convicted and incarcerated, the available data suggest that there are thousands of inmates who are behind bars for marijuana violations. State and federal prisoner data from 2004, for example, showed that marijuana violators made up a small, but substantial portion of the prisoner population. Findings from the 2004 Survey of Inmates in State and Federal Correctional Facilities showed that 12.7 percent of drug offenders in state prisons and 12.4 percent of drug offenders in federal prisons were serving time for drug law violations involving marijuana (Mumola and Karberg 2006). These percentages can be applied to other data from the Bureau of Justice Statistics (BJS) to estimate the number of prisoners in state and federal prisons who were serving time for marijuana violations. In 2004, there were over 249,000 drug offenders in state prisons, about 31,000 of whom were serving time for violations involving marijuana (Sabol et al. 2007; Mumola and Karberg 2006). Of the roughly 87,000 drug offenders in federal prisons in 2004, over 10,000 were serving time for marijuana violations (Sabol et al. 2007; Mumola and Karberg 2006). Taken together, these data suggest that over 40,000 people were serving time in state and federal prisons for violations involving marijuana in 2004 (see also Caulkins et al. 2012). These data are limited, however, insofar as they include marijuana violators who may have also committed other offenses (see Mumola and Karberg 2006).

Given that not all marijuana violators in state and federal prisons committed crimes that involved only marijuana, more complex analyses are needed to help estimate how many state and federal prisoners are serving sentences for which the primary offense was a marijuana possession violation. In a 2006 article published in the *Harm Reduction Journal*, researchers drew on 1997 prisoner survey data to show that there were an estimated 27,900 inmates in state and federal prisons serving a sentence for which a marijuana violation was the most serious offense (King and Mauer 2006). Among these prisoners, 23 percent were incarcerated for possession offenses, 15 percent for possession with intent to distribute, and 59 percent for trafficking. The authors further break down the data in order to determine the number of first-time marijuana offenders who were in prison for "low-level" offenses that did not involve importation, manufacturing, or distribution, and whose offense did not involve a weapon. Using these criteria, it was estimated that about 6,600 marijuana offenders were in state and federal prisons serving time for "low-level" marijuana offenses. This analysis appears to challenge the notion that only serious marijuana distributors are incarcerated in prison.

Incarceration Bias—All Drug Violations

Racial and sex/gender disparities also exist in the nation's prisons. However, there is some evidence that racial disparities in drug violation incarcerations may be decreasing. Bureau of Justice Statistics estimates from the year 2000 indicated that there were over twice as many black drug offenders as white drug offenders in state prisons (Harrison and Beck 2002). By 2014, there were nearly the same number of black and white drug offenders in state prisons (Carson and Anderson 2016). Likewise, in 2014 there were comparable numbers of white and black prisoners serving time in state prisons for drug possession alone (ibid.). However, given that African Americans make up only 13 percent of the U.S. population and use illicit substances at roughly the same rate as whites who make up about 61 percent of the U.S. population, it is evident that African Americans continue to be overrepresented among drug offenders in state prisons. State prison data from 2014 also show that there were over 6 times more males than females serving time for drug possession offenses (Carson and Anderson 2016).

Data also suggest that disparities exist in the population of prisoners serving time for drug offenses other than possession (including trafficking). As described earlier, 2006 data showed that 1.6 percent of whites and 2.8 percent of African Americans reported selling drugs in the past year (Fellner 2014). Given that African Americans make up only 13 percent of the population, these estimates indicate that there were about three and half times more white drug dealers than African American drug dealers in the United States at the time (ibid.). However, both state and federal prisons hold a disproportionate number of African American inmates for drug sales or distribution offenses. For example, in federal prison—where over 99 percent of drug violators are serving time for trafficking—black and Hispanic drug offenders far outnumber white drug offenders (Taxy et al. 2015). In state prisons, there is evidence that disparities in non-possession drug incarcerations have decreased since 2013. However, African Americans continue to be overrepresented among those prisoners serving time for drug violations other than possession (Carson and Anderson 2016).

Incarceration Bias—Marijuana Violations

Less data are available on the characteristics of those inmates serving time for marijuana violations specifically. However, there is some evidence that minorities are overrepresented among those who serve time for marijuana-related violations. In federal prison, for example, 60 percent of marijuana violators in 2012 were Hispanic, whereas 14 percent were black and 24 percent were white (Taxy et al. 2015). Moreover, in the analysis of New York City MPV arrests, researchers found that African American and Hispanic arrestees were more likely than their white counterparts to be convicted and sentenced to time served (Golub et al. 2007). The researchers found that almost all (99 percent) of MPV arrestees with no prior arrest record had their cases dismissed, and that the likelihood of conviction increased substantially with the number of prior arrests. However, even after taking into account prior arrests, African American and Hispanic MPV arrestees were still more likely than white MPV arrestees to be sentenced to jail.

Drug Control Disparities

In the United States, marijuana is the most commonly used illicit substance. In 2015, there were an estimated 36 million Americans ages 12 and older who used marijuana and there were 574,641 marijuana possession arrests. These data demonstrate that the probability of being arrested for marijuana possession is really quite low. However, the likelihood of being arrested for marijuana possession varies across social status groups. As the evidence in this chapter has shown, males and minorities are overrepresented among those caught and punished for marijuana violations.

There are several possible explanations that might help account for these disparate outcomes (see Spohn 2000). Of course, there is a possibility that overt racial or sex/gender discrimination by officials at various levels of the criminal justice system leads to these disparate outcomes. While racism and discrimination may exist, it is unlikely that the full extent of these disparities can be explained by personal animus. These disparities may also be the result of economic factors. For example, poor defendants, some of whom are minorities, may have less access to private attorneys and other resources necessary to successfully navigate the criminal justice system. It is also possible that males and minorities generally commit more severe drug crimes and specifically commit more severe marijuana violations.

An interesting line of research explores how neighborhood and community characteristics may contribute to disparate outcomes in the criminal justice system. For example, police often concentrate attention in high-crime urban neighborhoods, many of which are economically disadvantaged. As a result, residents in these neighborhoods may be more likely to come into contact with the police. Similarly, individuals who live in environments characterized by private space or undeveloped space may have an easier time using drugs discretely. These types of ecological factors may help to explain the evidence showing that African Americans are more likely to buy marijuana outdoors and from strangers, both of which may increase the likelihood of police intervention (see Nguyen and Reuter 2012). However, research from Seattle showed that even in mixed-race, outdoor drug markets a disproportionate number of drug delivery arrestees were African American (Beckett et al. 2006).

Disparities in drug arrests may also be due, in part, to unequal traffic enforcement patterns. Traffic stops are the most common means by which people come into contact with the police, and there is consistent evidence that disparities exist in traffic stop outcomes (Durose et al. 2005; Engel and Cohen 2014; Novak and Chamlin 2012). For example, BJS data from 2011 show that black drivers were more likely than white drivers to be pulled over and were also more likely than whites to be searched (Langton and Durose 2013). White motorists were searched 2.3 percent of the time, while African Americans motorists were searched 6.3 percent of the time, and Hispanic motorists were searched 6.6 percent of the time. That is, black and Hispanic drivers were more than twice as likely as whites to be searched during a traffic stop. Males were also twice as likely as females to be searched during a traffic stop. Despite being searched at higher rates, minority motorists are consistently less likely than whites to be found with contraband (Roh and Robinson 2009; Engel and Johnson 2006; Durose et al. 2005).

There is also reason to believe that prejudgments and biases on the part of police officers, judges, and the general public may contribute to disparate outcomes. The literature in this field is diverse but centers around the manifold ways that stereotypes, biases, and personal experiences affect decision making within the criminal justice system (see Engel and Swartz 2014). Simply put, many Americans, including some with legal authority, perceive minorities as more likely to commit crime. This perception endures for many reasons, including economic inequality, residential segregation, and mass-media characterizations. These perceptions, when held by police officers and judges, can lead to disparate outcomes in the criminal justice system. When these perceptions are held by the general public, they can serve to legitimize crime control strategies that focus on minorities and minority neighborhoods.

Relatedly, historical analyses highlight instances wherein minority groups have been linked to highly publicized drug scares. It has been suggested, for instance, that the first laws against opium were related to anti-Chinese sentiments in the 1870s, and that the Marihuana Tax Act of 1937 was passed against a backdrop of fears that the "killer weed" led to violence among Mexicans (see Q16). Similarly, the crack cocaine scare in the 1980s focused attention on urban, minority crack cocaine users. Whereas powder cocaine use had existed among a sizable minority of affluent people since the 1970s, it was the emergence of crack cocaine in urban neighborhoods that captured America's attention (Reinarman and Levine 1997). The crack cocaine scare coincided with the War on Drugs in the 1980s, and many people believe that racialized fears over crack cocaine fueled policy changes that continue to affect the criminal justice system. For example, the Anti-Drug Abuse Act of 1986, which codified a crack cocaine/powder cocaine sentencing disparity, has been linked to enduring racial disparities in the criminal justice system (Nunn 2002; Blumstein 2003).

FURTHER READING

Beckett, Katherine, Kris Nyrop, and Lori Pfingst. "Race, drugs, and policing: understanding disparities in drug delivery arrests." *Criminology* 44, no. 1 (2006): 105–137.

Blumstein, Alfred. "The notorious 100:1 crack: powder disparity—the data tell us that it is time to restore the balance." *Federal Sentencing Reporter* 16, no. 1 (2003): 87–92.

Boyum, David, and Peter Reuter. *An analytic assessment of U.S. drug policy*. Washington, DC: The AEI Press, 2005.

Carson, Ann E., and Joseph Mulako-Wangota. "Prisoners under the jurisdiction of state or federal correctional authorities, December 31, 1978–2015." *Bureau of Justice Statistics. Corrections Statistical Analysis Tool (CSAT)—Prisoners*. Accessed September 23, 2016. https://www.bjs.gov/index.cfm?ty=nps

Carson, Ann E., and Elizabeth Anderson. *Prisoners in 2015*. Washington, DC: Bureau of Justice Statistics, NCJ 250229, 2016.

Caulkins, Jonathan P., Angela Hawken, Beau Kilmer, and Mark A. R. Kleiman. *Marijuana legalization: what everyone needs to know*. New York: Oxford University Press, 2012.

Center for Behavioral Health Statistics and Quality. 2015 *National Survey on Drug Use and Health: detailed tables*. Rockville, MD: Substance Abuse and Mental Health Services Administration, Rockville, 2016.

Dorsey, Tina, and Doris James. *Drugs and crime facts*. Washington, DC: U.S. Department of Justice, NCJ 165148, 2009. https://www.bjs.gov/content/pub/pdf/dcf.pdf

Durose, Matthew R., Erica L. Schmitt, and Patrick A. Langan. *Contacts between police and the public*. Washington, DC: Bureau of Justice Statistics, NCJ 207845, 2005.

Edwards, Ezekiel, Will Bunting, and Lynda Garcia. *The war on marijuana in black and white*. New York: American Civil Liberties Union, 2013.

Engel, Robin S., and Derek M. Cohen. "Racial profiling." In *The Oxford handbook of police and policing*, edited by Michael D. Reisig and Robert J. Kane, 283–408. New York: Oxford University Press, 2014.

Engel, Robin S., and Richard Johnson. "Toward a better understanding of racial and ethnic disparities in search and seizure rates." *Journal of Criminal Justice* 34, no. 6 (2006): 605–617.

Engel, Robin S., and Kristin Swartz. "Race, crime, and policing." In *The Oxford handbook of ethnicity, crime, and immigration*, edited by Sandra M. Bucerius and Michael Tonry, 135–165. New York: Oxford University Press, 2014.

Federal Bureau of Investigation. "Crime in the United States." *United States Department of Justice*. 2016. https://ucr.fbi.gov/crime-in-the-u.s

Fellner, Jamie. "Race and drugs." In *The Oxford handbook of ethnicity, crime, and immigration*, edited by Sandra M. Bucerius and Michael Tonry, 194–223. New York: Oxford University Press, 2014.

Gettman, Jon. "Marijuana arrests in the United States. Arrests, usage, and related data." *The Bulletin of Cannabis Reform* 7, (2009): 1–24.

Golub, Andrew, Bruce D. Johnson, and Eloise Dunlap. "The race/ethnicity disparity in misdemeanor marijuana arrests in New York City." *Criminology & Public Policy* 6, no. 1 (2007): 131–164.

Harrison, Paige M., and Allen J. Beck. *Prisoners in 2001*. Washington, DC: Bureau of Justice Statistics, NCJ 195189, 2002.

Hockenberry, Sarah, and Charles Puzzanchera. *Juvenile court statistics 2013*. Pittsburgh: National Center for Juvenile Justice, 2015.

Johnston, Lloyd. D., Patrick M. O'Malley, Richard A. Miech, Jerald G. Bachman, and John E. Schulenberg. *Demographic subgroup trends among adolescents for fifty-one classes of licit and illicit drugs, 1975–2015* (Monitoring the Future Occasional Paper No. 86). Ann Arbor, MI: Institute for Social Research. 2016. http://www.monitoringthefuture.org

Kaeble, Danielle, and Lauren Glaze. *Correctional populations in the United States, 2015*. Washington, DC: Bureau of Justice Statistics, 2016.

Kearney, Melissa S., Benjamin H. Harris, Elisa Jácome, and Lucie Parker. *Ten economic facts about crime and incarceration in the United States*. Washington, DC: The Hamilton Project, 2014.

King, Ryan S., and Marc Mauer. "The war on marijuana: The transformation of the war on drugs in the 1990s." *Harm Reduction Journal* 3, no. 1 (2006): 1.

Langton, Lynn, and Matthew Durose. *Police behavior during traffic and street stops, 2011*. Washington, DC: Bureau of Justice Statistics , NCJ 242937, 2013.

Levine, Harry Gene, Jon B. Gettman, and Loren Siegel. *Targeting blacks for marijuana: possession arrests of African Americans in California, 2004–08*. California: Drug Policy Alliance, 2010.

Mitchell, Ojmarrh, and Michael S. Caudy. "Examining racial disparities in drug arrests." *Justice Quarterly* 32, no. 2 (2015): 288–313.

Mumola, Christopher J., and Jennifer C. Karberg. *Drug use and dependence, state and federal prisoners, 2004*. Washington, DC: U.S. Department of Justice, Office of Justice Programs, Bureau of Justice Statistics, NCJ 213530, 2006.

National Research Council. *The growth of incarceration in the United States: exploring causes and consequences*. Committee on causes and consequences of high rates of incarceration, edited by J. Travis, B. Western, and S. Redburn. Committee on Law and Justice, Division of Behavioral and Social Sciences and Education. Washington, DC: The National Academies Press, 2014.

Nguyen, Holly, and Peter Reuter. "How risky is marijuana possession? Considering the role of age, race, and gender." *Crime & Delinquency* 58, no. 6 (2012): 879–910.

NORML. "State laws." 2017. http://norml.org/laws

Novak, Kenneth J., and Mitchell B. Chamlin. "Racial threat, suspicion, and police behavior: the impact of race and place in traffic enforcement." *Crime & Delinquency* 58, no. 2 (2012): 275–300.

Nunn, Kenneth B. "Race, crime and the pool of surplus criminality: or why the war on drugs was a war on blacks." *J. Gender Race & Just.* 6 (2002): 381–446.

Office of National Drug Control Policy. *National drug control strategy*. Washington, DC: Office of National Drug Control Policy, 1989.

Reinarman, Craig, and Harry G. Levine. "The crack attack." In *Crack in America: demon drugs and social justice*, edited by Craig Reinarman and Harry G. Levine, 18–51. Berkeley and Los Angeles: University of California Press, 1997.

Reuter, Peter, Paul Hirschfield, and Curt Davies. "Assessing the crackdown on marijuana in Maryland." The Abell Foundation, Baltimore, MD, 2001.

Roh, Sunghoon, and Matthew Robinson. "A geographic approach to racial profiling. The microanalysis and macroanalysis of racial disparity in traffic stops." *Police Quarterly* 12, no. 2 (2009): 137–169.

Sabol, William J., Heather Couture, and Paige M. Harrison. *Prisoners in 2006.* Washington, DC: Bureau of Justice Statistics, NCJ 219416, 2007.

Snyder, Howard N., and Mulako-Wangota, Joseph. Bureau of Justice Statistics. (Arrests by race and age in the US). Generated using the Arrest Data Analysis Tool at https://www.bjs.gov/index.cfm?ty=datool& surl=/arrests/index.cfm

Spohn, Cassia C. "Thirty years of sentencing reform: the quest for a racially neutral sentencing process." *Criminal Justice* 3 (2000): 427–501.

Substance Abuse and Mental Health Services Administration. "Results from the 2012 National Survey on Drug Use and Health: Summary of National Findings." Substance Abuse and Mental Health Services Administration, NSDUH series H-46, HHS Publication No. (SMA) 13-4795, Rockville, MD, 2013.

Taxy, Sam, Julie Samuels, and William Adams. *Drug offenders in federal prison: estimates of characteristics based on linked data.* Washington, DC: Bureau of Justice Statistics, NCJ 248648, 2015.

Vaughn, Michael G., Jeffrey J. Shook, Brian E. Perron, Arnelyn Abdon, and Brian Ahmedani. "Patterns and correlates of illicit drug selling among youth in the USA." *Substance Abuse and Rehabilitation* 2 (2011): 103.

Walmsley, Roy. *World Prison Population List, Eleventh Edition.* Institute for Criminal Policy Research, London, 2016.

Q22. IS TREATMENT FOR MARIJUANA MISUSE NEEDED?

Answer: Yes. While the majority of people who try marijuana do not develop dependence or addiction, there is a subset of marijuana users who continue to use the drug in spite of experiencing social, psychological, and physical problems related to their marijuana use. Indeed, it is estimated that about 1.5 percent of the U.S. population ages 12 and older has misused marijuana in the past 12 months and about 9 percent of people who try marijuana will become dependent on it at some point in their lives (CBHSQ 2016; Anthony et al. 1994; Lopez-Quintero et al. 2011a). Although users of nicotine, alcohol, cocaine, heroin, and stimulants are at a greater risk of becoming dependent on those substances, the high rate of marijuana use in the population translates to a substantial number of people who misuse the drug or develop problems related to their marijuana use. Although many people who misuse marijuana will stop using marijuana on their own, others seek or require treatment. In addition to the people who seek treatment for marijuana misuse on their own, many people are mandated by the criminal justice system to enter treatment. Of the nearly quarter-million marijuana treatment admissions documented in the 2014 Treatment Episode Data Set, over half were criminal justice referrals (SAMHSA 2016).

Until recently, both researchers and laypeople commonly believed that marijuana users rarely developed problems significant enough to warrant treatment. However, the identification of a clinically relevant marijuana withdrawal syndrome gives credence to the belief that achieving abstinence can be difficult and uncomfortable for some marijuana users (see Q15). Yet, many individuals who misuse marijuana are able to recover without the assistance of formal treatment.

The Facts: Data from the Treatment Episode Data Set (TEDS), which presents national-level data on annual substance abuse treatment admissions, show that there were 247,461 primary marijuana admissions documented in state-licensed substance abuse agencies in 2014 (SAMHSA 2016). These admissions accounted for about 15 percent of all substance abuse treatment admissions documented in the TEDS data. The average age of admission for marijuana admissions was 26 years old. Roughly 52 percent of marijuana admissions in 2014 were criminal justice referrals, while only 18 percent were self-referrals. In contrast, 33 percent of alcohol-only admissions were self-referrals, and 57 percent of heroin admissions were self-referrals.

While marijuana treatment admissions are the least likely admissions to be self-referred, there is nonetheless evidence of a substantial unmet need for marijuana treatment. Indeed, studies that advertise treatment programs for individuals seeking assistance for problems related to marijuana use have shown that people will respond to these advertisements in order to receive treatment. In one study, researchers interviewed 225 individuals who responded to public service announcements directed at adult chronic marijuana users and found that nearly three-quarters were experiencing negative consequences associated only with marijuana use and 92 percent expressed interest in being treated (Roffman and Barn-hart 1987). Likewise, evidence from nearly 400 individuals recruited through media announcements showed that many respondents were using only marijuana, most were experiencing concurrent psychological distress, and only nine percent had previously sought help for marijuana use (Stephens, Roffman, and Simpson 1993). In a related study, researchers promoted a treatment research program for persons seeking assistance in abstaining from marijuana use and received over 1,000 phone calls, which yielded 510 eligible and interested participants (Copeland et al. 2001).

In addition to evidence showing that adults with marijuana-related problems will respond to advertisements for brief treatments, there is evidence that many people who meet the diagnostic criteria for marijuana abuse or dependence do not receive treatment. Drawing on data from the National Epidemiologic Survey on Alcohol and Related Conditions (NESARC), researchers found that relatively few individuals with life-time or past 12-month marijuana abuse or dependence ever receive treatment (Stinson et al. 2006). Only 9.8 percent of individuals with lifetime marijuana abuse and 34.7 percent of individuals with lifetime marijuana dependence ever received drug treatment; and receipt of treatment was even lower among individuals who met abuse or dependence criteria in the past year. It remains unclear how to interpret low treatment utiliza-tion among individuals who meet clinical criteria for marijuana abuse or dependence. On the one hand, it may be that some people who meet the diagnostic criteria do not desire or need treatment. On the other hand, it may be that many individuals who meet these diagnostic criteria require treatment but encounter barriers that interfere with treatment utilization.

COMORBIDITY

In the general population and among clinical samples, many people who misuse marijuana also suffer from other disorders—a phenomenon known as comorbidity. The prevalence of comorbidity among individ-uals with marijuana use disorders is disquieting and further compli-cates assessment and treatment. For example, drawing on data from the National Comorbidity Survey, researchers found that 90 percent of respondents with marijuana dependence had met criteria for a men-tal disorder during their lifetimes (Agosti et al. 2002). Data from the 1992 National Longitudinal Alcohol Epidemiologic Survey additionally showed that individuals with comorbid disorders were at increased risk for marijuana dependence. Compared to those not so classified, the odds of marijuana dependence were over two times greater among respondents with comorbid major depression, comorbid drug use disorder, or comorbid alcohol dependence (Grant and Pickering 1998). More recent nationally representative data also show that marijuana users (and users of other drugs) diagnosed with a mood disorder or personality disorder were more likely than those without these disorders to become dependent (Lopez-Quintero et al. 2011a).

In addition to evidence of comorbidity in the general population, there is evidence documenting the existence of psychiatric distress among patients in treatment for marijuana disorders. For example, researchers have observed that psychiatric distress is elevated among adults seeking treatment for marijuana use disorders (Budney et al. 1998; Copeland et al. 2001). Youth presenting for marijuana treatment exhibit high levels of psychological distress. Data from the 600 youth participating in the Cannabis Youth Treatment Study showed that over 95 percent of the youth self-reported one or more other problems, and 84 percent reported three or more other problems (Dennis et al. 2004). Moreover, 37 percent of youth in the study reported alcohol-use disorder; 18 percent reported major depression; 23 percent reported generalized anxiety disorder; 53 percent reported conduct disorder; and 60 percent reported a history of physical, sexual, or emotional victimization.

HOW LIKELY IS REMISSION FROM MARIJUANA USE DISORDER?

Researchers using data from the 2001–2002 NESARC study found that the lifetime cumulative probability of dependence remission (remaining free of dependence symptoms) for cannabis was 97.2 percent (Lopez-Quintero et al. 2011b). The achievement of dependence remission does not necessarily indicate that individuals achieved abstinence from marijuana, but rather that they eventually stopped experiencing the problems that qualified them for a dependence diagnosis. The probability of dependence remission was determined to be 83.7 percent for nicotine, 90.6 percent for alcohol, and 99.2 percent for cocaine.

Although the overwhelming majority of individuals with marijuana dependence will eventually stop experiencing the problems that qualified them for a dependence diagnosis, the process of achieving remission is often difficult, and many people relapse. In a further study of the NESARC data, researchers investigated the predictors of relapse among the 2,350 people with lifetime history of cannabis abuse or dependence who were in full remission at Wave I of the survey (Flórez-Salamanca et al. 2013). Results showed that 6.6 percent of individuals in remission from marijuana use disorder at Wave I had relapsed by the Wave II follow-up three years later. Individuals who had been in remission longer were at decreased risk of relapse, while individuals with a history of conduct disorder or a new onset of depressive disorder were at increased risk of relapse.

TREATMENT BARRIERS AND MOTIVES

Some people with alcohol and drug problems encounter barriers to substance abuse treatment. Common barriers to treatment include concerns about stigma or embarrassment, negative beliefs about treatment, the belief that the substance problem is not severe enough, and financial costs (see Sobell et al. 2000). The existing evidence indicates that many marijuana users believe that treatment is not necessary to reduce marijuana use or that their marijuana use is not a problem. In a 2012 study of nearly 500 regular marijuana users, researchers found that the belief that treatment is not necessary was the most commonly stated barrier to marijuana treatment, followed by users not being ready to stop using marijuana (Gates et al. 2012). Similarly, in a 2006 study of 25 daily marijuana users who quit on their own, researchers found that 80 percent of respondents reported that the most significant barrier to entering treatment was the belief that their marijuana use was not a problem or not enough of a problem to justify treatment (Ellingstad et al. 2005).

Researchers have also investigated the reasons why people use marijuana in hopes of developing targeted interventions (see Newcomb et al. 1988; Simons et al. 2000). This line of enquiry supposes that specific motives to use marijuana may be related to certain problematic outcomes and that these motives may be a key factor in helping individuals quit. Researchers (e.g., Simons et al. 2000) have generally focused on five common motives for marijuana use: enhancement ("I use marijuana to get high"), coping ("I use marijuana to forget my worries"), social ("I use marijuana to be sociable"), conformity ("I use marijuana so that others won't kid me about not using marijuana"), and expansion ("I use marijuana so I can expand my awareness").

Evidence from this line of research suggests that individuals who use marijuana to cope may be particularly at risk for adverse outcomes. This is perhaps not surprising, given the previous discussion on comorbidity, and that those individuals who use marijuana to cope may already suffer from distress. For example, in a study that sampled over 2,000 young Swiss adults, researchers found that marijuana users with coping motives had worse mental health and more distress than those adults who did not use marijuana (Brodbeck et al. 2007). On the other hand, participants who used marijuana for social reasons were no more distressed than those who did not use marijuana. Other research has similarly shown that using marijuana to cope is strongly associated with negative consequences related to marijuana use (see Fox et al. 2011; Simons et al. 2005). As a result, there is hope that interventions targeting marijuana users who use the drug in order to cope with distress may be able to help engender change among a subset of particularly vulnerable marijuana users.

Understanding why some people choose to quit using marijuana may also be an important factor in developing efficacious treatment interventions. Accordingly, researchers have looked at marijuana users both inside and outside of formal treatment in order to better understand what motivates different people to quit. As described in Q1, marijuana use peaks in young adulthood, and subsides thereafter. Those individuals who stop using marijuana in early adulthood may simply "age out" of marijuana use as they enter adult roles that are incompatible with illicit drug use (see Hughes et al. 2008). For these individuals, responsibilities related to work, marriage, and parenthood may supersede desires to use marijuana, and marijuana use may decrease with little effort. However, individuals who have difficulty quitting may find it useful to leverage certain motivations in order to increase the likelihood of success.

There is some evidence that motivations to quit marijuana vary across social groups. In a study of Canadian adolescents, researchers found that the most commonly endorsed reasons for quitting marijuana were "I was just experimenting and did not intend to use it again," "I have other things I enjoy doing," and "I am not interested in using it any more" (Goodstadt et al. 1984). In a study of 842 high-risk high school students from California, participants commonly cited quitting marijuana to avoid getting in trouble, because of a job, because of drug testing, and because they were bored with it (Weiner et al. 1999). Studies of adults suggest that they may have different reasons for quitting marijuana. Drawing on a sample of adult marijuana users who were not seeking treatment, researchers found that the most common reasons for quitting marijuana were related to health concerns, being a good example for children, and improving self-image (Copersino et al. 2006). Data from adult marijuana users who were seeking treatment showed that self-control and health concerns were the most common reasons for quitting marijuana (Stephens et al. 1993).

NATURAL RECOVERY

In spite of evidence showing that some individuals have difficulty abstaining from marijuana, most people who develop a marijuana use disorder are able to achieve abstinence or remission—and many do so without formal treatment (see Cunningham 2000; Copeland et al. 2016). This phenomenon is not exclusive to those with marijuana problems. In fact, evidence shows that individuals with a variety of drug problems have been able to recover in the absence of formal treatment. This process, known as *natural recovery, spontaneous remission,* or *self-change,* is well documented, and may help to explain low treatment utilization among marijuana users.

While several studies have examined natural recovery among marijuana *users,* fewer studies have investigated or observed natural recovery among individuals with marijuana *abuse or dependence.* Those studies looking specifically at natural recovery from marijuana abuse or dependence have found that it is not uncommon for individuals with a lifetime diagnosis of marijuana abuse or dependence to achieve remission or abstinence without the assistance of formal treatment. For example, an analysis of nationally representative data showed that fewer than half (43 percent) of the respondents who had remitted from marijuana dependence had utilized treatment services (Cunningham 2000). Of those who remitted from heroin dependence, over 90 percent had utilized treatment.

Evidence from individuals who successfully stopped using marijuana without formal treatment may point towards strategies that could be useful for other people interested in quitting. For example, in a 2011 study, researchers compared successful and unsuccessful marijuana quitters and found that unsuccessful quitters were more likely to use motivation enhancement strategies, whereas successful quitters were more likely to use coping strategies (Rooke et al. 2011). Specifically, individuals who found other ways to cope with their emotions, found other ways to relax, and set up a plan to use these techniques were more likely to maintain abstinence. Other research similarly highlights the efficacy of various pragmatic approaches to quitting marijuana. For example, in a study of marijuana abusers who successfully stopped using marijuana without formal treatment, researchers found that the majority of respondents developed or returned to activities not related to marijuana, avoided triggers, and made lifestyle changes in order to help avoid relapse (Ellingstad et al. 2005).

FURTHER READING

Agosti, Vito, Edward Nunes, and Frances Levin. "Rates of psychiatric comorbidity among US residents with lifetime cannabis dependence." *The American Journal of Drug and Alcohol Abuse* 28, no. 4 (2002): 643–652.

Anthony, James C., Lynn A. Warner, and Ronald C. Kessler. "Comparative epidemiology of dependence on tobacco, alcohol, controlled substances, and inhalants: basic findings from the National Comorbidity Survey." *Experimental and Clinical Psychopharmacology* 2, no. 3 (1994): 244.

Brodbeck, Jeannette, Monika Matter, Julie Page, and Franz Moggi. "Motives for cannabis use as a moderator variable of distress among young adults." *Addictive Behaviors* 32, no. 8 (2007): 1537–1545.

Budney, Alan J., Krestin J. Radonovich, Stephen T. Higgins, and Conrad J. Wong. "Adults seeking treatment for marijuana dependence: a comparison with cocaine-dependent treatment seekers." *Experimental and Clinical Psychopharmacology* 6, no. 4 (1998): 419.

Center for Behavioral Health Statistics and Quality. *2015 National Survey on Drug Use and Health: detailed tables.* Rockville, MD: Substance Abuse and Mental Health Services Administration, Rockville, 2016.

Copeland, Jan. "Cannabis use and its associated disorders: clinical care." *Australian Family Physician* 45, no. 12 (2016): 874.

Copeland, Jan, Wendy Swift, and Vaughan Rees. "Clinical profile of participants in a brief intervention program for cannabis use disorder." *Journal of Substance Abuse Treatment* 20, no. 1 (2001): 45–52.

Copersino, Marc L., Susan J. Boyd, Donald P. Tashkin, Marilyn A. Huestis, Stephen J. Heishman, John C. Dermand, Michael S. Simmons, and David A. Gorelick. "Quitting among non-treatment-seeking marijuana users: reasons and changes in other substance use." *American Journal on Addictions* 15, no. 4 (2006): 297–302.

Cunningham, John A. "Remissions from drug dependence: is treatment a prerequisite?" *Drug and Alcohol Dependence* 59, no. 3 (2000): 211–213.

Dennis, Michael, Susan H. Godley, Guy Diamond, Frank M. Tims, Thomas Babor, Jean Donaldson, Howard Liddle, et al. "The Cannabis Youth Treatment (CYT) Study: main findings from two randomized trials." *Journal of Substance Abuse Treatment* 27, no. 3 (2004): 197–213.

Ellingstad, Timothy P., Linda Carter Sobell, Mark B. Sobell, Lori Eickleberry, and Charles J. Golden. "Self-change: a pathway to cannabis abuse resolution." *Addictive Behaviors* 31, no. 3 (2005): 519–530.

Flórez-Salamanca, Ludwing, Roberto Secades-Villa, Alan J. Budney, Olaya García-Rodríguez, Shuai Wang, and Carlos Blanco. "Probability and predictors of cannabis use disorders relapse: results of the National Epidemiologic Survey on Alcohol and Related Conditions (NESARC)." *Drug and Alcohol Dependence* 132, no. 1 (2013): 127–133.

Fox, Courtney L., Sheri L. Towe, Robert S. Stephens, Denise D. Walker, and Roger A. Roffman. "Motives for cannabis use in high-risk adolescent users." *Psychology of Addictive Behaviors* 25, no. 3 (2011): 492.

Gates, Peter, Jan Copeland, Wendy Swift, and Greg Martin. "Barriers and facilitators to cannabis treatment." *Drug and Alcohol Review* 31, no. 3 (2012): 311–319.

Goodstadt, Michael S., Margaret A. Sheppard, and Godwin C. Chan. "Non-use and cessation of cannabis use: neglected foci of drug education." *Addictive Behaviors* 9, no. 1 (1984): 21–31.

Grant, Bridget F., and Roger Pickering. "The relationship between cannabis use and DSM-IV cannabis abuse and dependence: results from the National Longitudinal Alcohol Epidemiologic Survey." *Journal of Substance Abuse* 10, no. 3 (1998): 255–264.

Hughes, John R., Erica N. Peters, Peter W. Callas, Alan J. Budney, and Amy E. Livingston. "Attempts to stop or reduce marijuana use in non-treatment seekers." *Drug and Alcohol Dependence* 97, no. 1 (2008): 180–184.

Lopez-Quintero, Catalina, José Pérez de los Cobos, Deborah S. Hasin, Mayumi Okuda, Shuai Wang, Bridget F. Grant, and Carlos Blanco. "Probability and predictors of transition from first use to dependence on nicotine, alcohol, cannabis, and cocaine: results of the National Epidemiologic Survey on Alcohol and Related Conditions (NESARC)." *Drug and Alcohol Dependence* 115, no. 1 (2011a): 120–130.

Lopez-Quintero, Catalina, Deborah S. Hasin, José Pérez de los Cobos, Abigail Pines, Shuai Wang, Bridget F. Grant, and Carlos Blanco. "Probability and predictors of remission from life-time nicotine, alcohol, cannabis, or cocaine dependence: results from the National Epidemiologic Survey on Alcohol and Related Conditions." *Addiction* 106, no. 3 (2011b): 657–669.

Newcomb, M. D., Cp Chou, P. M. Bentler, and G. J. Huba. "Cognitive motivations for drug use among adolescents: longitudinal tests of gender differences and predictors of change in drug use." *Journal of Counseling Psychology* 35 (1988): 426–438.

Roffman, Roger A., and Robert Barnhart. "Assessing need for marijuana dependence treatment through an anonymous telephone interview." *International Journal of the Addictions* 22, no. 7 (1987): 639–651.

Rooke, Sally E., Melissa M. Norberg, and Jan Copeland. "Successful and unsuccessful cannabis quitters: comparing group characteristics and quitting strategies." *Substance Abuse Treatment, Prevention, and Policy* 6, no. 1 (2011): 1–9.

Simons, Jeffrey, Christopher J. Correia, and Kate B. Carey. "A comparison of motives for marijuana and alcohol use among experienced users." *Addictive Behaviors* 25, no. 1 (2000): 153–160.

Simons, Jeffrey S., Raluca M. Gaher, Christopher J. Correia, Christopher L. Hansen, and Michael S. Christopher. "An affective-motivational

model of marijuana and alcohol problems among college students."
Psychology of Addictive Behaviors 19, no. 3 (2005): 326.

Sobell, Linda C., Timothy P. Ellingstad, and Mark B. Sobell. "Natural recovery from alcohol and drug problems: methodological review of the research with suggestions for future directions." *Addiction* 95, no. 5 (2000): 749–764.

Stephens, Robert S., Roger A. Roffman, and Edith E. Simpson. "Adult marijuana users seeking treatment." *Journal of Consulting and Clinical Psychology* 61, no. 6 (1993): 1100.

Stinson, Frederick S., W. June Ruan, Roger Pickering, and Bridget F. Grant. "Cannabis use disorders in the USA: prevalence, correlates and co-morbidity." *Psychological Medicine* 36, no. 10 (2006): 1447–1460.

Substance Abuse and Mental Health Services Administration, Center for Behavioral Health Statistics and Quality. *Treatment Episode Data Set (TEDS): 2004–2014. National Admissions to Substance Abuse Treatment Services.* BHSIS Series S-84, HHS Publication No. (SMA) 16–4986. Rockville, MD: Substance Abuse and Mental Health Services Administration, 2016.

Weiner, Michelle D., Steve Sussman, William J. McCuller, and Kara Lichtman. "Factors in marijuana cessation among high-risk youth." *Journal of Drug Education* 29, no. 4 (1999): 337–357.

Q23. IS TREATMENT FOR MARIJUANA MISUSE EFFECTIVE?

Answer: It depends on the type of treatment and on how "effectiveness" is defined and assessed. While some people who use or misuse marijuana are able to achieve abstinence or symptom remission without formal treatment, a substantial number of people seek, require, or are mandated to formal substance abuse treatment for problems related to marijuana use. In 2014, marijuana was reported as the primary substance of abuse in 247,461 admissions to state-licensed substance abuse treatment facilities, accounting for 15 percent of all substance abuse treatment admissions in the Treatment Episode Data Set (SAMHSA 2016). In spite of widespread treatment utilization, there have been relatively few controlled trials evaluating the efficacy of various treatments for marijuana abuse or dependence. The research that does exist has primarily investigated psychosocial and pharmacologic treatment interventions. Psychosocial interventions for marijuana abuse and dependence have shown promise, while more research is necessary to determine the role of pharmacologic interventions.

The Facts: Considering the number of people in treatment for problems related to marijuana misuse, there is a need to match evidence-based treatment interventions with those clients in need of treatment. Yet research investigating treatments for marijuana misuse is still in its infancy, likely owing to the long-standing belief that people who use only marijuana rarely experience problems severe enough to warrant treatment. Recently, however, research on the treatment of marijuana misuse has expanded due to the growing recognition that some individuals do, indeed, experience problems related to marijuana misuse (see Q22).

Researchers and clinicians interested in how best to treat marijuana misuse are presented with several challenges. On the one hand, they are benefited by an ability to conduct randomized controlled trials which allow for strong causal inferences to be made regarding the efficacy of a given treatment. On the other hand, the identification of research participants and the selection of relevant outcomes are problematic. For example, marijuana users who choose to participate in research studies may be more motivated and more eager to make changes than other users, such as those in the general population or those coerced into treatment. Additionally, while the goal of many treatment programs is the reduction or cessation of marijuana use, there are other relevant outcomes which may result from treatment. For example, some treatment participants experience the remission of clinically relevant dependence symptoms even while continuing to use marijuana.

PSYCHOSOCIAL INTERVENTIONS

In spite of these challenges, researchers have investigated various marijuana treatment interventions. Most research has focused on psychosocial interventions already used in the treatment of other substance use disorders (Budney et al. 2007). Psychosocial interventions include a broad range of individual and group-based treatments aimed at engendering change in patients' drug use behaviors by taking into account salient psychological and social factors. These interventions address the manifold ways that biological, cognitive, emotional, interpersonal, or environmental factors can affect substance use problems (Jhanjee 2014; IOM 2015).

Although there are many interventions that may assist individuals with problems related to marijuana misuse, cognitive-behavioral therapy (CBT), motivational enhancement therapy (MET), and contingency management (CM) have received the most research attention. In addition, youth interventions often include a family component. CBT, which can be adapted for both individual and group interventions, focuses on helping patients alter learned behaviors and develop the skills necessary to recognize and manage triggering situations. MET, which can be delivered in brief or extended sessions, uses a variety of nonjudgmental approaches to help patients enhance motivation and overcome ambivalence related to change. Finally, CM approaches, which are often used adjunctively with CBT and MET, use incentives, such as abstinence-based vouchers that have monetary value, to further motivate client participation and adherence (see Elkashef et al. 2008; Copeland 2016; Budney 2007).

Adult Interventions

The first controlled study on marijuana treatment was published by Robert S. Stephens and colleagues in 1994 (McRae et al. 2003). The researchers advertised a treatment and research program for adults who wanted help quitting marijuana use, and compared a 10-session social support treatment with a 10-session cognitive-behavioral relapse prevention treatment (see also McRae 2003). Although there were no observed differences between the two interventions, 17 percent of participants reported abstinence and 19 percent had improved outcomes at a 12-month follow-up. The same researchers conducted a subsequent trial that assigned adult marijuana users to one of three treatments: a 14-session cognitive-behavioral relapse prevention support group, a two-session individual treatment using motivational interviewing, or a delayed treatment control group (Stephens et al. 2000). At the four-month follow-up, both treatment groups reported improvements, including fewer days of use, fewer times of use per day, fewer problems related to marijuana, and fewer dependence symptoms than the delayed treatment control group. Abstinence rates at the four-month follow-up were nearly identical for both treatments (37 percent), and significantly greater than for the delayed treatment control group (nine percent). These studies demonstrate that cognitive-behavioral and motivational treatments can lead to some improvements for adults who want help quitting marijuana, even when most participants do not achieve long-term abstinence.

Other studies have investigated cognitive-behavioral and motivational treatments among samples of marijuana-dependent adults. For example, a large randomized controlled trial conducted as part of the Marijuana Treatment Project Research Group compared two brief interventions for cannabis-dependent adults (Babor et al. 2004). In this trial, a two-session motivational enhancement intervention and a nine-session intervention that included MET, CBT, and CM were compared to a delayed treatment control group. Results indicated that both interventions reduced marijuana smoking more than the control condition; however, the nine-session treatment was most effective. At the 15-month follow-up, more participants in the nine-session intervention reported 90 days of abstinence (22.7 percent) compared to the two-session participants (12.5 percent). Reductions in marijuana use were also associated with reductions in symptoms of marijuana abuse and dependence. As in previous studies, this research suggests that improvement in abuse or dependence symptoms should be considered alongside complete abstinence as a meaningful treatment outcome.

Evidence also shows that relatively brief interventions can lead to improved outcomes among adults with marijuana use disorders. For example, researchers compared a six-session cognitive-behavioral intervention that included a motivational interview with a single-session version of the same intervention and found that participants in both groups reported better outcomes than those in the control group (Copeland et al. 2001). While participants in both treatment groups were more likely to report abstinence and reported significantly fewer marijuana-related problems than the control group, only a minority of all participants achieved continued abstinence. Likewise, a comparison of two brief interventions showed that a single session of personalized feedback utilizing motivational interviewing led to superior outcomes compared to a single session of multimedia educational feedback condition (Stephens et al. 2007). Compared to participants in the educational group, those receiving the personalized feedback utilizing motivational interviewing reported fewer days of use per week and fewer dependence symptoms at the 12-month follow-up.

Several studies have shown that abstinence-based vouchers can be added to cognitive-behavioral and motivational interventions to improve outcomes even further. In a 2000 study, researchers randomly assigned 60 adults seeking treatment for marijuana dependence to one of three treatment conditions: four sessions of MET, 14 sessions of MET combined with CBT, or 14 sessions of MET combined with CBT and a CM abstinence-based voucher program (Budney et al. 2000). The CM condition gave participants the opportunity to earn $570 in abstinence-based vouchers with consistent negative urine samples, and resulted in the highest abstinence rates during treatment. In a follow-up study, the same research team compared CBT, abstinence-based vouchers, and a combined treatment among 90 marijuana-dependent adults (Budney et al. 2006). The researchers found that abstinence-based vouchers led to superior rates of abstinence during treatment compared to the CBT treatment. However, the combined treatment that included both CBT and abstinence-based incentives engendered superior abstinence rates in posttreatment follow-ups.

Adolescent Interventions

The majority of research on marijuana treatment for adolescents focuses on cognitive-behavioral, motivational, and contingency management interventions. In addition, some studies have combined these treatments or included them as part of family-based interventions. While several studies have assessed treatment in the context of adolescent marijuana use, fewer studies have assessed treatment in the context of adolescent marijuana misuse. Nevertheless, from the limited studies that address marijuana misuse and from other studies that address marijuana use, there is evidence that existing interventions can help improve adolescent outcomes. In a 2011 meta-analysis, for example, researchers combined data from 15 studies and found evidence that both individual and family-based treatments were associated with moderate reductions in adolescent marijuana use (Bender et al. 2011).

Results from the Cannabis Youth Treatment Study, two inter-related trials evaluating interventions for adolescents with cannabis use disorders, showed that a variety of treatment modalities can be efficacious (Dennis et al. 2004). The 600 adolescent marijuana users in the study reported meeting at least one criterion for cannabis abuse or dependence, and were randomly assigned to one of five treatment conditions that included various combinations of MET and CBT sessions, Family Support Network sessions, the Adolescent Community Reinforcement Approach, and Multidimensional Family Therapy. All five interventions showed some efficacy and demonstrated significant treatment effects that were stable through the 12-month follow-up. Similarly, a 2008 study of 224 youth compared Multidimensional Family Therapy and CBT and found that both treatments helped reduce marijuana use (Liddle et al. 2008). While the treatments were similar in their effects on marijuana use, the Multidimensional Family Therapy resulted in superior reductions in other substance use as well as decreases in substance use problem severity.

Brief motivational treatments for young people who use marijuana have also received some research attention, and mixed results indicate that these interventions may hold promise as efficacious and cost-effective treatment options. For example, in a 2008 study, researchers assigned 40 adolescent marijuana users to either two sessions of a brief MET intervention or a delayed-treatment control group and found that the group receiving the motivational intervention showed greater reductions in marijuana use as well as greater reductions in the number of dependence symptoms (Martin and Copeland 2008). Similarly, in a study of 200 adolescent drug users, researchers assigned participants to either a one-hour single-session motivational interview or a control group (McCambridge and Strang 2004). Compared to the control group, those participants who received the motivational interview reported greater reductions in their use of cigarettes, alcohol, and marijuana. Moreover, a 2011 study showed that adolescents who received motivational interviewing during incarceration had lower rates of marijuana use after release (Stein et al. 2011). While research generally supports the use of brief motivational interventions for adolescent marijuana use, some research has shown mixed outcomes (McCambridge et al. 2008; Walker et al. 2006).

Other research shows that combining CM (i.e., abstinence-based incentives) and family-based treatments with other interventions can be efficacious and may further improve outcomes. For example, a 2009 study involving 69 adolescents and their parents compared a combined CBT and MET intervention to a similar treatment that also involved CM incentives for both adolescents and their parents (Stanger et al. 2009). The CM intervention resulted in enhanced abstinence during treatment. However, robust differences between the groups were not observed post-treatment. Both groups increased marijuana use following treatment; however, rates did not return to intake levels.

TREATMENT OF MARIJUANA USE AMONG INDIVIDUALS WITH COMORBID DISORDERS

Very few randomized controlled trials have investigated the efficacy of various treatments in reducing marijuana use among individuals with comorbid psychiatric disorders. The research that does exist has primarily investigated cognitive-behavioral and motivational interventions and has produced mixed results. For example, using data from a sample of people with psychotic disorders who reported hazardous alcohol or drug use, researchers evaluated a 10-session intervention that consisted of motivational interviewing and CBT (Baker et al. 2006). The results indicated that heavy users of marijuana benefited during treatment; however, marijuana use returned to previous levels following the intervention. Using a synthesized dataset from three randomized controlled trials, the same research team compared a one-session motivational interview to an extended 10-session treatment that included motivational interviewing and CBT (Baker et al. 2009). Results showed that the 10-session intervention was superior in reducing marijuana use at six months among participants with severe mental disorders. While motivational and cognitive-behavioral approaches appear to hold promise for treating comorbid marijuana use disorders, more research is needed.

PHARMACOTHERAPY

With the elucidation of the endogenous cannabinoid system, including the identification of endogenous cannabinoid receptors, and the development of synthetic exogenous cannabinoid agonists and antagonists, there is some hope that targeted pharmacologic interventions might be useful in the treatment of marijuana use disorders. Specifically, researchers have explored the use of medications to manage marijuana withdrawal symptoms, facilitate abstinence, and prevent relapse (see Elkashef et al. 2008 for review). Studies have evaluated the utility of THC, bupropion, lithium, divalproex, atomoxetine, naltrexone, and other medications; however, there is insufficient evidence demonstrating the efficacy of pharmacotherapies for marijuana misuse (Copeland 2016; Budney et al. 2007; Danovitch and Gorelick 2012). Nevertheless, based on the relative efficacy of pharmacologic interventions in treating other substance use disorders, researchers continue to examine whether pharmacologic agents could be utilized adjunctively with psychosocial interventions to treat marijuana use disorders.

RELAPSE

Given that many individuals who undergo treatment for marijuana misuse do not achieve continued abstinence, another line of research seeks to identify personal and interpersonal risk factors for posttreatment relapse (e.g., Haney et al. 2013). For example, there is evidence that anxiety symptoms at treatment discharge predict relapse to marijuana, indicating a need to understand and treat concurrent psychological distress among those individuals who achieve abstinence during treatment (Bonn-Miller and Moos 2009). Moreover, research has shown that social and environmental factors can affect the likelihood of relapse following substance abuse treatment. For example, a study of 552 adolescents who participated in outpatient treatment for marijuana abuse or dependence showed that individuals who associated with substance-using or delinquent peers were more likely to return to substance use (Godley et al. 2005). Finally, given that withdrawal symptoms may affect attempts to abstain from marijuana misuse, both pharmacologic and psychosocial interventions may be useful in ameliorating withdrawal symptoms and providing coping skills to avoid posttreatment relapse.

FURTHER READING

Babor, Thomas F., Kathleen Carroll, Kenneth Christiansen, Jean Donaldson, James Herrell, Ronald Kadden, Mark Litt, et al. "Brief treatments for cannabis dependence: findings from a randomized multisite trial." *Journal of Consulting and Clinical Psychology* 72, no. 3 (2004): 455.

Baker, Amanda, Sandra Bucci, Terry J. Lewin, Frances Kay-Lambkin, Paul M. Constable, and Vaughan J. Carr. "Cognitive–behavioural therapy for substance use disorders in people with psychotic disorders." *The British Journal of Psychiatry* 188, no. 5 (2006): 439–448.

Baker, Amanda, Alyna Turner, Frances J. Kay-Lambkin, and Terry J. Lewin. "The long and the short of treatments for alcohol or cannabis misuse among people with severe mental disorders." *Addictive Behaviors* 34, no. 10 (2009): 852–858.

Bender, Kimberly, Stephen J. Tripodi, Christy Sarteschi, and Michael G. Vaughn. "A meta-analysis of interventions to reduce adolescent cannabis use." *Research on Social Work Practice* 21, no. 2 (2011): 153–164.

Bonn-Miller, Marcel O., and Rudolf H. Moos. "Marijuana discontinuation, anxiety symptoms, and relapse to marijuana." *Addictive Behaviors* 34, no. 9 (2009): 782–785.

Budney, Alan J., Stephen T. Higgins, Krestin J. Radonovich, and Pamela L. Novy. "Adding voucher-based incentives to coping skills and motivational enhancement improves outcomes during treatment for marijuana dependence." *Journal of Consulting and Clinical Psychology* 68, no. 6 (2000): 1051.

Budney, Alan J., Brent A. Moore, Heath L. Rocha, and Stephen T. Higgins. "Clinical trial of abstinence-based vouchers and cognitive-behavioral therapy for cannabis dependence." *Journal of Consulting and Clinical Psychology* 74, no. 2 (2006): 307.

Budney, Alan J., Roger Roffman, Robert S. Stephens, and Denise Walker. "Marijuana dependence and its treatment." *Addiction Science & Clinical Practice* 4, no. 1 (2007): 4.

Copeland, Jan. "Cannabis use and its associated disorders: clinical care." *Australian Family Physician* 45, no. 12 (2016): 874.

Copeland, Jan, Wendy Swift, Roger Roffman, and Robert Stephens. "A randomized controlled trial of brief cognitive-behavioral interventions for cannabis use disorder." *Journal of Substance Abuse Treatment* 21, (2001): 55–64.

Danovitch, Itai, and David A. Gorelick. "State of the art treatments for cannabis dependence." *The Psychiatric Clinics of North America* 35, no. 2 (2012): 309.

Dennis, Michael, Susan H. Godley, Guy Diamond, Frank M. Tims, Thomas Babor, Jean Donaldson, Howard Liddle, et al. "The Cannabis Youth Treatment (CYT) Study: main findings from two randomized trials." *Journal of Substance Abuse Treatment* 27, no. 3 (2004): 197–213.

Elkashef, Ahmed, Frank Vocci, Marilyn Huestis, Margaret Haney, Alan Budney, Amanda Gruber, and Nady el-Guebaly. "Marijuana neurobiology and treatment." *Substance Abuse* 29, no. 3 (2008): 17–29.

Godley, Mark D., Jeffrey H. Kahn, Michael L. Dennis, Susan H. Godley, and Rodney R. Funk. "The stability and impact of environmental factors on substance use and problems after adolescent outpatient treatment for cannabis abuse or dependence." *Psychology of Addictive Behaviors* 19, no. 1 (2005): 62.

Haney, Margaret, Gillinder Bedi, Ziva D. Cooper, Andrew Glass, Suzanne K. Vosburg, Sandra D. Comer, and Richard W. Foltin. "Predictors of marijuana relapse in the human laboratory: robust impact of tobacco cigarette smoking status." *Biological Psychiatry* 73, no. 3 (2013): 242–248.

IOM (Institute of Medicine). *Psychosocial interventions for mental and substance use disorders: a framework for establishing evidence-based standards.* Washington, DC: The National Academies Press, 2015.

Jhanjee, Sonali. "Evidence based psychosocial interventions in substance use." *Indian Journal of Psychological Medicine* 36, no. 2 (2014): 112.

Liddle, Howard A., Gayle A. Dakof, Ralph M. Turner, Craig E. Henderson, and Paul E. Greenbaum. "Treating adolescent drug abuse: a randomized trial comparing multidimensional family therapy and cognitive behavior therapy." *Addiction* 103, no. 10 (2008): 1660–1670.

Martin, Greg, and Jan Copeland. "The adolescent cannabis check-up: randomized trial of a brief intervention for young cannabis users." *Journal of Substance Abuse Treatment* 34, no. 4 (2008): 407–414.

McCambridge, Jim, Renee L. Slym, and John Strang. "Randomized controlled trial of motivational interviewing compared with drug information and advice for early intervention among young cannabis users." *Addiction* 103, no. 11 (2008): 1809–1818.

McCambridge, Jim, and John Strang. "The efficacy of single-session motivational interviewing in reducing drug consumption and perceptions of drug-related risk and harm among young people: results from a multi-site cluster randomized trial." *Addiction* 99, no. 1 (2004): 39–52.

McRae, Aimee L., Alan J. Budney, and Kathleen T. Brady. "Treatment of marijuana dependence: a review of the literature." *Journal of Substance Abuse Treatment* 24, no. 4 (2003): 369–376.

Stanger, Catherine, Alan J. Budney, Jody L. Kamon, and Jeff Thostensen. "A randomized trial of contingency management for adolescent marijuana abuse and dependence." *Drug and Alcohol Dependence* 105, no. 3 (2009): 240–247.

Stein, L. A. R., Rebecca Lebeau, Suzanne M. Colby, Nancy P. Barnett, Charles Golembeske, and Peter M. Monti. "Motivational interviewing for incarcerated adolescents: effects of depressive symptoms on reducing alcohol and marijuana use after release." *Journal of Studies on Alcohol and Drugs* 72, no. 3 (2011): 497–506.

Stephens, Robert S., Roger A. Roffman, and Lisa Curtin. "Comparison of extended versus brief treatments for marijuana use." *Journal of Consulting and Clinical Psychology* 68, no. 5 (2000): 898.

Stephens, Robert S., Roger A. Roffman, Stephanie A. Fearer, Carl Williams, and Randy S. Burke. "The marijuana check-up: promoting change in ambivalent marijuana users." *Addiction* 102, no. 6 (2007): 947–957.

Stephens, Robert S., Roger A. Roffman, and Edith E. Simpson. "Treating adult marijuana dependence: a test of the relapse prevention model." *Journal of Consulting and Clinical Psychology* 62, no. 1 (1994): 92.

Substance Abuse and Mental Health Services Administration, Center for Behavioral Health Statistics and Quality. *Treatment Episode Data Set (TEDS): 2004–2014. National Admissions to Substance Abuse Treatment Services.* BHSIS Series S-84, HHS Publication No. (SMA) 16–4986. Rockville, MD: Substance Abuse and Mental Health Services Administration, 2016.

Walker, Denise D., Roger A. Roffman, Robert S. Stephens, Kim Wakana, and James Berghuis. "Motivational enhancement therapy for adolescent marijuana users: a preliminary randomized controlled trial." *Journal of Consulting and Clinical Psychology* 74, no. 3 (2006): 628.

Q24. IS MARIJUANA PROHIBITION EFFECTIVE?

Answer: The evidence is mixed. However, there is no overwhelming evidence that reductions in marijuana penalties are associated with increases in marijuana use.

Facts: Since the 1970s, marijuana policy reforms in the United States and elsewhere have provided researchers and policymakers with opportunities to examine the effectiveness of marijuana prohibitions. Evidence from within the United States and from abroad is largely mixed, and there is little consensus regarding the relative effectiveness of marijuana prohibitions. Inconsistent findings may be attributed to methodological differences in how studies are conducted. For example, studies vary in respect to how marijuana use outcomes are defined and how policies are categorized. Moreover, this research is complicated by the fact that policy reforms often occur in places that already have higher rates of marijuana use. On the other hand, there is evidence that marijuana prohibitions present substantial social and economic costs. While the empirical sciences can help to highlight the costs and benefits of marijuana prohibition, the empirical sciences cannot ultimately determine if the costs justify the benefits.

HISTORY OF MARIJUANA PROHIBITION IN THE UNITED STATES

During the "Reefer Madness" era in the early part of the twentieth century, exaggerated concerns over marijuana and the people who used it led to the first marijuana prohibitions in the United States. Over half of the states enacted marijuana prohibitions between 1914 and 1931, and the federal government followed suit by passing the Marihuana Tax Act in 1937 (Bonnie and Whitebread 1999). The Marihuana Tax Act restricted marijuana through a transfer tax, and this remained the means by which the federal government controlled the drug until the Comprehensive Drug Abuse Prevention and Control Act of 1970 (Musto 1991). Shortly after this new legislation affirmed the federal position on marijuana prohibition, several states relaxed or reduced marijuana penalties later in the 1970s (Pacula et al. 2003). Since then, more than half the states in the United States have legalized medical marijuana and eight states have legalized recreational marijuana (National Conference of State Legislatures 2016a, 2016b).

Deterrence—Benefits and Costs

The various policies in the United States and elsewhere that prohibit the use and sale of marijuana are based on the theory of *deterrence*. In simple terms, criminal deterrence theory suggests that marijuana laws will deter people from using marijuana by imposing, or threatening to impose, penalties against individuals who violate these laws (see MacCoun et al. 2009). Since the Enlightenment era, scholars have been interested in understanding the deterrent effects of official sanctions, and most have focused on how the *swiftness*, *severity*, and *certainty* of punishment influence human behavior (see Chalfin and McCrary 2017). Modern-day criminologists use empirical evidence to test deterrence theory, and have examined whether changes in the likelihood of arrest, and changes in the severity of punishment affect criminal behavior (see Nagin 1998). Although there remains considerable debate, several expert reviewers point to relatively strong evidence that the criminal justice system has an overall deterrent effect, with the best evidence showing that the *swiftness* and *certainty* of punishment are more influential in deterring criminal behavior than the *severity* of punishment (Chalfin and McCrary 2017; Tonry 2008; Nagin 2013).

In order to understand whether or not marijuana prohibition in the United States is an effective policy, it is important to consider that using criminal sanctions as a method of deterrence has both intended and unintended consequences. The intended benefit of marijuana prohibition is the reduction of marijuana use. Other chapters in this volume demonstrate that heavy marijuana use and marijuana misuse can have deleterious consequences, and marijuana prohibitions intend to minimize these consequences by enforcing a system of formal prohibitions. Marijuana prohibitions may also serve to make marijuana use less socially acceptable and may increase social disapproval. The extent to which these sanctions successfully minimize marijuana-related harms is a matter of debate, and the evidence necessary to evaluate the benefits of marijuana prohibition is oftentimes complex and inconsistent (see later in this chapter).

The prohibitions intended to deter people from using marijuana have economic and social costs that need to be considered. Although the total cost of marijuana prohibition is difficult to estimate, the respective costs of arrests and incarcerations are substantial. For example, the roughly 575,000 marijuana possession arrests in 2015—and the roughly 10.8 million marijuana possession arrests between the years 2000 and 2015—present both monetary and opportunity costs to U.S. taxpayers and law enforcement agencies. That is to say, marijuana arrests require considerable economic resources, and these resources could be used for other purposes. The resources spent to incarcerate marijuana violators are also substantial. Data from 2004 suggest that there were roughly 40,000 prisoners serving time in state and federal prisons for crimes involving marijuana, only some of whom were serving sentences for which a marijuana violation was the most serious offense (see Q21). Given that it costs about $31,286 per year to incarcerate a state prisoner (Henrichson and Delaney 2012), some estimates put the cost of marijuana incarcerations at a mark near $1 billion annually (see also Hall and Pacula 2003; Caulkins et al. 2012). Other estimates might be higher if they were to include the costs associated with pre-trial custody, legal proceedings, probation, and parole. On the other hand, some estimates might be lower if they were to account for the likely possibility that some marijuana offenders are serving time for offenses that included other crimes.

The social and personal costs of marijuana prohibition are more difficult to quantify, but no less important. While the majority of attention is paid to the manifold ways that individuals, families, and communities suffer personal, social, and economic costs during and after incarceration, it bears consideration that even an arrest without incarceration can nevertheless strain individuals and their families. Incarceration, specifically, has been linked to a host of negative outcomes related to education, employment, wages, earnings, health, discrimination, disenfranchisement, and family life (see Wakefield and Uggen 2010). Moreover, many of the social costs related to marijuana prohibition are disproportionately felt by males and by people of color, and likely to contribute to the existing structure of economic stratification and inequality (see Q21; Western 2006).

Marijuana Control Regimes

At the federal level, the United States maintains a policy of marijuana *prohibition*, and violations are considered criminal offenses. However, beginning in the 1970s, several states enacted reforms that reduced marijuana penalties. These state-level reforms are popularly referred to as policies that *decriminalized* marijuana; yet, several scholars have pointed out that this term is a misnomer because not all states removed the criminal status of minor marijuana offenses (e.g., Pacula et al. 2003). Thus, it is more accurate to categorize these early reforms as policies that *depenalized* marijuana (ibid.). However, because the term "decriminalization" is commonly used in both research and policy to categorize states that have reduced marijuana penalties, this chapter will do likewise. Twenty-nine states have also enacted *medical marijuana laws*, which allow patients to use marijuana for medical or therapeutic purposes; and eight U.S. states have *legalized* recreational marijuana, provisionally allowing for licensed retailers to sell defined quantities of marijuana to adults over the age of 21. State-level marijuana *legalization* provisions commonly include limits on the quantity of marijuana that an individual can possess as well as prohibitions against drugged-driving (Hall and Lynskey 2016).

STATE-LEVEL DECRIMINALIZATION

Several studies have investigated whether state-level decriminalization in the 1970s affected the prevalence of marijuana use. Methodologically, the best of these studies are those that compare marijuana use trends from before reforms were enacted with marijuana use trends after reforms were enacted, and subsequently compare these data with trends from other states (see Room et al. 2008). There are relatively few of these well-controlled longitudinal studies, and they generally indicate that state-level decriminalization in the 1970s did not significantly affect marijuana use (ibid.). For example, using data from the Monitoring the Future survey of high school students, researchers compared marijuana use in 10 decriminalized states with rates of use in the remaining states, and found that "decriminalization has had virtually no effect either on the marijuana use or on related attitudes and beliefs about marijuana use among American young people in this age group" (Johnston et al. 1981, 27). Other research from this period similarly indicates that penalty reductions in the 1970s did not lead to increased marijuana use in those states that enacted reforms (see Room et al. 2008; Single et al. 2000; Hall and Weier 2015).

Research on the effects of decriminalization from the 1980s and 1990s resulted in more mixed results. For example, an analysis of the 1984 National Longitudinal Survey of Youth did not find evidence of a significant relationship between decriminalization and the demand for marijuana (Pacula 1998). On the other hand, an analysis of Monitoring the Future survey data from the 1980s showed that marijuana decriminalization was associated with increases in past 12-month marijuana use among high school seniors, but decriminalization was not related to more recent marijuana use (Chaloupka et al. 1999). Drawing on nationally representative data from 1988 to 1991, other researchers found that marijuana decriminalization increased the probability of marijuana use among Americans ages 12 and older (Saffer and Chaloupka 1995).

Medical Marijuana Laws

Since the passage of Proposition 215 in California in 1995, a total of 29 states along with the District of Columbia have legalized medical marijuana. While the potential risks and benefits of medical marijuana continue to be debated (see Q12), there is also concern that medical marijuana laws might increase the nonmedical use and misuse of marijuana— particularly among young people. Specifically, some people worry that medical marijuana laws might provide increased access to marijuana or may send a normative message that marijuana use is relatively safe. There is some evidence to support these concerns. For example, adolescents in substance abuse treatment have reported using someone else's medical marijuana (Thurstone et al. 2011; Salomonsen-Sautel et al. 2012), and some research has shown that medical marijuana laws are associated with a decrease in the proportion of people who view marijuana as risky (Schuermeyer et al. 2014). However, other studies have not observed a link between medical marijuana laws and perceptions of risk (Harper et al. 2012). In spite of these concerns, public opinion data from 2016 indicate that roughly 89 percent of Americans believe medical marijuana should be legal (Quinnipiac 2016).

Several studies have shown that adolescent and adult marijuana use is more prevalent in states with medical marijuana laws, but this is not necessarily evidence that medical marijuana laws increase marijuana use. For example, in a 2011 comparison of past-month marijuana use among adolescents in states with and without medical marijuana, researchers found that the prevalence of past-month marijuana use was 25 percent higher in states with medical marijuana laws (Wall et al. 2011). However, the eight states that passed medical marijuana laws since 2004 already showed higher rates of adolescent use in the years leading up to the policy reforms. Similarly, a 2012 analysis of nationally representative data showed that medical marijuana states had significantly higher rates of marijuana use, and that individuals who lived in these states were almost twice as likely to report using marijuana in the past 12 months (Cerdá et al. 2012). However, because states with higher marijuana use may be more likely to pass medical marijuana laws, caution should be exercised before inferring a causal link between medical marijuana laws and recreational marijuana use.

Although more research is necessary, evidence from several studies suggests that the implementation of medical marijuana laws has not led to increases in adolescent marijuana use (see Ammerman et al. 2015). In a study published in *The Lancet Psychiatry*, researchers compiled Monitoring the Future data from over one million students surveyed between 1991 and 2014, and found that the implementation of medical marijuana laws did not increase adolescent marijuana use (Hasin et al. 2015). Consistent with prior evidence, this study showed that adolescent marijuana use was higher in states that passed medical marijuana laws. However, higher rates of use existed both before and after medical marijuana laws were passed. Similarly, a 2014 study examined 20 years of data from the Youth Risk Behavioral Surveillance Survey (YRBS) and did not find increases in adolescent marijuana use associated with the legalization of medical marijuana (Choo et al. 2014).

While the preceding evidence suggests that some consistency exists in the literature on medical marijuana laws and adolescent marijuana use, the broader literature is more mixed. For example, an analysis of nationally representative data from the NSDUH indicated that medical marijuana laws may affect adolescents and adults differently (Wen et al. 2015). Consistent with other studies (see earlier), these researchers did not find evidence that the implementation of medical marijuana laws affected the probability or frequency of past-month marijuana use among adolescents and young adults ages 12–20. However, they did observe a roughly 5 percent increase in the probability of first-time marijuana use among adolescents and young adults. This finding may indicate that medical marijuana laws increase experimental marijuana use among young people without increasing regular or heavy use. The same researchers observed a different effect among adults. There were no changes in marijuana use initiation among adults in medical marijuana states; however, there was a 15 percent increase in the probability of regular marijuana use among adults.

Results also vary depending on the specific dimensions of state-level marijuana laws being considered. For example, two research teams examined comparable data from the National Longitudinal Survey of Youth (NLSY) and the results indicated that medical marijuana policies differ in how they affect recreational marijuana use (Pacula et al. 2015; Anderson et al. 2012). Neither team found an overall association between medical marijuana laws and marijuana use outcomes. However, when one research team distinguished between medical marijuana laws that did and did not allow for dispensaries, they observed different patterns (Pacula et al. 2015). Compared to laws without dispensary allowances, laws with dispensary allowances were associated with an increase in the general prevalence of marijuana use, but dispensaries were not associated with an increase in heavy marijuana use. Other research similarly speaks to how dispensaries might affect marijuana use. Data from 50 California cities showed that the availability of marijuana through dispensaries and delivery services was positively related to current marijuana use and frequency of use (Freisthler and Gruenewald 2014). In contrast, when researchers incorporated dispensary information in their analysis of over 1 million students from the Monitoring the Future survey, such use was not affected (Hasin et al. 2015). Research on the impact of dispensaries remains a matter of debate (see Anderson and Rees 2014). However, there is little debate that medical marijuana laws vary substantially in how they are written, enacted, and enforced (Pacula et al. 2015).

There is also some evidence that medical marijuana laws might affect the prevalence of problematic marijuana use. For example, a 2015 analysis of nationally representative data found that the implementation of medical marijuana laws was associated with a 10 percent increase in the probability of marijuana misuse among adults (Wen et al. 2015). There is also mixed evidence that medical marijuana laws affect marijuana treatment admissions. For example, multiple analyses of the Treatment Episode Data Set (TEDS) have shown that medical marijuana laws in general are not associated with an increase in marijuana treatment admissions (Pacula et al. 2015; Anderson et al. 2012). However, when researchers investigated medical marijuana laws that allowed for dispensaries, they found that dispensary provisions, compared to medical marijuana laws in general, increased treatment admissions—including those that were not referred by the criminal justice system (Pacula et al. 2015). In addition, a 2014 study of male marijuana treatment admissions from 1992 to 2008 showed an increase in marijuana treatment admissions following the passage of medical marijuana laws (Chu 2014).

Recreational Marijuana Laws

As of early 2017, a total of eight states and the District of Columbia had legalized recreational marijuana for adults. Without exception, these policy reforms have resulted from voter initiatives and reflect the growing public support for marijuana legalization (see Q17). Researchers, policymakers, and advocates on both sides of the marijuana debate eagerly await research examining the impacts of these reforms; however, it will require many years of post-legalization data before strong conclusions can be drawn. This is especially true considering that it takes time for policies to be enacted, for markets and prices to adjust, and for social norms to change. In Colorado and Washington, for example, recreational marijuana measures passed in 2012; however, the first retail stores did not open until January and July 2014, respectively. Therefore, any research conducted in the absence of reliable multi-year trend data must be interpreted with caution.

The limited data that exist on the impact of state-level recreational marijuana laws, while insufficient for the purposes of making strong causal inferences, provide a starting point for understanding how marijuana use might be affected by these dramatic policy changes. In both Colorado and in the United States overall, past-month marijuana use among youth and young adults increased between 2006 and 2014, but rates in neither place were significantly different in 2014 than they were in 2011 (Reed 2016). Among Americans ages 26 and older in Colorado, rates of past-month marijuana use were higher in 2014 than they were in any year from 2006 to 2012. However, past-month use also increased among the larger population of Americans ages 26 and older during the same time period (Reed 2016). Additional data will help researchers answer important questions regarding the impact of commercialization and dispensaries on rates of use and misuse.

Some researchers predict that the legalization of recreational marijuana will increase marijuana use in the long run (see Hall and Lynskey 2016; Hall and Weier 2015; Pacula et al. 2010). Given that marijuana prices have fallen in some states with recreational marijuana laws, there is some reason to believe that marijuana use will increase as prices fall (Borchardt 2017; Pacula et al. 2014). The taxation of recreational marijuana could help keep prices from dropping excessively, but if taxation keeps marijuana prices too high it could have the unintended consequence of encouraging the illegal production or sale of marijuana (see Pacula et al. 2014). If marijuana use does increase following legalization, it remains to be seen which user groups will drive this increase. For instance, it is possible that legalization will result in more people experimenting with marijuana without becoming serious users, or it may be that serious users will choose to use marijuana in higher quantities or more frequently. As additional states legalize recreational marijuana and as more time passes, researchers will be able to sort through these complex data to assess if and how legalized marijuana affects marijuana use.

CROSS-NATIONAL EVIDENCE

Other countries have liberalized marijuana policies, and evidence from these countries has been used by both prohibitionists and protagonists to support their respective arguments regarding the effectiveness of marijuana prohibition. While much can be learned from policy experiments in Uruguay, the Netherlands, Portugal, and elsewhere, it remains that there is very little cross-national evidence regarding the impact of marijuana *legalization*. In 2013 Uruguay became the first country to legalize and regulate marijuana for nonmedical use, but the Uruguayan model differs from those in place in the United States and insufficient time has passed to evaluate the impact of this policy (see MacKay and Phillips 2016; Walsh and Ramsey 2016). The Netherlands adopted a system of *de facto* marijuana legalization, wherein the possession and sale of small quantities is tolerated; however, the nation continues to enforce laws against the sale and production of larger amounts (see Pacula et al. 2005; Reuter 2010). In Portugal, where the possession of all drugs for personal use has been *decriminalized*, marijuana possession is still considered an administrative offense (Hughes and Stevens 2010). As a result, there is scant cross-national evidence that will help predict what might occur in the handful of U.S. states that have legalized the regulated production, distribution, and sale of marijuana (see Pacula et al. 2014).

While cross-national evidence cannot be used to assess the impact of *legalization*, it remains that this evidence can still inform debates regarding the consequences of policy liberalization. For that reason, there is an expansive body of research—far too large to review here—that examines the consequences of policy reforms in other countries (see Room et al. 2008; Reuter 2010 for reviews). The evidence is largely mixed, and there is ongoing debate regarding how marijuana policy reforms in other countries have affected rates of marijuana use (see Hall and Weier 2015; Room et al. 2008; MacCoun 2010). It is worth noting, however, that some evidence indicates that the commercialization of retail marijuana markets may be an important factor related to subsequent increases in marijuana use (see MacCoun 2010). For example, a study by Robert MacCoun and Peter Reuter showed that policy reforms in the Netherlands had little effect on marijuana use among Dutch citizens prior to the expansion of retail marijuana outlets (MacCoun and Reuter 1997). However, marijuana use increased during the period of commercialization between 1984 and 1992. Although other researchers have disputed the "commercialization hypothesis" (see MacCoun 2010), this evidence may be taken in conjunction with the limited evidence on marijuana dispensaries in the United States as a caution to policymakers about potential consequences related to the commercialization of marijuana markets.

FURTHER READING

Ammerman, Seth, Sheryl Ryan, William P. Adelman, and Committee on Substance Abuse. "The impact of marijuana policies on youth: clinical, research, and legal update." *Pediatrics* 135, no. 3 (2015): e769–e785.

Anderson, D. Mark, Benjamin Hansen, and Daniel I. Rees. "Medical marijuana laws and teen marijuana use." *American Law and Economics Review* 17, no. 2 (2012): 495–528.

Anderson, D. Mark, and Daniel I. Rees. "The role of dispensaries: the devil is in the details." *Journal of Policy Analysis and Management* 33, no. 1 (2014): 235–240.

Bonnie, Richard J., and Charles H. Whitebread II. *The marihuana conviction: a history of marihuana prohibition in the United States.* New York: The Lindesmith Center, 1999.

Borchardt, Debra. "Marijuana prices fall in 2016 as growers flood the market." *Forbes,* January 31, 2017.

Caulkins, Jonathan P., Beau Kilmer, and Mark A. R. Kleiman. *Marijuana legalization: what everyone needs to know?* New York: Oxford University Press, 2016.

Cerdá, Magdalena, Melanie Wall, Katherine M. Keyes, Sandro Galea, and Deborah Hasin. "Medical marijuana laws in 50 states: investigating the relationship between state legalization of medical marijuana and marijuana use, abuse and dependence." *Drug and Alcohol Dependence* 120, no. 1 (2012): 22–27.

Chalfin, Aaron, and Justin McCrary. "Criminal deterrence: a review of the literature." *Journal of Economic Literature* 55, no.1 (2017): 5–48.

Chaloupka, Frank J., Michael Grossman, and John A. Tauras. "The demand for cocaine and marijuana by youth." In *The economic analysis of substance use and abuse: an integration of econometrics and behavioral economic research*, edited by Frank J. Chaloupka, Michael Grossman, Warren K. Bickel, and Henry Saffer, 133–156. Chicago: University of Chicago Press, 1999.

Choo, Esther K., Madeline Benz, Nikolas Zaller, Otis Warren, Kristin L. Rising, and K. John McConnell. "The impact of state medical marijuana legislation on adolescent marijuana use." *Journal of Adolescent Health* 55, no. 2 (2014): 160–166.

Chu, Yu-Wei Luke. "The effects of medical marijuana laws on illegal marijuana use." *Journal of Health Economics* 38 (2014): 43–61.

Freisthler, Bridget, and Paul J. Gruenewald. "Examining the relationship between the physical availability of medical marijuana and marijuana use across fifty California cities." *Drug and Alcohol Dependence* 143 (2014): 244–250.

Hall, Wayne, and Rosalie Liccardo Pacula. *Cannabis use and dependence: public health and public policy.* Cambridge: Cambridge University Press, 2003.

Hall, Wayne, and Michael Lynskey. "Evaluating the public health impacts of legalizing recreational cannabis use in the United States." *Addiction* 111, no. 10 (2016): 1764–1773.

Hall, W., and M. Weier. "Assessing the public health impacts of legalizing recreational cannabis use in the USA." *Clinical Pharmacology & Therapeutics* 97, no. 6 (2015): 607–615.

Harper, Sam, Erin C. Strumpf, and Jay S. Kaufman. "Do medical marijuana laws increase marijuana use? Replication study and extension." *Annals of Epidemiology* 22, no. 3 (2012): 207–212.

Hasin, Deborah S., Melanie Wall, Katherine M. Keyes, Magdalena Cerdá, John Schulenberg, Patrick M. O'Malley, Sandro Galea, Rosalie Pacula, and Tianshu Feng. "Medical marijuana laws and adolescent marijuana use in the USA from 1991 to 2014: results from annual, repeated cross-sectional surveys." *The Lancet Psychiatry* 2, no. 7 (2015): 601–608.

Henrichson, Christian, and Ruth Delaney. "The price of prisons: what incarceration costs taxpayers." *Federal Sentencing Reporter* 25, no.1 (2012): 68.

Hughes, Caitlin Elizabeth, and Alex Stevens. "What can we learn from the Portuguese decriminalization of illicit drugs?" *British Journal of Criminology* (2010): 999–1022.

Johnston, Lloyd D., Patrick M. O'Malley, and Jerald G. Bachman. "Marijuana decriminalization: the impact on youth 1975–80. Monitoring the Future. Occasional Paper Series, Paper 13." (1981).

MacCoun, Robert J. *What can we learn from the Dutch Cannabis Coffeeshop experience?* RAND Drug Policy Research Center, 2010.

MacCoun, Robert J., Rosalie Liccardo Pacula, Jamie Chriqui, Katherine Harris, and Peter Reuter. "Do citizens know whether their state has decriminalized marijuana? Assessing the perceptual component of deterrence theory." *Review of Law and Economics* 5, no. 1 (2009): 347–371.

MacCoun, Robert J., and Peter Reuter. "Interpreting Dutch cannabis policy: reasoning by analogy in the legalization debate." *Science* 278, no. 3 (1997): 47–52.

MacKay, Robin, and Karin Phillips. "The legal regulation of marijuana in Canada and selected other countries." Ottawa: Parliamentary Information and Research Service, Library of Parliament, 2016.

Musto, David F. "Opium, cocaine and marijuana in American history." *Scientific American* 265, no. 1 (1991): 40–47.

Nagin, Daniel S. "Criminal deterrence research at the outset of the twenty-first century." *Crime and Justice* 23 (1998): 1–42.

Nagin, Daniel S. "Deterrence in the twenty-first century." *Crime and Justice* 42, no. 1 (2013): 199–263.

National Conference of State Legislatures (NCSLa). "Marijuana overview." 2016a. Accessed December 8, 2016. http://www.ncsl.org/research/civil-and-criminal-justice/marijuana-overview.aspx

National Conference of State Legislatures (NCSLb). "State medical marijuana laws." 2016b. Accessed December 8, 2016. http://www.ncsl.org/research/health/state-medical-marijuana-laws.aspx#3

Pacula, Rosalie Liccardo. "Does increasing the beer tax reduce marijuana consumption?" *Journal of Health Economics* 17, no. 5 (1998): 557–585.

Pacula, Rosalie Liccardo, Jamie F. Chriqui, and Joanna King. *Marijuana decriminalization: what does it mean in the United States?* No. w9690. National Bureau of Economic Research, 2003.

Pacula, Rosalie Liccardo, Beau Kilmer, Alexander C. Wagenaar, Frank J. Chaloupka, and Jonathan P. Caulkins. "Developing public health regulations for marijuana: lessons from alcohol and tobacco." *American Journal of Public Health* 104, no. 6 (2014): 1021–1028.

Pacula, Rosalie Liccardo, Robert MacCoun, Peter Reuter, Jamie Chriqui, Beau Kilmer, Katherine Harris, Letizia Paoli, and Carsten Schäfer. "What does it mean to decriminalize marijuana? A cross-national empirical examination." In *Substance use: individual behaviour, social interactions, markets and politics*, edited by Björn Lindgren and Michael Grossman. Emerald Group Publishing Limited, 2005, pp. 347–369.

Pacula, Rosalie Liccardo, David Powell, Paul Heaton, and Eric L. Sevigny. "Assessing the effects of medical marijuana laws on marijuana use: the devil is in the details." *Journal of Policy Analysis and Management* 34, no. 1 (2015): 7–31.

Quinnipiac University Poll. Release Detail. June 6, 2016. Accessed December 8, 2016. https://poll.qu.edu/national/release-detail?ReleaseID=2354

Reed, Jack K. *Marijuana legalization in Colorado: early findings*. Denver, Colorado: Department of Public Safety, Office of Research and Statistics, 2016.

Reuter, Peter. Marijuana legalization: what can be learned from other countries? Baltimore, MD: RAND Drug Policy Research Center, University of Maryland (2010).

Room, Robin, Benedikt Fischer, Wayne Hall, Simon Lenton, and Peter Reuter. *The global cannabis commission report*. Oxford: The Beckley Foundation, 2008.

Saffer, Henry, and Frank Chaloupka. "The demand for illicit drugs." *Economic Inquiry* 37, no. 3 (1999): 401–411.

Salomonsen-Sautel, Stacy, Joseph T. Sakai, Christian Thurstone, Robin Corley, and Christian Hopfer. "Medical marijuana use among adolescents in substance abuse treatment." *Journal of the American Academy of Child & Adolescent Psychiatry* 51, no. 7 (2012): 694–702.

Schuermeyer, Joseph, Stacy Salomonsen-Sautel, Rumi Kato Price, Sundari Balan, Christian Thurstone, Sung-Joon Min, and Joseph T. Sakai. "Temporal trends in marijuana attitudes, availability and use in Colorado compared to non-medical marijuana states: 2003–11." *Drug and Alcohol Dependence* 140 (2014): 145–155.

Single, Eric, Paul Christie, and Robert Ali. "The impact of cannabis decriminalisation in Australia and the United States." *Journal of Public Health Policy* 21, no. 2 (2000): 157–186.

Thurstone, Christian, Shane A. Lieberman, and Sarah J. Schmiege. "Medical marijuana diversion and associated problems in adolescent substance treatment." *Drug and Alcohol Dependence* 118, no. 2 (2011): 489–492.

Tonry, Michael. "Learning from the limitations of deterrence research." *Crime and Justice* 37, no. 1 (2008): 279–311.

Wakefield, Sara, and Christopher Uggen. "Incarceration and stratification." *Annual Review of Sociology* 36 (2010): 387–406.

Wall, Melanie M., Ernest Poh, Magdalena Cerdá, Katherine M. Keyes, Sandro Galea, and Deborah S. Hasin. "Adolescent marijuana use from 2002 to 2008: higher in states with medical marijuana laws, cause still unclear." *Annals of Epidemiology* 21, no. 9 (2011): 714–716.

Walsh, John, and Geoff Ramsey. "Uruguay's drug policy: major innovations, major challenges." Foreign Policy at Brookings, Center for 21st Century Security and Intelligence, Latin America Initiative, 2016.

Wen, Hefei, Jason M. Hockenberry, and Janet R. Cummings. "The effect of medical marijuana laws on adolescent and adult use of marijuana, alcohol, and other substances." *Journal of Health Economics* 42 (2015): 64–80.

Western, Bruce. *Punishment and inequality in America.* New York: Russell Sage Foundation, 2006.

Index

absence of alternative explanations,
78, 139, 198, 210
  nonspuriousness, 139, 198, 210
  See also confounding
abstinence
  and aggression, 200
  from alcohol, 98
  from marijuana, 144, 147–148, 152
  marijuana treatment and, 233, 235,
    238, 241, 243–247
abstinence withdrawal procedure,
  151. *See also* antagonist-
  precipitated withdrawal
abstinence-based vouchers, 243–246
  contingency management (CM),
    242–246
abuse of marijuana. *See* marijuana
  abuse
accidental consumption of marijuana,
  82, 110
accidents. *See* automobile accidents,
  marijuana use and
acquired immune deficiency
  syndrome (AIDS). *See* HIV/
  AIDS

acute (short-term) effects
  of alcohol, 94, 97
  of marijuana, 82–83, 86, 207
  of other illicit substances, 109–110
acute toxicity
  of alcohol, 94
  of marijuana, 83
  of other illicit substances, 105–106,
    109
  of tobacco, 95
addiction
  marijuana and, 144–152, 232
  other substances and, 160, 168
addictive liability, 145, 147, 149
  dependence liability, 144
admissions, marijuana treatment,
  233, 241, 257
Adolescent Community
  Reinforcement Approach, 245
adverse events of medical marijuana,
  122
aerodigestive cancers, 139
African Americans
  and drug control, 228
  and drug sales, 220

and drug violations, 217, 221–224,
    226
and incarceration, 226–227
marijuana history and, 157, 159
and marijuana use/misuse, 13–23,
    220
age patterns of marijuana use/misuse.
    See patterns by age
agonist, 152, 192, 247
airway inflammation, 87. *See also*
    respiratory symptoms
airway resistance, 87. *See also*
    respiratory symptoms
alcohol
    acute effects of, 94, 97
    binge drinking, 94
    dependence, 149
    dependence remission, 235
    and dopamine, 148
    as gateway substance, 184–186,
        188
    and heart attack risk, 87
    morbidity, 97–98
    mortality, 96
    multiple criteria comparison, 99,
        111
    past-month use, 92–93
    poisoning deaths, 94
    public concern over, 178
    treatment admissions, 233
    withdrawal symptoms, 147
alcohol poisoning, 94
alcohol withdrawal, 147
alcohol-impaired driving, 205, 209,
    211, 213
all-cause mortality, 85, 97, 108
American Academy of
    Ophthalmology Complementary
    Therapies Task Force, 131
American Glaucoma Society, 131
American Medical Association
    (AMA)
    Journal of, 116–117, 132
    and Marihuana Tax Act, 166

position on medical marijuana,
    126–127
American Psychiatric Association
    (APA)
    diagnostic criteria, 2, 14, 25, 35,
        46, 56, 65, 145
    position on medical marijuana,
        132, 145
Ames test, 138
amotivational syndrome, 169
amphetamine-type stimulants
    dependence, 148–149, 233
    description, 103
    and dopamine, 148
    emergency department visits, 108
    health risks, 109–110
    morbidity, 109
    mortality risk, 108
    multiple criteria comparison, 111
    past-month use, 102–103
    scheduling of, x–xi
    toxicity, 105–106
anabolic steroids, 111
anal cancer, 140
analgesics
    marijuana, 117–118, 129
    opioid, 107
anecdotal reports, 113, 116, 126, 128,
    131
animal self-administration, 150–151
anorexia, treatment of, 115, 121
Anslinger, Harry J., 158, 163–166,
    168–169, 171, 197
antagonist, 121, 151–152, 247
antagonist-precipitated withdrawal,
    151–152
anticonvulsive, 131
Anti-Drug Abuse Act (1986),
    229
antiemetics, 117, 120–121
anti-inflammatory properties of
    cannabinoids, 130
antitumor effects of cannabinoids,
    140–141

anxiety
medical marijuana treatment of,
127, 132
and posttreatment relapse, 247
reactions to marijuana, 82
See also side effects: of marijuana
appetite change, 148. *See also*
marijuana withdrawal symptoms
appetite stimulation
and cannabinoids, 117, 121–122
medical marijuana and, 127
Armstrong, Louis, 162–163
army disease, 160
arrest rate, drug, 221–223, 225
Arrestee Drug Abuse Monitoring
(ADAM), 200
arrests. *See* arrest rate; drug arrests;
drug possession: arrests;
marijuana arrests in United
States
arrhythmia, 86, 109. *See also* side
effects: of marijuana
Ashworth scale, 119
Assassin of Youth. *See* Marijuana,
Assassin of Youth
Asthma
and cocaine use, 109
and marijuana use, 87
See also respiratory symptoms
Attention
and driving, 206
marijuana use and, 82, 198,
207–209
attention deficit hyperactivity
disorder (ADHD), 129
attributable risk, 82, 94
automobile accidents, marijuana use
and, 97, 205–206, 210–211
aversive effect of cannabinoids, 151

baby boomers, 179
back pain, medical marijuana
treatment of, 127
barriers to treatment, 234, 236

benzodiazepine
multiple criteria comparison, 111
withdrawal, 147
bias
in detentions, 224
in incarcerations, 226–227
personal, 228–229
binge drinking, 94, 97
bladder cancer, 140
blood alcohol concentration (BAC),
211
blood pressure, 83, 86, 96. *See also*
side effects: of marijuana
blood sample tests, 84, 210
body weight, marijuana use and,
121–122
Boggs Act (1951), 168–169
botanical marijuana, 115–118, 120,
122, 140
brain damage, 109
bronchial epithelium, 88
bronchitis, 87. *See also* respiratory
symptoms
Buerger disease, 86
buprenorphine, 111
Bureau of Justice Statistics (BJS),
225–226
Bush, George H. W., administration,
176
Bush, George W., administration,
177
butane, 111

cancer
alcohol use and risk of, 97
cannabinoid treatment of, 128,
137, 140–141
marijuana use and risk of, 97,
137–140
medical marijuana treatment of,
127
symptomatic relief of, 115, 118,
120–121
tobacco use and risk of, 98

cancer-related anorexia cachexia
    syndrome, 121, 127
cannabidiol (CBD), 114–115, 119,
    132
cannabinoid receptors, 114–115, 152,
    247
cannabinoids
    behavioral disorders due to use of,
        85
    and cancer, 137, 140–141
    conditioned place preference,
        151
    dependence and withdrawal,
        151–152
    gateway hypothesis, 192
    and immune function, 87
    in medicine, 113–122, 126–133
    pharmacotherapy, 247
    prevalence among fatal-crash
        involved drivers, 213
    self-administration, 150–151
    See also delta-9-
        tetrahydrocannibinol
cannabinol (CBN), 114–115
cannabis
    abuse and dependence, 2, 145–149,
        235
    in American history, 160
    description, 103, 115
    historical medical uses of, 113–114
    as medicine, 117–122, 127,
        130–131
    mortality, 97, 107
    multiple criteria comparison,
        110–111
    scheduling of, x
    toxicity, 83, 95
    withdrawal, 147–148
    See also marijuana
cannabis arteritis, 86
cannabis withdrawal syndrome,
    147–149
Cannabis Youth Treatment Study,
    235, 245

Cannador, 119
carcinogens, 81, 98, 137–139
cardiovascular death, 84
cardiovascular effects of
    cannabinoids, 82–83, 85–86
Carter, James, 170
Carter administration, 170, 175
case studies, 79, 83–84, 86, 116
causal inferences, 78–79, 193, 242,
    257
causation, 77–79, 138, 198, 210
cause of death, 84–85, 94, 106–107,
    110, 137, 205
Centers for Disease Control and
    Prevention (CDC), 84–85,
    94–96, 98
    CDC WONDER, 85, 106
central nervous system (CNS), 86,
    103–104
cervical cancer, 140
chemotherapy, 113, 115, 117, 120,
    126–127, 141
chemotherapy-induced nausea and
    vomiting (CINV), 120–121
chest tightness, 87. *See also*
    respiratory symptoms
China, prisoners in, 217
Chinese medicine, 113
chronic (long-term) effects
    of alcohol, 96–98
    of illicit substances, 108–110
    of marijuana, 85–88
    of tobacco, 95–96, 98–99
chronic obstructive pulmonary
    disease (COPD), 88, 98
chronic pain, cannabinoid treatment
    of, 117–119, 127
cigarettes
    association with marijuana use, 81
    electronic, 95
    gateway hypothesis, 185
    health risks, 95–96, 98–99,
        137–138, 140
    multiple criteria comparison, 99

public concern over, 178
statistically controlling for use, 140
See also tobacco
clinical trials, 116–117, 120, 122, 126–127
Clinton, William, 176
Clinton administration, 176
cocaine
    description, 104
    and dopamine, 148
    emergency department visits, 107
    health risks, 87–88, 106–109
    mortality, 85
    multiple criteria comparison, 111
    past-month use, 102–103
codeine, x–xi, 103, 105–106
cognitive behavioral therapy (CBT), 242–246
cognitive skills, marijuana use and, 198, 205–209
commercialization hypothesis, 259
comorbidity, 234–236, 246–247
compassionate care, 128
complicating condition, 127
Comprehensive Drug Abuse Prevention and Control Act (1970), 167, 170, 175, 251
conditioned place preference, 151
confounding, 78, 139, 201–202, 206
conjunctivae, reddening, 82. *See also* side effects: of marijuana
contingency management (CM), 242–244, 246
control group, 77, 189, 199, 243–246
Controlled Substances Act (1970), 175, 179
    Comprehensive Drug Abuse Prevention and Control Act, 167, 170, 175, 251
controlled substance schedules, x–xi, 80, 102, 126, 170–171, 175, 179
convictions, marijuana, 224–227
coordination, 206–207

coping
    and marijuana use motives, 236–237
    strategies, 238, 247
core based statistical area (CBSA), 25
coronary heart disease, risk factors, 97–98
correlation, 78, 187. *See also* statistical association
cough, 87, 114. *See also* respiratory symptoms
crack cocaine
    multiple criteria comparison, 111
    scare, 159, 176, 219, 229
    sentencing disparity, 229
    See also cocaine
craving, 146, 148. *See also* marijuana withdrawal symptoms
criminal justice referrals, 233
criminalization
    history of marijuana, 157–171
    public opinion on, 174–181
    See also decriminalization; marijuana prohibition
covarying, 201
Crohn's disease, 127, 130
cross-national evidence, 7, 188, 258–259
cyanide, 93

death certificate, 84, 106
decriminalization, 170, 175, 217, 253–254, 258
dehydration, 105
delayed treatment control group, 243, 245
delta-9-tetrahydrocannibinol (THC)
    and aggression, 199
    antitumoral effects, 137, 141
    conditioned place preference, 151
    dependence and withdrawal, 151–152
    description, 114–115

and dopamine release, 148
and driving, 205–212
and gateway hypothesis, 192
medical uses, 113–115, 118–121,
    129, 131, 247
mutagenesis and carcinogenesis,
    138, 141
health risks, 83, 106
self-administration, 149–151
See also cannabinoids; cannabis;
    marijuana
Democrats, 179–180
Department of Health and Human
    Services (DHHS), 12, 23, 33,
    44, 54, 63, 72
research, 96, 98, 107
Department of Justice (DOJ), 180
depenalization, 253. See also
    decriminalization
dependence liability, 144
addictive liability, 145, 147
dependence on marijuana.
    See marijuana dependence;
    marijuana misuse; substance
    use disorders
dependent variable, 77
depression
    clinical trials on cannabinoids and,
        132
    comorbidity, 235
    marijuana use as risk factor for, 132
    medical marijuana and, 127
    withdrawal symptom, 148
    See also marijuana withdrawal
    symptoms
detention, 224
deterrence theory, 251–253
Diagnostic and Statistical Manual of
    Mental Disorders (DSM)
    cannabis withdrawal, 147–148
    DSM-IV abuse and dependence
        criteria, 2–3, 145
    DSM-5 substance use disorder
        criteria, 145–146

direction of influence, 78. See also
    temporal association or
    sequence
discrimination, 227, 253
disease. See morbidity
divorce and marijuana use/misuse,
    64–65, 67–71
dizziness, 122. See also adverse events
    of medical marijuana
dopamine, 148
dosage of marijuana, 82–83, 116
dose-response, 201
driving simulators, 205–206,
    209–210
dronabinol, 115, 118, 120–122,
    140
drop-out drug, 169–170, 175
Drug Abuse Resistance Education
    (DARE), 176
Drug Abuse Warning Network
    (DAWN), 107–108
drug arrests, in United States
    disparities in, 221–223
    by drug type, 221
Drug Enforcement Administration
    (DEA), 171, 179
drug control disparities, 227–229
drug interactions, 116
drug panic. See drug scare
drug possession
    arrests, 219–221
    laws, 170, 175
    marijuana possession arrests, 217,
        227, 252
drug sales
    incarcerations, 226–227
    and race, 219–220
drug scare, 158–159
drugged driving
    detection of, 211–212
    prevalence of, 205
    prohibitions against, 211, 253
drug-naïve animals, 150–151
drug-paired environment, 151

drugs and crime, theories of, 197–199
dry mouth, 82. *See also* side effects: of
   marijuana

Ecstasy (MDMA)
   description, 104
   emergency department visits, 108
   health risks, 109–110
   multiple criteria comparison, 111
   party drug, 105
   past-month use, 102–103
   scheduling, x
edibles, 81–82, 110. *See also* route of
   administration
education level and marijuana use/
   misuse, 55–63
effect-based limits, 211–212
effective dose, 94–95, 105–106
Eighteenth Amendment, 160
electronic cigarettes, 95
emergency department (ED), 107–108
emesis, 120–121
emotional symptoms of marijuana
   withdrawal, 148
empirical evidence, xi, 75–76, 99,
   105, 144, 184–185, 251
   limits of, xi, 251
employment status and marijuana
   use/misuse, 45–54
endocannabinoid system, 86,
   114–115, 141
endogenous cannabinoids, 114–115,
   247
Enlightenment era, 251
epidemic, drug, 107
epidemiologist, 82, 93, 137
epilepsy, 127–128, 131
estimated human intake dose, 83, 95,
   105
ethanol
   animal self-administration, 150
   toxicity, 93
   See also alcohol
euphoria, 82

exercise tolerance, decrease in, 86.
   See also side effects: of marijuana
experienced users of marijuana, 208
experimental research design, 76–77,
   137–138, 149–150, 189, 199,
   206–207, 209–210
experimental use of marijuana, 237,
   256, 258
exogenous phytocannabinoids,
   114–115

family income level and marijuana
   use/misuse, 34–43
Family Support Network, 245
Fatality Analysis Reporting System,
   213
Federal Bureau of Investigation (FBI)
   arrest data, 177, 217, 219, 221
Federal Bureau of Narcotics
   campaign against marijuana, 114,
   158, 163–168, 170, 197
   establishment of, 114
federal prison
   disparities in, 226–227
   drug violators in, 176–177, 225
   marijuana violators in, 225–226,
   252
fibrosis (liver scarring), 87
Food and Drug Administration
   (FDA), 115–117, 120–121, 140

Gallup, 174–175, 178–180
gambling tasks, 207–208
Gaoni, Yechiel, 114
gateway hypothesis
   background on, 183–185
   causal explanation, 191–192
   common cause explanation,
   189–191
   first proposition, 185–186
   public perceptions of, 177–178
   second proposition, 186
   sociological or environmental
   explanation, 188

third proposition, 186–192
violations, 185–186, 188
generalizability, 79, 81, 150, 181
Generation X, 178
glaucoma, 127–128, 131
Global Health Risks report, 95–97
Goldstein, Paul, 198
gonorrhea, 114
Google Scholar, 79

hallucinogens
    description, 104
    emergency department visits, 108
    health risks, 105–106, 110
    multiple criteria comparison, 111
    past-month use, 102–103
    scheduling, x
harm reduction, 133
hashish, 160, 162, 165
head and neck cancer, 139
headaches, relief of, 127
heart attack. *See* myocardial
    infarction
heart disease, 83, 97–98
heart rate, increase, 82, 86. *See also*
    side effects: of marijuana
hemp, 160
hepatitis C, 86–87, 97, 127
heroin
    and crime, 200
    dependence, 149, 233
    emergency department visits, 108
    gateway hypothesis, 184–186
    health risks, 84, 105–106
    in medicine, 160
    multiple criteria comparison, 111
    past-month use, 102–103
    public concern over, 178
    stepping-stone hypothesis,
        168–169
    scheduling, x, 170
    substance use treatment
        admissions, 233, 238
high, marijuana use and, 82
Hispanics

and drug control, 228
and drug violations, 217, 223
and incarceration, 226–227
and marijuana use/misuse, 13–23,
    220
HIV/AIDS
    and appetite stimulation, 121–122
    cannabinoid treatment indications,
        115, 117
    intravenous drug use and, 109
    and medical marijuana, 127
human self-administration, 149
hypertension, 82, 97, 147
hyperthermia, 105, 110
hyponatraemia, 110
hypothesis, xi, 76–77. *See also*
        commercialization
        hypothesis; gateway hypothesis;
        stepping-stone hypothesis

immune function
    cannabinoids and, 87
    cigarettes and, 98
    malnutrition and, 121
impaired control, 145–146. *See also*
        Diagnostic and Statistical Manual
        of Mental Disorders: DSM-5
        substance use disorder criteria
impairment
    awareness of marijuana, 209–210
    cognitive and psychomotor,
        207–209
    compensatory behaviors related to,
        208, 210
    measurement of driver impairment,
        206, 210–212
    performance, 205, 208
    See also marijuana and driving;
        respiratory impairment
incarceration
    bias in, 226–227
    economic costs of, 252–253
    marijuana and, 224–226
    mass incarceration in United
        States, 159, 217

prisoner population in United
States, 218
social costs of, 253
incarceration rate in United States,
217
incidence, 82, 93
income level and marijuana use/
misuse, 34–43
Independent Scientific Committee
on Drugs, 99, 110
independent variable, 77
Independents, 179–180
India, 113, 162
Indian hemp, 114, 164
individual level, assessment of risk at,
82, 93, 106
inexperienced users of marijuana, 82,
208
infection, infectious disease, 85–88,
97, 104, 108–109, 117, 121
inflammatory bowel disease (IBD),
128, 130
inhalation, 81–82, 138
International Arrestee Drug Abuse
Monitoring (I-ADAM),
200
International Classification of
Diseases (ICD), 97
Internist, 140, 180
intervention
police, 228
in science, 77
substance abuse treatment,
236–237, 241–247
intoxication
acute effects of hallucinogens,
110
acute effects of marijuana/THC,
83–86, 161
alcohol and driving, 94, 209
marijuana and driving, 205–211
and violence, 198
intracranial administration, 141
intractable pain, 115, 127
intraocular pressure (IOP), 131

intravenous (IV), 104, 109, 150–151
irritability, 148. *See also* marijuana
withdrawal symptoms

Jazz, 158–159, 162–163
joint, 81. *See also* route of
administration

Kandel, Denise, 185
ketamine, 111
Khat, 111

La Guardia, Fiorello, 167
La Guardia Report (1944), 167–168
laboratory experiments, 77, 81, 87,
109, 137–138, 141, 149–150,
189, 199, 206–207, 209
legalization, ix, 114, 127, 171,
174
public opinion on, 5, 174–181
lethal dose, 83, 94–95, 105–106
levodopa-induced dyskinesia
(involuntary movements), 130
liver damage
alcohol and, 96–97
marijuana and, 86–87
longitudinal research, 191, 200–202,
254
LSD
description, 104
emergency department visits, 108
health risks, 105–106, 110
multiple criteria comparison, 111
scheduling, x
Ludlow, Fitz Hugh, 160
lung cancer
and marijuana, 88, 139
and tobacco, 98, 137
lung function, 88

magic mushrooms. *See* psilocybin
malignant glioma, 140
malnutrition, 121
mandated treatment, 233, 241
margin of exposure (MOE), 105–106

Marihuana, Weed with Roots in Hell,
164
Marihuana Tax Act, 114, 157–158,
163, 166–168, 170, 175, 197,
251
marijuana, 103
Marijuana, Assassin of Youth, 158,
165, 197
marijuana, introduction to United
States, 161
marijuana abuse
compared to use of marijuana, 3
DSM-IV criteria, 2–3
measurement of, 5
potential for, 80, 93, 102, 171
remission, 235, 238
treatment of, 234–236, 238, 241,
244–245, 247
See also marijuana misuse
marijuana and aggression
claims of, 157, 161, 163–164, 170,
197
evidence on, 199–201
theories of, 198
marijuana and crime
claims of, 114, 157, 161, 163–165,
169, 197
evidence on, 78, 196–203
theories of, 197–198
marijuana and driving
cognitive and psychomotor
research, 205, 206–209
driving simulators and closed-
course driving tests, 205,
209–210
methodological considerations,
206
observational evidence, 205,
210–211
prevalence of, 205
public safety, 212
roadside testing, 211–212
marijuana arrest disparities, 217,
222–223

marijuana arrests in United States,
163, 176–177, 217, 220–221
marijuana control regimes, 253,
258–259
marijuana dependence
animal models, 149–152
comorbidity, 234–235
controlled substance schedules,
ix–xi
DSM-IV criteria, 2–3
gateway hypothesis, 190
human evidence, 147–149, 151,
232
measurement of, 5
remission from, 235–236, 238
treatment of, 234, 241–247
See also marijuana misuse;
substance use disorder
marijuana in public view (MPV),
223–225, 227
marijuana incarcerations, 224–227
Marijuana Initiative, National Youth
Anti-Drug Media Campaign,
177
marijuana misuse
compared to use of marijuana, 3
definition of, ix, 2–3
and physical health, 80–88
relapse, 235–236
remission, 235
treatment of, 232, 234, 241,
243–245, 247
trends among population ages,
12 and older, 4
See also patterns by age; patterns
by sex
marijuana prohibition
benefits and costs, 251–253
history of, 161–171
and marijuana use, 253–258
public opinion on, 174–181
regimes, 253, 258–259
See also criminalization;
decriminalization

Marijuana Treatment Project
    Research Group, 243
marijuana use
    definition of, 3–5
    historical trends, 4
    See also patterns by age; patterns
    by sex
marijuana use disorder
    comorbidity, 234–235
    DSM-5 criteria, 145–146
    prevalence of, 149
    relapse, 235–236
    remission, 235, 238
    treatment of, 232, 234, 241,
    243–245, 247
    See also marijuana misuse
marijuana withdrawal symptoms, 148
marijuana withdrawal syndrome, 146,
    148, 200, 233
marital status and marijuana use/
    misuse, 64–72
mass incarceration, 159, 217–218
MDMA (Ecstasy). *See* Ecstasy
Mechoulam, Raphael, 114
media
    portrayal of drop-out drug,
    169–170
    role in Reefer Madness era,
    161–166
    as source of information about
    marijuana, xii
medical marijuana
    adverse events, 122
    commercialization, 259
    dispensaries, 202–203, 256–257, 259
    home cultivation, 202
    and marijuana use, 254–257
    state-laws, ix, 80, 114
    and traffic safety, 212–213
    variation in legal provisions,
    256–257
medical practitioners, views on
    medical marijuana, 140,
    180–181

memory, marijuana use and, 82, 198,
    207
mental health
    marijuana use as risk factor for, 132
    treatment with medical marijuana,
    128, 132–133
mephedrone, 111
meta-analysis, 79, 86, 108, 116, 132,
    139, 141, 200, 206, 210–211,
    245
metastasis, 141
methadone, 111
methamphetamine
    description, 103
    health risks, 105–106
    multiple criteria comparison, 111
    scheduling, x
method of exposure. *See* route of
    administration
Mexican immigrants, 159, 161–163,
    229
Michigan Cancer Foundation, 121
millennials, 178
minimum sentence, 168–170, 175
minorities
    and drug control, 227–229
    and drug scares, 159
    and gateway hypothesis, 185
    and incarceration, 226–227
    and marijuana use/misuse, 13–23
    and marijuana violations, 217,
    219–223
    in Reefer Madness era, 163
misdemeanor, 223–224
misuse, definition, ix, 2–3
misuse of marijuana. *See* marijuana
    misuse; patterns by age; patterns
    by sex
Monitoring the Future (MTF), xii,
    219, 254–256
moral panic, 158
morbidity
    alcohol use and, 97–98
    illicit substance use and, 109–110

marijuana use and, 85–88
tobacco use and, 98–99
mortality risk, 95–97, 108
motivational enhancement therapy
    (MET), 242–246
motivational interviewing, 243–244,
    246
motives
    to quit marijuana, 237
    to use marijuana, 236–237
motor control, 207
motor vehicle crashes
    and alcohol, 96, 205
    and marijuana, 108, 205–206,
        210–213
Multidimensional Family Therapy, 245
multiple causes of death, 84, 94,
    106–107
multiple criteria comparison, 99,
    110–111
multiple sclerosis (MS), 113, 115,
    117–120. *See also* relapse to
    multiple sclerosis
muscle spasms, 119, 127
mutation, mutagenicity, 138
myocardial infarction
    alcohol use and, 97
    cocaine use and, 109
    marijuana use and, 83, 85, 86, 87,
        98

nabilone, 115, 118, 120, 130, 133,
    140
nabiximols, 115, 118
narcotic
    animal self-administration, 150
    controlled substance schedules,
        x–xi
    in United States history, 160
    view of marijuana as, 163–165,
        168–169, 196–197
Narcotic Control Act (1956),
    168–169
National Commission on Marijuana
    and Drug Abuse, 170, 175

National Comorbidity Survey, 234
National Epidemiologic Survey on
    Alcohol and Related Conditions
    (NESARC), 149, 234
National Judicial Reporting Program,
    224
National Longitudinal Alcohol
    Epidemiologic Survey, 234
National Longitudinal Survey of
    Youth (NLSY), 254, 256
National Survey on Drug Use and
    Health (NSDUH), xii, 2, 3–5.
    See also patterns by age; patterns
    by sex
National Youth Anti-Drug Media
    Campaign, 177
nativism, 159
natural recovery, 237–238
nausea and vomiting, 113, 115, 117,
    120–121, 126–127, 140
neighborhood, 159, 228–229
neonatal abstinence disorder, 109
nervousness, 148. *See also* marijuana
    withdrawal symptoms
Netherlands, 258–259
neuropathic pain, 115, 117–118, 129
neurotransmission, 109
New York Academy of Medicine, 167
newspapers, 161–164, 197
nicotine
    addictive liability, 144, 149, 233
    animal self-administration of, 150
    dependence remission, 235
    and dopamine, 148
    toxicity, 95, 106. *See also* cigarettes;
        tobacco
Nixon, Richard, 170, 175, 218
Nixon administration, 175
non-cancer pain, 118
nonspuriousness, 139, 198, 210
    absence of alternative
        explanations, 78, 139, 198,
        210
    See also confounding
nutritional disorders, 109

Obama, Barack, 177
Obama administration, 177
observation, 75–76, 199
observational research
  and addiction, 149
  and alcohol, 96
  and cancer, 137–140
  causal inferences, 138, 198, 210
  and crime, 200–201
  and depression, 132
  description, 77–78
  and driving, 205–206, 210–211
  and gateway hypothesis, 189–190
  and medical marijuana, 113, 116,
    122, 126, 130, 132
obsessive compulsive disorder
  (OCD), 129
Ohio State Medical Society, 144
Oncologists, 140
opiate withdrawal, 147
opioids
  description, 103
  health risks, 84–85, 106–110
  medical use, 120
  multiple criteria comparison, 111
  scheduling, x–xi, withdrawal
    symptoms, 147–148
  See also heroin
optic nerve damage, 131. *See also*
  glaucoma
oral fluid testing, 212
O'Shaughnessy, W. B., 113–114
osteogenic sarcoma (bone cancer),
  120
outpatient treatment, 247
overdose deaths, 83–84, 94, 106–107,
  109–110, 193

pain
  cannabinoid treatment of, 113–115,
    117–118, 126–127, 129
  inflammatory bowel disease and,
    130
  multiple sclerosis and, 119
  Parkinson's disease and, 130

pain relievers
  past-month nonmedical use,
    102–103
  public concern over, 178
palpitations, 86. *See also* side effects:
  of marijuana
panic
  hallucinogen use and, 110
  marijuana use and, 82, 198
  See also side effects: of marijuana
paranoia
  hallucinogen use and, 110
  marijuana use and, 198
  See also side effects: of marijuana
Parkinson's disease (PD), 127–128,
  130
parole, 224, 252
patent medicine, 160
patterns by age, marijuana use/misuse
  ages 12 and older, 6–7
  and education level, 56–62
  and employment status, 46–53
  and family income level, 35–43
  and marital status, 65–70
  and population density, 25–32
  and race or ethnicity, 14–22
patterns by sex, marijuana use/misuse
  ages 12 and older, 7–12
  and education level, 62–63
  and employment status, 53–54
  and family income level, 43–44
  and marital status, 71
  and population density, 32–33
  and race or ethnicity, 22–23
peer review, xiii, 76, 79, 97
penile cancer, 140
per se limits, 211–212
perceptions of risk, 178, 255
Pew Research Center, 174,
  177–180
pharmacologic criteria, 145–146.
  See also DSM-5 substance use
  disorder criteria
pharmacologic interventions, 241,
  247

pharmacology, pharmacological, 94,
      105, 145–146, 151–152, 167,
      187, 192
pharmakon, 92
pharyngitis, 87. *See also* respiratory
      symptoms
physical health
   alcohol use and, 93–98
   challenges in making drug
      comparisons, 92–93, 104–105
   illicit drug use and, 105–110
   marijuana use and, 83–88
   tobacco use and, 95–96, 98–99
physical symptoms
   amphetamine-type stimulants use
      and, 109
   cocaine use and, 109
   Ecstasy use and, 109–110
   hallucinogen use and, 110
   marijuana use and, 86–87, 98
   medical marijuana and relief of,
      117, 119, 127–128, 130–131,
      140
   opioid use and, 109
physical withdrawal, 147–148,
      151–152
pipe, 81. *See also* route of
      administration
placebo, 116
Point Subtraction Aggression
      Paradigm, 199–200
population density, marijuana use/and
      abuse, 24–33
population level, assessment of risk
      at, 82, 84, 93, 105
Portugal, 258
possession with intent to distribute,
      226
post-traumatic stress disorder
      (PTSD), 132–133
posture, 119
potency, 116, 207
pre-cancer, 138
prevalence, xii, 82, 93. *See also*
      marijuana use

prison population, 217–218
probation, 224, 252
prohibition. *See* marijuana
      prohibition
prohibitionists, xi, 81, 145, 258
Proposition 215 (California 1995),
      254
prostate cancer, 140
protagonists, xi, 81, 145, 157, 258
psilocybin, 104–106, 111
psychiatric disorder, 132, 246
psychological distress, 234–235,
      247
psychological withdrawal, 147
psychomotor skills, 205–210, 212
psychosis, 132, 197
psychosocial interventions, 241–247
psychostimulants, animal self-
      administration, 150. *See also*
      amphetamine-type stimulants;
      cocaine
psychotic disorder, 246
public health data, 95–96
public opinion
   on illicit substances, 176–178
   marijuana legalization and,
      174–176, 178–179
   on marijuana risks, 177–178
   on medical marijuana, 179–181
pulmonary function. *See* lung
      function
punishment, 251–252. *See also*
      arrests; incarceration
Pure Food and Drug Act, 160
purity, 116

Quinnipiac University Poll, 174,
      178–180

race or ethnicity and marijuana use/
      misuse, 13–23, 219–220
racism, 159, 227
random assignment, 77
rave setting, 105, 110
reaction time, 206–209

Reagan, Ronald, 218
Reagan administration, 176
receptors, 114–115, 152, 247
recreational dose, 83, 94
recreational marijuana laws, 180,
    192, 251, 253, 257–258
red eyes. *See* conjunctivae, reddening
Reefer Madness, film, 164–165, 197
Reefer Madness era, 158, 164, 169,
    178, 197, 251
referrals, 233
relapse
    avoidance of, 238
    to cannabis use, 148
    to marijuana use disorder, 235–236
    prevention, 243, 247
    risk of, 247
relapse to multiple sclerosis, 122.
    See also adverse events of
    medical marijuana
relative risk, 82, 84, 93
remission
    Inflammatory Bowel Disease, 130
    marijuana use disorder, 235–236,
        238, 241–242
Republicans, 179–180
respiratory depression, 109–110
respiratory impairment, marijuana
    use and, 88
    tobacco use and, 98
respiratory injury, marijuana use and,
    88
    tobacco use and, 98
respiratory symptoms, 87
restlessness, 148. *See also* marijuana
    withdrawal symptoms
rewarding effect, 149–151
rigidity, 130
risk. *See* attributable risk; physical
    health; relative risk
risk taking, 189, 206–208
risky use, 145–146. *See also* DSM-5
    substance use disorder criteria
roadside testing, 211–212
route of administration, 81

safety
    driving under the influence of
        alcohol and, 205, 209
    driving under the influence of
        marijuana and, 205–213
    of medical marijuana, x–xi, 1, 80,
        122
    See also overdose deaths; physical
        health
safety ratios, 105–106
Schedule I. *See* controlled substance
    schedules
scientific consensus
    on effectiveness of marijuana
        prohibitions, 250
    establishment of, 76, 79
    on marijuana use and driving,
        211
    on medical marijuana, 180
    on toxicity of marijuana, 83
segregation, 228
seizures
    amphetamine-type stimulant use
        and, 109
    benzodiazepine withdrawal and,
        147
    cocaine use and, 109
    See also complicating condition;
        epilepsy
self-administration
    of cannabinoids, 149–151
    of illicit substances, 150, 192
self-change. *See* natural recovery
self-referrals, 233
set and setting, 94, 105
Shafer Commission. *See* National
    Commission on Marijuana and
    Drug Abuse
shortness of breath, 87. *See also*
    respiratory symptoms
side effects
    of marijuana, 82–83, 86
    of medical marijuana, 122, 131
    of opioids and chemotherapy,
        120

silent generation, 179
sleep disorders, cannabinoid
    treatments of, 127–129
sleep disturbances, 148. *See also*
    marijuana withdrawal symptoms
smoking
    association between marijuana and
        tobacco, 77–78, 139
    marijuana, 76, 80–81, 87, 104, 116,
        138
    See also cancer; cigarettes;
        physical health; respiratory
        impairment; respiratory injury;
        respiratory symptoms; route of
        administration; tobacco
snorting, 109
social impairment, 145–146. *See also*
    DSM-5 substance use disorder
    criteria
social support treatment, 243
somatic symptoms, 147, 152
spasticity, 113–115, 117–120,
    126–127. *See* multiple sclerosis
spontaneous remission. *See* natural
    recovery
spuriousness, 139, 198, 210. *See also*
    nonspuriousness
sputum production, 87. *See also*
    respiratory symptoms
substance use disorders, 128, 145,
    148, 242, 247
substituting, marijuana for other
    substances, 133
suicide, 85, 108, 110, 165, 179
standardized field sobriety test
    (SFST), 212
standardized mortality ratio (SMR),
    108
state prison
    cost per prisoner, 252
    disparities in, 226–227
    drug violators in, 225
    marijuana use among sentenced
        prisoners, 200

marijuana violators in, 225–226
statistical association, 78, 83,
    138–139, 184, 186, 190, 198,
    210
statistical "control," 78, 87, 140,
    190–192, 201–202, 254
statistical procedures, 189–190
statistics, xii, 3
steatosis (fatty liver), 87
stepping-stone hypothesis, 167–168,
    197. *See also* gateway hypothesis
stereotypes, 228
stiffness, 119, 130
stigma, 236
stimulants. *See* amphetamine-type
    stimulants
stroke, 97–98, 109
sublingual dose (under the tongue),
    131
substance use disorder
    DSM-5 criteria, 145–146
    treatment of, 128, 242–247
suburban and marijuana use/misuse,
    24–33
Survey of Inmates in State and
    Federal Correctional Facilities,
    200, 225
survival, 121
symptom management, 140
synthetic cannabinoids, 115–116,
    120, 130, 133, 150, 192,
    247
systematic review, 79, 85–86, 116,
    118, 122

tar, 138
Taylor, Bayard, 160
tea, marijuana, 81. *See also* route of
    administration
temperance movement, 159
temporal association or sequence, 78,
    138, 184–185, 187, 190, 201,
    210
    direction of influence, 78

tension, 148. *See also* marijuana
   withdrawal symptoms
testicular germ cell tumors, 139
tetrahydrocannabinol (THC). *See*
   delta-9-tetrahydrocannibinol
THC-COOH, 206, 210
therapeutic use of cannabinoids,
   116–122, 126–133
third variable, 187. *See also*
   confounding
tics, 129
tobacco
   correlation with marijuana use,
      77–78, 139
   dependence, 149
   gateway hypothesis, 184–186, 188
   health risks, 86, 88, 92–96, 98–99,
      137–138, 140
   multiple criteria comparison, 99, 111
   past-month use, 92–93
   public concern over, 178
   statistically controlling for use, 87,
      140, 192
tolerability, 116
Tourette's syndrome, 127–128, 129
Tower of London test, 207
toxicity
   alcohol, 93–94
   illicit substances, 105–107, 109
   marijuana, 83–84
   nicotine and tobacco, 95
traffic safety, 205–206, 210–213
traffic stops, 228
trafficking, 164, 168, 226
transitional cell carcinoma, 140
trauma, 110, 189
Treatment Episode Data Set (TEDS),
   233, 241, 257
treatment interventions, marijuana
   adolescent, 245–246
   adult, 243–245
   among individuals with comorbid
      disorders, 246–247
tremor, 119, 130, 147, 152

Trump administration, 177
tumor, 137, 139–141

ulcerative colitis, 130
unemployment and marijuana
   use/misuse, 45–54
United States Dispensatory, 114
United States Pharmacopoeia, 160,
   167
unmet need for treatment, 233
urban
   decay, 159
   and marijuana use/misuse in, 24–33
   police attention in urban
      neighborhoods, 228–229
urinary tract infection (UTI), 122.
   See also adverse events of
   medical marijuana
urine tests, 206, 210, 244
Uruguay, 258

vaporize, vaporizers, 81, 95, 110, 118
variables, 76–78, 138, 187, 190–191,
   198–199, 201–202, 210
ventricular tachycardia, 109
vipers, 162
virtual maze, 208
vomiting, 109, 113–115, 117, 122,
   147; cannabinoid treatment of,
   120–121. *See also* adverse events
   of medical marijuana; nausea
   and vomiting

war on drugs, 175–176, 218–219,
   221, 229
wasting illness, 117, 121, 127
water pipe, 81. *See also* route of
   administration
wheeze, 87. *See also* respiratory
   symptoms
whites (Caucasian)
   and drug control, 228
   and drug sales, 220
   and drug violations, 221–224

and incarceration, 226–227
and marijuana use/misuse, 13–23,
    219–220
Wisconsin Card Sorting Task, 207–208
withdrawal
    alcohol, 147
    benzodiazepine, 147
    marijuana, 144–149, 151–152, 200,
        233, 247
    opiate, 147, 160
World Health Organization (WHO),
    95

xenophobia, 159

young adults
    cardiovascular death among, 84
    impacts of medical marijuana on,
        256–257

and marijuana use/misuse, 1, 4,
    6–7, 11, 220, 237
See also patterns by age; gateway
    hypothesis
youth
    concerns over marijuana and,
        158, 162, 164, 166, 169, 175,
        197
    impacts of medical marijuana on,
        255–257
    and marijuana use/misuse, 1, 4,
        6–7, 11
    studies on, xii
    See also adolescent treatment;
        gateway hypothesis; patterns
        by age
Youth Risk Behavioral
    Surveillance Survey (YRBS),
    255

About the Authors

Karen T. Van Gundy, PhD, is associate professor of sociology, core faculty in justice studies, and a faculty fellow at the Carsey School of Public Policy at the University of New Hampshire (UNH), Durham. Funded by the National Science Foundation and the New Hampshire Charitable Foundation, her current research examines how social contexts shape physical, emotional, and behavioral health among rural and urban youth and emerging adults. Karen teaches undergraduate and graduate courses on drugs and society and has authored more than a dozen scholarly works concerning substance use or misuse in outlets such as the *Journal of Health and Social Behavior, Substance Use and Misuse,* and *Rural Sociology.* She was the 2012–2015 recipient of the UNH Class of 1940 Professorship, a university-wide award for outstanding interdisciplinary teaching and research. Karen earned bachelor's degrees in psychology and sociology from Virginia Tech, her master's degree in sociology at the University of Cincinnati, and her doctoral degree in sociology from the University of Miami.

Michael S. Staunton, MA, is a PhD candidate in sociology at the University of New Hampshire, Durham. He holds a BA in sociology from St. Michael's College in Vermont and an MA in sociology from the University of New Hampshire. Prior to pursuing his doctorate, he worked with adolescents in an intensive residential treatment program. Michael has since worked as a research assistant at the University of New Hampshire Carsey School of Public Policy and as an adjunct instructor of sociology. Michael received a dissertation year fellowship from the University of New Hampshire in 2016 and is currently working on his doctoral dissertation. His research focuses on stress processes, mental health, and substance use among rural youth.